HISTORY OF THE MINISTRY OF MUNITIONS

VOLUME V / II

WAGES AND WELFARE

Part I Control of Men's Wages

Part II Control of Women's Wages

Part III Welfare: the Control of Working Conditions

Part IV The Provision of Canteens

Part V Provision for the Housing of Munition Workers

The Naval & Military Press Ltd

in association with

The Imperial War Museum
Department of Printed Books

Published jointly by

The Naval & Military Press Ltd

Unit 10 Ridgewood Industrial Park,

Uckfield, East Sussex,

TN22 5QE England

Tel: +44 (0) 1825 749494

Fax: +44 (0) 1825 765701

www.naval-military-press.com

www.military-genealogy.com

www.militarymaproom.com

and

The Imperial War Museum, London

Department of Printed Books

www.iwm.org.uk

HISTORY OF THE MINISTRY OF MUNITIONS

VOLUME V

WAGES AND WELFARE

PART III

WELFARE: THE CONTROL OF WORKING CONDITIONS

1920.

PART III

WELFARE: THE CONTROL OF WORKING CONDITIONS

CONTENTS.

CHAPTER I.

The Establishment of a Welfare Policy.

CHAPTER II.

Welfare in Factories.

(3962) Wt.3643/AP5036 12/20 250 D.St. (Gp. 36)

CHAPTER VII.

Time-Keeping.

CHAPTER VIII.

A Few Local Examples of Welfare Regulation.

CHAPTER IX.

Conclusions.

APPENDICES.

INDEX.

CHAPTER I.

THE ESTABLISHMENT OF A WELFARE POLICY.

I. Introductory.

(a) THE IMPLICATIONS OF "WELFARE."

The paramount need for the supply of munitions led, under the Munitions of War Acts, to the system of State regulation of labour, recorded elsewhere,[1] in regard to wages, industrial disputes, trade union rules, the movements of workers from factory to factory, and the enforcement of workshop discipline by means of specially established courts. These restrictions were destined primarily to secure stability of labour and unbroken output. But in addition to this, the Ministry of Munitions developed a widespreading system of intervention into conditions of labour in the interests primarily of efficiency. State control of working conditions and of the workers' surroundings was already at the outbreak of war firmly established on the basis of the Factory Acts of the past century, the Public Health and Housing Acts and a mass of recent social legislation, while the initiative of employers and of organised labour had to a greater or less extent filled in the gaps in the compulsory system. But the needs of war production made it impossible to adhere wholly even to the national minimum of working conditions thus partially secured, and yet showed how imperative it was to maintain or raise this minimum. The measures taken by the Ministry of Munitions aimed at increasing the well-being, and, therewith, the efficiency, of labour under abnormal conditions. They were also a recognition (as was the regulation of women's wages) of the duties of a Public Department to those whose labour it employed or controlled on an unprecedented scale.

The Department had the advantage of a working programme for almost all the points with which it thus dealt, in the reports of the Health of Munition Workers Committee, an expert body appointed by the Minister of Munitions with the concurrence of the Home Secretary, in September, 1915, to advise on questions concerning "industrial fatigue, hours of labour, and other matters affecting the personal health and physical efficiency" of the munition worker. This committee represented the concentrated experience of the Home Office, of employers and labour, and of medical experts,[2] and supplied a

---

[1] See Vol. I., Part IV. ; Vol. IV. ; Vol. V., Parts I. and II., etc.

[2] The composition of the Committee was as follows : Sir George Newman, M.D. (Chairman) ; Sir Thomas Barlow, Bart., K.C.V.O., F.R.S. ; G. Bellhouse, Factory Department, Home Office ; Prof. A. E. Boycott, M.D., F.R.S. ; J. R. Clynes, M.P. ; E. L. Collis, M.B., Factory Department, Home Office ; W. M. Fletcher, M.D., F.R.S., Secretary of the Medical Research Committee ; Leonard E. Hill, M.B., F.R.S ; Samuel Osborn, J.P., Sheffield ; Miss R. E. Squire, Factory Department, Home Office ; Mrs. H. J. Tennant ; E. H. Pelham (Secretary).

scientific background, with much practical detail, for the greater part of the Department's work, both in administration and in propaganda, described hereafter.

If the Department was unable to follow up completely such a programme, this was to a great extent due to the difficulties of supply. Those who were responsible for output at high pressure, at first, at least, hesitated to adopt innovations in factory management or restrictions on working hours which might even temporarily retard output or add to the amount of apparently unproductive labour or equipment for which payment must be made ; while shortage of materials and of building labour and transport put great difficulties in the way of the erection of fresh "welfare" accommodation or housing.

With these two groups of considerations in the balance—on the one side the recommendations of its own expert committee, on the other, the needs and the severe practical limitations of supply—the Department developed by logical stages a "welfare" policy for munition workers. This policy consisted in practical and detailed provision for the health and well-being of very large numbers of workers, and was quite remote from the implications of patronage which attached itself in the minds of certain critics to the original meaning of the word welfare. The standards of comfort and of management at which the Department aimed were, indeed, in great part, by no means new, but represented the pre-war practice of a number of good employers. But the standardisation of such practice was of great importance, both for the sake of the employers and workers immediately concerned and of the assertion of principle involved.

(b) THE RELATION OF THE DIFFERENT BRANCHES OF WELFARE.

The production of munitions occupied ultimately at least 700,000 women and girls and 250,000 boys. Some of these were engaged in the same occupations that they had followed or would naturally have followed in time of peace, but the great majority were working or living under abnormal conditions within or without the factory. To provide for their comfort, efficiency and health, up to a higher level than that required in normal times by the Factory Acts, a special Welfare Section of the Ministry was built up, which (a) developed a policy, or in part, as has been said, gave effect to that of the Health of Munition Workers Committee ; (b) gave examples of carrying out this policy in the national factories and endeavoured to extend it among the " controlled " munitions firms, by moral suasion and by the supply of special facilities and information ; (c) organised or co-ordinated the care of munition workers outside the factory, by securing for them means of recreation, reasonably comfortable lodgings and travelling facilities, and provision, when this seemed necessary, for the care of their infants and older children.[1]

This work, with which the term "welfare" was primarily connected, was not originally destined for men munition workers,

---

[1] Chapters II and III.

who were often working under conditions of even greater stress, but whose trade union organisation gave them, in theory, the power to care for their own working conditions, and who had on this account been exempt from the greater part of the restrictions placed on the labour of " protected persons " in the previous seventy years.   The measures taken for the benefit of women and young persons, however, like the legal restrictions on their hours of work during the nineteenth century, reacted on the working conditions of men,[1] and were in the second half of the war beginning in a number of cases to work in with the industrial self-government movement fostered by the Whitley report of 1917.

The special medical work undertaken by the Welfare Section— work covering a large, and to a great extent a new, field of industrial hygiene—is described briefly in Chapter IV.

The attempt to balance the needs of output and the necessary relaxations of the Factory Acts with the results of scientific investigations of industrial fatigue,[2] was the work of an inter-departmental committee which dealt, in conjunction with the Home Office and the supply departments of the Ministry of Munitions and the Admiralty, with munition workers' hours of labour. This committee was inevitably concerned with diminishing overtime or minimising its ill-effects, so far as possible, rather than with the maintenance of physiological standards of hours of work during the stress of war. Its efforts, however, and the records of overtime and Sunday work performed, have a special retrospective interest, in the light of the reaction at the Armistice and the movement for the legal enforcement of a shorter working day. They have a further interest and importance in their connection with the problems of wage regulation during the war.

From the attempt to secure moderate hours of labour, in order that output should be maintained, there was an obvious transition to inquiries into the time-keeping of munition workers and to a system of attempts to improve this.   In its dealings with loss of time in munition works, the Department was brought into contact with problems of works discipline and with the possibility of co-operation with labour in its maintenance ; and was also led to consider the effect of health on regularity of work.[3]

The great migration of labour, fostered by the Department, brought, or threatened to bring, over-crowding, with ill-health and obvious loss of efficiency. To prevent this, and to make it possible to carry on the supply of munitions at all in certain areas, the Department undertook a series of housing schemes, built hostels, and helped to secure lodgings and to administer an Act passed in 1917 for the compulsory billeting of munition workers.[4] Further, it became

---

[1] Thus the Welfare Orders issued by the Home Office in 1917 and subsequently made no distinction in the age or sex of the persons for whose benefit they were intended. (See p. 17.)

[2] Chapters V and VI.

[3] Chapter VII.

[4] See Vol. V, Part V, Chap. III.

responsible, to an extent wholly new to a Government Department, for the social life and well-being of the entire population of workers in certain industrial centres.[1]

The connection of the different portions of the Department's policy for thus dealing with munition workers' industrial efficiency is obvious, although they were never administered from one section of the Department, and only in the last year's work from the Labour Regulation Department as a whole.

In thus dealing with munition workers, the Ministry of Munitions was inevitably brought into contact with many Departments and organisations already concerned with social and industrial welfare. In the promotion of the health and comfort of the workers, and in endeavouring to restrict their hours of work, it was approaching the sphere of the Home Office, which indeed alone exercised compulsory powers in this direction. In housing schemes it dealt with the Local Government Board, and in the provision of canteens with the Central (Liquor) Control Board ; the provision of crèches was arranged with the Board of Education. It came into touch with local authorities in connection with recreation schemes, the provision of housing, lodgings, and day-nurseries ; and with voluntary organisations (but not, to any considerable extent, with those of the working-classes), through all the varied forms of care for munition workers outside the factories. In pressing measures for welfare and housing, the Ministry of Munitions had the advantage of being the Department which controlled or ordered the supplies towards the production of which all these measures were ultimately directed ; and it had special opportunities for negotiating the financial concessions which met a great, if not the greater, part of the cost of the new extra-legal standard of industrial welfare which it advocated.

II. Welfare Organisation by the Ministry—First Stages.[2]

(a) Formation of the Welfare Section.

The Welfare Section of the Ministry was created by Mr. Lloyd George at the end of December, 1915, and Mr. B. S. Rowntree, who had had much experience of welfare organisation in the works of his firm at York, was appointed as its Director. Work in munition factories was being carried on frequently under great stress and under quite abnormal conditions, largely because works which had been equipped for other purposes were being reorganised and re-equipped to enable them to make munitions. Women were being introduced under the Ministry's policy of dilution into engineering works originally constructed with the idea that men only would be employed, and staffed only by men. New factories were rapidly springing up, and so great was the demand for munitions that workers were often busy and manufacture was begun in one part of a factory before it was completed,

---

[1] See Chapter VIII, and Vol. V, Part V.
[2] A considerable portion of this section is based on a memorandum by Mr. B. S. Rowntree, filed in Hist. Rec./H/346/1.

and before accommodation such as canteens, cloakrooms, etc., had been built or proper arrangements made for the transit of the workers. The employment of women in the engineering shops inevitably brought problems as to the best use of their labour—an unknown type to many managers, who were inclined either to allow the newly imported women to relapse into bad order and discipline, or to permit inexperienced and enthusiastic workers to overstrain themselves by too heavy work or over-long hours.[1]   Thus a grave danger arose that the tremendous demand for an increased output of munitions which was brought to bear on the supply departments, and on the managers of factories— a pressing demand which inevitably gave prominence to questions of output rather than of control of labour—might react disastrously upon the workers, and so defeat its aims.

The Health of Munition Workers Committee, in a memorandum issued in January, 1916, urged the need for attention to this side of the problem of production.[2]

"If the present long hours, the lack of helpful and sympathetic oversight, the inability to obtain good wholesome food, and the great difficulties of travelling are allowed to continue, it will be impracticable to secure or maintain for an extended period the high maximum output of which women are undoubtedly capable."

In their report on *Welfare Supervision*,[3] issued just previously, the Committee represented the need for increased care, if possible by means of "resident superintendents," for the well-being of workers— primarily, but not only, women and girl workers—in munition factories.

The labour employed in national factories and controlled establishments in October, 1916, was approximately as follows :—

Men.	Boys.	Women.	Girls.
1,253,000	205,000	340,000	69,000

Already, at the beginning of the year, the numbers were growing rapidly towards this level, and it was clear that the Department must become responsible for labour on a colossal scale. A few weeks after the establishment of the Welfare Section the Minister of Munitions formally expressed his desire that the conditions under which women worked in national factories should be as good as possible, and that for disciplinary purposes they should as a rule be under the control of women rather than men.   Beyond this, however, no definite directions were at the outset given to the new section, which was left to develop in a widening and necessarily indeterminate field.

(b) Powers of the Ministry.

Under section 6 of the Munitions of War (Amendment) Act of January, 1916, a section already discussed in detail in the history of Women's Wages, the Minister had power to give directions as to the

---

[1] Cf. Special Arbitration Tribunal Reports, Vol. V, Part II.
[2] Memorandum No. 5, *Hours of Work* (Cd. 8186).
[3] Memorandum No. 2, *Welfare Supervision* (Cd. 8151).

conditions of employment as well as the wages, of women workers to whom the leaving certificate regulations applied.[1] As regards women, therefore, the powers of the Department extended not only to national factories and controlled establishments, but also to a certain number of uncontrolled firms, and the extension of the power of regulation under the Munitions of War Act of August,1917, to " female workers employed on or in connection with munitions work in establishments of all classes" hardly widened the possible sphere of compulsory welfare. The Treasury Solicitor advised, in 1916, that the Minister had power under the section to give directions to a firm by order to appoint a " lady superintendent " and to supply the necessary buildings and appliances for the preparation, cooking and eating of food.[2] No " direction " was, however, given by the Minister under this section, for it was, according to the first Director of the Welfare Section, " the deliberate policy of the Department, with a view to achieving permanent results, to educate rather than to compel." The only exception to this was in the case of T.N.T. workers, on whose behalf powers were taken under Regulation 35 A.A. of the Defence of the Realm Act, of December, 1916, to insist on the appointment of a welfare worker, and the provision of canteens, cloakrooms, and washing apparatus, " approved by the Welfare Section."

Section 7 of the Munitions of War (Amendment) Act, 1916, gave similar powers to the Department for controlling the conditions of employment of semi-skilled and unskilled men and boys taking the work of skilled men in controlled firms ; but in their case also no advantage was taken of these undefined powers of enforcing improved working conditions, except in national factories.

(c) An Early Statement of Aims.

The aims of the Welfare Section were laid down virtually, though not formally, in the summary of the scope of welfare supervision given in January by the Health of Munition Workers Committee. After a few months' work these objects were summarised afresh in the department for the benefit of its officers. The object of the work of the Welfare Section was "to raise the well-being of the workers to as high a point as possible in all factories engaged in the manufacture of munitions of war." Such well-being might be considered under the heads of :—

(1) workrooms, which should be clean and wholesome, with work suited to the capacity of the worker ;

(2) food, for obtaining which there should be adequate facilities at reasonable prices under restful and wholesome conditions ;

---

[1] " . . . The Minister of Munitions shall have power by order to give directions as to the rate of wages or (subject so far as the matter is one which is dealt with by the Factory and Workshop Acts, 1901 to 1911, to the concurrence of the Secretary of State) as to hours of labour, or conditions of employment of the female workers so employed."

[2] Hist. Rec./H/346/1.

(3) a working day of reasonable length with suitable breaks in long spells ;

(4) wages, sufficient for efficiency, with a margin for reasonable recreation ;

(5) provision of cloakrooms and other accommodation, overalls, etc. ;

(6) reduction to the absolute minimum, of danger to life and health from unprotected machinery and from handling explosive or poisonous substances ;

(7) provision of such supervision as might be necessary to ensure in the factories a standard of behaviour such as would not offend an employee coming from a respectable home ;

(8) provision, where necessary, of suitable recreation, outside of working hours, especially for those working under strain or on monotonous employment.

These were the headings under which it was suggested that the position of workers inside the factories should be considered, with one important though indefinite addition, " the payment of due consideration to the workers as *individuals*, securing to each worker consideration · and absolute fairness of treatment." Outside the factory, the following objects should, it was urged, be considered :—

(1) The provision of adequate and reasonably comfortable means of transit to and from work.

(2) The provision of good conditions in hostels, where these were established.

(3) The provision of such supervision as might be necessary to ensure that girls and boys living away from home were not demoralised during their free time.

(4) Such supervision of lodgings as would prevent exploitation of the workers, and also prevent women and lads from lodging with disreputable people.[1]

The majority of these conditions came within the scope of the Welfare Section's influence though not of its executive responsibility. With some, such as those involving transit, recreation and care of workers outside the factory, it only dealt indirectly during the early stage of its work.

(*d*) ORGANISATION FOR DEALING WITH NATIONAL FACTORIES AND CONTROLLED ESTABLISHMENTS.

When the Welfare Section was formed, there already existed the nucleus of a welfare organisation within the supply departments. A woman staff inspector had, since August, 1915, been visiting the National Filling and Explosives Factories as they started work, and was in touch with Boards of Management with regard to the very important and varied questions of the welfare of women in this often dangerous work. Her duties included advice and help in the selection of women supervisors, in the training of the special types of labour

---

[1] HIST. REC./H/346/1.

required, and in the provision of doctors and nurses for its care. It had in January, 1916, just been arranged that a woman welfare officer should be provided for Woolwich Arsenal, and a complete scheme for her work and that of a staff of assistants had been drafted. The appointment of a woman inspector to deal with woman labour in National Shell and Projectile Factories, under the direction of Mr. West, was under consideration.[1] It was clearly a question whether direct responsibility for all welfare conditions should be centralised in the new Welfare Section of the Secretariat, or whether the supply departments, responsible for output from the national factories, should also be responsible for the control and working conditions of the labour employed. The latter view was put forward and was maintained strongly a year later by the Director of the Gun Ammunition Filling Factories Division on behalf of the National Filling Factories, to whose medical problems the Filling Division had given special attention.[2] The supply departments were, he represented, much stronger in executive powers with regard to the national factories than was the Welfare Section, the functions of which were mainly advisory, and the transfer of responsibility to the Welfare Section would involve " the separation of functions inseparably interconnected." " Output and efficiency of the means, whether human or mechanical, for obtaining output, should remain as heretofore, an undivided responsibility."[3]   A compromise in administration was, however, arranged for the first fifteen months of the section's work. At a meeting of Sir H. Llewellyn Smith, Mr. Beveridge, Mr. West, Mr. Geddes, Major Luck (representing the Secretariat and the supply departments concerned), with Mr. Rowntree in January, 1916, a few days after the appointment of the latter, it was agreed that the welfare officers already or about to be appointed to inspect National Shell Projectile or Filling Factories should do so as already arranged ; but that they should report both to their supply departments and to the head of the Welfare Section. The latter should only communicate with Boards of Management through the staff inspectors or their departmental chiefs, and these inspectors should only carry out Mr. Rowntree's suggestions with the approval of the supply departments.[4]   Similar agreements were made subsequently with the Trench Warfare Department and with Woolwich Arsenal.

These arrangements did not prove workable in practice, except in connection with the National Shell and Projectile Factories, and attempts to improve on them were unproductive. The argument for the necessity of undivided control of output and of labour appeared cogent, but it resulted in the course of the year in the emergence of a group of miniature welfare organisations within the Department, with no common policy as to the very serious medical problems that were developing, or as to the type of supervisor or the standard of welfare to be recommended.[5] When, therefore, the welfare work of the Department was reorganised in April, 1917, all duties of inspection were concentrated in the Welfare Section. The latter took over from

---

[1] M.W. 81954/2.   [2] See Chap. IV.   [3] L.R.W. 218/17.   [4] M.W. 81954.
[5] M.W. 162868.   M.W. 150529.

the supply departments their travelling officers, and assumed responsibility for the maintenance of standards of welfare (*e.g.*, with regard to the T.N.T. regulations) in national factories, although executive authority for carrying out the directions of the Welfare Section remained with the supply departments. This arrangement met the difficulty at first raised by the Filling Division that a section " divorced from close contact with the supply departments " would tend, from lack of the latter's intimate acquaintance with the real and ever-changing needs of production, to lay down " impracticable standards,"[1] and disposed on the whole satisfactorily of an administrative problem that recurred elsewhere in other matters, such as the adjustment of wages, local disputes and hours of work, in the allocation of functions between the supply and labour departments of the Ministry.

In dealing with trade firms, the Welfare Section was on ground untouched by previous organisation within the Department. The first step taken was to secure a list of all controlled factories in which as many as 20 women and girls were employed. While this was being done, a detailed questionnaire was drawn up in the section, relating to wages, hours, provision of canteens and messrooms, methods of engaging and supervising women workers, conditions of housing, transit, etc., and H.M. Principal Lady Inspector of Factories arranged for her staff to pay special visits to the factories and fill in the questionnaires for the use of the Welfare Section. These reports formed the basis on which the section took action, and for the purpose of such action a small staff of women travelling officers was appointed. This consisted on 1 March, 1916, of a senior and three other officers, whose number by January, 1917, had increased to 12. By 1 March, 1917, 1,228 factories (employing 275,000 women) out of 1,770 controlled establishments known to be employing over 20 women had been visited and reported on.[2]

(e) EARLY METHODS AND RESULTS.

Periodical visits were made to the same firm by the section's welfare officers when necessary, in order to secure improvement in working conditions. After the visits of the officers, and the receipt of their reports, letters were normally sent from headquarters to the firms whose works had been visited, to re-enforce the recommendations made verbally, a method of procedure obviously needing much common-sense realisation of factory conditions, and consideration of the individual firms' existing standards and capacities, together with careful selection and training of the travelling officers. If firms proved recalcitrant, which was not as a rule the case, pressure was brought to bear upon them by personal interviews with the section or by visits of the superintending engineers attached to the munitions area offices. The work was necessarily to some extent experimental during the first year, and its object was, according to the first Director of Welfare, " as much to enlist sympathetic interest in welfare as to make specific suggestions. It ranged from organising the welfare of a whole factory to advising the best

---

[1] L.R.W. 218/17.   [2] Hist. Rec./H 346/1.

way to handle a foreman opposed to women's labour ; from a question directly or indirectly affecting women's output, to a question of the most economical kind of soap to remove certain greases or dyes from workers' hands and faces."[1]

Such work is incapable of satisfactory statistical measurement. The following tables, however, summarise some of the results produced by March, 1917, and illustrate the trend of the section's pioneer activities with regard to controlled firms :—

The Creation of Welfare Staffs.

Nature of Appointments.	No. of Factories in which Appointments were :—		
	Made.	Promised.	Under Discussion.
Welfare supervisors	187	19	211
Assistant supervisors	32	6	16
Supervising women or charge hands ..	142	58	153
Matrons	42	10	41
Lady doctors	2	—	—
Nurses	42	6	15
Women with first-aid qualifications ..	81	38	104
Attendants for cloakrooms, etc.	58	27	48

The Provision of Welfare Accommodation.

Nature of Improvements. Provision made for :—	No. of Factories in which Improvements were :—		
	Effected.	Promised.	Under consideration.
Washing—			
(a) new	93	51	49
(b) improved	118	108	146
Sanitary conveniences—			
(a) new	37	18	44
(b) improved	44	46	53
Cloakrooms—			
(a) new	57	46	163
(b) improved	36	34	46
Canteens (per Canteen Committee, Central Control Board) and messrooms—			
(a) new	78	64	178
(b) improved	79	76	19
Rest Ambulance Rooms—			
(a) new	73	53	105
(b) improved	17	14	18
First aid appliances	55	43	44
Seats in workrooms	24	22	59
Supplies of overalls or other protective clothing	89	50	161
Supplies of caps	92	55	154
Supplies of safer pattern caps	8	1	12
Recreation facilities	15	1	5

[1] Hist. Rec./H/346/1.

In addition to the above appointments and to the improved accommodation secured, the travelling officers had, as has been said, visited for the first time 1,228 works employing 275,000 women and had revisited 812, employing 416,000. They had arranged training for welfare supervisors in 56 factories, arranged for firms to inspect model accommodation for women in 17 cases, had paid special visits to advise firms on difficulties arising out of the employment of women in 11 cases, had secured breaks for lunch and tea in long spells of work in 37 cases, had supplied memoranda, patterns of protective clothing, respirators, special gloves, etc., in a number of cases, and had referred a large number of complaints of breaches of regulation to the Home Office, or to the appropriate branch of the Ministry of Munitions.

The appointment of women welfare supervisors in factories heads the first of the foregoing summaries of results. It was one of the primary objects of the section to secure their appointment in all works in which the number of women employed and the conditions of their employment justified this, and it was, with this limitation, one of the almost invariable recommendations made by the section's travelling officers. In order to facilitate their appointment, the section formed a panel of suitable women, arranged for their interviewing, and when necessary for their training. During the year, 2,500 applications for posts as welfare supervisors were received and classified ; 2,000 were rejected as unsuitable or withdrew their applications ; 280 were placed on the selected list and classified as suitable for posts as welfare supervisors in large, small or medium factories, or as caterers or hostel matrons. The number of welfare supervisors appointed directly through the section was 205 (including those for national factories), and probably 200 more were appointed through the stimulus given.[1] No compulsion was exercised on controlled establishments with regard to the appointment of welfare supervisors, except (later), as has been explained, in the case of T.N.T. workers. Even in the national factories it was decided, in January, 1916, at the inauguration of the section, that the Boards of Management should only be " persuaded " by the inspectors of the supply departments to appoint supervisors and that the functions of such supervisors should be determined by the Boards appointing them.[2] The Minister, however, in April, 1916, ruled that supervisors should be appointed in all national factories where women or young persons were employed, and that they should be approved by the Welfare Section ; and in May all National Shell and Projectile Factories, with the exception of the Belgian Factory at Birtley, received an emphatic circular to this effect. The appointment of lady superintendents or welfare supervisors was pushed forward during the year in national factories, and served to some extent as a precedent for their introduction in controlled establishments.

In April, 1916, the section took up the question of welfare supervision for boys. Visits were made during the year to 346 out of 950 controlled firms known to employ more than 50 boys. A memorandum on welfare work for boys was drawn up and sent to employers. Thirty-

---

eight welfare supervisors for boys (15 from the section's panel) were known to have been appointed by March, 1917, and a number of employers had expressed their readiness to make appointments later. The dearth of suitable welfare supervisors for boys, at this stage of the war, inevitably hampered the development of this side of the section's work.

The inauguration of similar work among men was considered, and discussed with labour leaders and others, but nothing definite was attempted in the first year of the Welfare Section's operations.[1] The establishment of canteens, which was developing rapidly at this time by the action of the Central Control Board in conjunction with the Welfare Section, was, however, a very definite contribution to the increased comfort of men munition workers.

The section began the systematic inspection of hostels for women munition makers at the end of the year 1916, inspecting not only those in which the Ministry was directly interested, but also those managed by voluntary organisations. About 150 hostels were considered at this time to require inspection.[2]

The section, in its introduction of welfare work, was deliberately educational in its methods. For this reason it refrained, as has been explained, from forcing non-essential improvements on reluctant employers, and from insisting on their accepting welfare supervisors against their will, although it must be admitted that in some cases firms, large and small, stated that they only made such appointments in order to meet the wishes of the Ministry. " Real betterment of conditions," wrote Mr. Rowntree,[2] " springs in the last analysis from the conviction in the mind of the employer that here lies his plain duty, a duty which does not conflict with his business interests but promotes them, since it is obvious that workers who are in good health and are provided with the amenities of life are more efficient workers." In order to convince employers and workers and the world of consumers that the welfare movement in industry was really desirable, special measures were taken to secure publicity in the Press for the welfare policy of the Ministry of Munitions ; and from the summer of 1916 large numbers of articles on " Welfare " were contributed by well-known employers, such as Sir W. Lever and Mr. W. L. Hichens, by economists such as Professor Ashley, and others, and were inserted both in trade and labour journals and in the London and provincial papers. Perhaps the tone of these contributions appeared to critics to be too uniformly laudatory of the special " welfare " theories, and they certainly for this reason in some cases stirred the suspicions of labour. But they served a useful purpose as propaganda, and the section attributed to them direct results, such as applications for information and for help in securing supervisors, etc., as well as indirect effects in the formation of public opinion.

---

[1] L.R.W. 2433 ; M.W. 162868.   [2] HIST. REC./H/346/1.

III. Extension of the Work.

(a) Change of Personnel.

In March, 1917, Mr. Rowntree left the Department on his appointment to take up work on the Central Reconstruction Committee, and the work of the Welfare Section was reorganised and greatly expanded, although the principles laid down in the previous year remained as a basis. Dr. E. L. Collis, a Medical Officer under the Home Office and a member of the Health of Munition Workers Committee and the T.N.T. Advisory Committee, became Director of the section. The separate staffs of inspectors for National Shell and Projectile, Filling and Trench Warfare Factories, were amalgamated and became part of the Welfare Section, together with the Welfare Officers who dealt with controlled establishments. This change in administration was, wrote Dr. Addison on 19 April, " necessary in the interests of the State in relation to workers in order to consolidate the experience of those charged with welfare schemes, so as to evolve a well-considered and properly balanced policy and conduct."[1] It was, however, clearly stated in the general office memorandum which announced this reorganisation a week later that, " so far as ordnance and national factories are concerned, the function of the section is limited to inspection and is not executive ; *i.e.*, its business will be not to arrange for welfare and health, but to see that proper standards of both are maintained in the factories under the control of the appropriate Labour Supply Departments." The visiting of factories was arranged on a territorial basis, the inspectors or welfare officers in the service of the section being (with the exception of the small group who visited " medical factories " from headquarters, and of those responsible for the numerous " government examiners," who remained outside the Welfare Section) attached to the eight area offices and to the staffs of the chief investigation officers appointed at the end of the previous year to act as the local officers of the Labour Regulation Department. The work of the representatives of the Ministry concerned from different points of view in the local regulation of labour was therefore, to some extent, concentrated. At the same time the work of the section developed on more specialised lines than had been possible with the small staff of the previous year.

(b) Development of the Health Side of Welfare Work.

Greater insistence was laid on care for the workers' health as distinguished from their general well-being, and the section became known as the Welfare and Health Section.

In March, 1917, the regulations for T.N.T. workers to which reference has already been made had been issued, and the responsibility for a considerable portion of their observance had been placed on the Welfare Section. In May the Medical Officers of the Filling Factories Section joined the Welfare and Health Section, and a medical sub-section was built up (under Dr. W. J. O'Donovan) which (*a*) dealt with the health of workers on T.N.T. processes ; (*b*) supervised the

---

[1] L.R.W. 218/17.

appointment of factory doctors and the special welfare provision required for workers in dangerous occupations ; (c) carried out special inquiries, e.g., on maternity problems among munition workers. Factories and establishments where poison gases were manufactured or handled remained under the medical supervision of Dr. F. Shufflebotham who had had charge of this work from the first manufacture of poison gases and lethal bodies. At the same time a research sub-section (under Captain M. Greenwood) was inaugurated, which carried out investigations, supplementing those of the Health of Munition Workers Committee into such questions as food values for munition workers, factory wastage, tuberculosis in munition works and the medical causes of bad time-keeping. This sub-section was in special touch with the problems of restrictions on hours of labour, and was in 1917 under the direction of the secretary of the inter-departmental Hours of Labour Committee.

(c) Other Developments.

Other sub-divisions were made at this date in the work of the section. The care for munition workers outside the factory, the need for which had been already indicated by Mr. Rowntree and by the Health of Munition Workers Committee[1] was definitely organised, and a staff of " extra-mural " welfare officers was appointed. Boys' welfare received special attention, and Mr. R. Bray, chairman of the London Juvenile Advisory Committee, took charge of a new sub-section, with a small staff of local officers to visit firms on behalf of boys' welfare on lines similar to those already laid down with regard to women and girls.[2]

The inspection of hostels for munition workers developed in 1917 as a part of the section's " extra-mural " work. Five inspectors of private hostels and of those owned by the Ministry were at work during the following summer, and a number of local investigators into lodgings were appointed in the course of the year to relieve the discomforts of the imported munition worker. When in May, 1917, the

---

[1] Memorandum No. 17, *Health and Welfare of Munition Workers Outside the Factory* (January, 1917).

[2] The following table explains the distribution of the local welfare officers in the Chief Investigation Officers' local headquarters at the beginning of 1918. (In June, 1918, the work of the " extra-mural " and " intra-mural " officers was amalgamated :—

District.	"Intra-mural" officers (women).	"Extra-mural" officers (women).	Boys' officers.
London and S.E.	3	1	2
North-East (Newcastle)	1	1	1
South-Western (Bristol)	1	2	1
Scotland (Glasgow)	2	1	2
West Midlands (Birmingham)	3	4	2
Yorkshire (Leeds)	3	1	2
North-Western (Manchester)..	1	3	2
Barrow	—	2	—
Wales (Cardiff)	1	1	1
On probation ..	4	—	—
Total	19	16	13

" Billeting of Civilians " Act was passed, and a Central Billeting Board was formed, the section was associated with its work, and with that of the Food Section appointed in March, 1918, to take over, in the period of food shortage, the responsibility for munition workers' canteens, hitherto exercised by the Central Control Board.

The special organisation to secure publicity for welfare work was discontinued.

(d) ORGANISATION IN 1918.

As a result of these developments the organisation of the Welfare and Health Section of the Ministry consisted in the summer of 1918 in an expert staff at headquarters with a staff of local welfare officers stationed at various centres throughout the Kingdom. The work of the section fell into three main divisions :—

1. Medical work, described briefly above. A small staff of medical specialists at headquarters received reports from the doctors (full time or part time) attached to munition factories in which dangerous work was performed, and a separate staff of four or five women officers visited those factories in connection with their special welfare problems.

2. Welfare and health of women and girls, to deal with which there were five women officers at headquarters and forty-six stationed locally.

3. Welfare and health of boys, for which there was a staff of two at headquarters and fourteen in the country.

The work of the two latter divisions fell under the following main headings :—

(a) Securing the installation of welfare supervisors, and

(b) the provision, among other things, of canteens and messrooms, cloakrooms, washing accommodation, overalls, improved lighting, seats ;

(c) advising the keeping of personal records, referring especially to sickness and injury ;

(d) assisting and advising welfare supervisors in factories.

They also included the improvement of transit facilities and the provision of lodgings for munition workers and of relief for " stranded workers," the promotion of healthy recreation schemes of all kinds and educational classes, the establishment of crèches for munition workers' children and the provision, when necessary, of maternity homes. In connection with the two latter requirements a special staff of three at headquarters dealt with reports from the local welfare officers in collaboration with the Local Government Board.

In addition to this system of co-ordinated welfare work throughout the country and to the system of hostel inspection described above, the Welfare Section also maintained, by means of personal interviews and local interviewing boards, a panel of persons desiring to become welfare supervisors. By 30 November, 1918, 550 supervisors for women and 275 for boys had been appointed from the department's panel.

A table illustrating the visits to firms by the three groups of welfare officers is given, with the reservation previously made as to the value of such statistics.

	Week ending 28 September, 1918.				Weekly Average, February, 1917, to August, 1918.	
	First visits.		Revisits.		First visits.	Revisits.
	Firms.	Nos. em-ployed.[1]	Firms.	Nos. em-ployed.[1]	Firms.	Firms.
Welfare Officers for Women	19	5,885	55	14,500	24	54
Welfare Officers for Boys	17	1,117	46	4,600	17	35.
Welfare Officers for Medical work (May, 1917, to August, 1918).. ..	—	—	3	8,000	3	9

On these lines, the organisation and work of the section continued to the date of the Armistice. With the dissolution of the Labour Regulation Department of the Ministry, the Welfare and Health Section was gradually broken up. The sub-section for Boys' Welfare was on 1 December, 1918, transferred to the Training Section of the Ministry of Labour, and early in the following year the greater part of the remainder of the section was also attached to the Ministry of Labour, after much intensive work in assisting in the demobilisation of munition workers and in winding-up, or providing for the future of, existing welfare schemes.

IV. Relations with the Home Office.

(a) SPHERES OF WORK.

The welfare policy of the Ministry of Munitions inevitably brought its work into contact with that of other Departments, and primarily with that of the Home Office, whose administration of the Factory Acts was the foundation on which must be based any further care for the workers' health and comfort such as that promoted by the Ministry. For some years before the war the Factory Inspectors' annual reports had recorded the growing movement in factories towards a standard of hygiene and of amenities much above that prescribed by law, and the Home Office Inspectors were in January, 1916, the only officials in direct and constant contact with many of the problems taken up by the new Welfare Section. It has been explained how women Factory Inspectors made in the early months of 1916 the preliminary investigations which first served as an introduction to the work of the Welfare Section in controlled establishments.

The work of the Welfare Section was brought later into direct touch with that of the older Department by a transfer of officers. Thus one of the women Factory Inspectors was lent to the Welfare Section

---

[1] (Printed) *Weekly Report* No. 162, IX. (5.10 18). " Numbers employed " refers in the first and third lines to the number of women and girls, in the second line to the number of boys, employed in the factories visited.

in April, 1917 ; the second Director of the section was previously on the medical staff of the Home Office ; and in 1918 Miss Squire, the Deputy Principal Lady Inspector of Factories, became head of the Women's Branch of the Welfare Section. This did not, indeed, completely remove the difficulty of delimiting spheres of work, nor in adhering to these delimitations in practice. Definite attempts were, however, made to ensure this. When a staff of travelling officers for welfare inspection was formed by the Ministry of Munitions, special precautions were taken to prevent the overlapping of functions possible when two sets of officials were visiting factories for similar though not identical purposes. Welfare officers were instructed to "make no inspection with regard to matters within the province of the Home Office. If officers became aware during their visits of matters requiring the attention of the Factory Inspectors, such matters should be noted and sufficient inquiry made to enable the complaint to be reported to the Factory Department, but no other action, verbal or otherwise, must be taken. These matters might be defined as those within the requirements of the Factory Act and Orders and the special rules made thereunder." [1] (Sanitary defects or serious faults in ventilation would be examples of matters to be thus referred by welfare officers.)

Fundamentally, the functions of the welfare officer within the factory—with regard to such matters as clothing, rest rooms, and canteens—began where those of the Factory Inspector left off, and the border area in which overlapping was possible shrank as certain forms of welfare provision passed from the category of persuasion to that of compulsion.

(b) Welfare Orders by the Home Office.

The indefinite powers of compulsion possessed by the Department under the Munitions of War Act to induce firms to improve their working conditions were, as has been said, deliberately not exercised. Much more definite powers were possessed by the Home Office, under the "Police, Factories, etc., Miscellaneous Provisions Act," of August, 1916[2]; although these powers of enforcing welfare provision were during the war used almost as sparingly as were those of the Ministry of Munitions. Orders were, however, issued for the supply of drinking water in all factories and workshops employing more than 25 workers,[3] for the provision of first-aid equipment and ambulance rooms, at blast furnaces, copper and iron

---

[1] L.R.W. 1703. This delimitation of duties between welfare officers and Factory Inspectors was made more precise a few days before the Armistice. (Welfare Section circular 1113.)

[2] *Police, Factories, etc., Miscellaneous Provisions Act, Section* 7: "Where it appears to the Secretary of State that the conditions of employment in any factory or workshop are such as to require special provision to be made at the factory or workshop for securing the welfare of the workers employed therein in relation to the matters to which this Section applies, he may by Order require the occupier to make such reasonable provision therefor as may be specified in the Order.

"The following shall be the matters to which this Section applies :—

"Arrangements for preparing or heating and taking meals ; the supply of drinking water ; ambulance and first-aid arrangements ; the supply and use of seats in workrooms ; facilities for washing ; accommodation for clothing ; arrangements for supervision of workers."

[3] Statutory Rules and Orders No. 1068 (12/10/17).

mills, foundries and metal works[1] ; for the provision of protective clothing, cloakrooms, messrooms, and washing facilities in tinplate works,[2] and for the provision of seats for shell workers turning or machining shells or shell bodies[3] ; in addition to other orders which did not affect munition trades. Each of these orders represented a point which welfare officers had been previously directed to bring strongly to the notice of factory owners, and as each order took effect, the welfare officers ceased to intervene further in the provision which was thus made compulsory.

The future relation of welfare work to that of the Factory Inspectors' Department was left indeterminate at the date of its transfer from the Ministry of Munitions. During the war the latter possessed, as has been said, both as a great contracting Department and as an employer of labour on a scale unprecedented in the country, unique facilities for pushing forward and for directing the extension of industrial welfare. These facilities it utilised to give an impetus to existing schemes for improving working conditions in certain industries such as no other three-year period had produced.

V. Canteens and the Central Control Board.[4]

(a) ESTABLISHMENT OF CANTEENS IN MUNITION WORKS.

The provision of munitions canteens, which was the first step taken in securing the welfare of munition workers, originated outside the Department, and before the establishment of the Welfare Section. Historically, it was a by-product of the " prohibition campaign " launched by Mr. Lloyd George at the end of February, 1915. In the course of the debates in the House of Commons on the proposal to prohibit, or alternatively to limit, the drink trade during the war, it was more than once represented that the supply of reasonable opportunities for obtaining food in or near the works would diminish the force of the " lure of drink," which was said to be retarding production.[5] On 10 June an Order in Council was issued, under Defence of the Realm Act No. 3, establishing the Defence of the Realm (Liquor Control) Regulations, 1915, by which the Central Control Board (Liquor Traffic) was constituted " the prescribed Government authority for the purposes of the State control of the liquor traffic in areas to which the regulations are applied."

---

[1] Statutory Rules and Orders No. 1067 (12/10/17).
[2] Statutory Rules and Orders No. 1035 (-/10/17).
[3] Statutory Rules and Orders No. 824 (3/7/18).
[4] A fuller treatment of this subject will be found in Vol. V, Part IV.
[5] *Parliamentary Debates* (1915), *H. of C.*, LXXI, 354ff., 868 ff. Thus, Mr. Wilkie (of the Shipwrights' Society) in the Debate of 10 May, 1915, on the new Defence of the Realm Act, ended his protests against the character of the much-discussed White Paper on *Excessive Drinking in Shipbuilding and Munitions Areas*, which made men who " were doing the right thing feel they were maligned," with the very practical recommendations frequently made at the time by representatives of labour that every large works should, on the analogy of the Royal Dockyards, be provided with " an institution at which food and drink could be bought to meet especially the needs of workmen coming from a distance."

The work of the Central Control Board was a very large and important experiment in State control of the liquor trade, combined with constructive work in the provision of alternatives to the public-house, of a type often suggested, but not carried out, in time of peace. As such its history belongs elsewhere.[1] But, under the fifth liquor control regulation, the Board had powers to " maintain refreshment rooms," and it very early appointed a Canteen Committee to investigate the possibilities of this work. It was in its relations with this Committee which, under the chairmanship of Sir George Newman, undertook detailed responsibility for the establishment of canteens in munition works, that the Ministry of Munitions came into administrative connection with the industrial canteen movement.

In a letter to the Ministry of Munitions, on 24 August, 1915, the Board laid stress on the need for canteens in or near munitions works. They expressed the view that the duty of providing canteens rested primarily with the employers, and asked whether the Department could not see its way to provide such canteens in Government factories, and to encourage their provision in controlled establishments, especially such as were in the process of construction.[2] In further correspondence the Board pointed out the special need for canteens in the new Filling Factories, as their employees, being compelled to wear special factory clothing, could not leave the factory for refreshments. On 16 October a letter from the Ministry to the Central Control Board stated that the Minister was prepared to accept responsibility for the provision of canteens, where necessary, at national factories, and to encourage their provision at controlled establishments[3]; and on 19 November the Minister further stated that, by arrangement with the Treasury, capital expenditure on the provision of canteens by controlled firms might be written off against current profits for the purposes of Part II. of the Munitions of War Act of 1915, if such expenditure was approved by the Control Board.[4]

On 3 January, 1916 (when, it may be noted, the Welfare Section of the Department had just been formed), the Ministry of Munitions asked the Board to become responsible for the organisation of canteens in the Royal Arsenals and the National Projectile, Filling and Explosives Factories, where such provision had not already been made. The Ministry undertook " to provide the building, lighting, heating and equipment of canteens," and desired that " they should be run so as to be self-supporting, including the cost of staff."[5] The Board's reply, intimating willingness to accept responsibility, was dated 22 January. The Board made it clear that it would be no part of its functions to organise each individual canteen, and that, while in sympathy with the Minister's desire that the canteen should be self-supporting, they considered that this " should be regarded rather as an

---

[1] Cf. Reports I. to IV. of the Central Control Board, 1915 to 1919 ; and *The Control of the Drink Trade*, by Henry Carter (of the Central Control Board), 1918.

[2] M.W. 25683/1 and /2.

[3] M.W.28683/2.

[4] M.W.45309 ; C.R. 3235.

[5] M.W. 28683/7.

ideal than as a condition where women were employed."[1]   Sir George
Newman more than once subsequently represented that it might be
worth while, on educational grounds, to run industrial canteens at a
temporary loss in order to popularise the movement.   The Health of
Munition Workers Committee, under the same chairman, strongly
emphasized at the same time the value of canteens as an aid to
efficiency.[2]

In a circular announcing the arrangements that had been made,
which was sent to the heads of national factories on 16 February,
1916, it was made clear that the responsibility for the proper management of the canteen, when established, would rest with the responsible
authority in each factory, subject to the supervision of the Canteen
Committee of the Central Control Board.   The circular called attention
to the desirability of giving the workers some share in the control of the
canteen, and thus initiated in some factories the welfare functions of
the works committees subsequently organised.

(b) The Canteens Organisation of the Central Control Board.

The financial agreements thus reached were open to various
interpretations, and reference is made elsewhere to the understanding
on the point reached after detailed discussion in January, 1917.[3]
A special organisation for canteen work was developed by the Central
Control Board, and the Welfare Section of the Ministry of Munitions
referred to the Board all proposals for the establishment of canteens
discussed between controlled firms and the Department's welfare
officers.   The Board appointed trained inspectors, who investigated,
at a personal visit, the need for each proposed canteen, while H.M. Office
of Works scrutinised plans, specifications and bills of quantities,
insisting on the invitation of competitive tenders, and frequently
redrafting entire schemes.   This, it was claimed, undoubtedly resulted
in the saving of many thousand pounds, and in the erection of more
efficient canteens.   Neither the Ministry of Munitions nor the Board
intervened in the financial control of canteens once established in
controlled establishments.   It was, however, estimated that a large
proportion did not cover the cost of their working.

With regard to national factories, on the other hand, the Department took into consideration the question of running expenses.   In
March, 1917, it was found that the majority of these canteens were
working at a loss.   Special steps were therefore taken by the supply
departments to cover these deficits and prevent their recurrence.[4]
The provision of canteens, however, in both trade and national
factories often included messroom accommodation, which could hardly
be expected to pay its way.

[1] M.W.28683/8.
[2] Memoranda Nos. 3, 6, 11, 19 and *Final Report of Health of Munition Workers Committee.*
[3] See Appendix I.   [4] Hist. Rec./H/346. 1/3.

The Board's inspectors visited periodically canteens of both the national factories and controlled firms, and offered expert advice when necessary for their management. Such advice was further available, in complete detail, both in the pamphlets of the Health of Munition Workers Committee, who drew up their first report on canteens in November, 1915, and in a sixpenny booklet, *Feeding the Munition Workers*, issued in 1917 by the Central Control Board.

(c) THE FOOD SECTION OF THE DEPARTMENT.

The shortage of food in January, 1918, convinced the Minister that he must assume responsibility for feeding munition workers, and a Food Section was formed in the Labour Regulation Department, whose functions were to inspect canteens in national factories, and to advise the factory management on food questions, to advise controlled firms on the provision and maintenance of canteens, and to communicate with the Board of Inland Revenue on the finance of such provision ; and to act as the link between the Ministries of Munitions and Food on all questions concerning the feeding of munition workers.[1] To this body, accordingly, the canteens organisation of the Central Control Board, with its staff of inspectors, was transferred. For the last eight months of the war, therefore, the Department undertook both the maintenance of food supplies and the general superintendence of all munitions canteens.

VI. Finance.

Firms urged by the Department to make welfare provision for their workers often represented both that the cost of building work was exceptionally heavy during the war, and also that any provision made for canteens, rest rooms, etc., for women workers would have little or no value after the war, when the female staff would have dispersed, and the whole number of employees would probably have greatly diminished. To meet this objection a system was evolved by which a great part of the cost of such provision fell on the taxpayer, on the assumption that firms were being called upon to make special provision for the efficient output of munitions, and that this national need had perforce to be met without regard to convenient seasons, or to the future advantage of the employer. The cost of canteens, welfare accommodation, salaries of supervisors, recreation schemes for munition workers, etc., was therefore met to a greater or less extent out of excess profits, or rather, from the surplus on the year's working from which the excess profits tax or, earlier, the munitions levy, was drawn. Details of these provisions are given in Appendix I. Broadly, small expenses for such purposes, if approved by the Welfare Section, might be returned as a portion of the year's working expenses. In the case of larger expenditure on schemes approved by the Welfare Section, and of some permanent value to the firm, the difference

---

[1] HIST. REC./H/346. 1/2.   L.R.F. 120/129,

between their present and (probably diminished) post-war value to the firm was estimated, and, like the working expenses just referred to, might be deducted from the year's surplus liable to the excess profits duty.

The work of the Welfare Section was, as has been repeatedly said, to a great extent educational, and was improvised to meet an unparalleled emergency. As in other work meeting the requirements of a national emergency or of education, it might fairly be argued that its cost should be borne, or shared, by the community. Whether such assistance should be given by " allowance " from taxation or by direct grant was a matter of some controversy. The adoption of welfare measures was, however, much facilitated by the fact that financial concessions were secured after the creation of the Ministry of Munitions.

CHAPTER II.

WELFARE IN FACTORIES.

I. Welfare Work for Women and Girls.

(a) "Welfare" and "Welfare Supervision."

Welfare work in factories may be considered from two points of view—the provision of good conditions for the health and happiness of the workers, and the utilisation of such provision. The first is to a great extent a question of accommodation (including equipment for meals and for treatment of accidents and illness) ; the second involves problems of labour management in a wide sense, and of supplying the human element, without which the most elaborate accommodation may be useless. Welfare work, as organised by the Ministry of Munitions, was sometimes believed to consist only in the appointment by a firm of a new official, with anomalous functions, of a type known only to a few benevolent employers before the war, who should represent this "human" side of labour management. Although however, the welfare supervisor who, at the instigation of the Department, "looked after" the women and girls and boys in munition works, had, in many cases, an important part in the administration of the factory, yet his or her appointment was not an integral part of a welfare policy. To the supervisor was indeed entrusted much of the maintenance of a good standard of working conditions, because if a policy is to be effective it must normally be the duty of some one person or group of persons to carry it out ; but the work of securing the effective interest of managers in the well-being of their factory workers could take place without any formal system of welfare supervision, entrusted to one member of their staff. It was the main part of the work of the Ministry's travelling welfare officers to stimulate this interest, and to supply practical suggestions and information in order that it might have prompt results.

(b) Welfare Inspection.

When the Women Factory Inspectors of the Home Office undertook, in January, 1916, the preliminary inquiries into welfare conditions in munitions factories for the new Department, they supplied the Ministry of Munitions with a series of most valuable cross sections cut across the position of women·in industry in a year when that position was changing rapidly. The 1,396 factories (employing 200,000 women and girls) visited by them in the course of the year were roughly divided into three classes, of which Class A contained 31 per cent., Class B 49 per cent., Class C 20 per cent. Class A was satisfactory. B and C conditions meant, in varying combinations, partial or complete lack of messroom accommodation or facilities for cooking food ; inadequate or non-existent cloakrooms and washing appliances, even for dusty and greasy occupations ; lack of supply of seats ; need of first-aid and rest rooms ; supervision even of numerous young girls by men only, and other defects—in factories working mostly twelve hour shifts, and reached often by considerable journeys from the workers' homes.[1]

The duty of subsequent visitation, in order to secure improvements in such conditions, was at once taken over by the welfare officers of the Ministry of Munitions, who, as has been said, were in 1917 and 1918 stationed in some eight areas, with some 400 to 500 factories on the roll of each district. They visited at this time all controlled establishments, stores, and national factories employing over fifteen women (paying the first visit without, as in the previous year, awaiting a preliminary report from the Home Office), and went to factories or workshops with an even smaller number of women, on request for information by other Departments or on receipt of complaints. So far as was possible with a limited staff, factories received routine visits once in six months, but quarterly or more frequent visits were paid if there appeared to be special need, on account of bad working conditions which were in urgent need of remedy, or the appointment of an inexperienced welfare supervisor anxious for advice or help.

Women welfare officers were specially required to give attention to the following matters[2] :—

    1. The accommodation provided for the workers including—

        (a) Canteens and messrooms ;
        (b) Cloakrooms ;
        (c) Washing accommodation ;
        (d) Rest rooms.

    2. The health and personal records of the women employed, in so far as such records were kept.

    3. The nature of the work done and the method of technical control (by foremen or forewomen, charge hands, etc.).

    4. The method of engagement and dismissal.

    5. The supervision and control exercised over the women (on day shifts and night shifts).

    6. The provision and suitability of protective clothing.

    7. The provision of seats and lifting tackle.

They also reported on the supply of first-aid appliances, ambulance rooms, and drinking water, until, in the late autumn of 1917, the Home Office orders on these subjects placed the duty of securing the provision of these in a very large number of munition works in the hands of the Factory Inspectors.

The welfare officers found in their early visits, in accordance with the functions thus assigned to them, an exceedingly variable range of problems. Generally, though with some very marked exceptions,

---

[1] Cd. 9108 of 1918, p. 9.   [2] Hist. Rec./R/346/39.

good structural provision for the workers' comfort as well as for production had been made or was readily undertaken in large or new factories. Especially in the national factories, and (later) the new aircraft works, Boards of Management or owners were, normally, very ready to provide a high standard of accommodation. It was in the older factories, such as some of the long-established general engineering works, and the comparatively small firms engaged in the numerous marginal munitions industries, that there were serious difficulties in securing a good standard, on grounds of indifference (owing perhaps to the transitory nature of the employment of women), or of great pressure of business among the management, or of lack of sites for building.[1]

In some cases, rough working conditions for women and girls were the natural result of their taking on the work of men (e.g., in shipyards), who had acquiesced in discomfort as inevitable. A low standard of factory conditions was, however, also found to a marked extent in the districts, such as portions of the Midlands, in which there had been a large amount of industrial work by women before the war. There the factory in which munitions were made was often a building just complying with the regulations of the Factory Acts as to ventilation, etc., where the workers, in the times of greatest pressure, spent the hours from 8 a.m. to 7 p.m., or from 7 a.m. to 9 p.m. or more, with the statutory breaks of one or two hours for meals, taken beside the machines if they lived too far away to go home, with no facilities for resting, washing, warming food or drying clothes, or treating accidents. Such a low standard usually, though not always, coincided with a low level of wages.[2] The same discomforts had been accepted by generations of workers (men and women), but they were intensified during the war by the great increase of numbers employed, often in the same space, and by the much longer hours of work. The improvement of such conditions required the common-sense treatment of a number of semi-domestic details. The welfare officers' reports in connection with what has been called "structural" welfare indicated the need in many cases for great improvement, but also showed the changing attitude of employers, often under very difficult circumstances, to their workpeople's comfort. The following are some of the points on which the welfare officers reported to headquarters.

Canteens and Messrooms.—The provision of these had been warmly urged by the Health of Munition Workers Committee,[3] had been undertaken in national factories in the first autumn of the Ministry's work, and had been facilitated by placing the initial cost of them in controlled establishments to a very large extent upon the community.[4] Employers opposed to their construction explained

---

[1] The difficulty of finding space for improvements, which often before the war impeded the betterment of the older workmen's dwellings, applied equally to the factory in a crowded area.

[2] Cf. C.E. 1260/15 ; C.E. 1462/15 ; C.E. 152/15 ; C.E. 758/15, etc.

[3] See *Final Report of Health of Munition Workers Committee* (Cd. 9065, 1918) Section IX, and Appendix I, below.

[4] See Appendix I.

either that there was no room for them on the factory premises, or that, if established, their maintenance would add to the number of their unproductive employees ; that the workers lived near home and preferred to go back for their meals (obviously a valid reason, especially in the case of mothers of families), or that they preferred to eat separately, so that their neighbours should not see the food brought by them from home,[1] or, finally, that the workpeople were quite contented with existing conditions.   On the whole, however, employers became convinced of the desirability of some such provision, which was normally insisted on by the Home Office in granting permission for women to do night work[2]; and there was a growing demand for it among workers—a demand which increased with the rise in women's wages and with the food difficulties of 1917-1918.   Messrooms were, on the whole, more in request than canteens, except in very large factories.   The popularity of either depended, by universal experience, on their management.   If there was quick service and variety of food (in the case of canteens), cleanliness and good order, the women were said to be almost too ready to spend the whole of their meal times, even to the loss of opportunities of fresh air, in the canteen or mess-room.   Either type of room could form a centre for the social life of the factory, and could supply opportunities for concerts, dances, etc., when the arrangement of day and night shifts permitted.   Both normally gave most satisfaction when some kind of workers' advisory committee was attached to their management.   It was found that they were appreciated most by the younger workers (so that in some cases canteen takings fell off when the younger workmen had been called up for military service).

By the beginning of 1918 it was calculated that more than two-thirds of the factories visited by women welfare officers gave canteen and messroom facilities of some sort.   This was a very much larger proportion than that in the works occupied by men and boys alone.[3]

At the date of the Armistice, 733 controlled establishments (out of a total of 5,603), with 871,000 employees, were known to the Department to be provided with canteens.   The great majority of national factories also had canteens.[4]

Accommodation for Clothing and for Washing.—Cloakrooms in which the workers could leave their outer clothes were at first often not desired by the workers themselves, who preferred to hang their coats and hats beside their machines, so that they might be available promptly at breaks in the working day, and might also be safe from theft.   Clearly, however, it was much better to have facilities for

---

[1] " This feeling is so strong that in some North Country messrooms where tables are provided a strip of wood a few inches high is fixed down the centre of the table by way of screen." (Welfare Officer's Report, January, 1918. HIST. REC./R/346/133.) " We put up a special messroom which the workpeople will not use," replied a small firm near Birmingham to the representations of the Welfare Section in August, 1916. " They bring their own food and are not desirous of exposing what they have for dinner to their fellow workpeople. They do not always dine upon roast chicken, consequently they prefer to eat near their own machines where they have no overlookers." (C.E. 152/15.)

[2] Cf. Chapter V.   [3] HIST. REC./R/346/133.   [4] HIST. REC./H/346.1/2.

hanging them away from the workrooms where these were dusty or dirty, and for drying them if they were wet from outdoor work or the long journeys taken by many workers. When special working clothes were required, cloakrooms were obviously essential, and their care, for workers in "danger buildings," was safeguarded by elaborate regulations. Welfare officers found themselves called on to give frequent advice as to the best equipment of cloakrooms, and as to the appointment of cloakroom matrons to keep order and prevent pilfering. A good deal more than half of the factories visited by welfare officers had some such provision by the beginning of 1918.[1]

If a suitable place in which to keep outdoor clothes was desirable, even more so was provision for washing. "Good" firms had, indeed, realised the need for this before the war if they were to attract a satisfactory type of worker. Opportunities for washing were, however, almost universally found to be deficient at the early visits of the welfare officers, who found it often hard to convince employers, except in the best and most modern firms, that they had not fulfilled their duty in this matter by providing, perhaps, "one broken basin and cold water" to three hundred workers.[2] Here again the workers' own standard of demand reacted upon what was supplied to them. Employers frequently said, with apparent justification, that their workpeople were contented as they were, and had misused such provision of basins, soap and towels as had been made for them in the past. The Welfare Section, however, through its officers, laid much stress on the provision of proper washing accommodation, and supplied advice as to the kinds of soap and towels and of supervision required. It was found that with good conditions, including, where possible, a supply of hot water, the women and girls appreciated the provision made. In only about 30 per cent. of the factories was there, however, said to be really satisfactory provision in January, 1918.[1]

Protective Clothing.—With the employment of inexperienced women in explosives works, in the manipulation of poisonous chemicals as in the filling factories, in work with machinery however well fenced, in outdoor work—e.g., in shipyards, it became obvious that special clothing must be worn. The Home Office issued in 1917 an illustrated booklet showing the kind of clothing suitable for certain classes of work, and the Department of Explosive Supplies in the Ministry of Munitions arranged to supply overalls and caps at fixed prices, subject, of course, to market fluctuations, and by arrangement with contractors to quote prices for oilproof and waterproof aprons, munition gloves, clogs, boots (rubber and leather), oilskin coats and hats, and woollen serge and lasting cloth suits for acid workers. The welfare officers were able to supply information to firms about these, and helped, in conjunction with the factory inspectors, to design suitable protective clothing. They brought pressure to bear on firms to adopt caps and overalls, especially for shell workers. The wearing of overalls was recommended by the Department in the dilution Circular L. 6 in the autumn of 1915, but could not be enforced

---

[1] HIST. REC./R/346/133.   [2] C.E. 1227/15.

except in the case of T.N.T. workers. They were in some cases unpopular at first with the girls and the cause of temporary strikes ; but efforts were made to provide samples which should be becoming as well as useful, and they became accepted as the recognised uniform of munition workers. Employers as a whole were ready to accept the suggestion that they should be worn, and the Welfare Section secured financial help for their provision in certain cases. The question as to their provision and ownership as between the firm and the worker was, however, a source of friction in some cases.[1]

The provision of cloakrooms, washing basins or troughs and overalls was an apparently unimportant question. They represented, however, apart from the comfort or safety produced by their supply, an advance, even if small, in the " civilisation " of industry, and from both points of view were urged by the Welfare Section.

Rest Rooms, Ambulance Rooms, First Aid Appliances.—Under the special Welfare Order of 12 October, 1917, it became compulsory from December to provide ambulance rooms or first aid appliances in most of the factories with which welfare officers dealt, and their provision passed to the sphere of the Home Office.[2] Before this time, however, the Welfare Section had constantly pressed the need for them upon employers. The welfare officers were also frequently engaged in helping to secure good care of such first aid outfits as already existed in dusty corners of many factories, and the appointment of factory nurses and of welfare supervisors with first aid training gave value to such provision. Employers increasingly acknowledged the saving of time, and incidentally of payments under the Workmen's Compensation Acts, produced by prompt and regular treatment of accidents and minor maladies. It was probably this side of " welfare " which received the most unquestioning approval of men and boy munition workers, especially as disabled soldiers began to return to the workshops.

Seats.—The provision of seats, whenever production permitted, might seem an obvious means of preventing fatigue and increasing efficiency. Medical opinion, however, was not clear as to the general necessity for their provision, employers and foremen sometimes shrank from installing them as a possible encouragement to "slackness," and workers were not always anxious for them. Welfare officers, however, frequently drew the attention of employers to the desirability of their provision under certain conditions, and the section was prepared with recommendations as to suitable and conveniently fitted seats— *e.g.*, for lathe work. They were not, however, widely adopted. A special inquiry was made during 1917 by welfare officers with regard

---

[1] The provision of overalls for women and girls had some effect in raising the standard of men and boys, who had frequently in similar work avoided all " protective " clothing and acquiesced in discomfort. Thus at the first full dress hearing before the Committee on Production in July, 1917, of a claim for higher wages from the newly formed Chemical Employers' Federation, it was urged as a basis for such a claim that the workmen's clothes were destroyed by six or eight weeks of the most careful use on chemical work. (Cf. Committee on Production verbatim reports).

[2] See p. 18.

to the provision of seats for women engaged on shell manufacture. " Every operation involved was timed, and the possible sitting time for each was carefully estimated. The results were grouped so as to show those operations in which no sitting time was possible, those in which it was possible but was less than one-quarter of the actual machining time, those in which it was more than a quarter but less than half, etc."[1] This supplied data for the Home Office Welfare Order of August, 1918, for seats for women shell-makers—the first order rendering the provision of seats in factories compulsory.

Drinking Water.—The provision of this similarly became compulsory in October, 1917, in all factories employing more than 25 persons. Its supply had been previously advocated by welfare officers.[2]

In securing the prosaic and useful improvements just summarised, the Department facilitated their supply in controlled establishments, which it did not coerce, by securing the large financial concessions to which reference has been frequently made ; by helping to select sites for buildings, in conjunction with the Central Control Board and the Munitions Works Board ; by supplying (again largely through the Central Control Board) handbooks on food and canteen management ; by designing, in conjunction with the Factory Department of the Home Office, and securing supplies of protective clothing ; by providing busy managers with information about accessible welfare equipment (first-aid outfits, soapboxes, seats, etc.) ; and by assisting in the interchange of information between factory managers as to recent developments in welfare provision. This last function was at the time probably one of the most valuable performed by the welfare officers.[3]

The welfare officers and the Intra-mural Welfare Section at headquarters were to a great extent occupied with questions of accommodation and equipment. But a very important part of their work lay in helping to secure good use of such equipment, and, so far as they were concerned in this, the effective management of women's labour. This led normally (despite the fact already insisted on of the distinction between welfare provision and welfare supervision) to the recommendation of the appointment of a welfare supervisor who should, in the absence of any other organisation for the purpose, be

---

[1] Hist. Rec./R/346/39.

[2] " This is so elementary a need that we might have supposed it would be everywhere provided for. It is not. In some workplaces the only available drinking water for girls working on the fourth floor is in the yard down eight flights of stairs ; in others, a long walk to a distant part of the factory, involving loss of money as well as time to piece-workers (to say nothing of the foreman's displeasure) to ' get a drink.' Such difficulties lead not only to discomfort, and, in hot weather or in trades involving exertion to exhaustion, but to danger where the thirsty workers run the risk of typhoid by drinking water intended only for manufacturing purposes." (*Women's Trade Union Review*, January, 1917.)

[3] The Department sanctioned an exhibition by the Welfare and Health Section of a model rest room, dining-room, crèche, etc., at a " National Economy and Welfare Exhibition," in the L.C.C. Hall, in July, 1917. Propaganda work was done in connection with the Department's exhibitions of women's work under dilution held in different parts of the country during 1917. (L.R. 138.)

responsible for the effective employment of both accommodation and
labour.   In January, 1918, it was calculated that approximately
40 per cent. of the factories on the welfare officers' roll, employing
60 per cent. of women munition makers, had provided for the control
in some form of their women employees by a woman.   The proportion
of munition workers for whose welfare such provision had been made
at this date, was, it will be seen, noticeably larger in the case of women
and girls than among boy workers.[1]

No satisfactory statistics of the extension of industrial welfare
and the improvement in working conditions in munition factories
can be supplied.   The tables on page 10 give some numerical
indication of the improvements secured during the first year's work
of the Welfare Section, but with the gradual permeation of welfare
theories it became impossible to say to what agency specific improvements were due.   The welfare officers, however, recorded, in reports
from which the following quotations are taken, the change of attitude
which was apparent among employers at the beginning of 1918, after
two years' work.[2]   It is noteworthy that the process of education
which they described included that of workpeople as well as employers.

1. " The general standard of welfare conditions in the
factories of this area can be said to have been considerably
raised.   Factory managers on the whole now realise that the
provision of a certain amount of satisfactory accommodation
for women is expected of them, and is demanded by the good
type of workers.   It is not now so necessary to explain to firms
the principles of welfare work, as it has been brought to their
notice frequently, both officially and by public opinion.   Competition in certain areas plays an important part.   In our
experience, it is becoming more evident that the firms themselves
are recognising that well organised welfare conditions increase
efficiency by improving time-keeping and the standard of
health of the workers, and by creating an atmosphere of con-
tentment and well-being.   This would seem to be due more to
the personal element in good welfare work than to purely
mechanical organisation."

2. " Undoubtedly, during the last two years considerable
progress has been made in every direction in the Midland area.
A helpful sign is that the workers themselves are beginning to
demand better accommodation, and employers are waking up
to the fact that in order to secure the best type of labour they
must provide this organisation.   For instance, one firm, after
opening a canteen, found it was much easier to obtain labour.
In another case, where an employer was about to employ women
for the first time on work which demanded some skill and
intelligence, the women who applied for the work and whom he
would willingly have engaged, refused to come when they
ascertained what scanty provision was made for their comfort."

---

[1] Hist. Rec./H/346/39. See p. 42,   [2] Hist. Rec./R/346/133.

3. " One indication that good factory arrangements are now recognised as a necessary part of the employment of women is that in several cases firms about to take on women have invited a welfare officer to visit and discuss arrangements before engaging the women."

4. " During the year there would appear to have been very considerable progress both as to actual improvement of conditions and as to change in the point of view, so that the outlook is hopeful for further improvements."

5. " The progress noticed in factories in this area (Glasgow) is encouraging. We find that when factories have been visited and given the necessary stimulus, the management is in most cases very willing to take what steps are possible. In large factories this, of course, has been comparatively easy to obtain, as they are much in the public eye, but we have also noticed with satisfaction the great number of small places employing from 20 to 50 women where during the past two years conditions have been revolutionised. At the factories which are becoming well-known as having good working conditions, there are waiting lists which sometimes run into hundreds of applicants. The women workers, realising that good conditions are possible, are now looking for and expect a higher standard than they have ever had before."

This change of attitude, on which the welfare officers for boys also remarked, developed still further during the remaining months of the active existence of the Welfare and Health Section.

(c) WELFARE SUPERVISORS.

The functions of welfare supervisors in controlled establishments and national factories varied even more widely than did the interpretation of the term " welfare," as applied to industrial conditions. The position ranged from that of the promoted charge-hand in a small works, who combined technical supervision or production with some responsibility for the first-aid equipment, and perhaps the care of the messroom, to the "lady superintendent," an integral part of the factory's organisation, responsible to the directors or to the general manager, and recognised as the authority on all questions connected with woman labour. In between these two extremes there was every gradation.

The duties generally delegated to the supervisor included the following :—

1. The selection and rejection of candidates for employment, or the preliminary sifting of such applicants before passing them on to the foreman or forewoman for engagement on technical grounds.

2. The supervision of the women's accommodation, including canteens messrooms, cloakrooms, etc., and the engagement of their staffs.

3. The general supervision of the discipline of the women, either personally or through forewomen or cloakroom matrons, on day shift or night shift.

4. The supply and upkeep of protective clothing.

5. The investigation of workers' complaints.

6. Inquiry into absenteeism and bad time-keeping.

7. Inquiry before dismissal of a worker.

8. Care for the workers' health, especially in regard to ventilation, lighting, heating and cleanliness of the shops, the lifting of heavy weights, and the effect of long hours of work.

9. The supervision of first aid treatment by the factory nurses, if there was no factory doctor, and the administration of first aid treatment if there was no nurse.

In addition, the supervisor or her assistants sometimes undertook the visiting of sick workers, or of lodgings for workers in the factory, and the administration of war savings schemes, of benevolent and sick funds and convalescent schemes founded in conjunction with the workers. She organised recreation (such as dinner-hour concerts and dances in the canteen and outdoor games), supervised the factory crèche where this existed, and dealt with difficulties of transit to and from the works. In some factories she was consulted on, or directed, the transfer of women employees and the methods by which new work should be taken up by them. In many places the welfare supervisor was given the additional duty of supervising the boys employed.

Welfare supervision as described by the Health of Munition Workers' Committee in December, 1915, and as outlined in the first circular on the subject issued by the Ministry in 1916, included most of these varied functions. The appointment of a welfare supervisor or lady superintendent was summed up in this circular as meaning in effect that "the manager of a factory says : ' I want to be satisfied that the women and girls I employ are working under good conditions as regards both themselves and the business, but I myself have no time to go into every detail. I therefore appoint a lady superintendent or a staff of superintendents and I expect them to act for me in trying to ensure a satisfactory state of things. I wish them as a rule to be guided by their own tact and commonsense but to come to me when any defect cannot otherwise be remedied.' "[1]

A year later, as the result of experience, the position of the supervisor as defined by the section was made more precise, and more insistence was laid, as in the work of the Welfare Section as a whole, on her care for the workers' health. " The duty of a welfare supervisor is to obtain and maintain a healthy staff of workers, and to help in maintaining satisfactory conditions of work." She should, it was stated, on these grounds undertake the selection of the staff (with reference, if possible, to the certifying surgeon or panel doctor), the supervision of working conditions, of the canteen (probably in consultation with the trained manager in charge), of the

---

[1] Circular M.M. 13.

ambulance, rest room and first aid apparatus, of cloakrooms and the supply of overalls. She should, finally, be in touch with "the relation of health to efficiency" by access to the wages books and the time office, and by keeping records of ambulance cases and accidents.[1]

The welfare supervisors appointed in the first year of the section's work met with a good deal of comprehensible misunderstanding. Even when appointed from the official panel, their work was often ill-defined and their appointment was sometimes admittedly only the result of departmental pressure. There were difficulties with the manager or managers, often comprehensibly unwilling to delegate to a woman, normally inexperienced in factory life, powers of dealing with the staff. There was the possibility of opposition by foremen and forewomen, afraid of interference with their control of the workers from whom they were required to produce output. There was in some cases opposition from the workers, who distrusted the appearance of a new official. In the great majority of cases these difficulties disappeared in practice.

The success of the welfare supervisor's work depended largely on her own capacities, but also depended to a great extent on the position assigned to her by the management. It was chiefly owing to misconception of what welfare supervision should involve that failures occurred. Thus in a large shell works the management complained of the complete failure of "welfare" as represented by two nurses who had been installed to "look after the women" with ill-defined duties as to the division of control of the rapidly growing staff between themselves and the foremen. When, however, the general manager stated to the Department that he must dismiss his whole female staff in two days unless some improvement could be made in the resulting disorder, the Welfare Section promptly recommended a highly qualified superintendent, who was given a definite position on the administrative staff with an adequate number of assistants, and by the firm's admission wholly justified her position and that of the welfare movement, in fact if not in name.[2] In many munitions works, and especially in the national factories,[3] the functions of the welfare supervisor were early made definite. In all works, it is true, in which welfare supervision justified its existence a large portion of the supervision work remained perforce indefinite. Thus the receipt of workers' complaints, either on small details or on larger questions expressed by a deputation headed by a trade union secretary, might occupy a considerable amount of her time (to the advantage both of the firm and the worker in the removal of friction). Help in illness, etc., also opened an indefinite field of "human" relationships. After attempting to satisfy the workers' obvious and immediate needs, firms which had adopted welfare supervision tended to make some selection from the very wide field of possible activities. In some factories, especially in those in which dangerous work was performed, the health side of the work was

---

[1] Circular M.M. 13 (revised).

[2] HIST. REC./R/1122. 4/15 ; C.E. 804/15.

[3] Chapter VIII illustrates the position filled by lady superintendents in national factories.

emphasised. In others, the social side of welfare received most attention ; in others again the industrial side, as represented by the engagement and control of labour. This last function was of special importance if the supervisor was to enter into businesslike relations with the women for whom she was responsible, and to diminish the change in personnel—the " factory wastage "—which was a standing difficulty in the maintenance of an efficient staff.[1] Careful records were kept, in the national factories and in certain controlled establishments, of absenteeism among the women workers, as well as of their health, progress in the factory, etc., and bad time-keeping and unnecessary changes of work were checked by inquiry into their causes and by the removal of these as far as possible, while comfortable working conditions ånd a good " tone " in the workshop supplied an incentive to regular attendance.

The development of the functions of the welfare supervisor was due fundamentally, as has been said, to the need for entrusting the care for the human material in the workshop to some definite portion of the administrative staff of the factory.

The following account of her early work by the supervisor of a very large works is quoted as a typical illustration of this often disregarded fact. The writer explained that her experiences, which were typical of those of many others, might be taken as an instance of the impotence of welfare orders by themselves in securing " the spirit of welfare." When she began her work in 1916 in a controlled establishment engaged on T.N.T. work

"the provision for washing was good and adequate ; each worker was supposed to have her own overall which was washed every week ; the meal-room accommodation was also good, and milk and cocoa was provided in gallons and every regulation sent down was made an instruction by the management. The link that broke the chain was the executive one. One could hardly describe in official language the actual state of confusion, the abuse of every provision and privilege or the standard of behaviour, time-keeping or of work that prevailed. It did not follow that because milk was provided it was necessarily drunk, or that a comfortable meal

---

[1] The problem of the " disappearing woman " was an acknowledged difficulty of factory management before the war, and, despite the leaving certificate regulations, it continued as a phenomenon among women munition workers. Thus in March, 1918, Captain M. Greenwood of the Welfare Section supplied the Hours of Labour Committee with the following estimate of the length of service of women munition workers employed in any one factory at a given time. The figures, based on an extensive inquiry into the extent of wastage of female labour in munitions factories, indicate the transient nature of the population. (M.M. 197.)

Length of Service.				Number (percentage).	Length of Service.				Number (percentage)
1 month	..	..	..	13·33	7 months	..	..	..	5·89
2 months	..	..	..	9·66	8 ,,	..	..	..	5·67
3 ,,	..	..	..	10·00	9 ,,	..	..	..	5·87
4 ,,	..	..	..	11·61	10 ,,	..	..	..	4·06
5 ,,	..	..	..	10·04	11 ,,	..	..	..	5·59
6 .,	..	..	..	7·46	12 ,, and over		..		10·81

could be enjoyed because good accommodation was provided. At every break for a meal or change of shift the changing rooms were pandemonium, while each worker strove to get what she thought was a better overall or pair of gloves than her own. Hundreds of pairs of gloves and refills for respirators were used up every day, caps were lost by the dozen. Such supplies could be had for the asking, and yet we seemed to be making no headway against T.N.T. effects, nor any real headway with welfare."

Gradually order was evolved out of this chaos. "It seemed clear that the changing rooms could be made the real strategic point—and my own experience convinces me that next to the Employment Department the organisation and supervision of the women's quarters is all important ; the psychological effect of properly maintained quarters on the woman worker is tremendous—so that the new supervisor became for the time a glorified cloakroom matron ; the changing rooms, which were always very cramped and never boasted of separate lockers, at any rate assumed a businesslike appearance ; definite places were allotted and no trespassing was allowed. At first the girls resented any change in the old come-and-go-as-you-please method. But the innovations were so acceptable to the foremen, owing to the time saved in starting work and the different spirit shown in starting, that they not only gave unqualified support but gradually asked for co-operation in various other matters of general discipline.

" In like manner the meal room was tackled and comfort and cheeriness began to replace the previous noise and confusion. It is our pride that here, too, there was no change either in numbers or in personnel of the staff—we merely made different use of existing provisions."

Incidentally, bad time-keeping was cured. The welfare superintendent made or enforced a rule that no worker must begin work till she had had cocoa or milk ; this was served out just before 6 a.m. in the meal-room (by the superintendent) —" so that in the end no factory had such a record for prompt starting in the morning ; by 6.5. a.m. every girl was dressed and at work.

" I feel that it cannot be too strongly emphasised that welfare orders alone, invaluable as they are as tools, are nothing but tools. Not only are they powerless to secure real welfare ; they tend to have a contrary effect."[1]

The comprehensive functions of welfare supervision required a corresponding range of capacity in the supervisor, and it was not easy to improvise a supply of suitable candidates at the outset of the work of the Welfare Section. An official panel was, however, formed in the section in March, 1916, and interviewing boards for candidates were held in London and the provinces by representatives of the

---

[1] HIST. REC./R/346/41.

Welfare Section, the Home Office and the Ministry of Labour. Applicants were classified, after severe sifting, according to the degree of responsibility for which their previous experience had fitted them. From this panel employers were supplied with the names of suitable candidates, and 550 appointments were thus made up to December, 1918. Owing to the uncertainty as to the meaning of welfare supervision when the Department began to press it upon employers in 1916, appointments were at first frequently made of wholly unqualified candidates, and the Department undertook to receive, classify and distribute applications, partly in order to save trouble to employers in following the advice of its officers, but also in order to set a standard of qualification.

Brief courses of training were arranged by the Department in the early months of 1916 for the first contingents of supervisors, who, however, started work almost wholly on the strength of their existing qualifications, among which experience in social work or in almost any form of administration was found to be valuable. Subsequently, courses of training, lasting from three to twelve months, and including some study of industrial law and history, of economic theory and industrial hygiene, together with some opportunity of gaining practical experience in problems of working-class life and factory conditions, were organised at the London School of Economics and at most of the provincial universities, in order to prepare students for this virtually new profession for women.

The welfare officers, when asked to report on the general position of supervisors in the factories in their districts, gave at the beginning of 1918 reports which may be summarised as follows :—

In about 50 per cent. of the cases known to them the welfare supervisors' work was concentrated chiefly on the "domestic" side of their elastic range of duties, on the care, that is, of canteens, cloakrooms, first aid, clothing, etc. Welfare work was, however, very much more effective in other works where some form of specialisation was permitted and where much more responsibility, especially with regard to employment, was placed in the hands of the supervisor, provided that the latter was competent for the work. For this reason the welfare officers urged that the standard of qualification should be raised. (More than half the supervisors in their districts at the time had not been appointed through the Department's panel.) Employers justified themselves for not appointing welfare supervisors as follows :—

1. " The numbers of women employed do not justify the expense.

2. " There are sufficient non-productive women already engaged.

3. " The employment of women is only temporary and therefore there is no need to make such appointments.

4. " The employment of women is no new feature, and there is no need to change.

5. " The management fear that the foremen will resent such an appointment because it is likely to diminish their authority.

6. " Our employees are quite happy, and a welfaie supervisor would attempt too much and upset the factory.

7. " It is difficult to find the right type of woman with industrial experience and technical knowledge."[1]

When, despite these objections, a supervisor was appointed, in the great majority of cases the results admittedly justified the decision. The Department received constant reports from employers as to the " change of tone " in their factory and the practical advantages gained by the welfare superintendent's work. In work, however, so ill-defined as that of a supervisor, generalisations as to good or bad results produced in a short time are particularly misleading. The powers of survival of the system of supervision are the best test of its efficacy.

Over 1,000 supervisors of varying grades were working in munition factories at the date of the Armistice. Allowing for the fact that their appointment was compulsory in T.N.T. factories and practically compulsory in national factories, probably some 700 had been appointed voluntarily by heads of firms or boards of management.

When large numbers of munition works were shut down, the welfare supervisors in these works were, of course, discharged, although in some cases they were asked to remain until the factories should have been reorganised and the female staff returned. Some intermediate returns were obtained in the following year as to their position. Out of 733 factories in which welfare supervisors had been appointed, 249 were definitely retaining their supervisors and 42 more were to be retained so long as women remained on the staff. From 165 of the factories all the women had been discharged. The following is a summary of the position in certain divisions :—

	Factories with Supervisors during the war.	Factories retaining Supervisors.
London and South Eastern	140	60
West Midlands	76	39
Yorkshire and East Midlands	196	80
North Western	100	54

It was stated at the same time that in a number of cases the supervisors' work was being extended beyond the essentially " domestic " duties referred 'to above, and that in the London area the possibility of employing women as works managers had been discussed with a number of firms.[2]

Industrial conditions were still far from settled at the date of this return, and the office of the welfare supervisor, on which the Welfare and Health Section had placed so much insistence, may therefore be said to have proved its " survival value."

---

[1] Hist. Rec./R'346/133.

[2] *The Month's Work*, issued by the Ministry of Labour, May, 1919.

II. Welfare Work for Boys.

Welfare work for boys was organised by the Department on lines similar to those laid down for work among women and girls. The work was, however, carried out on a very small scale by the Welfare Section during the first year of its existence, and the period of its effective administration under the Ministry of Munitions only lasted for some twenty months. The problems inherited from pre-war conditions were to some extent similar in either branch of factory welfare work. A definite welfare policy was, however, on the whole adopted by firms less readily for boys than for women, because the employment of boys was by no means new in the factories producing munitions, whereas the novelty of much of the work performed by women was often held to justify special provision for their comfort.

(a) THE WORK OF THE WELFARE OFFICER.

" The welfare officer," it has been said,[1] " owed his position to two causes. Employers complained that boys were unmanageable, and that output suffered through this lack of control. ' My boys,' said one employer, are the sweepings from Hell, and nothing can be done for them.' The general public complained that the war had made life very difficult for boys, that there were clear signs of wide-spread deterioration, and that the fault lay with the industrial conditions of the time." From this two-fold complaint were born boys' welfare work and the welfare officer. His duties, following on these complaints, were of three kinds. In the first place he was called on to visit controlled establishments and ascertain facts. Secondly, he was asked to draw conclusions from the facts ascertained. And finally, he was required to suggest remedies. With the development of the work developed also the scope of the investigation. The office welfare inquiry form, at first a single sheet with a few headings, grew into a four-paged and elaborate questionnaire, covering the same points of structure and equipment enumerated in the previous section, and also such special points as the training and educating of munition boys. The officer was forced to realise that, in dealing with the problem with which he was confronted, he must regard as alien to his examination nothing which affected the general well-being of the working boy. Occasionally even wider views were entertained of his duties, as when one employer advocated that the State should take over the management of all the boys in industry, and another employer, in urgent need of assistance, addressed a communication to a welfare officer on the subject of the welfare of boilers.

(b) THE WAR AND BOYS' WORK.

The staff of travelling welfare officers, which increased from two in March, 1917, to fourteen at the beginning of the next year, found the same wide range of working conditions for boy munition workers as that which existed among women. A number of the firms producing munitions had before the war prided themselves on the completeness

---

[1] Memorandum on *Boys' Welfare in* 1917, by Mr. R. A. Bray. HIST. REC./R/ 346/39.

of their provision for the training, comfort, and recreation of their boy workers. In some cases these schemes were maintained and developed during the war without any stimulus from the Department. In others, however, the pressure of munition work inevitably caused the neglect of such schemes, while in the majority no system of training or special care for boy workers existed.

The position of boy munition workers was thus described in the welfare officers' reports in 1918.[1]

The boys employed fell, as in normal times, into two divisions, apprentices (whether indentured or not) and unskilled workers.

"As a rule," it was reported, "some attention is given by employers to the first class, though their conditions have changed for the worse during the war. The speeding up of output and the tendency to put apprentices to production work have not been favourable to training. There has been a marked decrease in their attendance at Continuation Schools, and not infrequently facilities for attendance have been withdrawn. The high earnings of the unskilled boys have led to a frequent breaking of apprenticeship. The call for military service brings the apprenticeship to a premature termination at the age of 18. The national loss entailed in the consequent diminished industrial efficiency of the artisan of to-morrow has not received the attention it merits, and the problem involved is as yet unsolved. Few new schemes of apprenticeship have been initiated since the war. As regards the unskilled boy, little attention is usually given to his training. He is considered a bird of passage, here to-day and gone to-morrow, and consequently of small permanent importance in the workshop."

The wages of boys taken as a whole had doubled since the war.

"The highest wage recorded as having been earned during any one week is £8. But anything approaching this figure is very exceptional. Cases of £3 to £4 a week are not uncommon. These large sums are obtained when employed on piece-work, and for this work a boy occasionally exhibits a remarkable quickness and gains accordingly. But the fact that such high wages have been earned becomes known and serves as an attraction which draws boys to the munition factory."

One welfare officer reporting on this question wrote :—

"The persistence with which the boys took up the trail to the great machine shops and to the great national factories or to anywhere where the processes were repetitive and the contracts ran into millions, can be likened almost to the rush to Klondyke. In their feverish eagerness boys spent their time wandering from shop to shop, from works to works, making short stays only, in search of the El Dorado. Indentures were thrown to the winds, places where useful trades could be learned were left behind, entreaties of considerate employers were rudely rejected, and parents treated with indifference."

---

[1] Hist. Rec./R/346/39 ; L.R. 168.

In spite, however, of common reports, the ordinary earnings did not reach any very surprising figures. A careful investigation in the Birmingham district among 250 boys aged 13 to 17 showed that in the spring of 1918 the average weekly earnings were £1 8s. 11d.[1]

Hours of work were, as a rule, the maximum allowed under the Factory Act. There had been a diminution of the long hours of overtime common in the early stages of the war, but boys were so frequently employed as helpers to men, that they tended to follow men's hours, so far as was legally possible, instead of sharing in the shorter day commonly worked by women in 1918.[2]

In spite of the recent increase in the number of canteens, such provision, or even that of a messroom, was not found in the majority of cases.

"In a group of firms connected with the iron and steel trades, a recent inquiry gave the following results :—108 firms employing 8,027 boys and 63,572 men had neither canteen nor messroom ; 59 firms employing 5,756 boys and 37,834 men had canteens or messrooms ; 19 firms employing 2,685 boys and 18,519 men were providing such places, as a rule at the suggestion of the section."

Opportunities for recreation had greatly diminished, since the majority of those responsible for the management of boys' clubs had joined the army.

"The effect," it was said, "of the decrease in the means of recreation, added to the dulness of repetition work, is seen in the large increase of gambling among boys both within and without the factory; employers have repeatedly called attention to the fact. One manager employing 100 boys informed the welfare officer that he had destroyed 34 packs of cards in a single week. A certain amount of gambling is natural among boys ; but gambling in excess, as now found, is an indication of the presence of an unhealthy monotony in their lives."

From these and very many other reports it was clear that boy life and labour had suffered greatly from the war. Therewith output had also suffered. An outstanding remedy offered to employers by the Department was the recommendation of the appointment of a welfare supervisor, as a "specialist" who should secure the individual care and consideration essential to the young worker.

(c) WELFARE SUPERVISION.

The Welfare Section formed a panel of men qualified for posts as welfare supervisors on the same lines as that formed for women.

[1] In two of the hostels for boys under 18 employed at Woolwich Arsenal, where wage rates as a whole were high, the earnings in April, 1917, averaged as follows:—Hostel A (200 boys), £1 12s.; Hostel B (86 boys) £1 8s. 6d. (HIST. REC. H 346 3).
[2] See Chapter VI.

There was a comprehensible difficulty in securing the right type of candidate for such work during the war, and those appointed had normally to take up work without any formal training.

The duties of a boys' supervisor, as suggested by the Department in its official memorandum on the subject, included the following :—

1. The interviewing of boys (and their parents) prior to their engagement, and their special supervision during the first week's work.

2. Questions of discipline, including time-keeping and complaints by and of the boys.

3. Arrangements for continued education.

4. Care for health, including some supervision of first-aid treatment and of canteens.

5. The organisation of savings schemes.

6. The organisation of recreation.

" The supervisor will be responsible for organising outdoor games, and for the management of a recreation room, if such exists. He will consider the question of forming a cadet corps or scout troop."

" The essence of the scheme," it was said, " lies in placing on some member of the staff the responsibility for the general well-being of the boys." Such work might be performed by a whole-time officer in a large firm ; by an officer specially appointed, but with other duties beside the supervision of boys ; or by an officer shared, as was not infrequently the case, by two or more firms. It was essential that the supervisor should co-operate with the local education authority, with the Juvenile Employment Committee, where this was in active operation, with club workers, and other outside agencies connected with boys.[1]

Accounts of their work given by the supervisors thus appointed showed the wide interpretation placed upon the suggested schedule of duties, and the essentially human problems involved therein.[2]

---

[1] Circular M.M. 13 B.

[2] The following is a specimen of a very complete scheme of welfare for boys, reported to the Department in October, 1918 :—

" The James Cycle Works, Birmingham, employing 160 boys, have initiated a welfare scheme the chief features of which are the establishment of a comprehensive athletic and recreation organisation, and co-operation with the local education authority for " continued " education. In connection with the former, the foremen and men in the works have consented to take charge of particular branches of recreation, which includes gymnastics, physical drill, boxing, football, swimming, cricket, photography, gardening, and running. The messroom is regularly used as a gymnasium, and on an evening in alternate weeks a popular lecture is given to the boys by members of the staff and others. Eighty of the boys have joined the special evening classes organised for them at the local technical school, and the welfare supervisor has made arrangements to receive from the school records of their attendance and progress. The management have specially notified the welfare supervisor that he is to pay particular attention to the health and development of the boys and provide where necessary free tonics and body building foods, such as cod-liver oil and emulsion."

(d) Progress of the Movement.

The boys' welfare movement made marked progress during 1918, and the number of local welfare officers for boys was increased to twenty in the course of the year, in order to cope with the work.

The number of welfare supervisors with firms known to the Department rose from 110 in January, 1918, to 275 on 1st December, 1918, when the Boys' Welfare Section was transferred from the Ministry of Munitions to the new Training Department of the Ministry of Labour.[1] The supply of potential supervisors on the official panel kept pace with the increased demand to some extent ; but the demands of the war still made it difficult to secure the right type of man in sufficient numbers for the work.[2] This was an inevitable difficulty ; but with the demobilisation of the army it became easier to secure the right type of candidate.

The number of firms with which the welfare officers of the section were in touch had risen to about 2,000 by December, 1918, and an average of from 50 to 60 visits were paid weekly to firms by these officers. The Birmingham Central Care Committee, in its annual report of 1918 to the City Education Committee, congratulated its citizens in that probably 10,000 local boys were now under definite welfare supervision, as compared with probably 500 a little over a year ago.

Apart from these increased appointments, a marked growth of interest in and comprehension of the aims of the section was reported from different quarters of England by the travelling officers. " The old attitude towards such work, which may be described as one of benevolent contempt, is much less met with than formerly, and there is not wanting evidence that welfare activity in one quarter of the town stimulates similar activity in another, and even produces here and there a sense of shame that arrangements in the works have so utterly ignored the human element and the possible effect of factory environment on the development of health and character," reported the Birmingham welfare officer in September, 1918.[3]

Welfare officers at the beginning of the year had repeatedly found almost complete ignorance among busy employers as to the number of their boy workers and the conditions under which they worked, but the results of propaganda were becoming visible by the end of the year.

---

[1] Hist. Rec./R/346/39. In December, 1917, out of 900 controlled establishments with 30 or more boy workers, nearly 20 per cent. of the firms (employing 40 per cent. of the boys in the whole number of factories) had appointed welfare supervisors or made some equivalent provision for welfare.

[2] Thus, when in June, 1918, advertisements were inserted in the Press asking for men with experience of working boys, and especially for discharged officers who had acted as scoutmasters or had experience in handling cadet corps, although 500 replies were received, comparatively few of the candidates proved suitable.

[3] L.R.W. 168.

" The revelation to employers of the actual number of boys they employ," reported a travelling officer, " has come as a result of the officer's visit, and in more than one case as a dramatic surprise.   One employer who guessed the number as 30 was startled to learn that there were 180 ; another, who thought he had only about 20, immediately on getting the information that he employed 70 walked with the welfare officer round the works to find them ; whilst a third, who guessed that he employed 70, exclaimed on getting the information that there were 500 in the works, ' Where do they all hide? ' In this way the management has in numerous cases, for the first time, been brought face to face with their responsibilities, and turned from an attitude of apparent unconcern to one of genuine interest." . Other firms came to realise the need of welfare supervision not so much from a heightened sense of responsibility for " the boy colony unorganised and ignored " in their works, as from sheer difficulties in management. The question of maintaining discipline among boys—especially those under 16, whom it was undesirable to bring before a munitions tribunal—was becoming increasingly difficult as the summer of 1918 advanced, as older men were called up, and as fresh relays of boys became accustomed to the high wages of munition work and the resulting independence.   The chief investigation officers were the recipients of many such complaints, and the suggestion of the appointment of a welfare supervisor was sometimes favourably received as a cure for disorder.[1]

Like the rest of the welfare policy of the Ministry, the methods by which the Department endeavoured to convince employers of the need for special provision for their boy workers were largely educational, and the cumulative effects of this education, done unobtrusively and by means of much spade work, were becoming increasingly visible by the date of the Armistice.[2]

The advance of the welfare movement for boys was also due to its coincidence with other movements which, despite war pressure, were developing in 1918 for the benefit of boys and girls.   The losses of the war were bringing home to the country the need for utilising its human material, and, at the same time, the shorter hours movement

---

[1] Not all supervisors were able to evolve order out of disorder, but frequent reports reached the section of the good effects produced by their appointment in firms whose discipline had become weak.   Thus the head of a large alkali works reported in June, 1918, that before the supervisor (a discharged officer) came the boys were " a lot of little hooligans," whereas since he came the whole position was changed ; nearly all the boys were members of a cadet corps, turning up " splendidly and keenly " for parades three times a week after work hours, while arrangements had been made both for a holiday camp for them and for opportunities for them to attend continuation school classes.   C.E. 2659/16.

[2] In May, 1918, an unofficial Boys' Welfare Association was inaugurated, which in November, 1918, began to issue a monthly journal for employers, welfare superintendents and others.   In the course of the year a number of local associations and a National Association of Welfare Supervisors were formed, with the approval and co-operation of officers of the Department.   The vitality shown by these extra-departmental organisations during the following year may fairly be quoted as a testimony to the efficacy of the Department's propaganda work among its controlled establishments.

made it more possible to put this into effect than it had been earlier in the war. Two results of this were the appearance during the year of a series of civic schemes for recreation for all the working-class members of the community in a number of industrial towns, and the establishment of Juvenile Organisations Committees under the auspices of the Home Office, which included the provision of recreation for boys and girls among their general objects of co-ordinating in each locality all " interests " concerned with the young. In these schemes the Ministry of Munitions took an active part, which is described in the following chapter.

In addition to these combined recreation schemes, there was a very general growth during the year of similar provision among individual firms, especially the larger firms engaged on munitions work.[1] Most large firms had their sports clubs, reported the welfare travelling officers in 1918, and increased provision was made for cricket, football, and swimming, in addition to the organisation of works orchestras, etc., and the provision of allotments. Both large and small firms had tended to omit provision in such schemes for the younger boys employed by them, and it was among those under 16 especially that the welfare supervisors in this year reported experiments in the organisation of " works troops " of boy scouts, in week-end and summer holiday camps,[2] in addition to schemes for furthering their education in its widest sense.

In questions concerning the training of boy workers, the welfare movement again coincided with a revulsion of interest outside. The strain of the first two or three years of the war had, as has been said, made attendance at continuation classes even more difficult for the working boy than it had been under pre-war conditions, and numbers of employers who had previously urged their young employees to attend such classes had, by their own admission, ceased to do this except, to some extent only, in the case of apprentices. Boys' supervisors were, however, able, in an increasing number of cases, to arrange, with their firm's approval, schemes for the encouragement of attendance at evening classes ; while the Education Act of 1918 and the debates leading up to it stimulated interest even among busy employers in the problem of continued education, and led to the organisation of works schools by various large firms—e.g., in the Birmingham and Manchester districts. This movement had not gone very far by the date of the section's transference from the Ministry of Munitions. The Act, however, clearly opened out a very wide field for work by welfare supervisors, in conjunction with local authorities (on the lines indicated previously by the Department), in care equally for the health, recreation, and formal education of boy workers. The need for such care was even more obvious among the boys engaged on unskilled or semi-skilled work than among apprentices, necessarily a small minority of those engaged on munitions work.

---

[1] L.R.W. 168.

[2] Thus it was reported in 1917 that a large Scotch firm had recently erected a hut on the banks of Loch Lomond where the boys in rotation spent their week-ends and special attention was given to the study of Natural History. (L.R.W. 168.)

With regard to apprentices, the work of the section again fell in with an industrial movement taking place outside. Apprenticeship systems, where such existed, had been inevitably shaken during the war. Senior apprentices had been upgraded to take men's work or to supervise women's specialised work, while younger apprentices had been frequently put on to repetition jobs, normally with increased pay. The loss of training was an obvious penalty paid by the boy worker (often to his own satisfaction) for the advantages to the country of repetition work, and was hardly avoidable, although the dilution officers of the Department from the summer of 1917 were instructed to arrange that boys should be put upon the less " dead-end " work when a choice was available, and to persuade employers, as far as possible, to keep purely automatic work for women, whose industrial future was unimportant. Special co-operation was arranged between the Ministry's dilution and welfare officers for this purpose.[1]

By the later months of 1917, however, employers began to work out fresh schemes, and to revive old schemes, for the better organisation of apprenticeship. Thus in the autumn of 1917 the Huddersfield Engineering Employers' Association produced an elaborate joint scheme for the progressive training, practical and theoretical, of their apprentices, with a scale of rewards for good time-keeping and general progress. Early in 1918 the Paisley Engineering Employers inaugurated a rather similar scheme. About the same time the Engineering Training Organisation, an association founded in October, 1917, and representing engineering and educational bodies throughout the country, began to develop a national scheme for the improvement of engineering training, which laid great stress, *inter alia,* on the need for a revival of apprenticeship. A system of co-operation was agreed upon between this organisation and the Welfare and Health Section of the Ministry of Munitions, which undertook " to supply information to its officers respecting the work and objects of the Engineering Training Organisation, to employ the term of ' apprentice-master ' instead of welfare supervisor in relation to the supervision of the broader education of boys in the engineering industry, and to instruct their officers to advocate the appointment of apprentice-masters in relation to engineering."[2]

The preparation of schemes for dealing with the broken apprenticeships of young soldiers called to the Colours was transferred from the Ministry of Pensions to the Ministry of Labour in December, 1918. The protracted negotiations with employers and workmen that led up to the framing of a scheme for each industry, suggested in a number of towns, where systems of apprenticeship were lapsing or were out of date, fresh possibilities of co-operative schemes for training in the future, while, at the same time, Juvenile Advisory and Juvenile Employment Committees were stimulated to local inquiries as to the existing means for boys or girls to enter trades in their own neighbourhood. The Welfare Section was able to help this growth of interest locally by active co-operation (*e.g.*, in Birmingham) and

---

[1] Minutes of Welfare and Health Committee (8 August, 1917).
[2] *Handbook for Welfare Supervisors and Apprentice-Masters,* p. 89.

centrally by the issue in January, 1918, of a *Handbook for Welfare Supervisors and Apprentice-Masters*, giving, beside much general welfare information, definite suggestions as to model indentures and detailed systems of " works " training for apprentices.

The position of welfare work for boys was well established by the date of the Armistice, even if it had not covered directly a very large proportion of the 250,000 boys in controlled establishments, and it suffered little in the process of demobilisation. Very few welfare supervisors were discharged along with the boys for whom they were responsible. Where discharges of boys were numerous, supervisors and welfare officers were able to assist, and in some cases to take the initiative, in the organisation of unemployment centres for their training and recreation.

The Welfare and Health Section for boys promptly became, as has been said, a part of the Training Department of the Ministry of Labour. As such it had growing possibilities of constructive work, since its sphere was no longer confined to workers in the munitions trades ; and the organisation by that Department of training schemes for demobilised soldiers whose apprenticeship had been interrupted brought its local officers into touch with problems of boys' work in many thousands of firms. The brief period during which the Ministry of Munitions pushed forward the development of welfare work among factory lads had demonstrated that such work was " no longer philanthropy, but good business."

III. Welfare Work among Men.

No systematic effort was made by the Department to deal with questions of "welfare" among men, although complaints as to accommodation were dealt with when referred to the section by men munition workers. Formal complaints were, however, seldom made, either by individuals or by labour organisations. Those of the former when made at all, referred to details such as canteen management, or the heating of workshops (a point which caused various small strikes during the fuel shortage of 1917-18). Demands of the latter, formulated at set hearings before the Committee on Production and other courts, almost invariably dealt with rates of wages and standards of living. In the exceptional cases (such as the negotiations with chemical employers in 1917) when reference was made to hard or unhealthy working conditions, such conditions were discussed by the men from the point of view of higher compensatory wages rather than of practical schemes for their improvement. No definite demand appeared to exist among workmen during the war for a general improvement of working conditions. It was felt by the Department that any attempt to take this question up actively would be liable to be misunderstood by the men themselves, and private conversations with prominent trade unionists confirmed this view. On the other hand, the question was not allowed to drop out of sight, and welfare officers were instructed to bear the matter in mind and, as occasion offered, to discuss it informally with employers, giving special attention to the possibilities of development by means of Works Councils.

It seemed probable, however, that welfare work among men would tend to develop spontaneously out of welfare work among boys, and, in particular, out of the appointment of welfare supervisors for boys. " In a not inconsiderable number of cases " reported the welfare officers, " the supervisor, usually on the request of the men, finds himself called on to deal with matters affecting their welfare. He naturally sees much of the men, and, if of the right type, soon establishes friendly relations with them. If a men's recreation club is started, he finds himself asked to undertake the organisation. If anything in the nature of a Men's Committee or Works Council is started, he has sometimes been thought the right man to act as secretary. Often he is in charge of the first aid equipment, and deals with men as well as with boys. Men tend to come and consult him in their various difficulties." One welfare supervisor in Scotland reported that in the course of a few weeks over two hundred men had come to consult him on various questions.[1] Men munition workers shared in the advantages of the first aid and messroom accommodation, which was sometimes provided, in the first instance, on the introduction of women to their factories, and it was frequently reported that their "standard of comfort" had been raised thereby. The administration of welfare provision for their benefit obviously involved different problems from those surrounding boys and girls and unorganised workers. These are discussed in the next section.

IV. Welfare and Organised Labour.

(a) TRADE UNION CRITICISMS.

The welfare movement as advertised during the war was watched with considerable suspicion by a section of organised labour, as a form of possibly undesired philanthropy on the part of employers. Opposition to improved accommodation could not endure long, especially when (e.g., in canteens) the workers were given a share in its control. It was round the position of the welfare supervisor, for boys as well as for women, that trade union criticism centred. It was said that the supervisor was a hybrid official, in the pay of the employer in order to increase efficiency and secure more output, but supposed to represent the interests of the workers. The welfare of the workers, it was said, should be the concern of the firm as a whole, and should not be " delegated to a paid official of anomalous position and divided interests."[2] The mere title, it was suggested, had a tinge of "hypocrisy." And apart from this, successful welfare work supervision was "a form of separatism," emphasising the relation of the firm to the individual worker, and weakening the sense of collective responsibility, in which the woman worker was being laboriously trained by trade union officials.[3] Thus, even after two

---

[1] Hist. Rec./R/346/39. M.W. 150529. Hist. Rec./H/346/1.

[2] *Women's Trade Union League Review*, April, 1917.

[3] " This need not be so ; but so far, the theory of the Ministry of Munitions seems to have gone little beyond this ideal of individualism and personal kindliness. In one case, the kindliness is accentuated (by a " good " supervisor) ; in another, the system is frankly one of intolerable personal meddling." (*Highway*, issued by the Workers' Education Association, June, 1917.)

and a half years' experience of welfare work, a motion was raised at the biennial conference of the National Federation of Women Workers in August, 1918, for the abolition of official welfare organisation. The personnel of the welfare workers and the ambiguity of their status as compared with that of the Factory Inspectors were criticised by the representatives of this women's trade union (which, however, included only a small proportion of the women in munition works), In the Home Office officials " the workers recognised the impartial representatives of the community ; in the existing welfare workers, merely a reflection of the wishes and disposition of the employer."[1]

There was some justification for these criticisms, both in theory and in practice, although they were increased by misunderstanding, and by the haste with which welfare work developed. The theory that the employer must not impose as from above improvements in working conditions without asking the co-operation of the workers was probably sound on educational grounds. It was impossible to wait for their co-operation in 1916, but means for securing it in future are discussed below. The criticism of the welfare worker as a hybrid official was the result of misconceptions, due, in part, to the early propaganda for welfare work. Insistence was increasingly laid by the Ministry of Munitions on the need for the welfare worker to become a definite part of the managerial staff, and the suggested change of title to " employment superintendent " or " establishment officer " avoided the possible taint of philanthropy or patronage attached to the word welfare.

In practice, while it is true that some of the hastily appointed supervisors showed, in dealings with individual girls and boys, an absence of that " tact " which was insisted on as a primary requisite for their difficult position, or from sheer ignorance of industrial organisation opposed trade union propaganda in the factory, these were only exceptional cases. In few instances was there any clash between the trade union officials and the supervisor, whose real functions were, as may be seen by their analysis in the previous sections, quite distinct. The normal shop steward had, for example, no desire to concern him or herself with the training of boys and women to a reasonable use of the welfare accommodation provided for them, which was one of the supervisor's most useful functions, and a *modus vivendi* could be, and was, readily arranged between the supervisor and the trade union official as to dealing with workers' complaints. Further, it must be remembered that trade unions had hitherto neglected the problems of boy labour except in connection with apprenticeship, and that the very large majority of women munition workers were unorganised. The welfare supervisor and her staff indeed helped to train a shifting population of workers—often young and irresponsible workers, to a great extent new to collective industry—in a sense of *esprit de corps* and good order, which, often for the first time, provided a possible basis for sound trade unionism.

---

[1] *Woman Worker*, October, 1918.

In April, 1918, a memorandum on "Welfare Supervision" (for men as well as women, boys and girls) was issued by the Woolwich Trades and Labour Council and Labour Party.[1] Its conclusion, after full consideration of the different points of welfare, may be quoted, in face of the criticisms of the movement by witnesses before the Commissions on Industrial Unrest of the previous summer. A Welfare Department, and even a system of welfare workers, might, it was held, prove beneficial, provided the functions of trade unions (e.g., with regard to wages) were not touched thereby. Any system of welfare supervision that should "win the full confidence and support of the workers" must, however, observe the following conditions :—

1. Welfare supervision must aim primarily at promoting the welfare of the workers and not at increasing the workers' output.

2. Welfare schemes and supervisors must be under a democratic system of control, in which the workers shall have equal participation with the employers.

3. The established field of operations of trade unions and their officials must be clearly and loyally recognised by welfare schemes and supervisors.

4. Welfare supervisors should be drawn, as far as possible, from among the workers.

5. Welfare supervisors should not be appointed without preliminary training or experience, such training to include a knowledge of trade union aims and methods.

6. If government control of welfare supervision is maintained after the war, such control must be transferred from the Ministry of Munitions to the Ministry of Labour.

7. As welfare supervision would probably become a permanent and extending element of the industrial system, there should be held in each industrial centre conferences convened by the local Trades Council or Labour Party, for the purpose of considering the aims, scope, and methods of welfare supervision ; and such conferences should be followed by a joint conference of the Trades Union Congress and the National Labour Party.

All these conditions were being approached in different forms of welfare work in 1918 and 1919.

(b) WELFARE AND WORKS COMMITTEES.

In the multiplying works committees among employees of controlled establishments, or, where these had not yet been established, in special *ad hoc* committees for the management of games or benevolent funds, experiments were being made in the "democratising" of welfare, which was asked for in this Labour report and others

---

[1] L.R.W. 682/17.

like it. No general statement is possible as to the relation of work-shop committees and welfare (or the control of working conditions) in the later stages of the war. The following arrangements in certain very differently placed firms illustrate the trend of possible development.

(1) In a National Projectile Factory (which had the distinction of working out, under conditions new to the engineering world, an apprenticeship scheme for its boy workers) a welfare committee existed from April, 1916. This committee, consisting of twelve representatives elected by the workers and one representative, also elected by the workers, of the management, administered a fund formed by weekly deductions at the rate of 1d. to 3d. in the £ from all wages. This fund was spent in subscriptions to various war funds and to hospitals and convalescent homes at which the workers might be treated, and in relief of distress due to illness among the workers. In the autumn of 1918 hospital subscriptions reached the rate of £600 a year, and grants, after investigation by members of the committee, to cases of distress through illness among the operatives averaged £25 a week. The funds further supplied newspapers and music for the canteen and purchased a piano for dinner-hour concerts.[1]

(2) The following is an example of an advisory welfare committee being superimposed on a particularly successful welfare organisation in a private firm :—"All welfare work in the firm is undertaken by the employment department, which consists of an employment manager, a lady employment manager, three assistants, and a clerical staff. The department is an integral part of the works, and is not regarded as an outside ameliorative agency." All labour was engaged by the department, the workers' progress was recorded there, and all questions of wages, hours of work, and working conditions were investigated there ; while the control of the dining rooms, cloak-rooms, etc., the dismissal of workers, the consideration of complaints, was in the hands of the department, which acted as a go-between for the workers and management, removing causes of friction in the works. An elected welfare committee had (in 1917) the right of sugges-tions about the general amenities of the place, the management of the dining-rooms, cloakrooms, and first aid, the ventilation, heating, etc. It had, however, no executive power.[2]

(3) The works committee of a Sheffield foundry developed the following welfare activities. This committee was reconstituted in March, 1918, " on a trade union basis." There were no repre-sentatives of the management, but the social secretary or welfare supervisor was unanimously invited " to become chairman, subse-quently secretary." It dealt, sometimes in conference with the directors, with the following matters during the summer :—A proposal of the directors to keep a week's wages in hand (agreed to) ; schemes for improving time-keeping and the enforcement of works discipline, referred to its members by the management ; arrangements for the summer holidays and for shortening the working day ; the provision of allotments ; the administration of war relief. A " junior works

---

[1] Hist. Rec./R/346/28.　　　　[2] C.E. 808/15 II.

council " was established, consisting of boy representatives from each department. Week-end camps were held under the care of the social secretary for groups of the firm's employees and for their children in a bungalow on the neighbouring moors.

(4) A striking form of developing responsibility among the younger workers appeared in a " Boys' Parliament," organised by a supervisor at the beginning of 1918 among the apprentices of Messrs. J. S. White & Co., shipbuilders, Cowes. This " Parliament," founded on strictly constitutional lines, was empowered to discuss all matters of welfare among the lads employed, and early distinguished itself by drawing up and sending in to the directors of the firm a scheme for the better training of the fitter apprentices.[1]

(5) Various interesting experiments in delegating the control of boys' welfare to the men working in the factory were reported during the year 1918. Thus a Birmingham firm making pens in peace time invited the men's works committee to undertake the welfare supervision of the boys. " The Chairman of the Committee," wrote the local boys' welfare officer in May, " is very sympathetic to the proposal and a suggested scheme is at present being worked out by the committee. The manager is a keen social student, and his relations with the works committee are very friendly. He has interested the members in the study of economics. He also conducts a works class for boys in the firm's time ; and for boys under 15 attendance at this class is compulsory."[2]

These are disconnected examples of the development of control by the workers of working conditions and amenities in munition factories during the war. They are typical of a process which had very wide possibilities of development.

The following were among the subjects suggested by the Ministry of Labour in January, 1919, for the consideration of the Works Committees established in connection with Joint Industrial Councils[3] ; the distribution of working hours ; breaks in spells of work, and systems of time-recording ; the provision of meals, drinking water, safety appliances, heating and sanitation ; discipline and conduct in the works ; the engagement of labour ; the training of young workers ; entertainments and sports, etc.

These suggestions sum up almost the whole of the activities undertaken by a welfare supervisor according to the recommendations laid down by the Ministry of Munitions. The services of an executive officer were, however, obviously required if these subjects were to be dealt with effectively, at least until such an organisation as was thus outlined for the joint control of industrial conditions had been perfected, and until the workers' own standard of such conditions had risen to a very much higher level than it had normally reached before the war.

---

[1] The scheme is described at length in the *Handbook for Welfare Supervisors and Apprentice-Masters* (1919).

[2] L.R.W. 168.

[3] Ministry of Labour, Industrial Reports, No. 4 ; *Industrial Councils*.

CHAPTER III.

WELFARE OUTSIDE THE FACTORY.

I. The Establishment of "Extra-Mural" Welfare Work.

(a) THE NEED FOR SPECIAL PROVISION.

In January, 1917, the Health of Munition Workers' Committee issued a report on the "Health and Welfare of Munition Workers outside the Factory,"[1] urging strongly the necessity of provision for the needs of the workers, especially the women and girls, who had moved from their own homes in order to take up work on munitions. Although their welfare was already to some extent under the care of local authorities, of voluntary agencies, and of semi-official organisations such as the Local Advisory Committees for Women's War Employment set up in connection with the Employment Exchanges, yet it was represented that "the time had now come to supplement and reinforce these by a larger degree of state action than had hitherto been deemed necessary." On the State, which had organised the transference of labour, lay the responsibility "not only for suitably housing these transplanted workers, but also for securing the safeguards needful for their health and morals, the maintenance of which is essential to the nation." Any work for these ends should take full account of existing organisations, official and voluntary. "The aim should be not to supplant the work of these various bodies, but by the appointment of special officers and by other means to supplement and co-ordinate." On this basis the Health of Munition Workers Committee offered a number of very practical suggestions about the provision of lodgings or hostels for imported workers, assistance to them in travelling, arrangements for their care in sickness, the widespread development of means of recreation for their leisure, while incidentally it was urged that, for the preservation of public order and for preventive work, women police should be appointed, and that the Central Control Board should be asked to consider and take action in local drink questions.

(b) ORGANISATION BY THE DEPARTMENT.

It had been realised in the Welfare Section from its establishment a year earlier that care for workers outside the factory was under war conditions an important aspect of industrial welfare work. To a certain extent welfare supervisors, as has been explained, supplemented their multifarious duties in the factory by care for the home

---

[1] This report (Memorandum No. 17) was not published. For an account of the general principles of extra-mural welfare see Section XIX. of the *Final Report of the Health of Munition Workers Committee* (1918).

conditions or recreation of the women or boys or girls for whom they were responsible. But there were limits to this expansion of their duties, both on account of the expenditure of time involved and. the suspicion felt by some workers, in theory if not in practice, of intrusion on behalf of the employer into their leisure hours. Apart from such isolated efforts, it had not been possible for the Department to effect much in this direction beyond arranging for grants to certain crèches and to a very limited number of clubs and of works recreation schemes, and initiating the inspection of munition workers' hostels. The problem, however, of the transported worker, which was unimportant so far as women were concerned at the beginning of 1916, was growing throughout the year as the demands of the new national and other munitions factories became effective. In March, 1917, the Employment Exchanges reported that the numbers of women being transferred monthly through their agency to work in other districts averaged 4,000 to 5,000. They were drawn from very many different sources. Thus in the previous month 5,000 women had been imported into eight large munition centres from 200 different Exchange areas. To one factory in the west midlands 772 women were imported from districts as far apart as Aberdeen and Penzance.[1] In addition, very considerable numbers of girls were, by this date, presenting themselves in the busy munitions districts, trusting to fortune or their friends to find them a job, without any application to the Employment Exchanges. In April, 1917, accordingly, when the work of the Welfare Section was reconstituted, a special subsection was created to look after the welfare of munition workers outside factories. Its activities covered almost exactly those outlined in the Health of Munition Workers Committee's report, although others were later added. At the beginning of January, 1918, the staff administering this branch of work numbered six at headquarters, besides 18 paid and three voluntary liaison officers, stationed in different industrial areas—normally, but not always the same (since they were technically on the staff of the chief investigation officer of each district), as those of the intra-mural welfare officers whose work has already been described. In addition to these, a small staff inspected hostels for munition workers, while the extra-mural welfare officers were allowed to employ a fluctuating number of temporary lodgings investigators.

From the establishment of this branch of the section's work special emphasis was laid on the fact that it existed to assist and not to supersede local effort. The extra-mural welfare officers were directed to co-operate with the Local Advisory Committees for Women's War Employment, where such existed, and with the officers of the Employment Exchanges, and to get into touch with the philanthropic and social agencies in the centre to which they were attached, to find out how far, if at all, their work required to be supplemented, and to recommend the means by which such supplementary work should be performed if it were required. Beyond this they were required to

---

[1] In 1914 the number of women who obtained employment in "other districts" through the Employment Exchanges was 32,988; in 1915, it was 53,096; in 1916 it was 160,000 (*Labour Gazette*, March, 1917).

give help with regard to lodgings ; where necessary to establish and control a systematic investigation and supervision of lodgings, paid investigators being appointed by the Ministry to work under their directions ; to investigate and report upon any welfare schemes, such as those described below, for which financial assistance was requested, and to keep the Welfare Section informed of the progress and development of such schemes. They also assisted in investigations required by the section, such as the condition of housing in their area, the holiday care of schoolchildren whose mothers were in munition works[1], or the provision required for maternity and other sick cases[2] ; and assisted, when necessary, in the organisation of convalescent homes, transit, recreation schemes, etc., to meet these needs.

Since the extra-mural welfare officers were installed in order to fill gaps, in so far as munition workers were concerned, in the network of official and unofficial agencies for improving social conditions, it was inevitable that they should become involved in a large number of directions. Thus an officer stationed in a country town whose existing resources had been heavily taxed by the opening, in the neighbourhood, of two large munitions factories, the employees of which had added 8,000 to the pre-war population of 36,000, was engaged in the course of a year with the following series of activities :—The establishment of " study circles " for social workers ; the proposed formation of a local guild of help ; the establishment of a convalescent home for munition workers ; the provision of evening play centres for their children ; the care for workers after a great explosion in the principal local factory ; the opening of a maternity home and crèche ; an inquiry into local housing and food conditions ; the supervision of " lodgings investigators " ; the organisation of recreation out of factory hours.

The welfare officers in general, as in this case, were on ground already partly covered by numerous local organisations. The efficacy of these, however, and their power of adaptation to the new demands upon them varied very greatly in different localities, and the work of the officers sent by the Welfare Section to their areas varied accordingly.[3]

" One officer," it was said early in 1918,[4] " has been invited by the local Medical Officer of Health and Health Visitors to address meetings on the care of infants ; another is assisting in the formation of a miners' orchestra ; another has been successful in arousing local

---

[1] L.R. 2258/4.

[2] Hist. Rec./R/346/129.

[3] In addition to the special provision for munition workers' needs initiated locally, central organisations such as the Y.M.C.A., the Y.W.C.A., the Church Army and the G.F.S. inaugurated schemes for their benefit. In February, 1917, the " Archbishop's Committee for Munition Workers " was formed, under the chairmanship of the Bishop of Dover. It started a comprehensive scheme for the material as well as the moral welfare of munition workers throughout the country, though primarily in crowded areas such as Woolwich. With such efforts the officers of the Welfare and Health Section co-operated.

[4] Hist. Rec./R/346/39. (Memorandum by Miss G. E. Hadow, who directed the extra-mural work from its inception.)

enthusiasm for the Girl Guide movement. . . . Their object is to stimulate local committees, to arouse local enthusiasm, and they have in many cases been successful in finding voluntary workers to take up the suggestions they have made and to establish welfare on a civic basis."

This extra-mural welfare work was financed in part by direct grants or by writing off allowances for certain definite purposes.[1] Its incidental expenses were met from a fund of £6,000 placed at the disposal of Mr. Lloyd George for the benefit of munition workers by the Maharajah Scindia of Gwalior in July, 1915. This sum was spent on objects such as pianos and books for munition workers' hostels and clubs, seeds and gardening tools to be used on the ground outside hostels, swings for munition workers' children, and, in larger grants, for courses of lectures organised by the Y.M.C.A. for munition workers, for salaries of games organisers and the cost of running factory boys' holiday camps, etc.[2]

II. Special Problems of Extra-Mural Welfare.

(a) TRANSIT.

The concentration of labour for the production of munitions necessarily involved difficult problems of transit. On the one side these bore upon the housing policy of the Department, since if workers were not to spend excessive amounts of time and money in travelling daily to their work, or in periodical visits to distant homes, the provision of housing or lodging accommodation for them near the factory was the obvious alternative.[3] On the other hand, the travelling difficulties experienced by munition workers had an obvious connection with the attitude of the Department and of employers to questions such as the hours of labour and fatigue in munition works, the organisation of canteens with opportunities for hot meals after long journeys, and the general well-being of the workers. It was from this point of view that the Health of Munition Workers Committee in February, 1916, drew the special attention of the Department to the strain and fatigue caused by their daily or nightly journeys to workers compelled to live at a distance from their work.[4]

" Often the fatigue due to long periods spent in travelling is greatly increased because trains, trams and buses are liable to be filled to their utmost, even standing room being often

---

[1] See Appendix I.

[2] A book of photographs of munition workers at play was despatched in 1918 by the Department to the Maharajah in India, in order that he might realise the pleasure conferred by his gift. (L.R. 487/8.) The fund was supplemented by two donations, of £50 and £20 respectively, sent as personal offerings to the Minister of Munitions in August and September, 1915 ; the first from a British resident in Greece, in token of regret at his inability to fight for his country, the second from a poor woman of 75, who wrote from a remote village that she had " made a sacrifice for our dear King and country in these trying times " (M.W. 55388). These two cases are typical of the offers of help and service to which the Department became accustomed in the months immediately following its establishment.

[3] See Vol. V., Part V.   [4] M.W. 60197/12.

difficult to obtain. Women and young persons may be compelled to wait until after the first rush has passed. The following
examples are typical of many that have come to the notice
of the Committee.

(i) " The length of time spent in travelling is a noticeable
feature in connection with this factory. This is partly due to
the fact that a number of workers come in daily by train from
outlying districts, but it is also largely attributable to the
exceedingly bad car service, about which there is universal
complaint. In the morning workers often have to allow twice
the time that would ordinarily be taken to travel the distance
to the factory, and even then they are frequently late. It is
said to be not uncommon to wait 20 or 30 minutes before being
able to get on to a car and then a worker considers herself lucky if
she finds standing room. . . . One girl . . . gets up every day
at 3.45 a.m. and does not get to bed till 11 p.m., spending
just on five hours in travelling and waiting about. Most of
these long distance workers prefer living at home, even with
these long journeys, to the idea of living in lodgings.

(ii) " Some workers come from a distance. One young
man leaves home at 4.45 and gets his first meal at 8.30 a.m. ;
he reaches home in the evening about 9.30 p.m., and after
food gets to bed about 10.30 p.m. He gets therefore about
six hours' sleep. Another man . . . leaves home at 5.5 a.m.
and returns at 9.15 p.m. Cross-country transit across a radius
of outer London would save much time lost in travelling into
London and out again.

" Again, a tired and heated worker is very liable to chill if
obliged to stand about after work and may be tempted to
enter a convenient public-house for rest and refreshment. . . .
A typical case is that of a worker . . . who, in order to start
at 8 a.m., must get up at 4.30 a.m. because no later train is
available. She reaches work at 7 a.m. and does her best to occupy
herself usefully during the waiting period. . . . In the evening
the men come out of the shops hot and have to wait for half
an hour. There is the danger of their waiting in the public-
house.

" In some instances much time is lost owing to the absence
of any direct means of transit. In some cities, such as
Birmingham, the trams radiate from the centre of the town,
and much loss of time and difficulty is experienced in getting
from one point on the outskirts to another.

" Where other means of transit are not available firms
have in many cases provided special brakes for conveying their
workers, but such facilities are often not available, so that the
workers are compelled to walk a considerable number of miles
before and after a twelve hours working day.

" Long periods spent in travelling to and from the works are not only in themselves productive of fatigue, but also make it difficult for the worker to get adequate food at proper intervals. An early start may mean not only a scrappy and hasty breakfast, but an interval of three or four hours at least before any adequate meal is obtained. . . . Further, in many factories it is still necessary for a worker to bring with him any food required during the day ; when the start is early the food must be put up over night and . . . it is likely to become stale and unpalatable before it is eaten.

" Wages are generally sufficient to cover the cost of transit, but this is not always the case with women, and their wages are sometimes barely sufficient to cover the cost of lodgings and transit, so that it is difficult to them to afford the occasional day off which may be essential to the maintenance of their health. Difficulty is experienced in obtaining workmen's tickets for night workers and others travelling outside the hours during which such tickets are usually available.

" The Committee fully recognise that the difficulties in improving these conditions are great. Railway, tram and omnibus companies are alike suffering from heavy reductions of staff through enlistment, and the railways at any rate are continually called upon to meet heavy and urgent military requirements. The problem in each area is different and must be considered separately in the light of local conditions and difficulties. No general solution is possible. Although difficulties of housing and transit are doubtless most severe in centres like Woolwich, Coventry, or Newcastle, where the numbers involved are large, it should not be assumed that the difficulties are confined to these places. The evidence before the Committee shows that there are many other cases where action is needed. . . . The Committee realise that the employer and his ordinary staff can afford but little time for the detailed investigations necessary, and they have therefore in their memorandum on *Welfare Supervision* given much prominence to the need for the appointment or designation of someone, one of whose special duties it should be to inquire into the difficulties of housing and transit and to seek their solution."

It was at once arranged, as a result of this letter, that an officer of the newly-formed Railway Transport Section in the Department should be responsible for questions dealing with the transit of munition workers.

The work of this section of the Department is described elsewhere.[1] The improvements which it effected in the different methods of conveyance used by munition workers may be summarised as follows.[2]

Lack of railway facilities were overcome by erecting halts at convenient spots, connecting works by sidings with the railway company's main lines and erecting alighting platforms inside the premises,

---

[1] See Vol. V., Part V.   [2] HIST. REC./ R /2020/2.

improving the accommodation at stations which had become too small to cope with the increased passengers, altering the existing train services to suit the hours of work at factories, and providing railway and motor bus services and increasing existing tramway facilities. In this connection, 56 halts and other works were constructed at an approximate cost of £150,000.[1]

In many cases improvements, such as loop lines, were secured in local tramways. Negotiations by the Department, involving numerous meetings with corporations and other public bodies, resulted in a number of motor omnibus services being started. Some of these services supplied districts remote from the railways and resulted in many workers being obtained who otherwise would not have been available.

The work of the section included river transport, and at Woolwich, by arrangement with the river authorities, a service of cross-river boats was provided which disposed to a great extent of the congestion complained of in the letter quoted above. " An additional ferry was constructed and two boats obtained from corporations in other parts of the country and a new service inaugurated. This shortened several thousand men's journey by forty minutes each way."

This organisation of transit was a very definite contribution both to the mobilisation of labour for munition work and to its well-being, although it was clearly impossible to overcome completely difficulties of travelling under the special conditions of the war. When the local welfare officers of the Department in 1917 and 1918 met with outstanding transit difficulties, from insufficient tram, omnibus, or train services, insufficient platform and waiting room accommodation, dark and overcrowded trains, etc., they referred these to the Transit Section for remedy. In some cases, equally, they were able to secure improvements locally, or to stimulate agencies, such as the Girls' Friendly Society or Young Women's Christian Association, to establish canteens or rest huts at suitable points.

For one problem of transit the extra-mural officers of the Welfare Section made special provision. Many of the women and girls arriving from a distance to make munitions were wholly unaccustomed to travelling, and set forth with no security as to lodgings on arrival. Also many of them, in spite of stringent directions by the Employment Exchanges, arrived almost penniless, and with no prospect of further funds until their first week's, or first fortnight's, wages were paid. It was found even in 1917 that would-be munition workers, " after long journeys, necessitating several changes or possibly crossing London, were arriving in the small hours of the morning, exhausted and dis-couraged, having had little or no food on the way, and not knowing how to find their lodgings."[2] To meet the needs of these inexperienced

---

[1] Thus at a Government factory in the north of England, 1¼ miles from the nearest station and 6½ miles from the nearest industrial centre, a halt was erected by arrangement with the railway company at a convenient spot adjacent to the works, and 50 special train services per day were provided for the 25,000 workers.

[2] Hist. Rec./R/346/39.

travellers, arrangements were made by the Welfare and Health Section in May, 1917, whereby, at a very small charge to the Department, girls were met and seen across London, or taken to their destination elsewhere by members of the Travellers' Aid Society. Further, it was arranged that any girl could, on the recommendation of the welfare officer or the officer of an Employment Exchange, be given a night's lodging at one of the " clearing hostels " established in the most populous munition areas by the Department and by voluntary agencies.

(b) LODGINGS.

Reports were at one time constantly received of the overcrowded and insanitary condition of lodgings in certain munition districts. In some cases firms had undertaken to make inquiries as to suitable lodgings, either through their welfare supervisors or through special investigators. Thus, Messrs. Vickers had, in August, 1915, begun to compile a register of rooms available at Lancaster.[1] In some towns local committees, such as those established by the Home Office and the Ministry of Labour in connection with women's war employment, had, at an early stage of the war, undertaken the work of finding and, to some extent, supervising lodgings. Except, however, in a very few districts, these efforts were in no way equal to the demand in 1917. To meet the need, such Lodgings Committees were, after the appointment of extra-mural welfare officers, established or strengthened ; and lodgings investigators, in some cases of the working woman class, were appointed to compile a register of lodgings, meet and take girls to them, and visit them periodically. It was found that such visits did much to smooth over any little difficulties between landlady and tenant, and to bring to light individual cases of hardship or distress among the lodgers. Detailed investigations of lodging conditions were made in certain towns.

> " The result of such inquiry was uniformly the discovery of a large number of additional lodgings. In many cases the people had not thought of taking lodgers, but were quite willing to do so when asked. Many of the most serious cases of over-crowding proved to be due not to the scarcity of lodgings, but to the fact that they were at some little distance from the factory or that the tram service was inadequate. In some cases comfortable hostels were found to be half empty, while lodgings were overcrowded, the girls preferring the homeliness of the kind of life to which they were accustomed to a new and strange community existence."[2]

It was found possible by thus getting a list of good lodgings to remove girls from bad surroundings.[3] In connection with this, hospitality committees were organised, at the suggestion of the welfare officers, in some towns, consisting of people ready to befriend the imported workers and invite them to their houses out of factory hours.

---

[1] HIST. REC./R/346/30.   [2] HIST. REC./R 346 39.
[3] Cf. *Final Report of Health of Munition Workers Committee,* pp. 114, 115.

In the provision and inspection of lodgings for munition workers the extra-mural welfare officers co-operated with the local billeting committees, which were appointed in twenty-nine " munitions " districts, under the Billeting of Civilians Act of 24 May, 1917. These committees in some cases took over the lodgings investigators previously employed by the Welfare Section. The local billeting officers had the right (which, however, they were not called on to exercise) of compelling householders to accept as lodgers, at authorised rates of payment, persons engaged on work of national importance. They operated with very little local friction, and had the advantage of definite organisation and powers for carrying out work elsewhere handled less authoritatively by the welfare officers.[1]

(c) HOSTEL INSPECTION.

In December, 1916, the Welfare Section was advised that the inspection of all hostels in which munition workers were housed fell within the powers of the section, inasmuch as " the way in which female workers are housed may be considered to be one of the conditions of their employment." Inspection was therefore started, and although no compulsory powers under Section 6 (1) of the Act of 1916 were used, it was found that in the " majority of cases the management was very willing to carry out the Department's recommendations." The Welfare Section was empowered to recommend financial help under certain circumstances.[2] Rates of board were fixed, as far as possible, at economic levels (*i.e.*, at rates only slightly below those charged locally in lodgings) ; but it was obviously difficult for hostels, admittedly put up for temporary use only, to cover all their establishment charges as well as their running expenses, and the majority of hostels were probably run at a loss.

Hostels were inspected with reference to the demand for accommodation, the building and construction, the charges made, the catering, the accommodation, management, general comfort and welfare of the tenants.

The hostels inspection fell, in 1918, into the following groups :—

OWNED BY		
Government.	*Voluntary Societies.*	*Private Owners.*
Housing Construction Department ... 67	Y.W.C.A. 56	Messrs. Vickers ' ... 68
Department of Explosives Supply ... 145	G.F.S. 27	Private Committees and Firms ... 112
National Filling Factory Department ... 3	Y.M.C.A. 8	
National Projectile Factory Department 4	Salvation Army ... 9	
Royal Arsenal, Woolwich 7	Other Societies ... 21	

Of these, 220 were men's hostels, 302 were for women, 2 were for boys, comprised in 236 estates and accommodating about 15,400 men and 25,400 women.

[1] See Vol. V., Part V.   [2] See Appendix I.

It will be observed that a large proportion of these hostels were either owned by private firms or by the Government Departments immediately responsible for the factories in which the workers were employed. There were theoretical objections to this from the standpoint of labour, just as there are to the " living-in system " or to employers' housing schemes, in the possibilities given to the employer of excessive control of the worker. In practice, however, it was found that these hostels filled quite as readily as those provided by voluntary agencies. The proportion of the total hostel capacity occupied was approximately two-thirds of the whole available in January, 1918, the rate being larger for women than for men, who found it, on the whole, more possible to secure accommodation for themselves and thus avoid the " institutional " life of a hostel.

As a result of the work of inspection, information applicable equally after the war to the needs of the normal industrial worker was acquired by the section, which enabled certain standards to be established, similar for men and women, and only modified in some cases for navvies, for the planning, equipment, finance, and food supply of hostels, a group of subjects little touched by pre-war experience. The inspection staff were able, in addition, to formulate extremely practical advice on these matters,[1] to develop a standard for the management of hostels, and to urge on those responsible for their establishment the importance of securing superintendents with the right personalities and at adequate salaries. As far as possible, managers of hostels were urged to form tenants' committees. These were in some cases very successful, although attempts to foster self-government did not make very much headway among women residents.

In addition to the inspection of lodgings and hostels the Ministry of Munitions was responsible for extensive housing schemes which involved the erection of both temporary and permanent houses, the provision of hostels and arrangements for the billeting of munition workers. These schemes are dealt with in detail elsewhere.[2]

(d) Sickness and Distress.

In dealing thus with munition workers' lodgings and hostels, cases of distress were inevitably found among women workers who had no obvious claim to local help, and found the 7s. or 5s. weekly sick pay under the Insurance Acts inadequate to support them when unable to work. Factory benevolent funds, organised by the workers or by welfare supervisors, helped numbers of such cases,[3] but did not cover all. To meet the need of these hard cases and those of workers stranded on their journey from one munition area to another, a small benevolent fund was given to the Welfare Section for emergency use by the welfare officers.[4]

---

[1] See *Final Report of the Health of Munition Workers Committee*, pp. 166-175.
[2] Vol. V., Part V.
[3] Cf. the scheme arranged at Dudley National Projectile Factory, Hist. Rec., R/346/28.
[4] See Appendix I.

In addition to the needs of sick and stranded workers, there was the very difficult question of provision for maternity among munition workers. The question was in itself by no means a war problem, but the need for its solution was intensified among women living often under overcrowded conditions away from home.

Two lines of treatment were considered : first, the provision of light work, so that a woman in need could earn as long as she was able to do so ; and second, the provision of maternity homes, etc.

With regard to the first line of action, a valuable experiment was tried at Leeds, where in April, 1918, the doctor in charge of the medical work at the three National Ordnance Factories organised, in consultation with employers and working women's organisations, a scheme under which women employed at these factories, and subsequently at other factories in the city, were, with their own consent, transferred some months before their confinement, first to light work at standard rates in a fuse assembling factory, and, secondly, to a special clothing store and sewing depot, in which factory overalls,, etc., were made, and in which special consideration could be given to the workers. The experiment paid its way, and was warmly received by the women for whom it was intended during the few months before the Armistice. Accommodation had at that date been secured for a hundred women at a time.[1]

With regard to the second point, a special report, drawn up by Miss Squire and Dr. Campbell for the Health of Munition Workers Committee, was forwarded, in September, 1917, by that Committee to the Welfare Section, calling their attention to the " urgent need for immediate action,"[2] since careful investigation had shown that the existing provision of maternity hospitals and rest homes, admittedly defective before the war, was wholly inadequate for the requirements of certain of the congested munition districts. Early in the following year informal assent was obtained from the Treasury towards expenditure for this purpose by the Welfare Section, and in March a grant was sanctioned, by way of experiment, to a maternity home at Norwood for London munition workers. In April, 1918, in response to representation by the Department as to the pressing need in some eleven specified munition areas, the Treasury gave their sanction in principle to an expenditure not exceeding £25,000 in twelve months for maternity hospital accommodation, under certain conditions, one of these being that each scheme should be submitted for separate approval by the Treasury, and that the Ministry of Munitions was satisfied as to the lack of local accommodation.[3] In accordance with this sanction, assistance was asked for schemes at Carlisle, Lancaster, Coventry, and for a hostel at Ealing for Hayes munition workers.

The Welfare and Health Section was in close touch with the Local Government Board in connection with these schemes.

---

[1] Cf. *British Medical Journal*, 21 September, 1918, and evidence of Dr. Rhoda Adamson before War Cabinet Committee on Women in Industry, Vol. II., p. 203.
[2] L.R. 2258/22.
[3] Treasury letter 14009/18 (L.R. 8003/2).

(e) CRÈCHES.

In 1917 an agreement was made with the Board of Education, by which the Ministry of Munitions undertook to pay 75 per cent. (if necessary) of the initial cost of day (or night) nurseries for munition workers' children, together with a payment of 7d. per day for each attendance made. The officers of the Ministry of Munitions would be responsible for investigating the need of a crèche in a munitions area, and for ascertaining the amount of local support available. The Board of Education undertook to superintend the initiation of an approved scheme, and to inspect munitions crèches along with the subsidised crèches already visited by its inspectors. Forty-one crèches received grants from the Ministry of Munitions under this scheme.[1] The advisability of promoting factory crèches, as in France and Italy at the same period, was considered in detail by the Welfare Advisory Committee[2] in the summer of 1918, but it was decided to make no recommendations thereon, on account of the theoretical objection to associating so vital a part of the worker's interests with her place of employment, and the practical difficulty of taking a baby on the long crowded journeys undertaken by many munition makers on their way to work.[3]

(f) RECREATION.

As the very long hours of overtime work, common in the early stages of the wai, were shortened, and the country realised that it was no longer possible to " sprint, as if for a short race," in the production of war material, it became clear that it was essential to have adequate opportunities for recreation among factory and other workers, by way both of wholesome occupation for leisure and relief from nervous strain.[4] The Home Office recognised this when, in October, 1916, it called together a representative conference of the leaders of boys' and girls' organisations, which was the nucleus of a standing committee established, in January, 1917, to promote opportunities of recreation for the young people whose lives had been disorganised by the war. As the local officers of the Welfare and Health Section began, in the summer of 1917, to consider the existing provisions for munition workers' leisure, it became clear to them, first, that there was a very great shortage of such provision (many of the pre-war schemes having died down for lack of workers) ; secondly, that such provision as existed did not always meet the present needs—the type of evening club provided, for example, had often not kept pace

---

[1] L.R. 2960. See Appendix I.

[2] A Welfare Advisory Committee was appointed in May, 1918, and was intended to serve as a Departmental Committee to carry on to some extent the work of the Health of Munition Workers' Committee. It had, however, few meetings, and ceased to operate after August, 1918.

[3] *A Report on the Welfare of the Children of Women employed in Factories in France and Germany*, drawn up for the Ministry of Munitions at this time, was published in 1919 by the Local Government Board.

[4] The Reports of the Commission on Industrial Unrest in July, 1917, drew special attention to the needs of recreation.

in its organisation with the very rapid change of outlook and the spirit
of independence produced in factory lads and girls during three years
of war ; and, thirdly, that there was much ignorance of each other's
objects and methods among the existing institutions, and little attempt
to deal with the very comprehensive problem of recreation as a whole.
In a few towns (such as Birmingham, where a Civic Recreation League
had been founded in the previous autumn) attempts had already
been made to co-ordinate and supplement the existing facilities ; in
a number of others, successful experiments had been made by voluntary
organisations in new types of recreation, such as those offered by
" mixed clubs " for boys and girls.   In none, however, was the provision adequate for the needs, and the welfare officers co-operated
actively in the development of existing schemes for its extension, and
in urging the introduction of new schemes when they were required.
On 21 July, 1917, leave was given by the Treasury for the cost of
recreation schemes approved by the Welfare and Health Section in
controlled establishments to be written off the sum contributed to the
Excess Profits Duty up to 10s. per head per year of those benefiting
by the provision made, and a similar undertaking was given for national
factories.[1]   With this provision, the development of recreation schemes
for industrial workers multiplied with great rapidity during the end
of 1917 and in 1918.

There were two alternatives in the organisation of recreation in
accordance with this concession, although the same financial provision
applied to both.   Schemes might, as under pre-war conditions, be
organised by firms for their workpeople, with a greater or less amount
of co-operation from the latter, or they might be developed and
controlled by some representative body.

The provision of recreation schemes by firms has been discussed,
in part, in connection with boys' welfare.   There were the same
objections to such provision as to that of factory crèches for the
workers' babies—the theoretical objection of possible interference
with the workers' leisure hours by the firm, and the practical difficulty
of distance if the workers' homes were scattered and far from their
work.   On the other hand, the *esprit de corps* fostered by common
employment often made the adoption of works schemes desirable.
These, indeed, had existed widely in times of peace, but they developed
very much during the last two years of the war, and a considerable
proportion of large firms then had their recognised athletic and social
clubs, embracing every variety of sport, etc., from cricket and football
and tennis to orchestras and pierrot troupes.   A few examples may
be given.[2]

---

[1] L.R. 4764. See also Appendix I.
[2] These examples may profitably be considered in connection with the industrial unrest of the early summers of 1917 and 1918.   The larger Coventry firms,
among whose workers unrest was constant, were well equipped with scout troops,
football clubs, orchestras, etc., for their boy workers at least.   Two of these firms
had cinemas ; three others had, in January, 1918, adapted canteens as theatres.
[(Printed) *Weekly Report*, No. 124, X (5/1/16)].

(1) A very complete scheme was submitted for the sanction of the Welfare Section by a Bath engineering firm in June, 1918. The firm proposed a complete scheme of recreation for 1,371 employees (987 men, 167 women, 190 boys). It was proposed to provide tennis, football (two grounds), hockey, cricket, a gymnasium, a boys' club, swimming competitions, papers for the canteen, a girls' club and other amenities, at a total cost of £1,022. The income from the employees' subscriptions was estimated at £185. In this case the Department recommended a grant at the rate of 9s. 10d. a head (£677).[1]

(2) Some schemes sent up for sanction were on a very much larger scale than this. Thus, late in 1918, a very large firm asked for an 8s. capitation grant for the benefit of the 10,000 workers in one of its numerous establishments. The firm proposed a comprehensive scheme which would cost £15,000 to introduce. Of this sum the firm proposed to bear more than two-thirds. The workers' subscriptions at 5s. per head were expected to produce £1,250 towards an estimated annual cost of £2,350.[2]

A State subsidy, direct or indirect, would obviously give a valuable stimulus to schemes of this type.

(3) In March, June and September, 1918, formal approval was given by the section for grants of 2s. 6d. a head of the employees concerned to finance a recreation scheme for the employees of a steel works near Birmingham. The neighbourhood provided very little opportunity of recreation of any kind, and the firm opened a canteen and social club, to be managed by a workpeople's committee, with a field for all kinds of outdoor games, together with a holiday resort on the Avon, at which batches of workers could stay for fishing and boating during the week-end. Out of the 748 employees (mostly men and boys, but including 170 women and girls) nearly half joined the social club during the first summer, paying 2d. a week. The firm, in applying in January, 1919, for a further grant towards the cost of a boat and fishing punt, etc., at the holiday home and the cost of upkeep of the cricket and football ground, expatiated on the great success of the scheme, which had already created a different atmosphere in the works, and was likely to be "the forerunner of similar good work among other firms in the trade." It had proved its value "not only in providing healthy, enjoyable exercises and recreation in a Black Country district where little or no facilities of the kind exist, but, almost equally important, it was providing a link uniting employers and employed, both working together for the common good."[3]

This expression of satisfaction was typical of many others received during 1918. Wherever possible, in dealing with applications for these grants, the Department urged the establishment of a democratic constitution for the management of recreation schemes, despite frequent representations by the firms concerned that management was simpler and more effective if not delegated. Democratic

---

[1] L.R. 1459/2.   [2] L.R.W. 208/5.
[3] L.R. 2245/18 ; C.E. 2323/15.

government would obviously not *per se* ensure the success of a recreation scheme, 'yet the outstanding cases of failure of carefully prepared plans and neglect of elaborate " institutes " very commonly coincided with autocratic management by the firm without consultation of the workers.

As an alternative to recreation schemes provided by and for individual firms, combined recreation schemes for the whole of an area developed in 1917 and 1918.   The Home Office had, in the summer of 1917, circularised a large number of towns, and had recommended the foundation of local " Juvenile Organisations Committees," in order to secure combination in dealing with the welfare of school-children and young people.   The welfare officers were already, in a number of towns, co-operating with or stirring up combined recreation schemes ; and the two Departments agreed in the autumn of 1917 to ask these Juvenile Organisations Committees to extend their scope of action to all classes, men and women, boys and girls, in munitions areas.[1]   As a result a number of civic recreation schemes were started.   These had very wide possibilities.   They ranged from proposals covering the whole of an area (such as that originated for the whole Merseyside district in April, 1918, where a very comprehensive organisation was developed, for strengthening and supplementing existing undertakings for boys and girls, developing schemes for men and women's recreation, *e.g.*, in mixed clubs, securing playing fields, so far as possible, and experimenting on the establishment of " social   institutes ") to more   limited   provision—primarily—for munition workers' needs, such as that made at Hereford, where a central club for munition workers, opened late in 1917, developed in the following year into a flourishing outdoor club, with a playing field for tennis, croquet, net-ball and skittles, with dancing and open-air concerts, at a payment of 6d. a week by each member.[2]

Many examples of such schemes could be quoted.   At Leeds a central recreation club for 4,000 workers was opened in 1918 ; in various districts of South Wales a Federated National Club Movement, fostered and inspired by the local welfare officer, took root, in order to " co-ordinate all existing efforts to promote social and educational facilities," with a central mixed club providing sports, musical and dramatic societies, educational classes, dances, whist drives, etc.

These collective schemes were usually formed under the presidency of the local Mayor, with a finance committee of business men to apportion the funds and with full representation of labour.   As has been said, they supplemented and strengthened existing agencies, and relied on local patriotism for their success.

The movement for the civic organisation of recreation had already, by the close of the war, large aims and possibilities of development, and the share of the Welfare and Health Section in its initiation was probably one of the most lasting forms of extra-mural welfare work. Combined recreation schemes sometimes took many months to mature, so that a good deal of the organisation undertaken by the section in 1918 was in effect a bequest to the period of peace.

---

[1] L.R.W. 1984.   [2] M.W. 11577/4.   L.R.W. 454,2.

(g) Public Order.

Indirectly, care for munition workers outside the factories included in its scope the promotion of public order ; and the provision made for recreation and for the transit and housing of imported workers was a very practical contribution to this end.   More direct action, of course, came within the sphere of the local authorities.   In this connection the extra-mural officers co-operated with the newly appointed women police and patrols, who were immediately concerned with the maintenance of order.   As many as 985 women police were supplied during the war by the " Women Police Service " to munitions factories, mainly for intra-mural work in National Explosives and Filling Factories. Twelve women police were provided by the Ministry of Munitions for outdoor work in the City of Carlisle and 164 were employed at Gretna.   Their work at the latter place was, on its cessation in 1919, warmly commended by the Chief of the Gretna Police as the inauguration of " a new and beneficent movement for the protection and guidance of young workers."[1]

III. The Character of Extra-Mural Work.

The Welfare and Health Section in its extra-mural work was meeting merely temporary needs much more than was the case in its organisation for the comfort and efficiency of workers inside factories. War pressure had uprooted working men in every part of the country and had, to a degree that had previously appeared impossible, removed the immobility of women's labour.   In safeguarding, to some extent, this process, the Welfare Section had to improvise practical and sympathetic treatment for the needs of the transplanted workers, treatment which involved consideration as much of their psychological as their material requirements.   In meeting these needs it inevitably came up against a series of outstanding social problems as they concerned working-class lives as a whole, and not only those of transient munition workers.   Further, it operated on a field already partly covered by the forces of local government and of voluntary organisations, and indeed largely developed this side of its work in order to fill in the gaps left by existing agencies.   Obviously, it could not attempt to give, in less than two years, lasting solutions of social problems, nor to act as other than a temporary stopgap in the organisation of social welfare.   It improvised, however, effective and unconventional treatment for a number of practical difficulties, and offered a valuable contribution towards the establishment of certain forms of welfare on a lasting civic basis.

---

[1] *Women Police Service*, 1919.   L.R. 682/16.

CHAPTER IV.

MEDICAL AND RESEARCH WORK.

I. The Establishment of a Factory Medical Service.

The precise position given to care for the workers' health varied in different schemes of welfare administration. In some factories, welfare supervision grew out of the work of factory nursing. In others, the welfare supervisor was responsible in a more or less definite sense for the organisation of first-aid and nursing in the factory ; and it was urged periodically that training for welfare supervision should consist very largely in matters of hygiene. Probably the establishment of efficient first-aid provision and nursing was one of the aspects of the official policy of welfare administration which was most readily accepted by employers and workers. More definite steps than the organisation of nursing and first-aid in factories were, however, taken by the Welfare and Health Section in its second year's work, in order to establish an organised method of attack on the health problems of factory life from within. Whole-time medical officers were, with the co-operation of the Ministry of Munitions, attached to the staffs of a number of factories to supervise the health conditions under which work was carried on, and to watch the health of individual workers. These officers, while primarily responsible to their own factory management, were also under the control of a medical staff at the headquarters of the Ministry, who visited the factories and advised the factory medical officers on problems that arose. The position of the factory doctor in relation to the factory management and to the Department was thus comparable to that of an army medical officer, in relation to his battalion Commanding Officer and to his administrative superiors in the aimy medical service, respectively.

The shortage of doctors during the war prevented the extension of this system beyond those munitions industries which subjected the workers to special risk, such as the factories for the manufacture or manipulation of T.N.T., lethal gases, and other poisonous explosives. The precautions taken for the safety of workers in these industries, however, brought medical men and women into intimate contact with the internal life of factories to a degree hardly possible before the war. The success of the special work of this factory medical service, together with the help given by research, during the war, in the solution of practical problems of workshop ventilation and lighting, the feeding and the regulation of the hours of work and time-keeping of munition workers, opened a new field for co-operation between medical science and the factory management of the future.

II. The Fight against T.N.T. Poisoning.

(a) THE SCOPE OF THE PROBLEM.

The technical side of the methods by which the Ministry of Munitions dealt with T.N.T. poisoning among munition workers is treated in detail elsewhere.[1] A brief account, however, of the Department's fight against the bad effects of T.N.T. work upon the workers must, omitting technicalities, find a place here, both on account of the intrinsic interest of the means taken to safeguard the workers' life and health, and because the Welfare and Health Section developed its care for matters of health primarily in connection with the very special problems of welfare which the use of T.N.T. originated.

Trinitrotoluene (T.N.T.) is a high explosive obtained by nitrating the coal tar product toluene. Before August, 1914, it had been little used, and was believed on expert opinion to be harmless " in ordinary use."[2] With the growing demand for high explosive ammunition, its use increased very greatly in 1915 and 1916. Munition workers were exposed to it both in its manufacture and in the filling of it into shells, bombs, mines, grenades, etc. Comparatively few workers were, however, required for its production, whereas very large numbers (chiefly unskilled workers, four-fifths of whom were, by 1917, women) were engaged directly and indirectly in the later processes. The filling factories producing for the Gun Ammunition Filling and the Trench Warfare Divisions of the Department were therefore the primary scene of action in the fight against T.N.T. poisoning.

It is impossible to estimate accurately the number of workers exposed at any given time to the action of T.N.T., for not all the National Filling Factories used the substance, and some of the workers, in those factories where it was employed, were quite remote from its use. Since, however, the incidence of illness from T.N.T. was not confined to those handling it, it might be argued that all operatives in factories employing T.N.T. in any of its different forms were exposed to its effects. In January, 1918, T.N.T. was handled by some or all of the operatives[3] in 29 trade factories, 10 national filling and 9 of H.M. factories engaged on the manufacture of explosives. The number of workers thus directly exposed to T.N.T. at this time was estimated at over 50,000 by H.M. Medical Inspector of Factories. Further, the wastage of labour, great in almost all munition factories among women munition workers, ranged from 60 per cent. to 100 per cent. per annum in filling factories in 1917,[4] being greatest among those of under six months' service, *i.e.*, the newcomers whom statistics showed to be specially liable to the different forms of illness produced by T.N.T. Therefore a much larger number came in one year within the poisoning range than the numbers employed in connnection with it in any one month would warrant, while it was recognised that " severe effects of T.N.T. might fall on the workers six months after all connection with the factory had ceased."[5]

---

[1] See Vol. X., Part V.

[2] Cd. 9108 of 1918. According to a Report of the Ordnance Board in 1908, there was " no reason to suppose any hygienic objection to its manufacture."

[3] HIST. REC./R/346/39.

[4] Circular M.M. 197, *Report of Hours of Labour Committee.*

[5] Dr. Legge, in the *Factory Inspectors' Annual Report* for 1917-18.

(b) The Early Methods of Working in T.N.T.

T.N.T. work in filling factories at the end of 1915, before its toxic properties were fully realised, involved mainly the following processes :—

(i) In the melthouse, T.N.T. with or without ammonium nitrate in crystals, was melted down and poured into shells. If this latter process was done carelessly or without proper equipment, the shells, the trucks in which they stood, and the floors were splashed with molten explosives, either T.N.T. or amatol (the product of T.N.T. and ammonium nitrate), and not only the shell fillers, but the cleaners of shells, floors, and trucks came into contact with the substance. The melting process, further, produced fumes which obviously affected the atmosphere.

(ii) In the presshouse, the same two substances, after being incorporated as a fine mixed powder by grinding in a mill, or the pure T.N.T. unblended, were then weighed out by hand and introduced as powder into the shells, partly by mechanical presses, partly by " hand stemming," or hammering in with a wooden mallet or stick through a loose funnel inserted in the shell opening. A thick layer of dust tended to accumulate on the ground, on the trucks on which the shells stood, and on the persons of the workers, whose exposed hair and skin became a tawny orange, while the air was filled with the same fine dust.[1]

The dry powder was also poured into small paper " exploder bags," which were then tied up by hand ; while the T.N.T. was pressed into pellets for gaine cavities, and filled into gaines, etc. These processes of manufacture gave full opportunity for the effects of T.N.T. working to tell on the operatives either by contact with the molten amatol, in liquid form and congealed on shells, trucks, floors, etc., or with the dust scattered in filling, or by inhalation of fumes or dust-laden air. Little attention was paid to these possibilities until the end of 1915, partly because current medical work held T.N.T. filling work to involve little danger, partly because a large proportion of the T.N.T. then used was of a very high standard of purity and therefore comparatively innocuous.[2]

(c) T.N.T. Illness in 1916 and Administrative Action.

Two or three cases of possible T.N.T. poisoning had been reported to the Home Office in 1915, but the first death officially recorded[3] as due to T.N.T. poisoning took place in January, 1916. This case was reported from a trade factory. In March, two deaths from T.N.T. poisoning were reported from Woolwich Arsenal and one from H.M.

---

[1] I.R.W. 218/17, and report by Dr. George Moore to the T.N.T. Committee in December, 1916, on the *Toxic Effect of T.N.T.*

[2] Hist. Rec./R/364 35.

[3] By order under section 73 of the Factory Act, toxic jaundice, if contracted in a factory, had on 27 November, 1915, been made notifiable by all medical practitioners to the Factory Department of the Home Office. The provision was, however, intended to secure notifications of this disease, not only when due to T.N.T., but also when caused by working in tetrachlorethane dope, by which much illness was caused until its abandonment in the summer, 1916.

Factory, Slade's Green. In May there were five cases with three deaths, in June eight cases with two deaths, in July sixteen cases with five deaths, seven of which, including two deaths, were of workers in National Filling Factories.

The Home Office, normally responsible for dealing with all matters in connection with dangerous trades, took action early in the year both to circulate information and directions to medical officers connected with the factories, and to secure investigation into the causes and prevention of this little-known form of poisoning. In July the Home Office, on the recommendation of the Medical Inspector of Factories, Dr. Legge, sent formal recommendations on the subject to the Ministry of Munitions, and accordingly the National Filling Factories and trade factories were at once circularised by the Department, urging that special attention should be paid to " clean " working until further precautions against T.N.T. danger could be perfected ; that alternation of workers from T.N.T. to other work should be arranged ; and that exploder bags (among the fillers of which six out of the eleven deaths recorded had occurred) should be filled with a smaller charge, in order to diminish the likelihood of spilling the powder. Most factories agreed to fall in with these recommendations, but one or two explained that they could not alternate their workers without reducing output, then urgently required.[1]

Early in July it was decided, on the recommendation of Dr. Legge, to attach a medical officer to the Gun Ammunition Filling Division ; and on 1 September Dr. W. J. O'Donovan, of the London Hospital, was appointed as supervising medical officer for the Ministry to collect information from the doctors attached to the various factories, to distribute the results of their investigations, to help them in laying down precautions against T.N.T. poisoning, and to advise the Department on devising means for preventing its occurrence. On 15 August Dr. Addison, at a departmental meeting of representatives of the supply departments, factory managements, and scientific bodies concerned in the use of T.N.T., stated that the Department must assume direct responsibility for dealing with the T.N.T. problems, since it had potential powers under the Munitions of War (Amendment) Act and the Defence of the Realm Act, and in the national factories the Department could exercise the rights of an employer. Colonel Milman, Controller of the Gun Ammunition Filling Division, then explained the precautions already taken. Medical superintendents had been appointed to all the larger National Filling Factories, and steps had been taken to appoint whole time doctors ; in the smaller factories local practitioners had been engaged to visit factories every third day. These doctors had received directions from the Home Office with regard to poisoning by T.N.T.[2]

Vigorous measures were continued by the Gun Ammunition Filling Division of the Ministry of Munitions throughout the autumn of 1916 to stem the tide of T.N.T. poisoning, which was rising steadily until the beginning of 1917, and to enlist the active co-operation of

---

[1] HIST. REC./R/346/35 ; L.R.W. 218/12.
[2] L.R.W. 218/13 ; HIST. REC./R/346/35.

factory managements and of workers in every possible way in its prevention. Draft regulations for T.N.T. work had been drawn up by the Health of Munition Workers Committee and had been discussed in detail with factory managers in August, and these served as the basis for action during the autumn and winter. A booklet of instructions to medical officers of filling factories was drawn up by Dr. O'Donovan in October, and a system of medical record keeping on a uniform basis was instituted.[1] The concluding paragraph of these instructions represents the attitude from which the danger to workers was approached by those responsible :—

> " The medical care of T.N.T. workers is of the utmost national importance. Men and women come to us ignorant of danger, the latter in the healthiest period of their lives ; we must spare no pains and no professional skill in preventing their leaving us, injured perhaps even for life."

(d) THE T.N.T. COMMITTEE AND THE " RULES FOR THE USE OF T.N.T."

At the end of October, 1916, an expert committee was appointed by Mr. Montagu, under the chairmanship of Dr. Morley Fletcher, with representatives of the Home Office (Dr. Legge and Dr. Collis), the Filling, Trench Warfare, Explosives Supply and Inspection Departments of the Ministry, and the Health of Munition Workers Committee, to advise the Minister as to the prevention and treatment of cases of poisoning in filling factories, and to make such inquiries and experiments as they might deem desirable for this purpose.[2]

As a result of the work of the committee during the next two months and of the investigations made on their behalf both in laboratories and factories, they presented in January, 1917, a draft code of rules to govern the use of T.N.T. in all factories. Owing to interdepartmental administrative difficulties, the proposed rules did not finally reach the factories till the end of March, 1917, but the active work of the medical officers attached to the Filling Division and the wide circulation of the results of the two committees' inquiries among the medical officers attached to the National Filling Factories, had already to a very considerable extent anticipated the provisions then made obligatory.[3]

---

[1] In December the trade factories also were asked to send to the Department weekly reports of T.N.T. illness. L.R.W. 218/9.

[2] L.R.W. 218/45.

[3] Serious alarm at the spread of T.N.T. poisoning was expressed in the press at this period, and spread to some extent to the workers, although, greatly to their credit, it did not result in labour shortage at the filling factories. Sickness, however, and fear of sickness led to considerable irregularity at work, and made it difficult to enforce strict discipline in this respect. (HIST. REC./R/346/35.) Thus Dr. George Moore (see p. 70) gave the following figures for absenteeism in one of the national factories on an average day in November, 1916 :—

			MEN.		WOMEN.	
			No. employed.	Per cent. absent.	No. employed.	Per cent. absent.
T.N.T. Buildings	Melt House	.. ..	668	25·4	469	42·9
	Press House	.. ..	808	28	498	33·3
	Mill	.. ..	196	18·4	—	—
Stores (no T.N.T.)		.. ..	1 077	12·9	951	25
Constructional Work		.. ..	2,000	2	—	—

The T.N.T. Regulations thus issued[1] (under Order 35 A.A. of the Defence of the Realm Act of December, 1916) laid down rules for :—

(i) " Clean " working and good ventilation in T.N.T. work shops ; and

(ii) Alternation, in periods of two or four weeks, of employment upon T.N.T. and other work, except when the factory medical officer held this to be unnecessary. (Alternation was adopted in all but one of the National Filling Factories until June, 1918, when the order for it was, with the consent of the T.N.T. Advisory Committee, revoked.[2])

(iii) Canteens must be provided, and half a pint of milk, or an approved substitute for it, given daily, gratis, to T.N.T. workers, who were forbidden to take food in any place where T.N.T. was handled or without washing. Much insistence was placed in practice on the need of good food for those engaged on T.N.T. work.

(iv) The management must supply working clothes, arrange for their being washed at least weekly, and provide changing rooms. (The Gun Ammunition Filling Department provided patterns of approved forms of overalls, and the Explosives Supply Department secured the supply of them through contractors.)

(v) A whole-time medical officer must be engaged for each factory with 2,000 workers, and one or more assistants if there were more than this number ; and a woman welfare supervisor, approved by the Welfare and Health Section, must be appointed in all factories and workshops employing women.

(vi) There must be adequate washing arrangements.

(vii) Records and returns, as prescribed, must be kept and supplied to the Department.

When these rules were issued it had already been decided to transfer the medical section of the Gun Ammunition Filling Division to the Welfare and Health Section, then in process of reconstruction.

The responsibility for enforcing the rules was therefore divided between the Supply Departments and the Welfare Section, acting through the Supply Departments, an arrangement which aroused much criticism at first from the Gun Ammunition Filling Division and from the national factories concerned,[3] but which caused less administrative difficulty than had been anticipated. The standard of these regulations was not, however, easy to maintain in the small trade factories, such as certain of those working for the Trench Warfare Supply Department. It was partly on this account that T.N.T. work was, in the course of 1918, concentrated in a comparatively small number of factories.[4]

---

[1] Cd. 8494 of 1917.   [3] L.R.W. 218/17.
[2] L.R.W. 218/50.   [4] L.R.W. 218/48.

(e) Statistics.

The following are the statistics for illness and death due to T.N.T. officially recorded during the war :—

	January to March.	April to June.	July to December.	October to December.	Total.
1916	6/4	16/5	73/21	86/22	181/52
1917	83/12	56/20	21/8	29/4	189/44
1918	13/4	6/2	5/2	10/2	34/10

(The figures in italics record deaths. Almost all the cases were toxic jaundice, though a few of aplastic anæmia are included.)

In considering the number of cases and the yearly totals it must be remembered that the numbers employed in the National Filling Factories, to which the great bulk of T.N.T. workers belonged, had increased from a monthly average of 30,000 in 1916 to 71,000 in 1917 (*i.e.*, by 140 per cent.), and had not fallen very much by the date of the Armistice. The most pressing danger of T.N.T. work was nearly ended after the midsummer of 1917, although the difficulties of diagnosis and the elimination of unfit workers from the factories after some brief experience of T.N.T. work make it impossible to dogmatise with complete confidence as to the after effects of exposure to T.N.T. The Department pointed out in June, 1918,[1] in a circular to the factories concerned, that whereas from October, 1916, to March, 1917, there had been 169 cases of serious illness, in the same period a year later there were 42 such cases ; while in April and May, 1918, there were four and one respectively. The minor forms of illness due to T.N.T—and Dr. Legge calculated[2] that 30 people suffered from these in proportion to each case of toxic jaundice—had died down. " In August, 1916, 11 per cent. of the operatives at the largest National Filling Factory were suspended by the medical officer for T.N.T. sickness ; in January, 1918, only 1 per cent. And at that date in all the other T.N.T. factories the percentage amount of T.N.T. illness could be represented in decimal fractions of the numbers employed."[3]

(f) Methods of Attack.

This very great improvement was ascribed by the Department in the circular just quoted to " close medical supervision of the workers, combined with improved methods of work and the substitution of mechanical processes wherever possible."

At the beginning of 1918 there were at the filling factories 15 whole-time and 28 part-time medical officers, responsible to their own Boards of Management, but with their duties, appointments, and salaries sanctioned by the Welfare and Health Section. This form of dual control was said to have caused little, if any, difficulty in practice. The factory doctors were " some of ordinary, some of expert qualifica-

---

[1] L.R.W. 218/50.
[2] *Factory Inspectors Report* for 1917, p. 23.
[3] Hist. Rec./H/346/2.

tions,"[1] and were in close touch with the headquarters staff, the members of which maintained close contact with current difficulties by periodical spells of residence and work at the factories, and secured expert laboratory assistance when needed in diagnosis. It was impressed upon the medical officers of filling factories that their work was essentially preventive, and that they were not required to undertake the care of " panel " ailments. Their duties were to inspect all workers on engagement and at regular intervals, whether ill or not ; to report to the Ministry all illness (not only toxic jaundice) apparently due to T.N.T., and to introduce definite arrangements for preventive or curative treatment.[2] Special arrangements were authorised by the Director-General of Munitions Finance in March, 1917, for in-patient treatment at local hospitals (at a cost of 3s. and 4s. per day), for persons suffering from toxic jaundice, and compensation was given on the scale of the Workmen's Compensation Act, with the 25 per cent. war addition of August, 1917, together with a diet allowance of 1s.·a day.[3]

Experts had not agreed even at the beginning of 1917 whether T.N.T. poisoning took place primarily through skin absorption or through inhalation. The one theory suggested primarily defensive clothing, the other good systems of ventilation, as a remedy. The less fumes and dust produced in work the less was, on either theory, the danger of poisoning. In the autumn of 1916, therefore, two small committees, representing the Supply Departments of the Ministry of Munitions and the Home Office, inquired in detail into the possibility of better ventilation and improved mechanical methods for T.N.T. work, and pressed them forward with much vigour and promptitude. Early in 1917 great improvements in both directions had already been made, both in the national and trade factories, despite the frequent changes in production required by changing demands for ammunition.[4] A year later, although T.N.T. filling by hand had not disappeared, Dr. O'Donovan reported as follows :—

> "A remarkable feature of T.N.T. work has been the rapid changes in processes which have come about. Melt filling, the method by which T.N.T. was melted in coppers and poured into shells by buckets or from spigots, has practically passed away. Hand stemming is gradually being superseded by horizontal and vertical filling machines, which convey the

---

[1] It was in practice impossible to confine their work within these limits. Thus at Hayes National Filling Factory, where the woman doctor with two assistants had a dispensary and a complete equipment of surgeries, each with a factory sister in attendance, the surgery visits from May, 1916, worked out as follows :—

	1916.	1917.	1918.
	Per cent.	Per cent.	Per cent.
Occupational diseases from T.N.T., C.E. and Fulminate.	17·6	9	4·6
Accidents, cuts, bruises and explosives ..	12·2	12·8	9·0
" Panel " illnesses from headache, etc. ..	70·2	78·2	86·4

In the case of workers without medical cards " panel illnesses " might be treated at the surgery to save loss of time. HIST. REC./R/1122. 3/34.

[2] HIST. REC./R/346/35.   [3] L.R.W. 218/2.   [4] L.R.W. 218/17.

powder into the shell by means of an Archimedian screw. The small exploder bags, holding a few teaspoonfuls of T.N.T. powder, which were formerly filled by hand, are now filled by machinery, but have to be finished and tied up by manual labour. This, too, will be superseded by a machine filling T.N.T. without any hand contact into stiff cartridge containers, and the finished article will fall from the end of the machine. This remarkable and rapid progress is largely due to the readiness with which engineers have listened to the urgent representations of the T.N.T. Committee and the Medical Department, and shows the seriousness with which the problem of T.N.T. poisoning is appreciated by all departments of the Ministry concerned."[1]

After the need for " clean " working, in a sense much more stringent than that of the ordinary danger building practice, was realised, workers had to be trained to wear the protective clothing designed for them, and workers and management had to learn precautions for avoiding contact with the T.N.T. This meant the adoption by the management of a very high standard of workshop " cleanliness," and the strict enforcement of discipline.

The following description by a welfare supervisor in a trade factory in the early stages of T.N.T. work records methods actually adopted by the unregulated worker, and indicates the need for special watchfulness :—

· "At the commencement of my work in June, 1916, we were still only beginning to be aware of T.N.T. dangers, and of the possibilities of averting them ; and it was an uphill fight those first few months. Munitions were needed so terribly ; the workers were all very closely linked up with soldiers at the front ; they were known to be having rough times, and each worker was inclined to take the attitude that output only mattered, and conditions of output must be overlooked. The day for filling exploder bags by hand—a process in which the factory had early developed marked success—will probably never return. One feels one owes a tribute to these girls who kept to that work so valiantly.

" Their workshops were wooden huts, scattered about a big untidy field. Cloakroom accommodation was totally inadequate, and so far away that the workers were obliged to wear their coats in going to the workshops, particularly at night, and, of course, then had to hang them in the Powder Huts. Canteen arrangements were hopeless ; at first the workers had had none. Food baskets had been brought into the shops ; as meal time approached, there would be a gradual drifting away towards the boiler house with tea pots ; and then when the tea was made the workers would wipe their hands on their skirts (overalls had not then been introduced), bring out their food from inside the T.N.T. boxes, which served as stools ; the work-bench became the meal table, and the picnic

[1] HIST. REC./R/346/39.

proceeded.   There was as little formality about starting work again as in leaving off, and, as it was all piece-work, very little time was wasted on meals.   The amount of work produced each day was marvellous.   I saw several other factories where exploder bags were filled, but whereas elsewhere 500 to 600 was considered a good daily record, 1,000 to 1,200, and 1,300, was a normal output for our old hands, with earnings from 10s. to 13s. 6d. a day, at a time when the ordinary daily rate was 4s. 2d. ; and the standard of work was always excellent. But health and welfare suffered proportionately.   It was not possible to start any traditions ; each day one took up the tussle anew—working before meals, wearing overalls, proper meal intervals and proper places for meals, as well as the ordinary rules for work in danger buildings—all the regulations were rather regarded as skittles, and it was part of the game to throw down as many as possible.   The doctor (not resident nor whole-time), however, warded off any real tragedy, and bit by bit the workers accepted the rules of the game, so that playing became easier, though the game was never won."[1]

This factory was admittedly exceptional.   At another much larger factory, the same supervisor found, a few months later, that precautions were increasingly observed and that the workers (who had been interested in a recent scientific inquiry carried on in their works, as to the effects of T.N.T.) were not, as in the previous case, wholly callous to precautions.

The reports of the medical officers and the special medical welfare inspectors, however, up to the beginning of 1917, illustrate the difficulties of introducing " clean " working.[2] " I know very few munition girls who do not love to spill, splash, and otherwise distribute melted T.N.T. . . .   The spigots constantly drip on to the floor, the collected amatol being removed by a worker, who kneels and scrapes the floor.   A fair number of cases are still cleaned by knocking them against the side of a bin . . . girls employed on this work sit round low tables and scatter the chippings over the table and over each other . . . the weighing room is very dusty, and the benches covered with powder, and the dust so caused is removed from the smaller shells by inverting them and knocking them on the benches ; this leaves a small lump of powder on the bench and cuts up the surface of the bench and renders it extremely difficult to clean." (January, 1917 ; a national factory.)

" Amatol mud on the benches and the floors.   The girls leave the gloves in the powder when they go off duty.   The benches are rather dusty ; the floors encrusted ; the machine is of a bad pattern and scatters dust far and wide." (September, November, December, 1916 ; a trade factory.)

" The process of filling grenades is incredibly dirty ;   T.N.T. mixture is spilt plentifully over the grenades and bench." (October, 1916 ; a trade factory.)

---

[1] HIST. REC./R/346/41.   [2] L.R.W. 218/14.

" Gloves soiled with T.N.T. and in a hopeless state of disrepair were used as a protection for T.N.T. workers." (November, 1916 ; a national factory.)

" The floors are deplorable, rough splintered wood, well sprinkled with T.N.T. grit ; dry sweeping ; the filling sheds are very dirty, benches and floors are uneven and covered with powder and pieces of amatol." (December, 1916 ; a national factory.)

Of one national factory in this group of reports it was, however, said (November, 1916) : " Physiological cleanliness is carried out wherever possible ; the floors are swept damp ; the benches are covered with non-splintering linoleum, and are cleaned with a damp mop at very frequent intervals."

Constant efforts were made from Headquarters, always in consultation with the management, to impress this standard of cleanliness upon workers and their supervisors alike, and a very high level was reached by 1917 in the great majority of factories.[1]

Welfare work in " medical " factories differed from that in the ordinary factory only in that it was more closely directed to the workers' health and was more directly subordinate to that of the factory doctor. Even questions such as clothing, feeding, tran-it, hours, recreation, must in factories of this type be considered with reference to the medical officer and danger building officer. On the other hand, it was particularly desirable to foster wholesome social activities, and especially outdoor games, such as hockey and football, among workers employed under the strict discipline and with the dangers involved in filling factories ; and the welfare superintendents of the national factories took this vigorously in hand in conjunction with the workers.

The purely official side of welfare supervision in a National Filling Factory employing at one time 8,000 women, but which held on its pay-roll 23,000 different women in three years, was thus described in 1919[2] :—

" A lady superintendent aided by an assistant was always on duty in each section of the factory. She assisted in the maintenance of discipline and enforcement of magazine regulations, helped and advised workers in difficulties and investigating grievances. She made arrangements for the transfer or discharge of workers, supervised the shifting houses and supply of necessary clothing, towels, etc., and the cleaning of shops and platforms. In addition she kept a card index of all the workers under her charge, on which was recorded their medical grade, time worked on C.E. or T.N.T., absence or unpunctuality, etc. She was also responsible for the distribution of milk and cocoa to workers on poisonous explosives and to all night workers."

With regard to the welfare inspection of these factories, the excerpts given above, if taken in connection with the standard of the T.N.T. regulations, illustrate some of the initial difficulties. A small expert

---

[1] HIST. REC./R/346/35.   [2] HIST. REC./R/1122. 3/34.

staff carried on the work from headquarters. The reports of the travelling officers, which dealt with many problems of occupational illness other than those due to T.N.T. work alone, were submitted to the chief medical officer for recommendations and then despatched to the trade firms or to the Supply Department concerned. The Welfare and Health Section was thus kept in touch with the constant changes in the manipulation of T.N.T. introduced by the changing requirements of successive Government Departments, while these " medical " welfare reports, often highly technical in character, were said to, be " of special value from the aspect of preventive medicine."[1]

III. Precautions for Lethal Gas Workers.

In preparing precautions for lethal gas workers, the Department had to some extent the advantage of earlier experience in dealing with the T.N.T. problem. It was at least not taken unprepared by illness resulting from an occupation believed to be harmless ; for it was clear from the outset that lethal gas must involve dangers from which the operatives must be safeguarded. The problems to be faced were quite new, but at the outset the Trench Warfare Supply Department secured the services of Dr. F. Shufflebotham of Newcastle-under-Lyme, who had had a large experience of industrial diseases and the conditions of labour in dangerous processes.[2]

(a) Special Character of the Work.

Special medical work[3] was carried out by the medical branch of the Welfare Section, in conjunction with the Trench Warfare Supply Department which controlled factories where lethal and lachrymatory bodies, liquid fire and coloured flares were manufactured, as well as the stations in which cylinders, shells, bombs and grenades were filled with these various bodies. These factories and filling stations could be classified thus :—

1. Chemical factories and filling stations, both controlled and national.

2. Controlled grenade filling stations.

3. The National Shell Filling Factories.

The actual manufacture of the chemical bodies used for lethal purposes was performed by men, the great majority of whom were either over military age or incapacitated for military service, while the filling was generally carried out by women and girls. The commonest dangers to which these men, women and girls were subjected

---

[1] Hist. Rec./R/346/39.

[2] Later Dr. Shufflebotham was assisted by Capt. G. W. Middlemiss, M.B., R.A.M.C., and Sir G. H. Pollard, M.P., M.D., while for some months Mr. E. Dudley, of the Local Government Board and subsequently of the Ministry of Health, was attached to this branch.

[3] Memorandum by Dr. F. Shufflebotham on Lethal Gas Factories and Filling Stations in 1917. Copy filed in Hist. Rec./R/346/39.

were those of (1) poisoning by the lethal and lachrymatory bodies ; (2) irritation of the skin, eyes and other exposed parts of the body caused by the handling either of the raw materials or the finished products, and (3) mechanical accidents. The latter, of course, occur in every branch of industry, but slight injuries, such as a bruise or a small cut, occurring to workpeople engaged in these factories might result in developments of the gravest kind, unless they secured prompt medical attention, on account of the poisonous character of the bodies handled or manufactured.

The section of munition workers employed in making the gas and other lethal bodies, and filling shells, cylinders, etc., were engaged unmistakably in the most dangerous processes known to either industry or medicine, and carried out their daily work with courage, cheerfulness and enthusiasm. In the face of the dangers involved the Department recorded with satisfaction that, though in some manufactories a large percentage of workers were " gassed " or affected by disease arising out of their employment, yet only seven fatal cases occurred in 1917, of which two were due to mechanical accidents and five to gas poisoning, and of these last cases one had already been gassed in France and one suffered already from organic disease. In 1918 up to the date of the Armistice, there were only seven fatal cases due to poisoning by the inhalation of poison gas or lethal fumes ; and the number of non-fatal casualties was small considering the very dangerous character of the processes. Special regulations were drawn up by Dr. Shufflebotham from time to time to meet different problems as they arose, in order to diminish the risks to which the workers were exposed.

(b) MEDICAL OFFICERS AND WELFARE ARRANGEMENTS.

A medical officer was attached to each of the factories and filling stations, attending thereat at stated times, with duties similar to those of the filling factory doctors. He determined the fitness of the applicant for the particular work ; examined all employees every fortnight, noting the result in a register, examined and treated employees who were ill or injured as a consequence of their employment ; and attended speedily on receiving summonses in cases of poisoning or injury, and arranged for their admission to local hospitals. He was also held responsible for the efficiency of the equipment of the ambulance station attached to each factory or filling station. Each officer had to make weekly as well as special reports to the Department upon his cases and in particular to advise as to any new aspects of poisoning by lethal bodies for which fresh precautions might be required. These medical officers, whilst attached for the above purposes to the various factories and filling stations, were in the direct employ of the Health and Welfare Department. In every instance they were men of the highest status alike as to qualifications and experience.

Fully equipped ambulance stations were provided at all the factories and filling stations. These stations were under the charge of fully trained nurses, who in a number of factories possessed assistants, the number of the latter in some instances running as high as three.   In the large factories where employees worked at night, a nurse was in constant attendance at the ambulance station.

Arrangements were made in each district where these factories and filling stations were situated for hospital accommodation for workpeople who sustained injuries or contracted illnesses arising out of their employment, with financial provision similar to that for T.N.T. workers.[1]

The welfare arrangements of lethal gas factories and filling stations were brought into line with those of other departments of the Ministry. Latterly, those in association with the factories and filling stations where secret processes were carried on were in the sole charge of a special travelling welfare officer.   The buildings in the factories and filling stations were so designed, the ventilation was so suited to the processes of manufacture, and the handling of raw materials and manufactured bodies was so reduced and protected, that the dangers of the various processes were reduced to a minimum.   All employees actually engaged in making or filling lethal and lachrymatory substances were supplied by the contractors or agents with suitable ove alls of an approved pattern ;   and, whenever the processes demanded it, they also wore helmets, respirators, gloves, goggles and clogs furnished by the contractors according to approved pattern.   It was an offence to take food of any kind into the workshops ;   and before eating and quitting the factory for home, all employees were compelled to wash their hands.   The overalls were doffed at each break in the work and left in a special room ;   strict injunctions existed against going outside of the shops in them, and the contractors were under obligation to wash them at least once a week.   At many large factories bathrooms were provided.   Messrooms and canteens were supplied except in cases where the workers preferred to go home to meals.   The National Filling Factories specially excelled in the canteen arrangements made for their workers.[2]

(c) NOTIFICATION OF ILLNESS AND PROVISION FOR COMPENSATION.

When the manufacture of poisonous gases and other lethal bodies was first contemplated, only the residuum of the male labour market could be obtained for this purpose.   All the young and healthy men had entered the Army and Navy, while skilled workers were employed in other directions ;   and it was therefore necessary to recruit for the manufacture of these poisonous bodies working people from those suffering from organic disease or disability which prevented them from entering the Services, or had been the cause of their discharge, or from those over military age.   Many men employed in these processes were subsequently found to be altogether unsuited for this particular

---

[1] See p. 75.
[2] Stringent regulations were made to impress upon workers the precautions necessary for safe working.   In the case, *e.g.*, of mustard gas (H.S.) work at the Hereford National Filling Factory, in 1918, the rules were to be read weekly to all employees.   Workers were directed to report at once to the surgery any symptoms of ill effects from their work.

class of work. These men were gradually eliminated, and instructions were given to medical officers of factories that no worker suffering from certain forms of illness or organic disease should be employed on lethal gas work.

In poison gas factories, a scratch on the hand or like simple injury, if neglected, might induce a serious case of blood poisoning ; and the inhalation of a small dose of poison gas, failing prompt remedial action, might result in perilous illness and even in death. It was therefore necessary even in cases of minor injuries, and in all gas poisoning cases, to secure prompt official notification, and in April, 1917, a series of regulations were issued which made such notification to the medical officer of the factory and to the Department compulsory upon all contractors and agents, in addition to the reports of accidents and poisoning required by the Home Office. The illnesses, thus to be notified, were set out as follows in the regulations :—Gassing ; eczematous ulceration of the skin due to the handling of the material, inflamation of the eyes caused by irritating fumes, etc. ; poisoning by lethal bodies used in the various processes (such as T.N.T.), and by lead, arsenic, phosphorus and dope ; all cases of mechanical injury arising out of the employment.

Such notification was required in part on account of compensation claims,. since, without a regular system of report and investigation, illnesses and deaths involving large claims against the contractors and the Government might occur without coming to the knowledge of the Ministry. Workmen's compensation for illness arising out of employment due to poisoning by gas or other lethal bodies was placed on the same footing as that for T.N.T. workers.

Among the cases of poisoning at the different factories and filling stations there was a wide field for medical research, and with the help of the medical officers such work was carried out. Exhaustive investigations were made into the pathology and treatment of many lethal bodies, with results greatly to the benefit, not only of the munition workers employed in these dangerous occupations, but also of soldiers gassed upon the battlefield.

IV. Other Medical Work.

In many other less specialised medical problems the Welfare and Health Section was called upon to give advice and to take action. The medical welfare officers were consulted in numerous cases of occupational illness, especially from factories where irritating or poisonous chemicals, such as tetryl, fulminate of mercury, or picric acid,[1] were handled, and their reports were frequently submitted for expert advice. " Problems of ·oil rashes in engineering shops ; of dermatitis due to caustic ; of weight lifting, and other questions incidental to the employment of female munition workers ; of the

----
[1] Cf. Memo. No. 8 of Health of Munition Workers Committee (Cd. 8214).

possibilities of poisoning by explosives, other than T.N.T.; of the maternity and other hospital accommodation in munition areas, were part of the routine of the work."[1] Reference has already been made to the last of these questions, in relation to "extra-mural" welfare. Dentists of military age were assigned by the Dental Service Committee, on which the medical sub-section was represented, to take up work in crowded munition areas, to give part-time service to hospitals, and take on posts at munition factories. Almost all the National Filling Factories had by March, 1918, provided adequate dental services for all the workers (the dentist at Hereford National Filling Factory was pulling out 1,200 teeth per month at that date). Dental treatment was facilitated as far as possible in all national factories, but especially in those where dangerous work was carried on. Hostels were visited in cases of infection. The Welfare Section had from its establishment urged the provision of suitable first-aid treatment in factories. When this was made obligatory in a large proportion of the munition trades by the Home Office Welfare Order of October, 1917, the officers of the section refrained from intervening in its enforcement in trade factories. but in the national factories steps were taken in conjunction with the medical sub-section to investigate the most effective means of carrying out the order.

A special branch of the section's medical work was the examination of workers claiming compensation for accident or injury on munition work. Doubtful cases were examined, if necessary in their own homes, and reported on to the Finance Department or to the Treasury Solicitor. In the case of an extensive factory explosion in the north, a medical officer spent a fortnight travelling up and down the Midlands and Wales, visiting the workers who had dispersed to their homes but had sent in written applications for compensation for the after-effects. By this means, the outstanding claims were quickly and satisfactorily dealt with. Many problems botn of preventive and curative treatment—in connection especially with young workers or with the infirm, discharged soldier or medical reject—were presenting themselves to the section in the summer of 1918, when the most pressing questions of dangerous occupations for munition workers had been disposed of ; but the close of the war left their further administrative treatment to other Departments.

V. Research Work.

On the expansion of the Welfare Section in 1917, a special branch was formed for scientific research in connection with problems of industrial health and welfare. In addition to utilising the pioneer investigations of the Health of Munition Workers Committee, the Department gained the services of several members of the Committee's expert staff. Thus Dr. H. M. Vernon, of Oxford University, continued his investigations into the relation of working hours and output,[2]

---

[1] HIST. REC./R/346/39.
[2] See p. 119 for an illustration of the administrative results.

initiated inquiries into the effect of working conditions on industrial accidents, and trained a staff of collaborators to continue such investigations. In addition to the physiological inquiries thus undertaken, it was felt that provision should be made for expert statistical treatment of the problems coming before the section, and a medico-statistical branch was formed, with a staff of three or four and a small laboratory, under Captain M. Greenwood, R.A.M.C. (Reader in medical statistics, University of London).   This branch carried out a large amount of research work in co-operation with members of the administrative staff—a combination which, it was urged, kept research work from developing too much on speculative lines and administrative work from becoming too stereotyped. The following were the main subjects of inquiry :—

(a) Food Investigation.

When the laboratory was established in May, 1917, although the food position was serious and it was clearly essential to secure the adequate feeding of munition workers, there was no accurate knowledge as to the sort of food being consumed by munition workers and its adequacy according to scientific standards.   A questionnaire was therefore drawn up and despatched to the managers of munitions hostels and canteens.   " At first hostel and canteen managers were extremely sceptical as to the value of the inquiry and a good deal of tact was needed before the forms were filled in at all, while still more tact and patience had to be exercised before they were filled in accurately."[1] In the end, however, the inquiry fully justified itself. A report was prepared and published[2] giving exact particulars of the diets consumed by a larger sample of industrial workers than had ever been studied before with an analysis of their scientific value.   " The hostel managers who had originally been sceptical found the advice of the Department so extremely helpful that there were times when it was found difficult to deal with the inquiries and requests for advice which came in."   The results were admitted to be of much value when the Food Section of the Ministry was established in 1918. Further information was collected and analysed during this year, and extensive use was made by the Food Ministry of data collected in the subsection as well as of the expert assistance of the staff in determining the sufficiency of various diets and the probable effects of various restrictive measures.   In the autumn of 1918 an important inquiry was begun into the food needs of munition workers by direct measurement.   This was cut short by the Armistice, but the report threw light on the fundamental need for the consideration of food requirements when fixing a minimum wage for industrial workers.

It was claimed on behalf of the subsection that " the officers of the Ministry of Munitions had made a more substantial contribution to the study of applied dietetics than any other civilian Department or laboratory during the war."[3]

---

[1] Hist. Rec./R/346/39.
[2] Special Report No. 13 of Medical Research Committee.
[3] Hist. Rec./R/346/39.

(b) Wastage of Workers.

A second problem considered by the section was that of the "missing worker." Out of 100 women who join a factory, how many will be still at work after one, two, three or more months ? What are the reasons for leaving ? What is the effect of such influences as age and nature of work upon the problem ? The research branch continued an inquiry into this matter, which had already been commenced under the auspices of the Health of Munition Workers Committee, and issued early in 1918 an exhaustive report on the *Causes of Wastage of Labour in Munition Factories employing Women*, dealing with the work of some 40,000 women, attention being paid to age, nature of work, incidence of sickness, etc.   This report, apart from its intrinsic interest as a contribution to a problem which had long perplexed those concerned with the factory women, was of direct administrative value when the effects of a "cut" in the munitions programme (due to shortage of material) was under consideration in February and March, 1918.[1]

(c) Other Inquiries.

Careful records were also kept of the extent and causes of lost time in national factories (*e.g.*, as to whether it was greater among married or single women).   The problem of accidents and their causation was studied statistically, and a report was issued in 1919, proving "that an important factor of accidents is personal susceptibility and that the rate can be diminished by a heedful elimination of unsuitable workers rendered possible by the system of ambulance records standardised by the Welfare and Health Section."   A special inquiry was organised into the prevalence of tuberculosis among munition workers, and a report was published early in 1919 showing the direct connection between factory employment and the incidence of tuberculosis, and the importance of structural condition, especially ventilation, in this respect.   A study was made of the influenza epidemic of the summer of 1918.   Further, two of the women welfare officers in 1917 carried through an inquiry into the provision of seats for women in shell factories which, as has been said, to a great extent served as the basis of the Home Office Welfare Order on that subject in August, 1918.

In addition to the researches above noted, the subsection was able to assist other Departments during the war.   The medico-statistical department of the Royal Air Force was organised by Captain Greenwood, and the subsection was frequently resorted to by

---

[1] In this case it justified a policy of *laissez-faire*.   The "cut" and discharge of workers bore most heavily on the filling factories, in which the wastage was in any case 60 per cent. to 100 per cent. per annum ; so that mere abstention from the engagement of fresh employees nearly satisfied the needs of a retrenchment in staff.   L.R. 6037/9 & /13.

the staff of the Royal Air Force in connection with statistical matters, as well as by special committees of the Local Government Board and the Royal Society.[1]

---

[1] The following papers were published by workers in the subsection wholly based upon the research work done therein :—

(1) A report on *The Composition of Dietaries of Munition Workers* (Earl of Antrim and Capt. Greenwood), published by the Medical Research Committee (Special Reports, No. 13).   (2) A report on *The Wastage of Munition Workers* (Capt. Greenwood), published by the Medical Research Committee (Special Reports, No. 16).   (3) and (4) two notes on *The Reduction of Dietaries* Capt. Greenwood and Miss Thompson), one published in "The British Medical Journal," the other in the "Journal" of the Royal Statistical Society.   (5) A paper on *The Physiology of Muscular Work* (Capt. Greenwood), published in the "Proceedings" of the Royal Society.   (6) A paper on *The Relation between Food Shortage and Disease* (Capt. Greenwood and Miss Thompson), published in the "Transactions" of the Royal Society of Medicine.   (7) A report on *Tuberculosis in Industrial Workers* (Capt. Greenwood and Dr. A. E. Tebb), published by the Medical Research Committee.   (8) *The Epidemiology of Influenza* (Capt. Greenwood), published in "The British Medical Journal."   (9) *The Causation of Industrial Accidents* (Capt. Greenwood and Miss Woods), published by the Fatigue Research Board.   (10) *Industrial Organisation from the Physiological Side* (Capt. Greenwood), published in the "Journal" of the Royal Statistical Society.

In addition, one complete paper on *Metabolism in Industrial Work* (Capt. Greenwood, Mrs. Hodson, Dr. Tebb) was ready for press, while other papers were being prepared, in March, 1919. A special investigation was also made by Dr. Tebb into the atmospheric conditions of iron-ore mines in Cumberland. for the Sub-Committee of the industry presided over by the Controller of Iron-Ore.

CHAPTER V.

HOURS OF LABOUR IN MUNITION WORKS, 1914-1916.

I. The Position before the Establishment of the Ministry.

(a) EXTENT OF OVERTIME WORKED.

Even in the outbreak of complaints of bad time-keeping raised in the spring of 1915 by a section of the Press and by certain employers (chiefly in the shipbuilding trades), all reasonable critics allowed that the great majority of the munition workers, except in certain limited areas, were doing all, and almost more than all, that could be expected of them. The White Paper of April, 1915, dealing with time-keeping in the shipbuilding trades, with their special difficulties for regular and prolonged work, showed by its statistics, in the midst of its damnatory conclusions, that a definite proportion of men in these trades were doing a 90-hours week.[1] The Secretary to the Admiralty, in his speech on the naval estimates in February, specially acknowledged the response of all the dockyard workers, " from the Admiral Superintendent to the yard-boy," under the strain of continuous nightshifts, overtime and Sunday work since the war began: " The Board of Admiralty had reason to be more than satisfied with the way the royal yards had answered the call of duty."[2] Mr. Asquith at Newcastle on 20 April said that the employees of the armament firms were working an average of 67 and 69 hours a week, and the labour Members of Parliament and trade union officials warmly endorsed this, quoting many instances of long hours—" 70, 80, up to 100 per week "—worked by men known to them, without a protest.[3]

From the end of August, 1914, overtime on munitions work became almost universal (although it coincided in the autumn of this year with some unemployment among engineers and shipbuilders). Some applications subsequently brought to the notice of the Department, from firms desiring the renewal of the Emergency Orders for overtime previously granted by the Home Office, may be quoted as detailed illustrations of the amount of weekly work actually sanctioned for women and young people in the first period of the war.[4]

---

[1] *Report and Statistics on Bad Time kept in Shipbuilding, Munitions and Transport Areas* (1 May, 1915). See Vol. IV., Part II., Chapter II.
[2] *Parliamentary Debates* (1915), *H. of C.*, LXIX. 1022.
[3] *Parliamentary Debates* (1915), *H. of C.*, LXXI. 297, 2298; (Cf. contemporary " Journals " of the Boilermakers, A.S.E. and Ironfounders).
[4] Minutes of Hours of Labour Committee.

(1) A very large Sheffield firm, in May, 1916, asked to be allowed to continue, under the following scheme, the employment of boys (aged 14 and over), and of women and girls in their works :—

	Boys in gun forge.	*Women and young people in shell works.*
	Day Shifts.	
Monday to Friday and Sunday	6 a.m. to 6 p.m.	6 a.m. to 5 p.m. (less 1½ hours for meals).
Saturday	6 a.m. to 12 noon	6 a.m. to 12 noon (less ½ hour).
Net weekly total =	68½ hours	62½ hours.
	Night Shifts (6 *per week*).	
	6 p.m. to 6 a.m.	5 p.m. to 6 a.m. (less 1½ hours for meals).
Net weekly total =	63 hours.	69 hours.

The week-end breaks at the weekly change of shifts were for 24 and 30 hours on alternate weeks.

These hours had been allowed since June, 1915, and had been worked almost to the full. The firm desired to continue thus till the end of the war. According to the reports of Factory Inspectors in September, 1915, and February, 1916, these hours had no apparent ill effects on the boys, who were said, on the whole, to come to work more regularly than the men.[1]

(2) A London firm of rifle makers proposed, in July, 1916, the continuance for boys over 14 of hours of work averaging 69 and 78 per week alternately. Their men could not work without boys ; the demand for rifles was urgent ; and the cessation of Saturday afternoon and Sunday work (urged by the Hours of Labour Committee) would reduce their weekly output of rifles from 2,000 to 1,750.[2]

(3) In January, 1916, a Manchester munitions firm reported on their hours of work as follows, explaining that the second winter's scheme was more successful than the first[3] :—

Hours Worked during Winter 1914-15.

Monday to Friday	..	6 a.m. to 10 p.m.
Saturday ..	.. ..	6 a.m. to 5 p.m.
Sunday ..	.. ..	Nil.

Total = 91 hours per week (including meal times).

Hours Worked during Winter 1915-16.

	First Week.	*Second Week.*
Monday to Friday	6 a.m. to 8 p.m.	6 a.m. to 8 p.m.
Saturday	6 a.m. to 5.30 p.m.	6 a.m. to 12 noon.
Sunday	6 a.m. to 5.30 p.m.	Nil.
Total (including meal times) =	93 hours.	76 hours.

(4) In a departmental report in October, 1916, on hours of work at Woolwich Arsenal since the outbreak of the war, the following statements were made :—

" Men have been employed on the shift system on 27 days out of 28."

---

[1] C.E. 1021/13.   [2] C.E. 641/13.   [3] C.E. 818/13.

" Women, girls, and boys have worked on 13 (sometimes 13½) days out of 14."

" Women have been frequently employed on seven consecutive night shifts,—normally of 12 hours."

" Men on overtime have sometimes worked up to 96 hours per week and boys up to 75."[1]

When, as was often the case, long daily or nightly journeys in overcrowded trains and trams were added to work in the factory, the munition worker's day spread through much the greater part of the 24 hours, and, as the Health of Munition Workers Committee urged early in 1916, the fatigue involved became excessive.[2] The provision of housing and improved transit for munition workers after the spring of 1916 diminished, but in no way removed, this difficulty. The long hours specially affected the foremen and skilled workers, such as toolsetters and gaugemakers, whose scarcity made it impossible for them to be spared. "At one time cases of such men working as much as 90 hours per week were common ; more recently there has been a tendency to reduce hours, but even so, weekly totals of 70 to 80 hours are still frequent," reported the Health of Munition Workers Committee in their fifth memorandum in January, 1916.[3] Even where the daily hours were not excessive, the workers (as in the cases quoted in detail above) frequently had no weekly rest. In many works the Sunday shift was comparatively short. But in many " seven day labour was the rule." Thus, at the works of Messrs. Vickers, Barrow, in October, 1915, 2,500 girls were working an eight hour shift for a seven day week, with one Sunday off in four, while the men employed did a 12 hours' shift on the same basis.[4]

(b) The Pre-War Movement for a Shorter Working Day.

A large number of similar illustrations of extremely long working weeks might be given. In gauging their significance it must be recalled that there had, for at least 20 years, been a continuous agitation in the trade union world for the reduction of hours of work, and a fairly continuous tendency towards their actual reduction, sometimes as a result of strikes, more often by negotiation. Many employers had found the economy of the shorter working day, especially in the skilled trades, and it was realised increasingly that continuous working of overtime in trades so laborious as some of those connected with engineering and shipbuilding was extravagant from the point of view both of capital and labour.[5] The Factory Inspectors' reports had for a number of years recorded with gratification the movement towards

---

[1] Minutes of Hours of Labour Committee. C.E. 1947/13. Woolwich Arsenal had had a normal 48 hour week since 1894.

[2] M.W. 60197/12. Cf. p. 55.

[3] M.W. 60197/4.

[4] C.E. 1013/13.

[5] The " Agreement " of 1907 between the Engineering Employers' Federation and the principal engineering trade unions recommended that " not more than 32 hours overtime should be worked in any four weeks."

the reduction of the normal working week in certain industries. The motion for an eight hours day had for many years appeared annually at the Trade Union Congress, and it had been the objective of many workers in the engineering trades,[1] whose members almost uniformly worked long hours during the first years of the war. It is true that high rates of pay for overtime, night and Sunday work, compensated, or more than compensated, in cash for the extra time worked, and that overtime work was on this account often regarded as a privilege to be reserved, e.g., for good time-keepers. The extra payments, however, could not compensate for the sacrifice of strength, health, and comfort by a large proportion of the workers, and as the pressure of demand for munitions diminished there was a return, for some months before the Armistice, of the movement for a shorter working week.

(c) THE REGULATION OF OVERTIME.

Official cognisance of overtime extended, under the Factory and Workshop Act of 1901, only to protected persons, i.e., to women, and to boys and girls under 18. The maximum number of hours worked by these persons might not normally exceed 55½ hours per week in textile and 60 hours in non-textile factories, excluding meal times.

Overtime might be worked by women on not more than three days a week for not more than thirty days in the year, up to the limits of a 12-hour working day in certain specified non-textile factories, as against 10½ hours daily maximum normally permitted.

Sunday work was forbidden for any woman, young person or child, except in a very few workplaces such as creameries, and night work was also forbidden to them, although boys over 14 might under

---

[1] Since November, 1913, the Federation of Engineering and Shipbuilding Trades of the United Kingdom, then representing 3i societies and 600,000 members, had carried on negotiations with the Engineering Employers' Federation on the subject of a 48-hours' week (without reduction of wages) and had endeavoured unsuccessfully to do the same with the Shipbuilding Employers' Federation. The latter had refused categorically to discuss the subject with the unions (in June, 1914) ; the former also, after two conferences with the men and after consulting its local associations, replied to the Federation of Trades that they could not agree to any reduction in the working day, though they were. open to negotiations on the subject. This reply was received a few days before the outbreak of war, and a conference of delegates from the trades concerned at Liverpool on 7 August, 1914, agreed that the question must be suspended till the termination of the war, though it authorised its representatives to continue negotiations on the subject in the future with the Engineering and Shipbuilding Employers' Federations. The question of the 48-hour week had, however, by this time been discussed in the district organisation of every trade concerned ; and it was beginning to be accepted by the rank and file, as well as by their leaders, as an end to be attained within a reasonable length of time. (*Annual Report of Federation of Engineering and Shipbuilding Trades*, 1915.) The arguments in favour of the movement w̧re summarised in 1914 by Mr. Brownlie, Chairman of the Executive Committee of the A.S.E., in a pamphlet entitled, "The Eight Hours Day."

special conditions be employed at night in blast-furnaces, iron mills, paper mills, letterpress printing and glass works, and boys over 16 might, by special order, be so employed in any non-textile factory or workshop in which continuous work was required.[1]

These were the statutory limits of work under the normal conditions of peace. If, however, the maximum output was to be secured from the inadequate amount of machinery and adult male labour in readiness for the munitions trades in August, 1914, Sunday work, overtime, night work, had all to be made permissible for protected persons, since the efficient work of the men concerned in almost all cases involved their co-operation. This became an increasing necessity as the dilution of male labour progressed.

To meet this urgent need, extensive use was made, during the first months of the war, of Section 150 of the Factory and Workshop Act of 1901, by which the Secretary of State has power, "in case of any public emergency, to exempt from the Act, by Order, to the extent and during the period named by him, any factory or workshop in respect of work done on behalf of the Crown."

This power was reinforced on 10 June, 1915, by Regulation 6A under the Defence of the Realm Act, which extended the power of the Secretary of State under Section 150 to "any factory or workshop in which the Secretary of State is satisfied that by reason of the loss of men through enlistment or transference to Government service, or of other circumstances arising out of the present war, exemption is necessary to secure the efficient carrying on of work in the national interests."

The Factory Inspectors' Annual Reports for 1914 and 1915 described the procedure with regard to application for exemption under these powers. In the earliest stage of the war when a number of trades were affected by the sudden demand for war material, "big guns to boot nails, blankets to tape, motor wagons to cigarettes," while at the same time the quantity of unemployment and underemployment was considerable, short exemption orders were given for one month at a time, "allowing two hours overtime, but, save in exceptional cases, no extra hours on Saturday and no Sunday employment," and letters were sent to contractors urging them to obtain extra hands and plant. After two or three months, however, as the supply of some forms of labour grew short and the demand for equipment of every kind became urgent, exemption orders were given more freely. In the first six months of the war special orders were given to 151 firms engaged on munitions in the narrow sense—explosives, ammunition, shells, mines, grenades, ordnance, aircraft, and to nearly 200 other firms in the shipbuilding, electrical and metal trades. With regard to these, Mr. Bellhouse, H.M. Superintendent Inspector of Factories, wrote, "it had to be recognised at once that latitude on a very wide scale must be permitted. Orders were granted allowing employment on day and night shifts, and also extended overtime both on

---

[1] Factory and Workshop Act (1901), Sections 49, 34, 23ff, 54 and 55.

weekdays and on Saturdays and Sundays, and the permission thus granted extended to boys of 14 years of age and upwards as well as to women and girls over 16."[1] After some months' experience the situation was reviewed and a general order was issued which covered the great majority of the smaller firms, and most of those where metal equipment and accessories, electrical apparatus and transport wagons and fittings were made, leaving for separate consideration the bigger firms and others with exceptional conditions.

The General Exemption Order for Munition Work, 1915, provided four schemes for the employment of protected persons by which :

(a) boys over sixteen might work up to a maximum of 67½ hours a week, with the provision that the period of employment should not exceed fifteen hours on any day (inclusive of overtime and meal times), and this only when overtime was worked not more than three times a week ;

(b) women, girls over sixteen, and boys over fourteen, might work up to 65 hours a week, with a maximum of fourteen hours in any one day, while in certain processes of the manufacture of guns, ammunition, etc., women might work up to 67½ hours per week ;

(c) three shifts of eight hours might be worked during the twenty-four hours by women and girls over sixteen and boys over fourteen, with an interval of at least sixteen hours between shifts for each worker ;

(d) day and night shifts of twelve hours each were sanctioned, subject to certain conditions, such as that no girls under eighteen should be employed on night shifts and boys under sixteen only with the consent of the Superintending Inspector of Factories, and that the working of overtime "should not be made a condition of employment for any woman or young person."

Many special exemption orders were also issued, especially for the large munition firms.[2]

Each engineering factory as it engaged on munition work and got its contract applied "almost automatically" for an overtime order. The Factory Inspectors' Reports of 1914 and 1915 recorded increasing doubts on the part of the employers as to the efficacy of Sunday labour and overtime work. As a whole, however, no widespread ill results were reported at the time, partly as a result of patriotic enthusiasm which checked fatigue, partly on account of the higher earnings and standard of living reached by a large proportion of the workers. "The general opinion seems to be," wrote the Chief Inspector in his annual report issued in May, 1916, "that reasonable overtime does yield increased output, though the increase is not in full proportion to the extra hours worked."

---

[1] *Factory Inspectors' Annual Report for* 1914. Cd. 8051 of 1915.
[2] Cd. 8276 of .916.

" Whatever may be the future effects," it was stated in the Factory Inspectors' Report for 1914, " there is at present no sign that workers have been injuriously affected. There can be little doubt that the knowledge that they were taking an active share in the struggle in which the country is engaged and the feeling that they were thus ' doing their bit ' has enabled workers to carry on under conditions that in normal times would be insupportable. Employers, too, in almost every case, have used their overtime in a restrained and reasonable way." The women inspectors urged the necessity of constant vigilance as to the effect of long hours of work on young girls and boys, if not on the women, employed under war conditions.[1] But the experience of the early years of the war provided no data for wholesale condemnation of carefully regulated overtime work, undertaken as an emergency measure.

II. The Position after the Establishment of the Ministry.

(a) ARRANGEMENT BETWEEN THE MINISTRY OF MUNITIONS AND THE HOME OFFICE.

During the first year of the war, the regulation of hours of labour, at least for " protected persons," was wholly in the hands of the Home Office, which endeavoured with the utmost care to balance the nation's need for munitions with the workers' need for rest. From July, 1915, however, the engineering establishments engaged on munitions successively became controlled by the Ministry of Munitions, and it was a question whether the regulation of hours of work should be added by the Ministry to the other limitations which it undertook to enforce on capital and labour.

In August, 1915, Mr. Wolff, then head of the General Labour Section in the Secretariat of the Ministry, explained the arrangement made between his Department and the Home Office as follows :

" The Home Office refers to the Ministry applications from firms contracting for us and for the War Office (other than the Quartermaster-General's Department) for orders relaxing the Factory Acts. The Home Office supplies a report on the circumstances of the workers, the healthiness of the surroundings and type of work. After obtaining a report as to the urgency of the work, we refer to the Labour Exchange for a report as to whether there is enough labour available in the neighbourhood to make the working of the proposed extended hours necessary. If there is not and the work is urgent, we advise the grant, or the extension of an order. In the case of controlled establishments it is necessary to ascertain whether the firm is or is not accepting war munitions volunteers. If this assistance is not accepted the order is either refused or granted for a very limited period."[2]

---

[1] Cd. 8051 of 1915.   Cd. 8276 of 1916.
[2] Weekly Sectional Reports, August, 1915.

Executive power with regard to hours of labour thus remained in the hands of the Factory Department of the Home Office, and the Ministry of Munitions, in the first months after its establishment, intervened very little in their control. The pressure of demand for certain forms of munitions was so intense that the supply sections of the Ministry could hardly contemplate shortening the number of working hours available for their production.[1]

At intervals during this period the Home Office drew the attention of the Department to the need for effective co-operation in regard to hours of work between their respective officials. Thus, on 22 September, a letter was sent from the Home Office to the Ministry of Munitions enclosing a copy of a report from one of H.M. Factory Inspectors, that in consequence of an urgent order for trench bombs, 12 women had been employed by a firm continuously from 8 a.m. on 30 August to 5.50 p.m. the following day, with only a few intervals, the longest of which was two hours, and representing that " it should be impressed on the officers of the Department that such hours as were worked in this case must inevitably reduce the productive capacity of the workers and that nothing could justify them except a situation in which the immediate completion of a particular order was a matter of far greater importance that a continuous supply of war material."[2]

To this the Ministry of Munitions replied that its officers had been instructed to keep in touch as far as possible with the Home Office inspectors.

On 8 December the Home Office again wrote to call attention to the fact that officials of the Ministry of Munitions had directed firms to alter their hours, in contravention of the Factory Acts.

" The Secretary of State would be glad if the Minister of Munitions would at once take steps, by the issue of further instructions or otherwise, to prevent a repetition of the action complained of. The Ministry will, of course, understand that he does not take any exception to responsible officers of the Minister of Munitions giving instructions to firms to prolong hours of work in a case of vital urgency where there is no time to consult the District Inspector of Factories beforehand, but in such cases the Inspector or the Home Office should be informed immediately of what has been done.

" The Secretary of State is informed that in consequence of what has occurred an impression already exists in certain quarters that the authority of the Home Office in regard to the enforcement and administration of the Factory Acts has been superseded."[3]

These representations pointed to the need of some system of co-ordinated action such as that introduced early in 1916.

---

[1] Thus, on 17 September, 1915, the Machine Tool Committee circularised the firms with which it dealt, asking them if, in view of the urgent necessity of increasing the supply of machine tools, they were working on Saturday afternoons and Sundays, and if not, why not ? This circular later caused some natural perplexity to those responsible for the Ministry's later policy with regard to Sunday work. (M.W. 60197/4).

[2] M.W. 49529.   [3] M.W. 49529/2.

(b) GROWING CRITICISM OF SUNDAY LABOUR AND OVERTIME WORK.

During the autumn of 1915, the interest of other persons, beside the producers themselves and the Government Departments concerned in the supply of munitions, began to be directed towards the limitation of hours of labour.

In September, a report on *Fatigue from the Economic Standpoint* was presented to the British Association, and gave the results of a number of valuable investigations on conditions of factory hygiene, in connection with industrial fatigue and accidents. The report was suggestive and stimulating, if (by its own admission) not very conclusive, and it drew a considerable amount of public attention to the subject. In the same month, the Ministry took one of the most important steps in its policy of utilising the service of experts, by appointing, with the concurrence of the Home Secretary, the Health of Munition Workers Committee, to which reference has already been repeatedly made.[1] The need for expert advice on questions of industrial fatigue and hours of labour which the committee was primarily called on to consider, was brought home to the Department by the great expansion of munition work for which it was responsible in the latter months of 1915. The Ministry of Munitions was brought into touch with the industrial needs of a constantly increasing number of women and young persons, for whom even the limited amount of overtime legally permissible was only doubtfully expedient. Many men also, drawn into heavy munition work from other occupations or recalled to the factories in spite of advanced years, obviously needed some protection against overwork if their efficiency was to be maintained, although the desire to " back up the men in the trenches " and the satisfaction of high earnings had so far prevented any general demand for a reduction of overtime.

The Admiralty had already taken action with regard to Sunday work. In the previous April, an official letter had been sent to the home dockyards and contractors, ordering the discontinuance of Sunday labour on Admiralty shipbuilding and engineering work, except in cases of extreme urgency, since " recent experience seemed to show that over a long period more work would be done without Sunday labour than with it." In July the Admiralty sent out a further letter to the same contractors, stating that " systematic Sunday labour is to be entirely discontinued as far as hull work is concerned, though urgent fleet repairs and items employing only a small number of workmen may be permitted." A protest received from an important firm, which complained of much dissatisfaction among their workpeople at Barrow owing to the discontinuance of Sunday labour and loss of earnings, led the Admiralty on 5 October to write to the Ministry of Munitions, explaining their desire to put a complete stop to Sunday labour, and drawing attention to their difficulties in enforcing this in face of its constant use by the Ministry of Munitions and the War Office. Some uniform policy, they urged, was desirable, and, if required, they would be pleased to place at the

---

[1] See p. 1 for the composition of this Committee.

disposal of the Minister of Munitions the experience in the matter gained on Admiralty work, experience which had led the Admiralty to decide, " after careful and repeated consideration," to stop Sunday labour.[1]

This communication coincided with a letter to Dr. Addison from the chairman of the Health of Munition Workers Committee,[2] to the effect that after three weeks' work their inquiries already showed both the drawbacks of Sunday labour and the realisation of these drawbacks equally by employers and employed.   The trade union officials who had been consulted were clearly of opinion that the men were beginning to get "fed up," nervous and irritable.   Could not the Minister of Munitions, it was asked, take some definite restrictive action on behalf of controlled establishments, since an isolated employer could not afford to take an independent line ?

In the following month (November, 1915) the Health of Munition Workers Committee presented their first formal report,[3] explaining that they felt impelled thus to forestall a report on the other points of their terms of reference on account of the urgency for action with regard to Sunday labour.   The great majority of employers whom they had approached were, they declared, unfavourable to work on Sundays on administrative, economic, religious, and social grounds. Supervision on Sundays was difficult to arrange and imposed a severe strain on the foreman.   Yet deputies were not easy to obtain ; the double pay for Sunday work made it expensive and often led to bad time-keeping and slackness—" Six days' output for seven days' work on eight days' pay," according to one foreman's formula[4]—and on all grounds a weekly rest was wholesome for the worker.   Although, however, " employers generally were opposed to Sunday work, it had been widely adopted

(a) on account of the heavy demands for output, or

(b) because employers had been forced into it by a desire of their workpeople to obtain the increased pay."

The Committee, as a result of evidence received, urged strongly that Sunday work should in future be confined to emergencies and cases of real necessity.

In conclusion, the Committee emphasised their conviction " that some action must be taken in regard to continuous labour and excessive hours of work if it were desired to secure and maintain, over a long period, the maximum output.   To secure any large measure of reform it might be necessary to impose certain restrictions on all controlled establishments, since competition and other causes frequently made it difficult for individual employers to act independently of one another."

---

[1] M.W. 60197/6.   C.P. 73401/15.   C.P. 59930/15.

[2] M.W. 60197/5.

[3] Memorandum No. 1, *Sunday Labour.*

[4] Memorandum No. 7, *Industrial Fatigue,* p. 7.

(c) Issue of a Departmental Circular (L. 18) on Sunday Work.

As a result of the statements in this report, which was considered at a meeting of heads of departments on 28 October, 1915,[1] a circular (L.18) was sent by the Ministry to controlled establishments, quoting the conclusions of the Health of Munition Workers Committee, and stating that "the Minister is of opinion that it is necessary, in the interests both of the workers and of production, that a weekly rest period—preferably Sunday—should be secured to all workers," and that the working of a moderate amount of overtime during the week was preferable to a seven days' working week. Controlled establishments were asked to report immediately on the possibility of discontinuing Sunday labour, and to indicate the possible effect upon output of such discontinuance. The Minister would, it was stated, when desired, endeavour to arrange, in conjunction with the Labour Exchanges, for the supply of voluntary week-end labour to firms discontinuing Sunday work among their own employees, and would undertake to obtain prompt sanction from the Home Office for emergency Sunday work by women and young people, when such work or resumption of work was really necessary. The circular concluded by indicating the possibility of compulsory limitation of all Sunday work under Section 4 (5) of the Munitions of War Act, in so far as such limitation was not carried out voluntarily.[2]

Some 200 replies to this circular were received, many of them acknowledgments only, though seven firms wrote that they intended to give up Sunday labour as a result of the suggestions made.[3]

III. Formation of an Hours of Labour Committee.

(a) The Sunday Labour Committee.

To deal with these replies, and with applications for the supply of week-end labour or for the sanction by the Home Office of emergency Sunday work, a small interdepartmental committee was formed.[4] In January, 1916, this Committee consisted of Mr. Wolff (Chairman), representing the Secretariat ; Mr. R. R. Bannatyne, of the Home Office ; Mr. Lee Murray, Sir Maurice Levy, Mr. B. S. Rowntree, who represented respectively the Supply Departments of the Ministry at Armament Buildings and the newly formed sections in the Secretariat dealing with the time-keeping and welfare of munition workers.

---

[1] M.W. 60197.

[2] The Admiralty, in continuance of its previous policy, concurred in the issue of this circular to firms engaged on Admiralty work, but insisted that it should retain "complete and independent discretion in regard to Sunday labour and overtime work," since emergencies in work of the Admiralty type often made it essential for the authorities on the spot to make arrangements as to extra work. Firms engaged in Admiralty work were accordingly instructed to apply to the Admiralty for sanction to resume Sunday labour in any case when it had been discontinued. (M.W. 60197/5.)

[3] M.W. 60197/5.

[4] M.W. 60197/3.

Within the next six months, representatives of the Admiralty, the Explosives supply department of the Ministry, the Dilution Section, the National Projectile Factories, and the section which dealt with week-end relief labour were added, and were joined later by other representatives of the supply departments, in order to co-ordinate the policy of those interested from different standpoints in the hours of work and the output of munition workers. Departmental office instructions[1] were sent out in February, in order to check independent action, such as that previously complained of by the Home Office, with regard to sanctions of overtime issuing from the Ministry.

> " The Home Office have requested that instructions shall not be given by any officer of the Ministry to any firm to exceed the hours of labour permitted by the Factory Acts without previous consultation with the local Factory Inspector. In cases of vital importance, where such previous consultation is absolutely impossible, a strictly temporary instruction may be given, provided the matter is at once reported to the Factory Inspector. All questions relating to hours of labour and conditions of employment are dealt with in the Secretariat ; and for this purpose a small committee . . . has been set up to consider applications for exemption from the provisions of the Factory Act."

Questions of this nature arising in other departments of the Ministry should, concluded this memorandum, be referred to Mr. Wolff, the Chairman of this committee. With co-ordination thus facilitated between the Home Office, which administered the Special Orders under which the hours permitted by the Factory Acts could be exceeded, and the different departments of the Ministry, it became possible for the Labour Department to attempt to formulate a policy about the hours of labour of munition workers as a whole. When, in June, 1916, the original committee formed to deal with the Sunday labour circular of the previous December decided to change its name to that of the " Hours of Labour Committee," it had already for some months been dealing with many questions about the reduction of overtime, the duration of shifts and spells of work, and the conditions under which night work should be carried on, in addition to those of its original terms of reference.

(b) PROCEDURE OF THE COMMITTEE.

As a basis for action, a questionnaire (L.31a) was, in January, 1916, and subsequently, sent to all munition works as they became controlled, asking for detailed information as to the extent of Sunday labour, the working hours, the arrangement of shifts, and the meal intervals in each firm's works. This was supplemented by a further series of questions as to overtime, short time, and Sunday work included in the comprehensive schedule (L.31) which was sent monthly by the Labour Department to all controlled establishments.

---

[1] Office Memorandum (Whitehall Gardens) No. 39.

The replies to these questions were not always very complete, nor were they wholly accurate, since certain firms misunderstood the wording of the question as to overtime in its original form, and sent in returns giving the number of hours paid for, *e.g.*, at " time and a half." On the whole, however, they supplied a valuable body of statistics as to the amount of time spent in the production of munitions in the country.

Supplementary questionnaires were issued from time to time, to be filled in either by firms direct, with information on special points, such as the amount of productive work as distinguished from the inevitable repairs to machinery done on Sundays, or by the local investigation officers, who were appointed by the Labour Regulation Department at the end of 1916.[1]

Further information was supplied by the Welfare and Dilution Sections in the course of their work. The Home Office drew the attention of the Department to cases in which "protected persons" appeared to be working too long hours in munition factories ; while the Hours of Labour Section supplied the Home Office with monthly lists, based on the " L.31 " returns, of cases when " protected persons " were working on Sundays, in order that inquiries might be made, when necessary, by the Factory Inspectors' Department. Excessive hours of labour shown by such reports and by the monthly returns were frequently curtailed after correspondence between the Department and the firm concerned. The Home Office also referred to the Joint Hours of Labour Committee applications from individual munition firms for special orders or for the renewal of special orders giving leave for overtime and Sunday work, when it appeared possible that such orders might be justified by urgent demand for the firm's output. These applications were considered, after reference to the supply departments for which the firms concerned were working. Sometimes a special report as to conditions of work was asked for from the district Factory Inspector, or a representative of the firm was invited to attend before the Committee, and only after such consideration was the Home Office recommended to sanction or refuse the firm's application. Thus the Hours of Labour Committee did not attempt to use fresh compulsory powers on behalf of the Ministry, although, under Section 6 of the Munitions of War (Amendment) Act, 1916, the Department possessed such powers. It relied on persuasion and negotiation, backed by the coercive powers administered by the Home Office under the Factory Acts. The existence of a representative committee of this type provided the Home Office with a rapid means of ascertaining the extent to which the legal limits of working hours, defined for " protected persons," after decades of legislation, should or should not be enforced in the face of the demand for munitions.

(c) Problems before the Committee.

The Ministry of Munitions was faced in the spring of 1916 by the very difficult problem of adjusting hours of labour in the interests of efficiency, and, if possible, of diminishing hours of work without

---

[1] See Chap. VII.

diminishing output.   The whole efforts of the munition works of the country were being concentrated on preparations for the offensive of 1916, and on its support after this had been begun.   The urgency of these needs were quoted in support of the policy of dilution, a policy which was sometimes said by its opponents to be clearly unnecessary if it were possible to risk a loss of output by shortening hours of labour.

The pressing need for output, especially of heavy guns and large shells, was urged as the ground for the limitation of holidays at the New Year and Easter and for their postponement at Whitsuntide, in August, and at the dates of all the traditional summer " wakes " and " weeks of factory operatives."   In addressing trade union representatives on this subject at the end of May, Mr. Lloyd George said :—

> " The French workmen have turned out every day a sufficient quantity of shot and shell to fill the chasm of the artillery at the front.   Every day their guns are emptied by the evening and the French workmen fill them by the morning. They are turning out every day the amount consumed by the gunners.   Any moment that may be the experience of our soldiers.   In a few months I will guarantee to tell you whether we can afford a few days' holiday.   We cannot now.   We simply cannot.   We want to pile up the ammunition day by day until our soldiers are in such a position that they need not spare shells at the expense of life."

A few days earlier he had addressed a gathering of employers to the same effect.[1]   These and other more formal utterances indicated the tension at which both labour and capital were called on to produce munitions, at least until the autumn of 1916.   It was on account of this tension that it was impossible for the Ministry to adopt a consistent line of action with regard to the hours worked by munition makers. On the one side, the experts on the Health of Munition Workers Committee urged the necessity of diminishing Sunday labour and overtime ; on the other, manufacturers and the Supply Departments of the Ministry, in the face of the pressing need of increased output, insisted on the importance of utilising as many " machine hours " as possible. The Hours of Labour Committee had as far as possible to reconcile these two points of view.   They were indeed fully reconcilable, on the principle theoretically adopted by the committee from March, 1916, that, other things being equal, shortened hours of work and adequate rest periods produce in the long run greater efficiency in the worker and therefore no loss of output.   It was not, however, always easy to convince those responsible for the supply of munitions (as the history of Woolwich and of the National Projectile Factories in 1916 showed) of the truth of this in time of war.   Owing to this pressure of demand, proposals made early in the year by the Home Office for the reduction of the hours of work permissible to protected persons under the general Order of 1915, did not take effect until October, 1916, and even then constant exceptions had to be made, in succession, for the needs of special trades, such as the makers of machine tools, of heavy guns,

---

[1] M.W. 89791 3.

of aeroplanes ; and in the case of establishments whose output was held to be essential, such as Woolwich Arsenal, where work was for many months carried on in excess of the limitations of the Factory Acts and unsanctioned by a special order from the Home Office.[1]

If the demands of supply made the curtailment of work difficult, the attitude of employers and of workpeople was often not helpful in this respect. The employers with whom the Ministry of Munitions and the Home Office corresponded were, indeed, frequently opposed to Sunday labour on principle, and pointed out to the Ministry that they had only adopted it as a war necessity, or as the result of pressure from the Supply Departments for the rapid fulfilment of contracts. The burden of such work often fell even more heavily on the staff than on the workpeople. Yet having begun Sunday work on grounds of emergency, they found it hard not to continue it as a matter of routine, partly because of the exigencies of completing contracts, partly because of difficulties, anticipated or actual, with workpeop'e over wages. It was (as Messrs. Firth, of Sheffield, pointed out in May, 1916) very difficult for any one firm to take isolated action on this point, as in other matters which concerned labour, since workmen, dissatisfied with the stoppage of their Sunday work and wages, might, despite the leaving certificate regulations, go elsewhere. Skilled workmen had frequently left their families in other towns and come to the munition centres, attracted by the high earnings with increased rates for overtime work, which more than covered the cost of keeping up two homes. Discontinuance of Sunday labour would certainly mean decreased output, if the workmen were tempted thereby to seek other employment.[2] Government contractors on building work, who were normally unprotected from losing labour by the provisions of Section 7 of the Munitions of War Act, urged this difficulty very strongly. It was for this reason that the influence of the Ministry, even without coercion, was valuable in securing group action among employers in diminishing both Sunday and overtime work.

From the workpeople's point of view, the desirability of stopping Sunday and overtime work was largely a matter of wages. Sunday work in most though not in all industries, by tradition or agreement, received double pay ; it was therefore proportionally valued by certain classes of workers, and in some cases (as at Messrs. Armstrong's, at Newcastle)[3] it was found that the workers preferred that the twenty-four hours' rest urged by the Ministry of Munitions should be taken on a week-day, paid at normal rates, rather than on the highly-paid Sunday.[4] In the same way, it was sometimes represented on behalf

---

[1] Hist. Rec./H/343/2.   [2] C.E. 1658/13 ; C.E. 439/13.   [3] C.E. 828/13.

[4] A well-known Derby firm admitted, in submitting their time table in 1916 for approval by the Home Office, that they felt that they might well be asked : " Why don't you work all day Saturday and play all day Sunday ? " They had, however, deliberately arranged to stop work punctually at noon on Saturdays, and to work (on three Sundays out of four) from 8.30 to 5 on Sundays, and they felt that their system might well be copied. The men, or at least the great majority of them, did not go to church or chapel, whereas they could amuse themselves and get fresh air on Saturday, in a way which Sabbatarian prejudices would prevent on Sundays. If a full day's work on Saturday were substituted for Sunday work, the men would constantly ask for or take their Saturday off. (C.E. 828/13.)

of women munition workers that a Saturday holiday gave them opportunities of shopping, which a free Sunday would not provide. Despite this and similar examples, the rest day secured to munition workers was normally the Sunday. Where the intention to stop Sunday work was duly explained beforehand to the workpeople in accordance with the provisions of Schedule II of the Munitions of War Act, labour trouble was only reported to the Ministry in isolated cases. In some cases, increased overtime work on week-days partly met the difference in earnings ; in others, the stoppage of Sunday work was made the excuse for further general demands for increased wages. The workers of the country had no desire for a seven days week on other than patriotic or pecuniary grounds.

The wages question, however, largely influenced the attitude both of employers and employed with regard to long working hours on week-days. Thus, skilled tool-room men were reported periodically to insist on long hours of work, in spite of obvious fatigue, in order to compensate in some measure for their lesser opportunities of earning as compared· with pieceworkers, while they urged, reciprocally, that wage rates must rise if overtime was, as seemed probable in 1916, to fall off, since it was only the extent of overtime earnings that had camouflaged the fact that their standard rates had not risen in proportion to the rise in the cost of living.[1]   At the other end of the scale, labourers on time-work often asked to be employed on overtime ; and munitions tribunals dealt with a number of cases in which such low-paid workers demanded their leaving certificates because of diminished opportunities of increasing their earnings by overtime work for the firm which thus employed them.   The tribunals on various occasions in dealing with such appeals expressed the hope that the men in question would be given fresh opportunities of overtime employment.   And in the case of women workers, low wage rates were often quoted as a justification for long hours of work.   To the woman or girl living just on the margin of subsistence on the 14s. or 15s. weekly wage common before the Ministry began to regulate the wages of women on " women's work " in the second half of 1916, the increased earnings procurable by overtime work might more than compensate for the resultant fatigue by the better food and lodging thereby secured.   The greatly improved standard of living among large numbers of women, and to a less extent among men munition workers, undoubtedly contributed to the power of endurance shown by them.[2]   More than once, however, the Wages Section of the Ministry was called in to negotiate for a rise in rates of wages paid by a firm, before the Hours of Labour Section could take action to

---

[1] C.E. 372/13, C.E. 1352/13; Hours of Labour Committee Minutes, 23 March, 1916 ;   Committee on Production reports, etc.

[2] Cf. the " Canteen " reports of the Health of Munition Workers Committee, with their comments on the modification in the tea and bread and butter diet of the woman worker as a result of increased wages and canteen facilities.

diminish the hours worked by its employees.[1] And even when a minimum wage rate had been laid down for women on men's work the same reason tended to make the shorter hours of the eight-hour shift system unpopular, since the £1 minimum guaranteed to women taking men's work was, until December, 1916, based on the 53 or 54 hours week common in the engineering trades, and received a proportionate reduction when only 48 hours were worked.[2] This question of earnings was on various occasions brought forward as a reason for abandoning or refusing to adopt an eight hours day for women munition workers. A certain type of apparently well-paid workers, both men and women, clamoured for long hours of work and opportunities of high earnings and resented the efforts of the Government or of employers to curtail these. This attitude was frequently and quite comprehensibly reported among the Belgian munition workers, especially in their first months of English factory life.[3] As a whole, however, a desire for further rest became general both among employers and employed in the course of the year 1916. Exceptions to this were found principally, though not exclusively, among the less well-paid of the time-workers. Especially in the case of women workers, hours of labour clearly could not and cannot be settled satisfactorily without reference to the wages paid.

The vexed question of the relation of the standard weekly wage to the working week is considered later in connection with the claim for a reduction of normal hours, as distinct from that of overtime work.

IV. First Recommendations of the Health of Munition Workers Committee.[4]

The memoranda of the Health of Munition Workers Committee coloured the policy of the Hours of Labour Committee so largely, that a summary of certain of them is almost essential for comprehen-

---

[1] Thus in June, 1916, a Birmingham firm, with which the Hours of Labour Committee and the Home Office had prolonged negotiations for two years, reported much difficulty in inducing its women workers (whose hours of work had been reduced from 77 to 66½ per week) to accept a further reduction to 58½ hours, since this would diminish the adult workers' time earnings from £2 3s. 9d. to 18s. 8d. In July, 1916, an application from a Birmingham wire rope firm for leave to change from a 45-hour week to a week of 55½ hours per day, 50 per night, was sanctioned, on the firm's explanation that by this means the wages of its women workers would be raised from an average of 16s. 9d.—based on the normal rates in the trade—to 19s. 6d. (C.E. 1016/13; C.E. 1250/13.)

[2] See Vol. V., Part II.

[3] One of the complaints made to a small commission, appointed in August, 1915, to enquire into alleged grievances among Belgian munition workers in English factories, came from a group of Belgians employed at Coventry, and was to the effect that they were only employed for 54 instead of 78 hours a week as they had expected. [M.W. 54772.]

[4] Reports issued by the Health of Munition Workers Committee bearing on hours of labour :—Memorandum No. 1, *Sunday Labour* (Nov., 1915) ; No. 2, *Welfare* ; No. 4, *Employment of Women* ; No. 5, *Hours of Work* (Jan., 1916) ; No. 7, *Industrial Fatigue* ; No. 10, *Sickness* (Feb., 1916) ; No. 12, *Output in Relation to Hours of Work* (July, 1916) ; No. 18, *Further Statistics on Output in relation to Hours of Work* (Aug., 1917) ; No. 20, *Weekly Hours of Employment ;* *Industrial Efficiency and Fatigue*, Interim Report (Feb., 1917, Cd. 8511) ; *Industrial Health and Efficiency*, Final Report (1918).

sion of that policy. On 7 March, 1916, the Hours of Labour Committee definitely "adopted" the Health of Munition Workers Committee's programme. It must be admitted that the pressure of demand from the Supply Departments led in the course of the year 1916, and subsequently, to very many gaps in the consistent administration of such a policy.

(a) SUNDAY LABOUR.

The Health of Munition Workers Committee recommended, in its first memorandum, that the discontinuance of Sunday labour should be of universal application, and should extend to all classes of workers. Except where the work was necessarily continuous, Sunday labour should be confined to special emergencies,[1] including the occasional making up of arrears in particular sections, and to repairs, tending furnaces, etc., the men so employed being given a corresponding period of rest during some part of the week. The first circular on Sunday labour issued by the Ministry to controlled establishments (in December, 1915) accordingly urged that not more than 12 single shifts or 24 double shifts should normally be worked. Meanwhile the Committee urged that if this complete discontinuance could not be secured, one Sunday shift should be dropped (or two shifts if three were normally worked) ; that Sunday work should be cut down for overtime workers ; that alternate Sundays off should be given, or a complete 24 hours' rest at some period in the week ; and that week-end volunteers should be used for Sunday reliefs.

(b) OVERTIME

With regard to overtime, the Committee urged, in their fifth memorandum on *Hours of Work*, that the average weekly hours of labour, including overtime, should not exceed 65 to 67 for men and 60 for women. They suggested that it might be desirable to differentiate to some extent between different kinds of work, since investigation already indicated the very comprehensible conclusion, later demonstrated statistically, that the normal working hours should be shorter on heavy than on light occupations. They did not, however, offer any detailed information on this point, because at the time they had not sufficient data at their disposal to warrant definite conclusions. In successive reports they drew attention to the extravagance of excessive overtime work.

> " Even during the urgent claims of a war the problem must always be to obtain the maximum output from the individual worker which is compatible with the maintenance of his health. In war time the workmen will be willing, as they are showing in so many directions, to forgo comfort, and to work nearer the margin of accumulating fatigue than in time of peace, but the country cannot afford the extravagance of paying for work done during incapacity from fatigue, just because so many hours are spent upon it ; and the further

---

[1] See p. 97.

extravagance of urging armies of workmen towards relative incapacity by neglect of physiological law. . . . Taking the country as a whole, the Committee are bound to record their impression that the munition workers in general have been allowed to reach a state of reduced efficiency and lowered health, which might have been avoided, without reduction of output, by attention to the details of daily and weekly rests. (The signs of fatigue are even more noticeable in the case of the managers and foremen, and their practical results are probably more serious than in the case of the workmen.) "[1]

In their report on the *Employment of Women* the same Committee drew attention to the bad effects, both on health and output, of prolonged overtime among women workers. " The importance to women of a wise limitation of their hours of work and an appropriate distribution of the pauses in those hours, can hardly be overstated."[2] Further detailed investigations into the relation of hours of work and output, carried out on behalf of the Ministry during 1917, only confirmed the more general conclusions quoted from these earlier reports.

(c) SHIFTS AND SPELLS OF WORK AND NIGHTWORK.

With regard to the general question of the reduction and adjustment of hours of work, apart from overtime, the Health of Munition Workers Committee made many suggestions, especially for the benefit of the new army of women factory workers.

In one of its early reports the Committee expressed an opinion, as yet unsupported by definite statistics, on the subject of shifts.

" The three systems of employment most commonly adopted for women in munition works are as follows[3] :—One shift of 13-14 hours (the overtime system) ; two shifts of 12 hours ; and three shifts of 8 hours.

Of these, the system of eight-hour shifts appears to yield the best results in the long run. The strain of night work, indeed strain generally, is sensibly diminished, greater vigour of work is maintained throughout the shift, less time is lost by unpunctuality or illness, and there is less liability to accident. More hours of actual work are available out of the twenty-four, and in the eight-hour shift each hour has a sustained value, in contrast to the diminishing value of the later hours in a twelve-hour shift. The Committee recommend the adoption of the three shifts system, without overtime, whenever a sufficient supply of labour is available. Where the supply is governed by difficulties of housing and transit, the committee are of opinion that every effort should be made to overcome these difficulties before a less serviceable system be continued or adopted."

---

[1] Memorandum No. 7, *Industrial Fatigue*, January, 1916.
[2] Memorandum No. 4, *Employment of Women*.
[3] Memorandum No. 4, *Employment of Women*.

The strain of prolonged spells of work, even if they did not exceed the legal limit of five hours, had been frequently pointed out by Factory Inspectors before the war.   The Health of Munition Workers Committee drew attention to the great value of pauses, well distributed, in averting breakdown and in giving an impetus to output.   " With a five-hour spell," they urged, " there should certainly be a break for a cup of tea or cocoa."

The Committee recognised that the employment of women on night work was undesirable but inevitable in time of war.   They therefore recommended that provision of canteens and of responsible supervision of rest rooms should, so far as possible, be enforced when protected persons were engaged on night work.[1]   The objections to night work were personal and social rather than industrial. Subsequent investigations, carried out indeed on a limited scale, failed to show any real inferiority in output from night work.

> " There is no significant difference between the rate of output in night and day shifts managed on the discontinuous system.   The time-keeping, too, of women and girls over or about nineteen years of age working alternate weeks of day and night shifts appears to be even better maintained than when they worked on permanent day shifts."[2]

The Committee, however, made it clear that any conclusions reached by them on the subject of night work applied only to war conditions, and that they were not prepared to dogmatise on the question of the industrial efficacy of night work in general.

---

[1] Memorandum No. 4, *Employment of Women*, pp. 4, 5 and 6.
[2] *Industrial Efficiency and Fatigue*, p. 5 (February, 1917).

CHAPTER VI.

THE CONTROL OF HOURS OF LABOUR, 1916-19.

I. Sunday Labour.

(a) THE EXTENT OF SUNDAY MUNITION WORK IN 1916.

The Ministry of Munitions gradually and with marked exceptions approached in the controlled establishments and national factories the standard of hours of work set by the Health of Munition Workers Committee.

When replies were received in February, 1916, to the questionnaire sent out to controlled establishments (excluding the High Explosives and Chemical Factories, where work was normally continuous) it was found that 812 employed Sunday labour, while 1,434 did not do so. Throughout the early months of the year, the Hours of Labour Committee considered at their weekly meetings the names of firms which had given up Sunday labour or proposed to give it up shortly. In May a list was produced of 89 firms which had discontinued Sunday labour in December, January, February and March, the first four months of the Ministry's activity in the matter, and of 76 others which pursued the alternative policy of giving twenty-four hours' rest during the week.[1] Among the latter were important engineering and shipbuilding firms such as Messrs. Hadfields, Armstrong Whitworth, Thorneycroft, Harland and Wolff, White and Poppe.

At the end of this month the Hours of Labour Committee sent a letter to firms which had thus ceased Sunday labour, asking them for their views on the effect of this discontinuance upon their employees' output, health and regularity of attendance, and also for information as to any resulting changes in earnings, or in the hours worked during the week. Two months later answers had been received from 65 of these controlled establishments, with supplementary reports from Home Office Inspectors who had visited the firms. No very valid statistics could be supplied, as in many cases the work had varied during the period. As a whole, however, the reports coincided remarkably with the findings of the memorandum on *Sunday Labour* of the Health of Munition Workers Committee. All reported improved health among their workers, except in one case, where absences (with doctors' certificates) multiplied, owing to the "holiday feeling" produced by a free Sunday. On the whole a marked improvement in time-keeping was reported, though four firms reported a deterioration in time-keeping which they ascribed to the unfortunate influence

---

[1] *Parliamentary Debates* (1916), *H. of C.*, LXXXII., 2711.

of the "holiday spirit." Twenty-two firms said that their output had been maintained, and seven that it had been increased by the stoppage of Sunday work, though admittedly it was difficult to isolate this influence among the constant changes in personnel, methods and conditions of work, in the first half of the year 1916.[1]

Forty-two firms had met no wages difficulties. Ten others had disposed of these by arranging opportunities for overtime work and earnings during the week. These results, even if inadequate statistically, were sufficiently satisfactory to suggest that an experiment might now be tried in a more general stoppage of Sunday labour.

(b) Proposed Stoppage of Sunday Work at Sheffield.

It was suggested that such an experiment might be made in the Sheffield area, where very long hours had been worked for many months, and a number of representative firms were asked for their views. Already 105 out of 187 munition firms at Sheffield reported to the Ministry at the end of May, 1916, that they did not employ Sunday labour. It was felt that if some half-dozen leading firms, such as Messrs. Firth, S. Fox, Vickers, Hadfield and Cammell Laird would agree to stop work on Sunday, others would follow their example, and a valuable object lesson would be given to other districts. Some of the replies received from the firms approached were not discouraging. Thus, Messrs. T. Firth and Sons replied in favour of the stoppage of Sunday work from their own point of view, and reported that other firms in Sheffield were also in sympathy with the desire to put a stop to week-end labour on production, although they urged that, owing to the wages difficulty to which reference has already been made, any instructions as to discontinuing Sunday labour should be given nationally if at all.[2] The Supply Departments of the Ministry, however, when consulted, replied that it was quite impossible to sanction the stoppage of Sunday labour at Sheffield at the present. The pressing demand for steel and for 6-in., 8-in., and 9·2-in. shell was quite unsatisfied, and the Minister was then actively engaged in securing the postponement of all holidays till August, so that the output of munitions of all kinds should continue unbroken. Messrs. Firth and Hadfield, amongst much output of different types, were supplying large quantities of steel plates for helmets. It was essential that Firth's especially should not be closed down for an hour a week until huge reserve stocks of munitions had been built up. Sheffield was, therefore, not selected for an experiment in the effects of the local discontinuance of Sunday labour. In its stead, the North East Coast area was chosen.

---

[1] Thus the Austin Motor Co. reported a steady increase in their weekly output of 13-pdr. and 18-pdr. shells from August, 1915, to March, 1916. This, the firm said, was due largely to increased experience among their employees ; but the monthly increase had been larger since Sunday work was dropped in November, 1915. (C.E., 158/13.)

[2] C.E. 439/13. Reports of discontent among the skilled day-workers in Sheffield munition works constantly reached the Department during the first six months of 1916, and were the subject of a special enquiry by the Wages Section, and of a "hearing" before the Committee on Production on 9 August.

(c) Discontinuance of Sunday Labour on the Tyne.

On 19 July the names of 81 firms on the Tyne and 54 on the Tees were returned as having already ceased to employ Sunday labour. Messrs. Armstrong, at the same time, reported very favourably on the effect of the change of hours which they had introduced at their works in February, on the representations of the Ministry. This change, though it did not, owing to the employees' opposition, involve a complete Sunday off for any worker, yet gave a clear 24 hours' rest to both day and night shifts. There had been, the firm reported, no diminution in output and no wage difficulties, but a reduction in time lost and in accidents. On 14 September, 1916, with the advantage of this large scale local example, a letter was sent by the Ministry to each of the principal engineering and shipbuilding establishments in the North East Coast district (except those engaged on the manufacture of 6-in. and heavier shell, then in urgent demand), stating that " the Minister would be glad " if the firm addressed would arrange for the discontinuance of Sunday labour, and notices were a few days later sent to the Press, calling attention to the Ministry's attitude towards Sunday labour, and to its discontinuance on the Tyne.

Sunday labour was accordingly generally stopped in this district, except by firms engaged on continuous process work or requiring repairs. The change took place smoothly, and when, at the end of the year, a special inquiry into its results was held by the local factory inspectors, and by the Ministry's Chief Investigation Officer, in conjunction with the local Labour Advisory Boards, the reports received were almost uniformly satisfactory. There had been little difficulty as to wages ; there was, according to the Labour Advisory Boards, "no desire to re-start or extend Sunday labour, except among certain sections of workers who desired it because it gave them increased earnings." Time-keeping on the whole had improved, allowing for the recent very bad weather, and there was no evidence of decreased output. The different works belonging to Messrs. Armstrong stopped at noon on Saturdays and started on Sunday night or Monday morning, and the chairman of their directors had recently publicly expressed his satisfaction at the change.

(d) General Reduction of Sunday Labour in 1917.

The Committee thus had the desired precedent of the successful discontinuance of Sunday labour throughout a large area. This could now be quoted in proposals for the extension of such discontinuance. Unfortunately for such a policy, at the beginning of 1917 there was a recrudescence of demand for Sunday labour, owing to the urgent need for additional output of certain forms of munitions, so that the Committee could not at once attempt to secure any further limitation of work. At the end of December, 1916, 890 controlled establishments, including those engaged on continuous processes, were employing Sunday labour on production or on repair work, and the National Filling Factories received permission to work every Sunday up to 31 March, provided that the maximum of 60 hours for women and young people was not exceeded. Eight of the principal firms engaged on the manufacture of guns and gun carriages also obtained leave to work every Sunday. At the same time, however, it was decided to collect the opinions of the different Supply Departments with regard to the further stoppage of Sunday labour. In March the replies from these Departments were considered. They showed a marked change of attitude from that of the previous year. Almost all, including the Admiralty, which had steadily discountenanced Sunday labour except on repairs since April, 1915, and the War Office, were in favour of a general stoppage of Sunday work, provided that adequate provision was made for urgent repairs and for " emergencies." The only dissentients were the Air Board, which did not consider it possible for the aircraft firms to discontinue Sunday work, except in individual cases ; and the Director-General of Ordnance Supplies, Sir Charles Ellis, who agreed that Sunday work should be discontinued except among special firms, which, for his department, included all those engaged on guns and gun carriages, together with two large rifle manufacturers.[1]

Under these circumstances the Hours of Labour Committee decided to communicate with all controlled establishments which were employing Sunday labour, pointing out to them the views of the Department on the subject, and instructing them to discontinue all Sunday work from the beginning of May, except for the necessary repair of machinery or for work of exceptional urgency, or for shifts starting on Sunday night or ending on Sunday morning. (Exemptions might, however, it was explained, still be obtained in times of great need.)

A circular to this effect[2] was accordingly sent out in April, 1917, to all controlled establishments except a certain number known to be engaged on work of special urgency. The Hours of Labour Committee was thus able to give effect to the principles which it had adopted more than a year earlier. Sunday labour still continued, but the numbers so employed shrunk to comparatively small proportions in the course of the year.[3]

(e) STATUTORY PROHIBITION OF SUNDAY LABOUR ON BUILDING WORK.

In dealing with one class of labour, performed by workmen who were not technically engaged on munition work although they were most important to its output, the Department obtained definite statutory powers to check Sunday work. A special order (Statutory Rules and Orders, No. 912 of 1917), issued in July, 1917, under Regulation 8E of the Defence of the Realm Act, prohibited the employment of Sunday labour for building and construction work, except in so far as such work was authorised by the Government Department for which the work was being carried on, or was undertaken on an occasion of sudden emergency, subsequently reported to the Ministry of Munitions, such " sudden emergency " not to include " mere urgency for the completion of work." In accordance with this order, builders engaged on private work could only employ Sunday labour by special licence from the Building Labour Committee, an inter-

---

[1] M.W. 60197/41.   [2] Circular L. 86.
[3] See Appendix II for statistics of Sunday labour on " non-continuous processes " in controlled establishments.

departmental committee established in October, 1915, to secure uniformity in policy between different Departments in dealing with the difficult problems of competing contractors and unstable labour supply in the building trade, so far as it concerned the production of munitions.[1] Government Departments, however, still retained considerable latitude for permitting Sunday work on construction which they held to be of special importance, and exercised this with no obligation except that of reporting to the Building Labour Committee when Sunday work was sanctioned for their contractors. This power was curtailed by an order issued in December, 1917, by the War Priorities Committee of the War Cabinet, to the effect that from 14 January, 1918, no Sunday labour, except in sudden emergency, would be permitted to contractors and employees for Government Departments, " subject to the right of appeal to the Works Construction Sub-Committee of the War Priorities Committee, in cases of special hardship, this prohibition to apply equally to controlled establishments. " Other works of construction requiring licence should only be approved by the Works Construction Sub-Committee on the condition that Sunday labour was not employed."[2]

Objections to Sunday labour for building work did not proceed so much from the resulting overstrain to the workers, as was the case in the engineering trades, since building work is often inevitably stopped by bad weather, or carried on for comparatively short hours during, at least, the winter months. It was urged by the spending Departments rather on grounds of economy, and of preventing the not infrequent poaching of labour by competing building contractors through offers of Sunday work at double pay. The conclusion, however, that a seven days' working week tends to waste of time and money was borne out by experience equally in building and in munition work.[3]

---

[1] HIST. REC./H/321/2.   [2] L.R. 1089/10.

[3] The following letter received in May, 1916, by the Ministry from the local office of a trade union near a recently established national factory, where work was continuously carried on upon Sundays, illustrates the sabbatarian point of view with regard to Sunday labour :—

" I should like to try and say a few words. . . . This old England of ours, what a mighty nation it is, with its millions of money, a grand defence, we could not do without it. Then with its mighty Fleet . . . what a defence, we could not do without it. And then with its mighty Army that has made the world to shudder again, could we do without this ? Oh no ! What a wall of defence it is, we could not do without it. But with these three mighty defences we are next thing to helpless ; we must have something to go with them, and this brings me to the thing which I want to say, we must have a bit of the spirit to help these great forces. We are living in an age of work and no time to refresh the spirit. Although it had been clearly demonstrated on purely physical grounds that a day of rest was a national necessity, and unless a man, let alone a woman, had her quiet seasons their inmost and truest life would run to waste. Here we have a few hundreds of women working in a district where it is a new thing and where they have been in the custom of going to Sunday school and they find it hard. They are' supposed to have a day off in the week, but they all prefer Sunday when they can be refreshed and come with new vigour on the Monday morning to go forward and do their best. Hoping you will consider the matter, which would be a great improvement."

It was explained to the writer of the above letter that all workers in this factory had one day off per week, and that anyone preferring a Sunday to a week-day rest could have it. (C.E. 3522/13.)

(*f*) SUNDAY LABOUR ON "CONTINUOUS PROCESSES."

Firms engaged in the manufacture of chemicals and explosives, and those which involved continuous processes, such as blast-furnaces, were inevitably exempt from pressure to close down on Sundays. The disadvantages of even a short stoppage of work in the production of explosives had been represented in December, 1915, by the Explosives Supply Department. " Apart from the question of loss of plant capacity " (and a twenty-four hours' stoppage would involve a loss of 30 per cent. of output in the case of sulphuric acid chamber and concentrating plant) " the waste of time while slowing down and speeding up chemical plant, and the consequent loss of output . . . is very great, and the only economical method is to work continuously on three shifts."[1] Such shifts were organised in most of H.M. Explosives Factories for all the women and for a large proportion of the men engaged. Special directions[2] were accordingly issued by the Department for such factories, urging that one or more shifts per week should be dropped for each worker in compensation for the full Sunday rest.[3]

The managers of these works were confronted by a special difficulty with regard to their workpeople—a difficulty caused by a concession to sabbatarian feeling made in the course of the debates on the Munitions of War (Amendment) Act.[4] Under the resulting amendments of February, 1916, to the Munitions Ordering of Work Regulations, no penalties could be imposed by a munitions tribunal on a man or woman refusing to work on Sundays. It was possible therefore for an indispensable workman to absent himself from his work on Sunday in the midst of a " continuous process " without detriment to himself. The Hours of Labour Committee considered the position in the autumn of 1916, and admitted the difficulty in which the group of ironmasters who had raised the question were placed, but agreed that no remedy could be provided short of an amendment to the Act.[5]

(*g*) WEEK-END RELIEF LABOUR.

Where Sunday labour either on the single or double shift system could not be stopped completely by closing down the works for 24 hours, the Hours of Labour Section had to be content either with urging a firm thus hardly pressed to drop one shift on Sunday, so that only 26 out of the possible 28 double shifts should be worked per fortnight, or to employ special week-end relief labour. Such relief shifts were provided in some few cases by the engagement of an extra number of women or boy workers, so that those who worked on Sunday could have a corresponding amount of time free in the week. This was arranged for a short time by Messrs. Vickers at Barrow at the end of 1916.

Another alternative was to employ persons not normally engaged on factory work, such as those organised independently by a " Volunteer Munitions Brigade," which, just before the establishment of the

---

[1] M.W. 60197,2.   [2] Circular M.M.10.

[3] Thus at H.M. Guncotton Factory, Queensferry, eight women were engaged to do the work of seven, so that each could have one whole day off per week.

[4] See Vol. IV., Part II.

[5] An attempt was made to deal with this difficulty by an agreement made by their employers with the Cleveland blast-furnacemen for the improvement of time-keeping in 1917. (See p. 152.)

Ministry of Munitions, enrolled some 15,000 members in the London area, and from the end of June, 1915, sent for many months regular detachments of volunteers for Saturday afternoon and Sunday work at Woolwich Arsenal. During the first year of its existence this brigade supplied 7,300 workers for employment in the London area, and 275,000 six-hour shifts of work were performed by its members.[1] A similar organisation on a smaller scale, the " Women Munition Workers," recruited and supplied after brief periods of training some 2,000 " educated " women for Sunday factory work in the neighbourhood of London. Other bodies of volunteers offered themselves independently during the early summer of 1915, and were employed by a few firms in the provinces, for example, at Glasgow, at Paisley, and Newcastle.[2] These workers were normally drawn from the professional classes. They were engaged in non-manual work during the week, and their Sunday labours were an expression of the desire for national service which in the first stages of the war had been often repressed for lack of object. Some suspicion of the movement was at first shown by organised labour, but this was met by a generally accepted undertaking that " voluntary " workers would be paid at the same rates as those whom they relieved, and that if material was short they would not be employed to the detriment of the regular workers.[3] Their work was almost always unskilled or at most semi-skilled, since the majority of workers had no time to spare for preliminary training, and few opportunities for training were in any case available. The Volunteer Munitions Brigade, however, included a certain number of members with engineering experience who undertook skilled work at Woolwich Arsenal and elsewhere.

The Ministry endeavoured during the year 1916 to popularise the employment of such week-end labour, both by circulars to controlled establishments, by the recommendation of its own officials, and through the agency of the Labour Exchanges, whose officers in September, 1916, conducted a detailed inquiry into its actual and potential use.[4] A special subsection of the Secretariat, under Mr. W. H. Cowan, M.P., was formed in January, 1916, in Mr. H. E. Morgan's section, to deal with the supply of week-end labour, and attention was drawn to its existence more than once by questions in the House of Commons.[5] Circulars sent to controlled establishments by the Labour Department of the Ministry in June, 1916, pointed out that the voluntary labour of " persons who from patriotic motives offered themselves for week-end work in the production of munitions " was already being employed in certain repetition and other processes with satisfactory results in a number of important

---

[1] In May, 1916, the Department took over the control of this Brigade. (M.W. 60436. O.F./Gen./202.)

[2] M.W. 60197/27. C.E. 187/13. C.E. 682/13.

[3] M.W. 91889, 60436 ; C.E. 1049/13. Thus volunteer tentmakers in Earl's Court gave up their Sunday work in November, 1915, because members of the Workers' Union held, with apparent justification, that the relief workers were taking away work which could well be done by themselves.

[4] M.W. 60197/27 ; L.E. 9738. Board of Trade Circulars C.O. 2607, 3/8/16 ; C.O. 2681, 14/9/16.

[5] M.W. 94863 ; Parliamentary Debates (1916), H. of C., LXXX. 1173.

establishments. Firms which either employed or proposed to employ Sunday labour were accordingly urged to apply to the Divisional Officer of the Labour Exchanges for a supply of special relief workers in order to secure rest for their regular staff.[1]

No enthusiasm was shown in anticipation by employers as a whole for volunteer labour, though a few who made the experiment expressed very warm approval of the results. The objections commonly raised in advance were (1) that such workers would be unpunctual and unreliable (a usual, if unjustified, criticism of " voluntary " workers) ; (2) that they would be likely to damage valuable tools and machinery ; (3) that their employment could not release the foremen and toolroom staff from Sunday labour, whereas these formed the class most in need of rest. The difficulties in providing skilled superintendence, and of securing, in the shortage of training facilities, preliminary training for unskilled volunteers, were the causes which prevented volunteer labour being widely utilised. In the second half of 1915, however, and the first half of the succeeding year, the voluntary workers secured a week-end break for a considerable number of overworked munition makers and also the extended use of machines for output. Their readiness to serve as substitutes gave point to the Department's representations as to the need of rest for the regular workers, and where employers refused point blank (as in the case of the National Projectile Factory managers in August, 1916,[2] and of various private firms a month or two earlier) to consider their employment even in repetition work, claims for special leave to continue Sunday labour among the existing workpeople were obviously weakened.[3]

---

[1] Circulars L. 18 ; L. 50 ; L. 50b.

[2] Minutes of National Projectile Factories Committee.

[3] The extent of organised Sunday relief work in September, 1916, was reported by Labour Exchange officials to be as follows :—Some half-dozen provincial firms employed small numbers of relief workers. In the London area, nine firms, excluding Woolwich Arsenal, were employing small bodies of men and women volunteers (some 500 in all) on Saturday afternoon and Sunday work. Six other firms had used such labour, but had discontinued it. The relief workers actually engaged were mostly doing unskilled work. Thus Messrs. Vickers at Crayford had some 70 members of a local Volunteer Training Corps who came weekly to clean up the shops. At Erith the same firm employed 100 volunteers on similar work and 18 women on shell machining. A firm of engineers at Bow Bridge had 70 men, recruited by its own managers among the " bank clerk and newspaper type of man," who were said to do good work in machining 6 in. H.E. shells and shell noses. The London Small Arms Company employed some 50 men, recently introduced by Mr. Cowan at the request of the Hours of Labour Committee, in order to secure rest for the boy employees, whom the firm had proposed to employ for 68¾ and 77½ hours on alternate weeks. At Woolwich Arsenal some 1,300 of the Volunteer Munition Brigade were still employed every week-end. This Volunteer Munition Brigade had the largest record for voluntary munitions work during the war. Up to 21 December, 1917, when its services at Woolwich ceased owing to the general decrease in Sunday work at the Arsenal, its members had put in 400,000 shifts each of six hours. They were employed, with certain skilled exceptions, either at "labouring" work, porterage, etc., or in the Small Arms Cartridge Factory and elsewhere on machines which, though requiring no special degree of skill, needed attention. They were said to do this latter work very well, though not to reach the output of the normal workers. Beside work at Woolwich Arsenal, they had then given week-end help at 17 factories, and had on one occasion, in the autumn of 1915, supplied nearly 5,000 men for such work. (M.W. 60197/27 ; L.E. 48511.)

By the end of 1916 practically no demands for volunteer relief work in munitions factories had been received by the Labour Exchanges, and its use had almost ended, except at Woolwich Arsenal. Other opportunities of part-time voluntary work multiplied in the course of the following year and were summarised in a comprehensive publication issued by the Ministry of National Service. At the same time the supply of potential relief workers in factories declined, as women who had earlier offered part-time work were absorbed in whole-time employment, and business men found their staffs curtailed and their own labours increased, while the demand for their help shrank with the general decrease in Sunday munitions work. In November, 1917, the Department intimated that its connection, financial and administrative, with relief labour, even at Woolwich, would end in the following month.

The offer of week-end relief work was only a small side issue in the organisation of munitions labour supply. It is, however, worth record, both as a successful attempt to utilise voluntary effort and as a factor in the hours of labour policy of the Department.

II. Overtime Work.

(a) The Limits under the General Munitions Orders of 1915 and 1916.

It was even less easy for the Ministry to formulate and make effective a definite policy for the limitation of overtime work than for the abandonment of Sunday labour. The legal position was defined for munition workers by the general and special orders issued by the Home Office. The general order, which held good from July, 1915, to October, 1916, established a legal maximum, as has been said, of 65 hours a week for women and girls and boys under 16, and 67½ hours for boys over 16. In practice, however, these limits were exceeded. Thus at Woolwich Arsenal, for the first six months of 1916, protected persons were frequently employed for 13 12-hour shifts per fortnight, which meant a week's work of 63 and 73½ hours alternately.[1] At Dudley National Projectile Factory, the Factory Inspector reported in September, 1916, that the day shift had for some months worked 15 turns per fortnight (13 of 11 hours and 2 of 8 hours, including meals) ; and the night shift 14 turns (13 of 11 hours and 1 of 8).[2] At the Electric Ordnance Company's works at Birmingham, 77 hours and 68 hours a week were worked by women in the latter part of 1915 and the beginning of 1916.[3] Systematic overtime was worked in almost all the munition trades, and especially in the engineering trades, in which, according to the monthly returns obtained from controlled establishments, overtime by men employed on overtime averaged from 12 to 11 hours per week, and by women so employed from 7½ to 6½, between September, 1916, and July, 1917.[4]

When the Hours of Labour Committee received reports that excessive overtime was being worked by firms which supplied munitions, it was often able, by merely drawing the attention of the manage-

C.E. 1947/13.   [2] C.E. 2631/13.   [3] C.E. 1016/13.   [4] See Appendix III.

ment to the terms of the general order for munition workers, to reduce the hours within these limits. The "sanction" of the Factory Acts always remained in the background for production to recalcitrant firms. And as each "special order" came up for revision by the Home Office at the close of the period for which it was granted, it was, after January, 1916, in case of doubt, referred to the Joint Hours of Labour Committee, so that its continuance might be reconsidered with the representatives of the Supply Departments and of the Home Office. This gave useful opportunities for issuing instructions to firms as to the adjustment of shifts (especially at the weekly or fortnightly "change over" from day to night work) and as to the maximum number of hours to be worked in any one day.

Under the General Munitions Orders of 1915 and 1916 no woman, or girl or boy under 16, was permitted to work more than 14 hours in any one day. In applications for special orders, however, firms frequently, in 1916, submitted schemes which involved very heavy days or nights of work, even if the prescribed weekly total were not exceeded. Thus at a very large Sheffield works[1] boys of 14 and upwards at this time commonly worked 13 hours for five or six night shifts during the week; while at an important cable works[2] (strained to the utmost in the first half of 1916 to produce field telegraph cables) five day shifts of $13\frac{1}{2}$ hours were worked by women and young persons for five days a week, in addition to a Saturday shift from 7.30 to 12.30 or 6 p.m. in special emergency. In April, 1918, women and girls over 14 were found to be working up to 78 hours a week on munitions in a Blackpool factory, and the day shift at a Government cartridge factory was working seven days and 70 hours a week.[3]

The limit of 14 hours' work in any one day for all "protected persons" except boys over 16 was retained, although it affected an arrangement of overtime, common in Scotland, by which normal working hours were adhered to on three days of the week, while on the other days three hours of overtime were worked, say from 6 to 9 p.m. In spite of applications from individual firms, the 14-hour limit was, however, adhered to in the granting of exemption orders, though older boys were permitted to fall in with the practice of the men with whom they worked. For the same reason boys were sometimes called on to work along with the men whom they were helping for 18 hours at a stretch, according to a common system by which the weekly or fortnightly change over from the night to the day shift was carried out by requiring those employed to work their own shift and half that of the other workers.[4]

---

[1] C.E. 1021/13.
[2] C.E. 896/13.
[3] HIST. REC./R/343/106.
[4] Other and more extreme cases were reported periodically to the Ministry. Thus in January, 1917, the Hendon Aircraft Co. was reported to be employing men for 20 hours at a stretch on doping. (C.E. 109/13.) In May of the same year, the factory inspectors were informed that another aircraft company had been working a body of 18 women for consecutive periods of 29, 34, 23, and 37 hours, with intervals for meals but for no other rest. (Hours of Labour Committee Minutes.)

Under the General Munitions Order issued by the Home Office in October, 1916, the weekly maximum, except in ship repairing, was reduced to 60 for women, girls and boys under 16, and to 65 for boys over 16. There was therefore less incentive to employers to arrange for such long stretches of work on any one working day.

(b) OVERTIME AND INDUSTRIAL UNREST IN 1917.

The amount of overtime worked by " unprotected " persons fell slightly, but only slightly, in the course of 1916-17. There was a decrease in the number of overtime hours worked in controlled establishments as a whole ; but the amount worked by each man employed on overtime remained fairly constant, falling by only three-quarters of an hour per week on an average for those employed on overtime in controlled establishments between September, 1916, and July, 1917. In certain large factories, such as those of Messrs. Hadfield and Messrs. Firth at Sheffield, and Messrs. Beardmore at Paisley, the majority of the employees still worked from seven to eighteen hours weekly overtime in the first five months of 1917 (a fall, it is true, from the 74 and 76 hour week recorded by these three firms in the stress of June and July, 1916).[1] Messrs. Vickers' engineers at Barrow were working, just before their strike in March, 1917, an average of 13½ hours overtime above the normal week of 53 hours in their shipbuilding yards, and 13½ hours overtime above the normal engineering week of 53 and 57½ hours. The men so employed in the two branches of the firm numbered 3,600 and 12,000 respectively. Six thousand of the men, but only a very small number of women, were working on Sundays in February, 1917. In the previous November some 11,000 men from the engineering works and 1,381 women were doing 12 hours weekly overtime, and this had continued for many months. The attribution of contemporary industrial unrest to overstrain among other causes[2]—an explanation given in the House of Commons during the discussion of the general engineering strike and the unsuccessful Munitions of War Bill of April and May, 1917,[3] and again by the special commission which reported in July of the same year—is fully comprehensible.[4]

---

[1] C.E. 3568/13 ; L.I.B. files.

[2] C.E. 1013/13.

[3] *Parliamentary Debates* (1917), H. of C., XCII. 2790 ; XCIII. 1392.

[4] A member of the National Brass Workers and Metal Mechanics Society, in a hearing before the Committee on Production in August, 1917, referred as follows to the relation of long hours of work to the admittedly high earnings in his trade.

" If you were to see the casters after they have done their week's work as I have seen them, you would say they are entitled to it. They go home after they have been working from 7 a.m. to 9 p.m. and say they are ' skint.' I myself have worked on an average 8½ days per week for two years and after my work I only feel inclined to lounge about and go to bed. . . . The Government have told us to push on : the caster has pushed on and many casters have made themselves wrecks in doing so while this war has been on, just to help the Government, and some of them, the fathers, thinking of their sons in the trenches." (Committee on Production, verbatim reports, August 23, 1917.)

(c) Reduction of Hours in Relation to Output.

In April, 1917, those of the men employed in munition works who were working overtime were still doing from 8 to 15 hours above the normal working week in government establishments, and an average excess of 10½ hours in controlled establishments. As a whole, however, employers and workers and the contracting Departments were by this time becoming equally convinced of the inadvisability of prolonged overtime work, unless the sudden needs of the armies at the front made this inevitable. Instances of improvement in health and time-keeping without diminution of output were reported by firms which had shortened their hours of work. The encouraging results from the Tyne firms who gave up Sunday labour have been quoted. In May, 1917, Messrs. Hadfield reported that their National Projectile Factory at Sheffield had dropped one night turn and Saturday afternoon work, without loss of output ; and in the following August the same firm reported that one of the shell machining shops at their East Hecla Works had reduced the hours worked by 17 per cent. (from 69 to 57½ per week) with no loss of output, and in some cases with a slight increase. In one of the cartridge factories at Woolwich, a similarly marked increase of output was recorded on the reduction of hours in November, 1916.[1]

As an illustration of the manner in which experience showed the expense of long hours of work, and of working on the normal weekly holiday,[2] these statistics may be quoted from a National Shell Factory where heavy overtime and Sunday work had for many months been carried on.

During six weeks, in the early part of 1917, the progress records of the factory showed an output of 11,998, 11,502 and 9,102 units on the afternoons of Tuesday, Thursday and Saturday respectively. The loss of output on Saturday as compared with the two other afternoons ranged from 14 per cent. to 34 per cent. in the processes involved. This might be due to fatigue or to the " holiday spirit." The result on prices, owing to overtime payments on Saturday afternoon, was a rise of from 2·4d. to 4·54d. per unit of production. The manager was anxious to drop Saturday afternoon work, but was informed by the district munitions committee that the demand for 18-pounder shell was too great for this to be permitted, in spite of expense.[3]

In 1917 some striking statistics on the relation of output to hours of work were prepared by Dr. Vernon, and were issued by the Health of Munition Workers Committee as a supplement to their fifth

---

[1] C.E. 497/13 ; Hours of Labour Committee Minutes.

[2] By the General Order of September, 1916, a step was made towards the restoration of the Saturday half-holiday. No overtime was permitted for protected persons on Saturdays, and overtime was only to be sanctioned for boys by the superintending inspector of factories on condition that their work should end at 2 p.m. The section of the Welfare Department concerned with boys urged the importance of keeping clear one afternoon for them, and every effort was made to insist on this when applications for special exemptions were considered. With certain establishments, however, under great pressure for output, the young workers' and the women's half holiday had to be given up.

[3] M.W. 170142.

memorandum—*Hours of Work.* Very detailed studies of various groups of workers—men, women and youths—engaged on operations on fuse bodies over periods of over 13 months were described in detail and showed conclusively that, in the examples selected, reduction of hours, even by 18 or 20 per week, increased net output.

Such results, even if not generalised, confirmed with the weight of detailed observation the growing feeling that long hours of work should be reduced in the interest of all parties concerned in production.   Accordingly,[1] Mr. Winston Churchill, soon after his appointment to the Ministry of Munitions, sanctioned a proposal from Mr. Wolff that the Hours of Labour Committee should be called on to examine and report on the possibility of extensive reduction of hours of work for men, as well as for the " protected persons " in whose interests hours of work had primarily been reduced.[2]

(d) PROPOSALS FOR A GENERAL RESTRICTION OF HOURS OF WORK IN 1917.

Strengthened by the generally spreading opinion that prolonged hours of overtime led to inefficiency and industrial unrest, by scientific data as to the comparative inefficiency of long hours of work in special instances, and by statistics as to the amount of overtime actually in progress in the munition trades, the Hours of Labour Committee considered the possibility of a compulsory limitation of hours of work for men, an unprecedented step, except with regard to coal miners, in the history of State control of industry in the country. It was decided in the course of the summer to recommend the establishment of a 63-hour maximum working week for men munition makers, this number of hours to exclude meal times but to include overtime, and to represent a limit not to be exceeded, except for the purposes of urgent and necessary repair work or work on a continuous process, unless special permission was obtained from the Ministry.   Such a working week would not mean drastic interference with the average number of hours actually worked by the majority of firms, but would limit the firms which maintained very long hours to some ten hours overtime per week.

This proposal was, however, rejected on 27 September by the " L " Committee of the Munitions Council, primarily on the ground

---

[1] Minutes, Hours of Labour Committee (8 August, 1917). (HIST. REC./R/ 343/100).

[2] According to a statement based on returns from controlled establishments in the four northern counties and the Middlesbrough district, overtime was worked in the middle of July, 1917, as follows : Out of 218,757 workpeople (157,687 men and 28,032 boys under 18, 21,869 women and 4,869 girls under 18), 49,337 were employed on overtime. Only a small minority of these (3,147) were women, who were employed for an average working week of 57·1 hours, *i.e.*, for 5·8 hours overtime per week.   The men and boys on overtime, 46,190 in number, were employed for an average working week of 63·3 hours, including 10 hours overtime.   The greatest amount of weekly overtime by men was worked in the following trade groups :   electrical engineering, 15·8 hours (only 653 men were, however, involved) ;   shipbuilding and iron and steel trades, 10·5 ;   chemicals, 13·5 ; engineering, 10·2.

of earnings. The position of the skilled time-worker was even then being considered on behalf of the Ministry by a special committee,[1] whose report led in the course of the autumn to the notorious grant of a 12½ per cent. statutory bonus on earnings to successive classes of time-workers. " Any cutting down of overtime," it was represented, " concurrently with the proposed increase in time-rates for skilled men, would be represented as taking away with one hand what has been given with the other. Serious discontent would be unavoidable." The Hours of Labour Committee had decided, in drawing up its recommendations, that no increase of hourly rates ought to be enforced to compensate for the limiting of overtime work. It was true that overtime earnings were often looked on by the time-worker as a standing bonus, which, to some extent, compensated him for his low income as compared with the piece-worker. He had, however, clearly no vested interest in the continuance of overtime work, though " overtime " was often claimed either as a right or a privilege on these grounds.

The consideration of a general curtailment of hours of work was therefore postponed till the beginning of the next year. The wages question had again impeded the " scientific " adjustment of hours of labour.

Meanwhile, the Health of Munition Workers Committee prepared and issued a summary of their latest conclusions with regard to hours of work for munition workers.[2] In Memorandum No. 20 they recalled their recommendations made in Memorandum No. 5, issued in January, 1916. At that time, in the absence of definite data as to the relation of hours of work to output, and to fatigue upon the worker, the committee had recommended a maximum working week of 65 to 67 hours for·men and boys over 16, and of 60 for women and girls. In the two years that had elapsed since the appointment of the committee conditions had changed :—

(1) The strain of work and of the war had increased for all classes of the community.

(2) In many cases the same work was being done·by older or less fit men, or more difficult work was being done by women than they had attempted on their introduction to munition work.

(3) Scientific investigation had shown conclusively that shorter hours, varying according to the nature of the work performed, in some cases definitely increased output, especially when the curtailment of the working day meant that no factory work was done before breakfast.

The Committee therefore in October, 1917, recorded its conviction " that the maximum limits of weekly employment provisionally suggested are too high, except for quite short periods, or perhaps in cases where the work is light and the conditions of employment exceptionally good." They therefore urged strongly, in the concluding

---

[1] See Vol. V., Part I.

[2] Memorandum No. 20, *Weekly Hours of Employment* (October, 1917).

paragraph of their report, that "the time is now ripe for a further substantial reduction in the hours of work.   If this be effected with due regard to the varying conditions prevailing in different branches of industry, they are satisfied that reduction can be made with benefit to health and without injury to output." The same recommendations were made in brief and dogmatic form in a small handbook, issued by the Committee at the end of the year, summing up in a compact form their principal conclusions, "for the benefit of directors, managers, foremen, and others in authority in munition works."[1]

A practical object lesson in the effects of a short working week on the one break system was proposed in the course of the autumn. It had been urged strongly in some quarters in the previous September that instead of the 63 hour weekly maximum proposed, a week of 44 to 50 hours should be established experimentally in industries such as the manufacture of shells and fuses and shell filling. This was not held to be desirable ; but an alternative proposal by Mr. B. H. Morgan, of the Dilution Section, for an experimental reduction of the working week to 48 or 50 hours in six National Shell Factories, for a period of four months—such reduction to be accompanied by careful record of output, individual and collective—was sanctioned by the Minister early in November.   The proposal was not received with enthusiasm by the Boards of Management concerned when it was laid before them.   They accepted it, however, when reassured as to the immediate effect of such an experiment upon local rates of wages, and the consultative committee of the Engineering Employers' Federation raised no objection provided the working week was not less than 50 hours.[2]

In September, 1917, when it was officially decided not to proceed further with the limitation of overtime for men, it was urged that the question of overtime employment for women should receive special consideration at once, since they were not affected by the contemplated advance in skilled time-rates.   Accordingly, in January, 1918, the Hours of Labour Committee, after consultation with the Women's Trade Union Advisory Committee, drew up and submitted to the

---

[1] *Health of the Munition Worker*, prepared by the Health of Munition Workers Committee, 1917.

[2] There were many administrative difficulties in getting the experiment of a 50-hour week under weigh, and it was ultimately fully carried out only at the Workington National Shell Factory, where a 50-hour week was introduced on 11 February, 1918, in place of the previous 53 and 52½ hour week.   A comparison for two periods of 13 weeks before and after the change gave the following results. (Printed) *Weekly, Report,* No. 168, IX. (16 November, 1918).

	Before change.	After change.
Hours worked	130,916	119,827
Shells produced	44,000	45,500
Percentage lost time	8·9	6·5
Time occupied per shell	2 hrs. 58 m.	2 hrs. 38 m.
Cost per shell	8/4·09	7/5·54

Within this limited field, therefore, the results of the experiment confirmed the thesis that a reduction of hours increases output.

Employers' Consultative Committee[1] formal recommendations for a reform in the general Munitions Order of 1916, by substituting 13 for 14 hours as the maximum to be worked by a woman in any one day, and by the reduction of the maximum of 60 hours per week to 65½ hours per week for women engaged on the heavier classes of work. The practical effect of this reduction would be that where the double 12-hour shift system was worked only five full turns could be worked at night, and that employers would be encouraged to substitute for the longer " turns " double shifts of eight, nine, or ten hours, so that six day and night turns could still be worked if necessary.

This proposed limitation of hours coincided with past recommendations of the Health of Munition Workers Committee and with the regular practice of the Home Office in sanctioning schemes of work in the non-munition industries.   There were, however, difficulties in shortening the daily or nightly periods of work for those women munition workers who, as "labourers" or as "skilled" toolsetters, turners, etc., were acting as assistants to men.   It was on account of their fellow-workmen that the Ministry had been compelled to ask the Home Office to sanction 13-hour night shifts for women employed at Barrow and elsewhere, and that strong opposition was reported from more than one National Shell Factory when shorter hours for women were proposed in 1917.   The difficulty was not of wide extent, for only 48 applications to employ women for more than a 12-hour night shift had been sanctioned at the end of 1917, and of these only 18 extended to the full 13-hour shift.   Long hours were, however, in certain salient cases, the penalty that women had to pay for their invasion of " men's work."

Hours of work were generally shortened during the year 1918, although the requirements of the Army in March and April, 1918, inevitably produced a temporary return to overtime work.   The adjustment of wages in proportion to a reduced working week was considered for women as for men, and a clause providing for this was submitted by the Department in January to the Special Arbitration Tribunal for insertion in the Consolidated Women's Wages Order of that spring.[2]   The clause was not, however, inserted, and the question was left indeterminate for women as well as for men munition workers at the date of the Armistice.

III. Shifts of Work and Night Work.

(a) THE PRE-WAR SHIFT IN ENGINEERING WORKS.

At the outbreak of the war, work in engineering shops was normally carried on under the single shift system.   The workmen spent from 7 a.m. to 6 p.m., or from 6 a.m. to 5 p.m. in the shop on the first five days of the week, and from 6 to 1 or 7 to 2 on Saturdays, with breaks of 1½ hour for breakfast and dinner.   The actual distribution

---

[1] L.R. 6037/2. These Committees had been formed in the course of the previous year in order to keep the department in touch with organised employers and with women's labour organisations respectively. (Cf. Vol V., Part 11.)
[2] M.W. 6037/2.

of the hours of work varied in different localities, but the engineer normally put in the 53 or 54 hours of his working week under this system.[1]   If there was a sudden press of work he worked overtime, generally for an extra " quarter," *i.e.*, from 5 or 6 p.m. to 8 or 9 p.m., at " time and a quarter " or " time and a half " rates of wages. Local agreements regulated the length of night shifts when these were necessary ; but the day shift of 11 hours gross or $9\frac{1}{4}$ hours net, with a short day on Saturday and evening overtime to be worked when necessary, was the normal arrangement of the working week. This system was carried on into the first period of the war, with the very important modification that all limits on overtime were, by agreement between the employers and men, suspended from August, 1914. It was thus that the very heavy working hours, such as those at Woolwich, where men on single shift were employed for many months from 6 a.m. to 9 p.m. for six and seven days a week alternately, became possible for skilled men.

(b) THE TWO-SHIFT AND THREE-SHIFT SYSTEMS.

On the establishment of the Ministry of Munitions, and the inauguration of the campaign for increased output and for dilution of skilled labour, pressure was brought to bear on employers, as has been said, to introduce a double shift system. Some firms had already organised a regular night shift. It was pointed out to others, on behalf of the Ministry, by office circular and by the labour officers and area engineers, that only thus could the engineering machinery of the country and the skilled labour available (both inadequate at the time for the demands upon them) be fully utilised. The double-shift system, with two shifts normally of 12 hours each, was therefore increasingly adopted in the autumn and winter of 1915-16. The day shift and night shift workers could thus hand over their job without a break to their successors, so that work could be carried on without interruption, an arrangement which had obvious advantages for the foremen and those responsible for production. In some firms and areas the 24 hours were divided into a day shift of 11 hours and a night shift of 13 hours, and special sanction for such an arrangement, in so far as protected persons were concerned, could be given under the General Order for Munition Workers. This division involved a very heavy spell of night work, but was said to have the advantage of leaving intact previous working agreements, normally based on 11 hours gross for the day worker, while it ensured an extra hour's pay at the higher rates for night work to compensate for its inevitable drawbacks.

With the increasing introduction of women into the engineering works, efforts were made—and were warmly encouraged by the Minister—to spread the adoption of the system of three eight-hour

---

[1] A few areas had by 1914 secured a 48-hour or 50-hour week with a single daily break, and certain firms made a practice of demanding less than the standard district working week from their men. This made a different system of " breaks " possible, but did not otherwise affect the arrangements of the working day.

shifts.[1]   Dilution Officers were instructed, after consultation with the Hours of Labour Committee, in February, 1916, to recommend the adoption of the three-shift system where possible in munition works and the Home Office, through its inspectors, continued its endeavours to bring before managers the advantages of an eight-hour day for women and girls.[2]   In their fifth memorandum—*Hours of Work*— issued in February, 1916, the Health of Munition Workers Committee noted with satisfaction the increasing use of this system.   " It is the more important," the Committee wrote, " to establish the eight hours shift for women workers, because there are being attracted into munition works women who hitherto have been entirely unaccustomed to factory life, and who are on that account not unlikely to find the strain of a 12-hour day too great, while they could work readily and effectively through an eight-hour period."   " Unfortunately, a shortage of workmen and the difficulties of supervision, as well as problems of housing and transit, to a large extent exclude eight-hour shifts from practical consideration, so far as male workers are concerned."

An advantage of the three-shift system from the point of view of the employer was that only one half-hour break was legally necessary during the eight-hour period.   Allowing for three such breaks in the three spells of work, and for some waste of time at the change of shifts, yet the number of " machine hours " available during the 24 hours under such a system was clearly greater than under the system of two 12-hour shifts, in each of which two " breaks " of an hour and half an hour, with their inevitable accompanying dislocation of work, were legally required.

In spite of the possible advantages both to employers and employed, the three-shift system was not widely adopted in munition works, except in those producing explosives and in chemical works.   Only a small proportion of the controlled establishments of the country employed three shifts of workers at any time, and a number of those which started doing so abandoned the system.

(c) Objections to the Three-Shift System.

The objections raised by employers turned chiefly on points of organisation :   (a) the inconvenience caused to the foremen and toolsetters, since there was not sufficient skilled labour available for the separate supervision of three shifts of workers, and it would therefore be necessary for each section of the skilled workers to be responsible for one shift and half the succeeding shift—a division of labour which clearly gave opportunities for friction and misunderstanding ;   (b) the difficulty of working two systems simultaneously, since, even if the women workers wished for a short working day (and this was not invariable), the men employed were almost invariably anxious to work and earn for a full 12 hours shift, while it was very

---

[1] M.W. 94863.
[2] M.W. 87176 ;   Cd. 8276 of 1916.

difficult to synchronise the coming and going of two sets of workers;[1] (c) the question of housing accommodation. It was true that the large available surplus of women ready to work on munitions made it comparatively easy to secure the increased number of workers necessary for three rather than two shifts ; but the congestion of lodging and railway accommodation in the large munition areas constantly made the importation of further numbers of women a serious problem. This housing difficulty was quoted by Messrs. Vickers at Barrow, and by the management of the Huddersfield National Shell Factory as a main reason for changing from a three to a two-shift system ; and it was pointed out to the Hours of Labour Committee, in May, 1916, by the Chief Superintendent of Woolwich Arsenal, that this obstacle made it quite impossible to adopt their suggestion for the introduction of eight-hour shifts among the women employed there. Where special provision could be made for housing and transit this objection was removed. Thus at Gretna a large proportion of the many thousand operatives, for whom the Ministry constructed a special colony among the moors, could without difficulty be employed on three eight-hour shifts.

Women workers also, paradoxically, often opposed the introduction of the system which was destined to secure them a shorter working day, giving the following as their reasons :—The possible loss of wages ; the upset of family life, since it was impossible for the worker so employed to have meals at the same time as other members of the family employed under more normal conditions ; the fatigue of doing the housework which was expected before or after the eight-hour shift, whereas, under the longer system even the mother of a family of children had often perforce to evade domestic work after factory hours ; the inconvenience of the hours for coming on or off duty, especially for those on night shift, who would start at 10 p.m. or 11 p.m. and come off at 6 a.m. or 7 a.m. ; and the complaints made by landladies and managers of hostels over the variable hours at which the three-shift workers left and returned to their lodgings.

---

[1] Thus, Messrs. Vickers in May, 1916, submitted the following time table, illustrating the extreme inconvenience of the scheme of work then in force at Barrow, with the men on a 12-hours' and the women and girls on an 8-hours' day :

" 6 a.m., men change shifts.
6.30 a.m., girls change shifts.
9 to 9.30 a.m., breakfast (for all workers).
12.30 to 1.30 p.m., half the men go to dinner.
12.30 to 12.37 p.m., girls have seven minutes break.
1.30 to 2.30 p.m., half the men go to dinner.
2.30 p.m., girls change shifts.
5 p.m., men change shifts.
5.30 to 6 p.m., girls' tea interval.
8.20 to 9.20 p.m., half the men go to supper.
8.30 to 8.37 p.m., girls have seven minutes break
9.20 to 10.20 p.m., half the men go to supper.
10.30 p.m., girls change shifts.
2 to 2.30 a.m., late supper.
4.30 to 4.37 a.m., girls have seven minutes break.
6 a.m., men change shifts."

These practical and domestic difficulties could be illustrated in detail by the experiences of a number of firms—notably Messrs. Vickers at Barrow and Erith, and the Huddersfield and Leeds National Shell Factories—which in the course of 1916 asked and obtained the reluctant consent of the Department to change from a three-shift to a two-shift system.[1] Such changes, only sanctioned after full inquiry by the Home Office, and on the assurance of the acquiescence of the majority of the employees in this extension of their working day, showed the difficulty in applying even tested theories of betterment to industrial conditions in war-time.

As a whole, the experience of the three-shift system of working was not very encouraging, though the explosives works carried it on with success ; and the National Projectile Factories of Messrs. Hadfield at Sheffield and Cammell Laird at Nottingham dealt successfully with the difficulty of combining a 12-hour shift for men with an 8-hour shift for the women employed.[2] The small extent to which it was adopted affords no precedent for industrial organisation in times of peace, since the main drawbacks to it came from the special war conditions of shortage of skilled workmen, which involved them in a longer working day ; of urgent demand for output, which made it difficult to arrange the change-over of shifts so as to ensure a complete Sunday rest ; and of the difficulty of housing the extra number of employees required in towns already overcrowded with war-workers.   The failure or success of the three-shift system in the production of war material is obviously no criterion for the desirability of the eight-hour day under normal circumstances.

The adoption of a double ten-hour shift, involving nine hours actual work per day and a 50-hour week, was tried increasingly, and with success, in the later stages of the war, both in some of the national factories and by private firms.   The nine-hour day had the advantage,

---

[1] C.E. 1013/13 ; C.E. 1017/13 ; C.E. 573/13 ; C.E., 718/13.

[2] An example of the successful " synchronising " of the 8-hour shift for women with the 12-hour shift for men is given in detail, and may be compared with the unsuccessful attempt recorded above. (The women here were on piece-work and only actually employed for 6¼ hours on two shifts. Men were the supervisors on time rates.)

Leeds National Ordnance Factories, Armley and Hunslet (1918).
Women :   6 a.m. to 1 p.m.
           2 p.m. to 9 p.m.
          10 p.m. to 6 a.m.
Men :   6 a.m. to 6 p.m.
          6 p.m. to 6. a.m.
   6 a.m., in together.
   9 to 9.30 a.m., breakfast together.
   1 p.m., men off to dinner.   (Shops then clear.)
   2 p.m., men and second shift of women return together.
   5.45 p.m., women to tea.
   6 p.m., men's day shift come out.
   6.15 p.m., women return from tea.   (Men's night shift then at work.)
   9 p.m., men and women off together.
   9 to 10 p.m., men to evening meal.
   10 p.m., third shift of women come on, together with men.
   1.30 to 2 a.m., off together for a meal.
   6 a.m., men and women change shifts.

from the employers' point of view, of only necessitating one break for meals, and from that of the worker of avoiding work before breakfast.

The extent to which single, double, and treble shifts were actually worked in national factories during the longest period of continued pressure for output, is summarised in Appendix IV.

(d) NIGHT WORK FOR " PROTECTED " PERSONS.

The General Munitions Orders of 1915 and 1916 had made heavy inroads into the safeguards provided by the Factory Code for boy and girl workers, and pressure on individual firms and trades made it necessary for the Ministry to acquiesce in, and for the Home Office to sanction by special orders, still further exceptions to these safeguards.

Boys' Work. By the General Munitions Orders of both 1915 and 1916 no boy under 16 might be employed on night work except with the approval of the superintending inspectors of factories, who were instructed that such employment should "be avoided as far as possible." According to a Home Office report of May, 1916, leave had been given, "and was then in force," for night work by boys under 16 in 39 cases at Manchester, 35 at Leeds, 8 at Glasgow, 40 at Birmingham, 12 at Bristol, 35 in the South-Eastern district.[1] Boys under 16 were regularly so employed at the same time at Woolwich.

During the preparation of the new general order for munition workers by the Home Office in 1916, proposals for limiting the power of the superintending inspectors to give special permits to firms for night work by boys under 16 were considered in detail. But after local inquiry and consultation between Home Office inspectors and the Ministry's area engineers, it was agreed to leave the discretionary powers of the inspectors unaltered.[1] Some firms found that boys appeared to prefer the high pay and comparative freedom from discipline of night work, and worked as well as or better than their elders ; others, such as those working for the Trench Warfare Department at Glasgow and Newcastle, stated that the employment of young boys at night was at the best "a disastrous makeshift" from the point of view of the employer. "Boys when used in this way seem to imagine that night work is not so stringent as that of the daytime, and the foremen complain that they need much more looking after in consequence. . . . Masters seem to find boys of this age almost impossible to deal with. Boys go out on strike and hold up the whole of the shop and seem more trouble than any other wage earning class."[2]

---

[1] M.W. 49529/6.

[2] A well-known Surrey firm in applying in June, 1916, for a special exemption order for their workers, asked leave to give only two half-hour breaks instead of the hour and a half usually necessary in a 12½ hour night shift to their boy employees between 14 and 18. "The boys would misuse longer meal intervals ; they had already destroyed a neighbouring farmer's property ; the night watchman now locked them into a room during meal times, where they gambled and smoked." (A representative of the Welfare Section was detailed to interview the firm in this case.) (M.W. 117901.)

In spite, however, of drawbacks both of discipline and health, the power to permit the employment of such boys at night was still necessarily retained, since their labour was in certain firms said to be indispensable to the men with whom they worked. Boys over 16 were allowed, without question, to do work under the normal 12-hour shift system, with its possible variation of a 13-hour night shift and an 11-hour day shift.

In the autumn of 1917 the Hours of Labour Committee, after the failure of the attempt to limit overtime for men, considered the possibility of diminishing the employment of boys under 18 at night. The consideration of such employment for boys over 16 was postponed until the question of men's hours could be considered, on the ground that it was hardly possible to separate their work from that of men. There were at the time, however, 14,000 boys of 14 to 16 years of age employed at night in national factories and controlled establishments. Of these about half were working as assistants to men. Some 4,000 were so employed, under the normal provisions of Sections 54 and 55 of the Factory Act, in iron mills, blast furnaces, etc., while 10,000 were working, mainly in small arms ammunition, shell, and fuse factories, under the special provisions of the General Munitions Order.[1]

The Hours of Labour Committee drew up detailed proposals, which were approved by the Supply Departments concerned, for further restrictions on night work by boys under 16, and laid them in January, 1918, before the Engineering Employers' Consultative Committee for their comment. The latter, however, opposed the alteration on the ground that boys employed in shipbuilding and marine engineering were expressly excluded from these proposals and that there should be no differentiation between different classes of boys ; while the Shipbuilding Employers were equally clear that with the existing pressure for output there should be no curtailment of the hours worked.[2]

Girls' Work. Night work was permitted, under the General Munitions Orders of 1915 and 1916, for girls over 16, but only under narrow restrictions. Under the three-shift system their employment for an eight-hour night shift was allowed ; under the two-shift system, which was far more frequently adopted, they might, according to the general order of 1916, only be employed for a twelve hours night shift, subject to the approval of the superintending inspectors of factories.

In the early stages of the war, girls of 14 and 15 were employed at night on munitions work ; and even after the general order of 1915 came into effect, instances of such work were at intervals reported to the Ministry of Munitions. In each of these cases, stringent directions were sent that such employment must cease as soon as the firm

---

[1] L.R. 5321, and *Parliamentary Debates* (1917), *H. of C.*, XCIX. 1017.
[2] L.R. 5321 ; L.R. 6037/4.

could find substitutes.[1] Night work by girls between 16 and 18 never reached a high figure in national factories and controlled establishments. In November, 1917, it was stated in the House of Commons on behalf of the Home Office that about 8,000 girls were so employed, mainly in small arms ammunition and fuse factories, but that none of these were under 16 years of age.[2] The Hours of Labour Committee represented to the Employers' Consultative Committee in January, 1918, that no further girls should be engaged for night shift work and that steps should be taken to stop within three months the employment of those under 17, at present working at night, on any longer night shifts than eight hours. No regulations were made on the subject, but the Home Office took steps to restrict by administrative action the employment both of boys and girls at night to the lowest point practicable.[3]

Women's Work. Night work was only permitted for women, under the General Munitions Orders, for six nights in the week and for a weekly maximum of 60 hours. The curtailment of these night shifts to five per week was strongly urged by the Hours of Labour Committee at the close of 1917. In both general orders provision was made that such employment should be, in the case of all " protected " persons, " subject to the provision, to the satisfaction of the factory inspector, of proper facilities for taking and cooking meals, and in the case of female workers, for their supervision " by a welfare worker or a responsible forewoman. It was explained by the Home Office, in the covering letter to the order of 1916, that much importance was attached to this provision, and that " arrangements of a high standard would be insisted on." Firms were referred to the memorandum on *Welfare Supervision* drawn up by the Health of Munition Workers Committee, and were informed that the Welfare Branch at the Ministry of Munitions would be glad to furnish names of persons suitable for appointment as welfare supervisors. The introduction of night work among women and boy and girl munition workers was, therefore, directly accompanied by the spread of the welfare policy in industrial management.

IV. Holidays.

In 1915 and 1916, at the instance of the Ministry of Munitions, the holidays of munition workers were both postponed and curtailed, in order that there should be no shortage in the supply of munitions. The connection, obvious though hard to reduce to statistics, between

---

[1] In the case of a large Birmingham firm employing a considerable number of girls under 16 as late as 1917, the management protested that their labour was essential to the older women because their fingers were nimble and specially adapted for the light work required ; that every provision was made for their welfare, and that they actually suffered less by night work than their elders. In this the factory inspector concurred. These young girls were " always bright and alert at their work. The difference between them and the older hands between 5 and 6 a.m. was remarkable. Older girls suffered most from night work because they spent too much of their free time in shopping and recreation rather than rest." (C.E. 607/13.)

[2] *Parliamentary Debates* (1917), *H. of C.*, XCIX., 1017.

[3] L.R. 6037/4.

holidays, industrial fatigue and factory ou put, brings the special regulation of the first of these within the scope of the Department's policy about hours of labour in munition works.

The process of changing the recognised holidays proved to be curiously complicated (owing to the interdependence of the munition and non-munition trades, and the extent to which holiday arrangements are interwoven with the social life of the country), and involved two series of representative conferences both in London and the provinces with employers and employed, two royal proclamations, a special order under the Defence of the Realm Act, and two orders under the Munitions (Ordering of Work) Regulations.[1] The results may be summarised briefly as follows :—

During the summer of 1915 the Ministry of Munitions issued letters to the small number of munitions firms then controlled, and to a number of uncontrolled firms, urging that not more than a week's holiday, or three days in the case of machine tool firms, should be taken.[2] In some cases hardly pressed firms made their ow.: arrangements with their men for a shortened stoppage of work ; in others, such as some of the Clyde firms, the week's break extended to ten days. At the end of the year special efforts were made to ensure that the holidays should be the minimum necessary for the health of the workers, and circulars were sent by the Ministry to all controlled establishments urging that not more than three or four days' holiday in all should be given or taken at Christmas and the New Year.   At Easter, 1916, the holidays were, by the recommendation of the Ministry, limited to three days.   This amount was generally taken south of the Tweed, and in some cases exceeded by individuals or firms strained by over-work.   As a result there was a heavy drop in the output of shell and other munitions urgently needed by the army.   Accordingly at the end of May, after explanations of the position by the Minister and the Secretary to the Admiralty at hastily summoned conferences of employers and trade unionists, arrangements were made for the post-ponement (by royal proclamation under the Bank Holiday Act of 1875) of the Whit-Monday Bank Holiday to August, while as far as possible the intervening holidays held in normal times in June by some districts and by the Royal Dockyards were stopped.   This stoppage of holidays was intended to apply to all workers, including the teachers and children at the elementary schools, and not only to the makers of munitions.   The representatives of employers and workmen acquiesced readily in the change, and undertook to explain the need for it in their own localities.   Dr. Macnamara's question at the trade union conference of 29 May, " How will they be spending Whit-Monday at Verdun, at Vimy, at Souchez, at Ypres, at Kut-el-Amara ? " admitted of only one application when the munition workers were assured that unbroken output was essential.   The men's leaders, indeed, showed some resentment, as in previous discussions on good or bad time-keeping among their members, that there should be any

---

[1] M.W. 56790 ; M.W. 89791 and sub-files ; M.W. 127166 and sub-files.
[2] M.W. 54954 ; M.W. 87991.

suggestion that workmen as a body were taking more holidays than were necessary, and that, therefore, special public appeals were required. " There is an impression going abroad that the workers are not interested," said the secretary of a union whose members had been doing much and continued overtime work in shipbuilding. " The great bulk of the workers are just as much interested as you (the Minister) are yourself."

Arrangements were therefore made in detail by local conferences throughout the country for the dates at which the postponed holidays should be held, a subject requiring considerable negotiation, since the holiday makers of the crowded industrial areas must, perforce, travel at different dates. In the middle of July, however, it was decided by the Ministry of Munitions and the Admiralty, on the strong recommendation of their supply departments, that the August holiday must be postponed till the end of the summer, by which time it was hoped that the needs of the summer offensive would be satisfied. A further series of conferences arranged the details of this postponement, which was accompanied by a proclamation, based on a new regulation under the Defence of the Realm Act ; while posters, containing facsimiles of a message from the Commander-in-Chief and cartoons illustrating enemy trenches before and after bombardment, were despatched to controlled establishments. Many trades and areas sacrificed their local summer " wakes " and " weeks," as well as their statutory holidays, although employers in, for example, the textile and dye trades protested in advance that it would be difficult to convince their workpeople that they, like the munition workers, were helping to " win the war " by so doing. No compulsion was applied on either occasion to induce any class of worker to forego their holiday ; but the Department guaranteed the payment of wages at extra rates for some portion of the abandoned holidays, and thereby became involved in the complications of local and trade variations in such payment throughout the country.[1]

Attempts were made by the Department at the beginning of August to arrange or recommend " relay " holidays for factory workers, but no scheme that was really practicable could be devised. Towards the end of the month a considerable number of workers, both in the munitions and non-munition trades, took unauthorised holidays—the first, in a good many cases, after continuous overtime work since Christmas. At the end of September the pressure for output lessened, and a final regulation, issued under Section 4 (5) of the Munitions of War Act, provided that three days' rest should be given to the workers and the staff of controlled establishments on 28, 29 and 30 September.

[1] The Department undertook that extra payments thus made should, under certain conditions, be allowed to employees as an expense to be deducted in determining the profits under the Limitation of Profits rules. (M.W. 89791 15. M.W. 1271/66.) Considerable friction was caused in some districts in deciding the rates at which the holiday payments should be made, especially in unorganised trades with ill-defined agreements. The Committee on Production arbitrated in two or three cases of such disputes. (Cf. Award 431 of September, 1916, and A.S.E. *Journal*, September, 1916.)

There was no further general curtailment of munition workers' holidays, although workers at special times of pressure (e.g., at Easter, 1918) spontaneously put in extra work in certain trades. At Christmas, 1916, directions similar to those of the previous year were sent out to controlled establishments, providing either for three or four days' rest or for two clear week-ends, and arranging for cheap fares for munition workers during the holiday period. In July, 1917, the Commission on Industrial Unrest reported strongly on the need of further rest for workers, to which the Health of Munition Workers Committee had earlier drawn attention ; and the Department indicated its desire that the normal summer holidays should be taken by munition makers.

The machinery used to induce the workers to forego their holidays was, as has been said, complicated ; but this was because the suspension of holidays was voluntary, and was arranged at short notice among very large numbers of workers. The suspension was a trivial matter compared with the reasons that led the supply departments to require it ; but it coincided with what was probably the hardest period of Sunday and overtime work, and it cut with great completeness across the workers' domestic life, trade union traditions or lack of tradition, and local custom. In the non-munition trades, especially in the North of England, the second suspension was only partially observed, if at all. With many of the munition workers the sacrifice of holidays was made with enthusiasm for the men at the front. With the exceptions who insisted on their holiday, this was in some cases the result of fatigue ; in others it was probably due to the conviction (common in other problems that appeared after August, 1914) that the action of one individual or of a group could not possibly affect the progress of the war.[1]

V. The Movement for a Shorter Working Week in 1918.

(a) THE WAGES QUESTION.

The proposal for a general shortening of hours either by limiting overtime or by altering the agreed working week to 50 hours was held up in 1918, partly on account of the renewed pressure of demand from the forces which in March, 1918, made it inevitable that overtime

---

[1] On 26 March, 1918, appeals were telegraphed from the Minister to firms producing certain types of guns and shells as well as tanks and machine-guns, calling on them not to cease work during the Easter holidays and acknowledging the " spontaneous assurances already received from the men in many districts that there will be no loss of output." " Now is the time," concluded the message, " to show the fighting army what the industrial army can achieve."

The following was one of many replies received :—
" Sir,

In answer to your appeal to Munition Workers to give up their Easter Holiday, I would like to say that we [at Park Royal] do so without a murmur ; proud to make some slight sacrifice in this our solemn hour. Know that, whatever the needs of our army, we women of England will never desert her, never, never, never.

God save our King and Country.

Yours truly,
A. B. (A Worker)."

should continue to be worked in certain industries, especially in the production of aircraft, small arms ammunition and tanks, but also, and fundamentally, on the ground of wages. Demands for increased wages in the munition trades were normally refused by the Committee on Production in 1918, except in so far as the 12½ per cent. and the 7½ per cent. advances of the previous autumn and winter permeated to almost all munition workers. A tendency therefore began for the men to ask for a shorter working week with unchanged weekly wages. In some cases this was a revival of the pre-war movement referred to in the previous chapter; in others it was virtually a demand in a different form for higher wages, since the actual hours worked per week must apparently remain unchanged so long as the war lasted, and a shorter " normal " week would mean the earlier beginning of payment at overtime rates. This opened very important questions as to standard hours and wage rates — questions which had been left in abeyance during the war, but which it became increasingly clear must be faced immediately the war ended.[1]

The Engineering Employers' Consultative Committee in December, 1917, expressed to the Department, as has been explained, their acquiescence in an experimental 50-hour week in National Shell Factories (without reduction of pay),[2] and in the summer of 1918 the Bradford Engineering Employers' Association arranged for their district a 50-hour week, also without reduction of pay, " piece rates to be settled by mutual agreement," while the Huddersfield branch renewed a similar agreement made the year before. Further reductions of hours were being widely asked for in trades without as well as within the sphere of munitions;[3] railway engine drivers agitated for a 48-hour week in August, 1918 ; coalminers in Scotland and South Wales were asking for a shorter week at the same time ; the Joint Committee of the Scottish Parliamentary Committee of the Trade Union Congress, with the Scottish Advisory Council of the Labour Party, issued in the same month a manifesto asking for a 44-hour working week in Scotland (hours, 8 to 12 and 1 to 5 from Monday to Friday, 8 to 12 on Saturday, with 20 minutes break in each spell), and urging that the Government should institute a strong Committee to inquire into the subject " with powers to act speedily." At the last recorded meeting of the Hours of Labour Committee on November 5, 1918, it was agreed to press for a vigorous departmental inquiry into the working of the " one-break " system (in connection with the proposed 8 or 9-hour day) and the relation of hours to output. This was the more desirable since, partly owing to this question of wages, the proposed experiment in the establishment of a 50-hour week in selected national factories had been only to a small extent effective.[4]

---

[1] The Committee on Production on 13 July, 1916, in the case of the Clement Talbot Co. and the A.S.E., definitely refused to take up the question at that time. (L.R. 6037/2.)

[2] L.R. 6037/4.   L.R. 5581/14.

[3] L.R. 6037/34, etc.

[4] L.R. 6037/44. Cf. p. 121.

(b) THE POSITION IN NOVEMBER, 1918.

At the date of the Armistice there existed a very widespread desire in all trades for a shorter working week—a desire which was receiving active expression by the workers of other countries—and also a considerable amount of isolated evidence—analysed in some cases by expert physiologists, and borne out in others by the experience of firms both in war and peace—that shorter hours produce, *cæteris paribus*, increased output. There was, however, no comprehensive body of evidence on this point, and employers as a whole were by no means convinced as to its truth.[1] There was, further, a general agreement among workers that no reduction of the week's wages must accompany such a reduction of hours, and that hourly wages must therefore rise. The relation of piecework payments to hours of work and output must obviously vary in each trade and in almost each works (as the Yorkshire coal strike of July, 1919, showed), and there was therefore less unanimity about the required alteration of piece-rates.

The proposals for a shorter week, based on the general desire for more leisure, involved very difficult problems of the settlement of wages and the incentive to industrial efficiency under normal conditions. It was inevitable that the Ministry of Munitions should, in its control of the wages and hours of munition workers, come to some extent into contact with these pre-war (and post-war) problems; but their solution was clearly outside the province of a temporary Department established to meet abnormal needs.[2]

(c) THE SUSPENSION OF EXEMPTIONS IN 1919.

The wholesale reduction of hours of work consequent on the Armistice made it obviously unnecessary to maintain a system of special sanctions for overtime work, or an interdepartmental committee to consider such sanctions. On 5 December, 1918, the Home Office, in correspondence with the Ministry of Munitions, raised the question of revoking the general exemption order of 1916 for munitions works, and, on 26 February, 1919, reported, after inquiry by the Factory Inspectors, that the overtime concessions under the order were by that date hardly used at all, and that the regulations as to shifts were effective only "in a comparatively small and rapidly diminishing number of cases." No inconvenience or hardship would be given by the revocation of the order. The Home Office therefore revoked the order (with the concurrence of the Ministries of Labour and Munitions) as from 29 March, 1919, leaving it to any individual firm to apply for latitude in case of need.

So ended the period of abnormal employment.

---

[1] Cf. the establishment in 1918, on the invitation of the Home Office, of the " Industrial Fatigue Board," by the Department of Scientific and Industrial Research and the Medical Research Committee.

[2] In claims under the Fair Wages clause, the Department was occasionally called upon to determine the length of the normal working week, when workmen such as builders and cabinetmakers, with different working rules, were engaged together upon, *e.g.*, boxmaking. These were, however, exceptional cases. In the aircraft trade, the same difficulty of " mixed trades " with varying standards of hours reappeared, and was met in part by the Skilled Aircraft Workers Order of Feb. 8, 1918. [L.R. 4914, etc. See Vol. V., Part I.]

CHAPTER VII.

TIME-KEEPING.

I. The Problem of Lost Time.

(a) POSITION BEFORE THE MUNITIONS OF WAR ACT.

The second of the model rules for controlled establishments, issued in the interests of " a proper standard of efficiency " under section 4(5) of the first Munitions of War Act, provided for the enforcement of good time-keeping.

> " Every person employed in the establishment, whether on time, piece, or otherwise, shall attend regularly and work diligently during the ordinary working hours of the establishment, and a reasonable amount of overtime, if required, unless he has previous leave of absence for holidays or otherwise, or is prevented by sickness or some other unavoidable cause which shall be immediately reported."

Complaints of the breach of this rule might be made before a local munitions tribunal, either by an employer or on behalf of the Ministry of Munitions, and fines up to £3 might be inflicted by the tribunal.

This was the new disciplinary machinery added by the Department to the varying methods of dismissal, suspension, exclusion for periods of the working day, small fines within the limits of the Truck Acts, and loss of time-keeping bonus, by which employers had before the war penalised irregularity of attendance by their workers. The shortage of labour during the war rendered the first of these penalties almost useless, in so far at least as skilled and fit workmen were concerned ; the second again was difficult to enforce in the case of a pivotal man, whose absence might hold up others' work,[1] and the remainder were admittedly only of moderate efficacy. Earlier volumes of this history have described the storm of criticism of the workers' time-keeping aroused in May, 1915, by the publication, during the total

---

[1] The Department discouraged the use of suspension as a penalty, at least among skilled men, in so far as it was brought to its notice. Thus in September, 1915, Messrs. Hans Renold, Salford, were refused permission to substitute in their works rules the suspension of an offender for his prosecution before a local tribunal, on the ground that in the present state of the labour market and need for production the Ministry could not countenance such loss of time. (C.E. 808/2.)
As late as June, 1918, the employees of a South Wales firm alleged before a munitions tribunal that they had been suspended from work for a day because they had been absent from work the previous day without leave, and claimed that therefore their contract of service had been terminated. The firm stated that one of their works rules gave them the right to prohibit employees who lost a day from working the next day. The tribunal dismissed the men's claim, but the chairman criticised the rule strongly. (Printed) *Weekly Report* No. 148 iX. (29 June, 1918).

prohibition campaign, of the white paper, " *Bad Time kept in Ship-building, Munitions and Transport Areas,*" and the answering comments of labour in Parliament and through the trade union leaders ; the establishment of the Central Control Board, with its constructive treatment of one cause of lost time ; and the local schemes for the reduction of lost time drawn up in the early summer of 1915 by the Armament Committees on the Clyde and Tyne. The establishment of munitions tribunals, consisting of an " appointed " chairman and assessors, the latter representing employers and labour, was agreed on in consultation with the men's leaders, largely in the interests of workshop discipline, and model works rules were, after consulta-tion with the two principal employers' federations concerned and with the National Advisory Committee, issued in August, 1915, providing for the maintenance of workshop discipline under the headings of obedience to orders, co-operation in the suspension of trade union restrictions, and sobriety, good order and time-keeping.[1] The last of these was, throughout the war, the heading under which by far the larger proportion of charges for the breach of works rules were brought before the tribunals.

The further intervention of the Department into a matter so domestic as that of the regularity of attendance of men and women at work, is an illustration of the unprecedented but yet limited State regulation of labour which was evolved in the relation between the Ministry and the controlled establishments.

(b) Early Attempts under the Ministry to Improve Time-keeping.

In the months immediately following its establishment, the Department took little administrative action to improve time-keeping. A number of wholesale prosecutions of workmen by their employers took place before the tribunals under the model rules in the course of the autumn, and supplied the Press with telling but not really repre-sentative details of the cumulative loss of time among munition workers,[2] especially in shipbuilding.

When managers, generally of small firms, at this period consulted the Department as to the improvement of their workers' time-keeping, their attention, if they were controlled, was either drawn to the

---

[1] See Vol. IV., Part II., Chap. I.

[2] Thus a great shipbuilding firm (Cammell, Laird) on 18 September, 1915, at a prosecution of 69 platers, drillers and electricians, stated that the average number of their workmen per day who lost a " quarter " was 1,552, and besides this 1,090 men lost a whole day per week. This represented a total loss of possible working days during a continuous period of over 1½ millions, and a week's work of over 20,000 men. (As against these portentous figures, it was urged on behalf of the men that they had recently completed a battleship in four and a half months within the scheduled time). (C.E. 292/5.) A month later the same firm reported that on the last Monday for which records were available, out of 11,400 men on the books, 3,820 were absent during the first quarter, and 1,200 of these did not come in for the whole day. (*Liverpool Journal of Commerce,* 22 October, 1915.) Messrs. Vickers, at Barrow, produced similar statistics before the local tribunal in October, 1915.

possibility of prosecution before a tribunal, or hortatory letters were despatched for transmission by the firm to offenders. In the case of uncontrolled establishments, printed copies of an appeal for increased production, drawn up in July, 1915, by the National Advisory Committee, were sent to bad time-keepers, or the latter committee asked the delinquent's trade union officials to use their personal influence for his improvement.[1] The labour officers appointed in August and September to represent the Ministry locally were directed to interview and admonish bad time-keepers, but their manifold duties of dealing with labour disputes, promoting dilution and supplying information to headquarters about munition workers' badges and the instalment of War Munition Volunteers, did not in 1915 leave them leisure, except at Glasgow,[2] for much work in this direction. A speech made by the French Minister of Munitions (M. Thomas) on a visit to England, and a report on the output of munitions in France, which stated incidentally that in that country "loss of time was practically negligible," were issued in order to stimulate the British worker,[3] and Members of Parliament were despatched by the "Munitions Parliamentary Committee " to make dinner-hour appeals to workmen for the highest possible output. By the end of the year, however, the following conclusions became clear : (1) that the great majority of workers were, by the employers' reports, " doing splendidly," and that the minority who lost time were not affected by wholesale appeals to their patriotism ; (2) that prosecutions before the tribunals were having some deterrent effect ; and (3) that the long standing problem of lost time in factories, brought into sudden prominence by the war, involved highly complicated questions as yet quite insufficiently explored.

(c) SOME CAUSES OF BAD TIME-KEEPING.

Employers consulted by the Department during the war ascribed bad time-keeping, in itself an elastic term, to some of the following causes: sickness and accident (the most frequent cause, but obviously hard to define) ; transport difficulties (also a very common cause) ; bad weather, especially for outdoor workers ; shortage of material ; ill-health of discharged soldiers (in the later stages of the war) ; domestic duties of married women ; old age and infirmity ; indifference or lack of imagination ; drink (it was stated that loss of time was certainly diminished by the operations of the Central Control Board) ; overtime and Sunday work resulting in the loss of " morning quarters " ; after effects of holidays and of air raids ; high wages, and the separation allowances of soldiers' wives.[4]

Clearly it was very difficult to classify such heterogeneous influences. Attempts to make a primary distinction between them as avoidable and unavoidable required very careful discrimination, owing

---

[1] Cf. M.W. 48893, M.W. 55918.
[2] See Vol. IV., Part II., p. 33.
[3] *French Munition Workers' Sacrifices and Aims: A message to British Workers from the French Minister of Munitions* (October 6, 1915), and *Report on the Output of Munitions in France.* (Cd. 8187, 1916.)
[4] HIST. REC./H/345/1.

to the differing standards of definition and the imperfect records of many firms. Even in the case of sickness, variations in the form of medical certificate, if this was required, often made returns invalid, and wholesale statistics as to lost time, even those supplied by controlled establishments as a basis for investigation, must, as the Department admitted, be received with extreme caution. Three reasons for loss of time, however, stand out during the war period, and may.be kept in view in considering the attempts of the Department to improve time-keeping among munition workers.

Difficulties of management.—The very large number of new workers engaged, and the constant leakage among them, despite the leaving certificate regulations[1]; the loss of foremen, the appearance of new managers and staffs, and the indefinite expansion of existing staffs ; the need for engaging and retaining workers who on grounds of morals, efficiency and physique would not have been engaged for similar work before the war—these things often made the maintenance of good " tone " in a workshop difficult, and showed up any latent weakness in the powers of foremen and under foremen to enforce discipline under the circumstances. (" Time sheets often reflect the character of the management," it has been said, and the incursion of the State into the domestic concerns of workshops, with the publicity given to tribunal cases, threw a flood of light on the highly variable character of contemporary workshop organisation.)

Health.—Men and women worked admittedly over-long hours, although it was hard to prove statistically a connection between overtime work and lost time. The men were, as the war went on, more and more of a low physical category, or, if over military age, were tried by persistent long hours of work. Lost time investigations pointed clearly to the need for further study of industrial hygiene.

The personal factor.—Lost time was, as was early realised, in part due to the faults of character or lack of imagination of the worker ; to his (or her) inability to realise the cumulative effect of abstention from work by many people, and his reluctance in certain cases to exert himself further after his standard of living was satisfied by his earnings. In this respect the problem of lost time was partly psychological, partly a reflection on existing methods of payment for labour.

---

[1] Thus in a large and exceptionally well organised London engineering (shell and ordnance) works, the following figures were given as late as 1918 in *Engineering* :—

Length of service of 2,878 present workmen.   *Men leaving during the past year.*

	Per cent.				
Three years and over ..	449 ⎫		Own accord	..	608
Two years and under three	865 ⎬ 64		To join H.M. Forces	..	132
One year and under two ..	526 ⎭		Continued absence	..	253
Six months and under one			Expiry of notice ..	..	802
year	415	14½	Summary dismissal	..	146
Under six months	623	21½	Deceased ..	..	24
					1,965

These figures compared favourably with those for the women employees.

II. Administrative Action.

(a) ORGANISATION IN THE DEPARTMENT.

A small department was formed as a section of the Secretariat in January, 1916, under Sir Maurice Levy and Mr. H. O. Quin, to deal with time-keeping in controlled establishments. Its officers at first concentrated attention on obtaining information by visits to industrial areas, by discussion with employers and workers, and by statistical inquiry, as to the extent to which bad time-keeping was a serious problem in the supply of munitions.[1]

The general questionnaire (L. 31) sent out monthly to controlled establishments, and returnable under section 4 (3) of the Munitions of War Act, contained clauses requiring information as to the amount of time lost by munition workers. It was found in these returns that over 80 per cent. of the time-keeping in controlled establishments was held by employers to be quite satisfactory. In September, 1916, and subsequently, a separate questionnaire was sent out by the Time-keeping Section to firms which had not hitherto replied or about which special information was desired.[2] If more than 5 per cent. (later 4 per cent.) of time was lost per employee, or if the number of individuals losing over six hours per week was very high, a letter of inquiry was sent to the firm, and recommendations were made, if this seemed desirable, either for a formal admonition by the firm, reference to the representatives of the offender's trade union, or prosecution by the firm or the Ministry of Munitions. Alternatively, attempts were made to remove obstacles such as travelling difficulties, or to induce firms to suspend rules for admission which appeared overstrict for war-time. Detailed replies had been received by the end of November, 1916, from 2,648 firms, in 340 of which over 5 per cent. of time was lost.

When the local organisation of the Ministry was rearranged and developed in November, 1916, with the appointment of separate dilution and investigation officers for each of the eight administrative areas, it was made one of the duties of the latter group of officers to attend to questions of time-keeping in munition works. A new and more definite policy then developed. The investigation officers were supplied with the names of firms in which, according to the monthly returns to headquarters, time-keeping was bad. They were directed to visit the controlled establishments concerned and to discuss with the management the causes of irregularity ; to interview, with the firms' permission, the individuals who were keeping bad time, to inquire from them their reasons, giving full opportunity for excuses, and, with

---

[1] HIST. REC./H/345/1.

[2] The questionnaire (MM 72) asked for the number of (a) employees ; (b) persons on overtime and hours of overtime actually worked by such persons ; (c) hours of normal working time lost (i) through all causes, (ii) through sickness, accident, or leave of absence ; (d) employees losing more than six hours per week from causes other than sickness, lack of material, etc. It also required (e) the normal weekly working hours of the firm ; (f) its rules for the admission of late comers ; (g) general remarks, e.g., as to delay caused by journeys or as to the special classes of workers affected. A monthly report on " Time-keeping in controlled establishments " was based on these returns and printed for official use.

the firms' consent, to admonish them when in fault, or to warn them formally of the probability of prosecution, at the same time "endeavouring to enlist their sympathies in favour of good time-keeping with a view to maintaining output at a high level." The officers were further desired to arrange with the employers for subsequent records of the conduct of a man thus admonished, and if necessary for his report either to his trade union or to a Labour Advisory Board, or to the Ministry for prosecution. In the latter case they were responsible for conducting the prosecution before a munitions tribunal. They were to suggest to employers the slight relaxation of very rigid rules as to punctuality if the morning start was as early as 6.30 a.m., and were "generally to assist employers in all matters regarding time-keeping," without any approach to officiousness or interference.

Special insistence was laid on the keeping by the chief investigation officers, of careful records, both of individual and general time-keeping in the cases referred to them, and of following up cases of men warned or prosecuted.[1]

(b) Prosecution and Co-operation with Employers.

No prosecution on behalf of the Ministry of Munitions was sanctioned from headquarters without formal warning either by a Labour Advisory Board, a trade union official or an officer of the Ministry of Munitions; nor was it normally allowed under any conditions (according to a departmental notice of May, 1917) when the worker was under 17 or over 60, or when the worker had during the period under consideration worked 60 hours or more per week. The prosecution of women for lost time was dropped by the Ministry at this time[2] although it was continued by some private firms. Very few prosecutions for lost time were in fact recommended by the investigation officers under the official time-keeping scheme evolved in 1917. Thus in June of that year, while 1,827 records of the time-keeping of individuals were inscribed on the card indices of the chief investigation officers' offices, only 62 cases were recommended for prosecution. This proportion was said by the investigation officers to be a testimony to the effect of moral pressure and careful watching on avoidable loss of time.[3]

During the debate on the second reading of the Munitions of War Bill in April, 1917, attention was drawn to the frivolous cases brought into court by employers, causing loss of time, ill-feeling and a sense of grievance. In March, said Mr. W. C. Anderson, out of 965 cases at the Sheffield tribunal, 254 were dismissed apparently as being frivolous or unproved while 256 others were adjourned on probation. "It is very doubtful whether a man feels most irritated if his case is dismissed or if he is found guilty. If the case is dismissed it means that he has been brought there for nothing." Sir Tudor Walters equally emphasised

---

[1] See L.R. 107/107 *passim*.

[2] L.R. 232. A year later (May and June, 1918) the duty of investigating time-keeping cases among women and boys was formally handed over to the welfare officers, acting under the immediate instructions of the chief investigation officers.

[3] L.R. 107/107.

the discontent caused by numerous trifling prosecutions, which were not, he urged, normally brought by the large, well-organised firms.[1] The Employers' Consultative Committee urged during the consideration of the revised Munitions Bill during the summer of 1917, that prosecutions for breaches of works rules should be undertaken in future, not by firms, but by the Ministry (or the Admiralty) alone.   At the time, there were about 2,000 time-keeping prosecutions per month before tribunals, and of these about 60 per cent. ended in convictions.[2] Only some 3 per cent. were at the time initiated by the Ministry, but these cases, being carefully prepared and sifted, were seldom dismissed by the tribunals.   It had been repeatedly urged since the early autumn of 1915, that it would conduce to better discipline and remove friction, and also save waste of time in unnecessary hearings, if the Department would initiate all proceedings.   With the withdrawal of the leaving certificate regulations under the Munitions Act of 1917, employers were comprehensibly anxious not to risk the loss of men through the enforcement of works rules, if the responsibility for this could be undertaken by a public authority. Accordingly, Section 10 of the new Act[3] took this power wholly from employers, and responsibility for receiving employers' complaints, investigating them and arranging, if necessary, for prosecutions with the sanction of headquarters, was left to the chief investigation officers.

In the meanwhile a separate procedure was begun in May, 1917, for the treatment of avoidable loss of time among men of military age by co-operation with the Labour Enlistment Complaints Committees described below.   The withdrawal of exemption from military service was a more effective method of coercion for the inveterate bad time keepers (a small minority, it must be repeated, among munition workers) than was moral suasion or the infliction of small fines by the tribunals.

A large increase in the penal work of the investigation officers naturally resulted from the Act of August, 1917, and the number of prosecutions instituted by them rose from 45 in September, 1917, to 373 in October, when the effects of the Act became visible. In the ten months that passed between the adoption of this process and the end of June, 1918, the investigation officers had received 9,314 formal complaints from 2,606 firms. After exercising their right of summary dismissal of complaints, the officers referred 4,825 of them to the Labour Enlistment Complaints Committees and instituted 3,698 prosecutions.[4]

An attempt was made in 1918 to systematise further the treatment of bad time keeping in controlled establishments, and employers were circularised in March urging their increased co-operation and explaining

<hr/>

[1] *Parliamentary Debates* (1917), *H. of C.*, XCII. 2772, 2790.
[2] L.R. 107/13 ; L.R. 5581.
[3] " Proceedings against a person for contravening or failing to comply with regulations made by the Minister of Munitions under subsection (4) of Section 4 of the Munitions of War Act, 1915, shall not be instituted except by the Minister of Munitions or the Admiralty or by a person acting on his or their behalf."
[4] (Printed) *Weekly Report* No. 148, IX. (29 June, 1918).

in detail the present procedure of the Department (described below in connection with the Labour Enlistment Complaints Committees). The procedure consisted ultimately in individualising bad time-keeping with the help of the employers, by means of personal interviews and enquiries and by the maintenance of card records over considerable periods for the attendance of such men. This in itself involved a severe strain upon the chief investigation officers' staff, since it was said that one investigation officer could not scrutinise and assist to improve effectively the time-keeping of more than 12 firms per week. It was, however, represented by the officers themselves that the scope of their activity was perforce limited, since it was obviously impossible to give "admonition" or to conduct detailed enquiries into time-keeping in certain phases of the labour unrest that in 1918 still followed the adoption of the $12\frac{1}{2}$ per cent. bonus on earnings.[1]

The following figures summarise the time-keeping officers' extramural activities for October, 1918, among 4,875 controlled establishments :—

Firms dealt with	816
Firms under special observation (with their own assent)	518
Individual records kept	2,685
Warning letters for prosecution	497
Warnings for removal of protection	1,353
Referred to Labour Enlistment Complaints Committees for prosecution	337
Referred to Labour Enlistment Complaints Committees for withdrawal of protection	132
Prosecutions instituted for bad time-keeping	129
Labour Enlistment Complaints Committees' recommendations to withdraw protection	59
Protection withdrawn by the Ministry	34

The Ministry's work in connection with time-keeping was clearly ended abruptly by the Armistice, and as an instance of prompt discontinuance of war activities it may be recorded that instructions were sent on 13 November, 1918, by the Department, to its local officers, to the effect that "no further action will be taken by the Ministry in connection with the improvement of time-keeping in controlled establishments."

III. Methods of Preventing Lost Time.

It is worth while to enter into some further consideration of methods of dealing with the munition worker who failed to put in the full working week, partly as an illustration of departmental dealing with the individual, partly because of the connection of the problem of lost time with other problems of labour regulation.

(a) "ADMONITIONS."

The efficacy of the "admonitions" and formal warnings delivered to bad time-keepers by chief investigation officers and others obviously depended largely on the personality of the admonisher and admonished.

---

[1] L.R. 107/58.

In some cases of unjustifiable time losing, appeals to the workers' patriotism and to the needs of the men in the trenches did their work, in the opinion of those most qualified to judge ; in others no lasting effect was produced until the exhortations became warnings with penalties behind them.

(b) Munitions Tribunals.

In the first months after the establishment of these courts, prosecutions before them for loss of time were on the whole held to be effective by the munition firms and the Admiralty officials with experience of them.[1]   In the second year of the Department's work there was considerable criticism of their effectiveness in enforcing workshop discipline.   While some large firms, such as the Coventry Ordnance and Beardmore's,[2] regularly sent their bad time-keepers before them, others said that the loss of time involved in arranging for attendance at the court of a foreman and witnesses as well as the delinquent, together with the bitterness sometimes left by a conviction, made it not worth their while to use them.   They further said that the publicity of the hearings and their press reports acted as a deterrent to the self-respecting workman but not to the really bad case who gave trouble in the workshops, and that the scale of fines, especially if paid by instalment—variable within the £3 limit—was insufficient penalty for workmen earning from £5 to £10 a week.

To meet this last criticism, special inquiries were made in the first half of 1917 from the chairman and clerks of local munitions tribunals as to their practice in dealing with time-keeping cases.   Their replies supplied the following facts.[3]   .

In January, 1917, 2,681 time-keeping cases were dealt with by the tribunals.   Fines were inflicted in 1,744 (65 per cent.) cases ;   147 (5·4 per cent.) cases were dismissed with a caution ; 172 cases were adjourned.   The level of fines varied greatly in different districts.   The average was £1 3s. 8d. throughout the country, ranging from 6s. 10½d. at Bradford to the full £3 at Huddersfield.   (A considerable number of women and boys were involved at one centre—Birmingham—and this kept the average fine low.) 237 (13·5 per cent.) of the fines were under 10s. in amount, and 623 (35·7 per cent.) of the larger fines were payable in weekly instalments of under 10s.   The Metropolitan local munitions tribunal inflicted fines of 60s. in 24 cases, 40s. in 25, 30s. in 11, 20s. in 89.   The Sheffield tribunal, spoken of by employers as very effective, had in this month most cases (502) ; next to this, the largest number of time keeping cases were at Birmingham (383), the Metropolitan Court (297), Glasgow (207), Coventry (197).   The time-keeping cases from January to June averaged 2,122 per month among 53 local munition tribunals.   Of these cases only 56 per month were on an average brought by the Ministry.

The clerks and chairmen were consulted in March as to their practice in assessing fines and fixing the weekly instalments by which

---

¹ Weekly Sectional Reports.   ² M.W. 160760.   ³ L.R. 107/32.

they might be paid (*i.e.*, deducted by the employer from the delinquent's wages). Their replies were to the effect that it was difficult to be wholly consistent owing to the varying constitution of their boards of assessors, and that no definite rule or principle could be laid down for the fixing of fines. Cases must be dealt with on their merits, with due consideration of the earnings and circumstances of the person charged as well as his character and past record. " The main point in Birmingham had been to secure as large instalments as practicable, subject to two considerations, (*a*) the fine should be levied so as not to fall on the family instead of on the offender, (*b*) the fine should not drive the men away from the work altogether. The average of fines was much higher than a year ago, and the chairman thought it impossible to increase this without imperilling the unanimity of the tribunal, the maintenance of which he considered of the highest importance." " We keep prominently before us," reported the Blackpool munitions tribunal, " the desire by our decision to induce the man to put his best into his work as well as to make the penalty deterrent to others."[1]

A few months later, when the desirability of abandoning work before breakfast was frequently urged, the officials of tribunals were similarly consulted as to their practice in regard to prosecutions for lost " morning quarters." Very varying customs were reported among the firms which approached the tribunals.[2] At Leeds the court attached great importance to the enforcement by employers of the rule as to " quartering " (the exclusion of late comers till the first break in the morning's work). There would be an entire lack of discipline without such strictness, though in fact many employers gave a quarter to half an hour's grace. At Birmingham the local practice was said to vary from exclusion for half an hour to a whole day. In such an extreme case as the latter the chairman " not seldom " invited the employer to make provision for some elasticity lest he should be compelled to dismiss a charge or grant a certificate. At Liverpool, it was thought that locking out (the common rule in shipyards) was not *per se* nearly sufficient penalty.

One frequent cause of difficulty in settling time-keeping cases before the tribunals lay in the difficulty of obtaining satisfactory medical certificates. The efforts of the Department to standardise medical certificates were not successful. Early in 1917 a very large number of model certificates were printed by the Department for use in controlled establishments. It was, however, found that busy panel doctors, while they were prepared to give, *e.g.*, a written statement that "A.B. is unable to follow his occupation," commonly refused to make the detailed diagnosis required for the completion of these certificates, unless they were allowed to charge much more than the normal working-class fee for the purpose.[3] To meet this difficulty tribunals were directed to obtain medical referees to whom at a small fixed charge (7s. 6d.) doubtful cases could be sent ; or they could require the attendance, at a fee of £1 1s., of the defendant's doctor.

[1] M.W. 160760 ; M.T. 132/3 ; M.T. 129/3 ; L.R. 107 sub-files.
[2] L.R. 107/22.
[3] L.R. 107/74 and 107/79. A copy of the certificate is given on page 178 of the *Final Report of the Health of Munition Workers Committee.* (Cd. 9065 of 1918.)

Statistics of fines and isolated descriptions of procedure do not give a fair indication of the tribunals' work in the enforcement of good time-keeping or of other branches of factory discipline. It was often claimed by employers that prosecutions had a deterrent effect on very many who were not brought before the courts, although it was admitted that convictions and fines were powerless against the confirmed " slacker." But, apart from deterrence, they gave a fair opportunity for the expression of grievances, and for explanation of the difficulties of punctual attendance due to ill-health, crowded trains, admission rules, for which in the press of munition work in busy firms there was no guarantee of a hearing. The local munitions tribunals were essentially domestic courts, ready to hear, in the presence of assessors representing both capital and labour, any detail of workshop organisation, of family difficulties, and the unnecessary discomforts of working-class life, that might account for irregularity at work.[1] On the other hand, they gave opportunity for a definite statement by the employer of the dislocation of work by bad time-keeping, and to some extent enforced the point of view that regular work was national service.[2] Their efficacy obviously varied in accordance with the personality of the local chairman and the selection made from the rota of assessors. Large numbers of employers never had recourse to them ; but in the absence of other machinery, their influence was valuable ; and, incidentally, experience of their working helped to establish the permanent value of a new kind of industrial court.

A charge was raised in certain engineering workshops during the autumn of 1915 that the enforcement of works rules by an external tribunal inaugurated a form of widespreading tyranny over the worker. It is worth while to record, therefore, that in 1917, when the tribunals reached their maximum of rather over 2,000 time-keeping cases per month, there were some 2,000,000 workers subject (with their employers) to the Munitions of War Acts.

(c) Withdrawal of Military Exemption : Labour Enlistment Complaints Committees.

" Labour Enlistment Complaints Committees " were established in January, 1917, simultaneously with the first attempts to give effect to the contentious Trade Card Exemption scheme for members of the

---

[1] One such case, typical of very many others, may perhaps be quoted. At one of the early sessions of the Newcastle local tribunal (September, 1915) an admittedly bad time-keeper explained his lateness at work by sleeplessness due to ill-health, the presence of twin babies at home, and the fact that he lived opposite to a steel works, " and every time that the lights went out " (this was in a month of local air raid alarms) " the men working there came outside and sang and played mouth organs." In this case no fine was inflicted. (*Weekly Tribunal Reports*, September, 1915).

[2] " Many firms," wrote a woman assessor at a munitions tribunal in a large provincial town, " use the courts freely as a means of making their workers keep good time. I have seen firms bring up 20 or 30 women for unpunctuality and loss of time. Constant unpunctuality in coming to work is always severely dealt with. Occasional loss of time in a worker who has a good reputation is not generally severely treated, but the girl who has a record of unpunctuality is sure to get into trouble sooner or later." *Women in the Munitions Courts : Hints for Women Workers* (Labour Press ; 1917).

skilled trade unions,[1] " to deal with cases of alleged victimisation of
skilled men by employers in substitution and debadging, and with all
allegations of improper enlistment " ; and consisted of the chief dilution
officer in each of the eight employment exchange divisions as chairman,
with representatives of the War Office, the Admiralty, and the Ministry
of Labour, and three or four representatives of labour nominated
by the Labour Adviser to His Majesty's Government.   They reported
to a special section of the Labour Supply Department, under the direction of Mr. W. Mosses (secretary to the National Advisory Committee,
and formerly general secretary of the Federation of Shipbuilding and
Engineering Trades), and offered another example of the joint committee
on which the official and labour element were equally represented,
which appeared in many spheres of administration during the later
stages of the war.

When in May, 1917, it was arranged to refer to these committees
cases of bad time-keeping among men of military age, for consideration
of the removal of their military exemption certificates,[2] the following
procedure was evolved. Complaints of bad time-keeping among
exempt munition workers, whether these were received direct from
firms by the district chief investigation officer, or were referred to him
by headquarters, might, after personal investigation by the chief
investigation officer or his deputy, be reported, with the employer's
written approval, to the area Labour Enlistment Complaints Committee.[3] The latter were directed to fix a day for hearing the case ;
to summon the man to attend (with his trade union representative
if he desired), explaining that his travelling expenses would be paid,
and that if he did not appear, it would be assumed that he had no
further explanation to give of his irregular attendance ; to consider
the evidence, and to report thereon to headquarters. If the local
committee recommended the withdrawal of exemption, the Labour

---

[1] Protests against the alleged over-representation of the A.S.E. on these
committees were raised by members of the general unions, on whose behalf it was
claimed that they included 450,000 munition workers as against 190,000 in the
A.S.E.
    " The Trade Card scheme was in the first place suggested and forced upon
the Government by the A.S.E., and intended by them to crush all other unions
to which they objected—and there are only one or two unions to which the A.S.E.
do not object in the engineering world.
    " But why worry if the A.S.E. should presume to rule the Trade Union world,
even as its exemplars—the Prussians—aspire to rule the states of the world ?
There comes a day when over-reaching ends, because it incurs universal condemnation. And evolution supplies the brake sometimes so suddenly that the road-
hoggishly driven vehicle turns turtle."   (Article on " Prussianism in the Trade
Union Movement " ; *Workers' Union Record*, August, 1917).
    [2] The schedule of protected occupations of May, 1917 (MM.130) stated
(note 6) ; " Any men found to have a bad record for absence from work will obtain
no protection by reason of being employed in an occupation covered by the
schedule."
    The Trade Card Agreement of 22 November, 1916, between the Govern-
ment and twenty-five " skilled " unions was abrogated on 1 May, 1917, and the
Labour Enlistment Complaints Committees from that date heard claims to
"protection" under the new Schedule (Printed) *Weekly Report* No. 87, XII.
(14/4/17.)
    [3] L.R. 107/107.

Enlistments Complaints Section of the Ministry, if they concurred, at once took action for the removal of the exemption certificate, formal sanction to this being reserved to the Parliamentary Secretary. The local committee were empowered, if they desired, to ask for a medical certificate from a specially appointed medical adviser, and were specially instructed to take into consideration sickness, or other reasonable cause, in deciding whether the case was one where protection should be withdrawn.   If the man concerned had not been convicted before a munitions tribunal, but was reported on good grounds to be a bad time-keeper, the investigation officer, after personal inquiry, was directed to send a formal warning to the offender, explaining the position, and quoting from the latest schedule of protected occupations to the effect that " The national need at the present time does not permit of the retention on Admiralty, War Office or munitions work of any man of military age who does not devote his whole time and energies to the work."[1]

The fullest opportunity of protest and of defence against any possible form of " victimisation " was given to the workman. Only after three or four weeks had elapsed from the date of the warning, and its result had been carefully noted, was a time loser to be reported to the Labour Enlistment Complaints Committee. The latter was directed to report specially to headquarters (though without appearing to offer censure without full inquiry)[2] if a firm's methods of management appeared to conduce to bad time-keeping ; and its members were directed to report to the chief investigation officer any cases of invidious selection of bad time-keepers by an employer.

Explanations of the scheme were sent to employers in June, 1917, and again in April, 1918, in the latter case urging strongly upon firms the desirability of at once and regularly reporting to the chief investigation officers the names of the small percentage of workers who habitually kept bad time, delaying and setting a bad example to their neighbours, in order that they might either be prosecuted before a munitions tribunal or sent into the army. Employers not infrequently said that with the shortage of skilled men they would rather have one who was a bad time-keeper than none at all, and that since the removal of the leaving certificate regulations, prosecution might lead to the loss of the workman.   It was, however, pointed out to them that it was unfair to other men to protect bad time-keepers of military age from military service, and that the notoriously bad time-keeper above military age was still liable to prosecution on the strength of his record if he transferred his services to another firm. To meet a criticism that the national factories were not similarly sacrificing their skilled men in the interests of regular work, the controllers of national factories were similarly called on to report their bad time-keepers to the chief investigation officers and Labour Enlistment Complaints Committees.   A poster explaining the effect of the revised schedule of occupations was sent out in May, 1918, to firms desiring to exhibit it.

[1] L.R. 107 and sub-files.   [2] M.S. 34808.

The chief investigation officers reported good effects from the increased stringency of the methods of dealing with bad time-keepers in the summer of 1918. In Glasgow, especially, the chief investigation officer declared that the last warnings had been very effective ; the employers had backed up their efforts in supplying records, and had not found their men leave them. The system was now simplified as follows[1] :—A bad time-keeper received an official letter of warning ; after three weeks, if he had not improved and if he lost at least one hour per day, his record was sent to the Labour Enlistment Complaints Committee. The man was summoned to the next meeting of the committee within ten days ; the committee's decision was given in a week or ten days. Four or six weeks later the papers reached the recruiting office.

The following table[2] shows the number of bad time-keeping cases which were referred to Enlistment Complaints Committees, and the manner in which these were dealt with from 7 May, 1917, to 3 November, 1918 :—

Bad time-keeping cases referred	955
Protection withdrawn	548
Protection not withdrawn	173
Under consideration by the Committees	69
Under consideration by the Ministry	145

The total number of men posted to the Army under this procedure up to 3 November, 1918, was 372.

The very small number of men actually affected by the procedure described is a testimony both to the shortage of male labour in the last year of the war and to the extent to which good or bad time-keeping is dependent on health. It was clearly not worth while to claim, for military service, munition workers of a very low medical class. The provision for the removal of exemption from bad time-keepers was a concession to the workers' sense of justice rather than an additional means of securing men for the Army.

(d) CO-OPERATION WITH LABOUR ;—TRADE UNIONS, LABOUR ADVISORY BOARDS, WORKS COMMITTEES.

It has been shown how, in the discussions with trade union representatives in May and June, 1915, and in the debates in Parliament which led up to the passing of the first Munitions of War Act, emphasis was laid on the necessity of enlisting the help of labour in securing good time-keeping and factory discipline.[3] The constitution of the local munitions tribunals, with their equal representation of capital and labour on either side of the chairman, was intended to give effect to this. In the criticisms of the working of the tribunals that preceded the passing of the first Amendment Act in January, 1916, it was pointed

---

[1] L.R. 107/56.
[2] (Printed) *Weekly Report* No. 166, IX. (2 November, 1918).
[3] See Vol. IV., Part II., Chap. I.

out that this partnership was not really effective,[1] and it was urged that intermediate councils should be established to settle, with even more promptitude than was shown by the tribunals, petty disputes and points of workshop discipline.[2] No formal proposal was, however, made, and the employers informally consulted were against any such intermediate councils. The second year of the war, with its preoccupations and its heavy demands for overtime work, was not a time in which to convince employers of the advantages of devolution in control, or to educate the trade union rank and file in the principles and details of workshop administration.

Labour Advisory Boards.—Some attempts were, however, made by means of the Labour Advisory Boards to utilise the labour leaders' readiness to give a lead to those of the rank and file who appeared indifferent to the output of war material.

These boards were designed, according to their formal constitution, to act as the district agents of the National Advisory Committee, " reporting to that committee on matters arising there, taking up questions with local representatives of trade unions, and co-operating with the labour officers of the Ministry, so as to secure the most effective use of labour on the production of munitions of war." They consisted of seven members elected by representatives of the trade unions locally concerned in munition work. One of their specified functions was to deal with lost time.

" The Labour Advisory Boards shall investigate cases of bad timekeeping reported by employers, either directly by the firm or through the local labour officer, and take such action as may appear possible and desirable with a view to improving time-keeping."[3]

The Labour Advisory Boards came slowly into existence, largely owing to trade union dissatisfaction at their constitution, which gave equal representation to all munitions trade unions, irrespective of their membership, and expressly stated that no union should have more than one member. Representatives of the A.S.E. explained this at the conference on 31 December, 1915, with the Minister on the Munitions of War Amendment Bill (" What certain of our members

---

[1] " Why," asked Mr. Wilkie of the Shipwrights' Society, in the debate of 4 January, 1916, " was there not an effort at partnership ? " " Instead of getting those domestic courts which were promised, we have got these other courts with most ridiculous decisions." The Shipwrights' Society had established committees in all the large shipbuilding firms in the North of England to deal with the managers and foremen. " If these committees had received more encouragement from the Minister of Munitions and his officials, they would ·have been of much more power for good and less cases would have gone to the tribunals." *Parliamentary Debates* (1916), *H. of C.*, LXXVII. 862, 863, and *A.S.E. Journal*, December, 1915, and January, 1916.

[2] M.W. 72469/4.

[3] The Central Munitions Labour Supply Committee in the early autumn of 1915 represented that avoidable time losing should be reported to the local labour officer so that offenders might come under the influence of the Labour Advisory Board, not instead of, but before, referring them to munitions tribunals, and the head of the Time-keeping Section of the Ministry agreed, after discussion with the secretary of the National Advisory Committee, at the beginning of 1916 to make use of the Labour Advisory Boards when advisable. (M.W. 88872.)

have refused to do is to appoint one man to represent 20,000.   Probably
the bricklayers or the plumbers, or some other small association
representing about 50 men, has joint representation with us ") ;   and
again, on 14 March, 1916 (" The trades which are being called upon
to release their rules and make sacrifices are not adequately represented ").   Members of the A.S.E. urged the establishment in their
place of joint committees (shop committees, works councils, and district committees) for the engineering industry.   These proposals,
the germ, perhaps, of a later industrial constitution, were not, however,
officially formulated, and though considered at intervals throughout
the year, no action was taken upon them.[1]

The Labour Advisory Boards, therefore, were limited in action
and devoid of any compulsory powers ;   and it is safe to say that they
never fully realised the nebulous duties assigned to them.   At their
early meetings, of which, according to instructions, brief records were
sent to the National Advisory Committee, they were chiefly concerned
with very minor points of dilution and wages questions, the position
of men released from the colours, and the subsistence allowances of
War Munition Volunteers.   At the beginning of 1916 a few of the
Boards took up the question of time-keeping among munition workers,
on the suggestion of the National Advisory Committee, and those
which evolved a vigorous policy with regard to it were the only
boards to survive their first year in any state of health.

The most effective board in this respect, though not the first to
take action, was that at Coventry, which developed a system commended
by the Department as an example to the similar boards throughout the
country.   It developed the following procedure, a procedure, it may
be observed, based almost wholly on the efficacy of "moral suasion."
At the end of April, 1916, one of the large engineering firms in the city
wrote to ask its help in dealing with lost time.   The chairman and
secretary interviewed the management, and next week reported
on their agreement.   They undertook to send a warning circular
to all workmen reported to them whose average loss of time exceeded
four hours per week, and a letter to all losing more than 30 hours per
month, summoning the latter to appear before the board.   Until
the men had had the opportunity of doing this the firm agreed not to
prosecute before the tribunal.   The trade union officials, representing
ten or twelve trade unions, and the local branch of the Engineering
Employers' Federation agreed, in the course of the summer, to co-
operate with this scheme, and for a few weeks in the autumn of 1916
the board had informal meetings three or four times a week to deal
with the men reported to them, interviewing separately some 15 men
per night.   The great characteristic of these meetings was the individual treatment of each case.   The delinquent stated his case, gave
good grounds for his unpunctuality, or listened to reminders by his fellow-
workmen of the needs of " the men in the trenches."   Reports were
sent to the employer on the result of the interview, exonerating the
man who had been charged, or recommending his prosecution or

[1] M.W. 72469/4.

further probation, as the case might be.[1] Local employers testified
to the real efficacy of this board; and a few other boards, *e.g.*,
those at Luton and Bristol, followed its example with vigour.

It must, however, be admitted that the boards were not effective
in dealing with time-keeping cases, despite the support given to them
by the Department. There was easily explicable jealousy of their
position among trade union officials, while in some cases, employers
comprehensibly disliked asking the help of trade unionists in matters
of works discipline. Further, the boards depended for their efficacy
in a disagreeable task on the personality of their members, and,
granted that this was satisfactory, they were not effective outside
the sphere of personal influence. There was, therefore, obviously
little scope for them in districts in which, unlike Coventry, controlled
establishments were either very numerous or widely scattered.

Trade Unions.—The schemes of the two Armaments Committees in
1915 for improved time-keeping, and that of the Admiralty in 1916,
expressly involved the co-operation of the trade unions. The Boilermakers' Society, in particular, undertook to give this, thus reviving an
obsolete system under which their officials had, before the war, in theory
at least, interviewed, or if necessary fined, bad time-keepers reported
to them by the shipbuilding firms.[2] In the engineering trade it was
difficult to produce any such definite extension of functions, although[3]
in January, 1916, at the monthly York conference between the Engineering Employers' Federation and the engineering trade unions,
the latter agreed that they would take special steps to deal with cases
of bad time-keeping. Wherever possible the investigation officers
were directed to make use of the good offices of the local trade union
officials, in order to bring pressure upon their members. In Scotland,
the Chief Investigation Officer said, early in 1917, that this would be
impossible,[4] and reference was seldom made to trade union secretaries, for very obvious reasons, based equally on the relationship of

---

[1] A vivid description of an evening's session of the Coventry Board by
Mr. Harold Begbie in the *Daily Chronicle* was reprinted by the Department and
circulated to other boards and to employers.
  In June, 1917, only 14 Labour Advisory Boards out of 62 nominally existent,
made returns to the chief investigation officers. They had in the last month
summoned 223 delinquents from 30 firms to their meetings. Of these, 189
appeared before them and were admonished, while three were recommended for
prosecution. At this time even the Coventry Board only dealt regularly with
bad time-keepers from 11 or 12 out of the 65 controlled establishments in the city.
Some seven boards were, however, dealing with lost time cases. Next year, they
were largely superseded by the Labour Enlistment Complaints Committees,
bodies with a far more definite status than had ever been allotted to the boards.
In July, 1918, boards were still surviving at Bristol, Barrow, Blackburn, Wigan,
Cowes, Coventry, Rochdale, St. Helens, Swindon, and Warrington, holding
irregular meetings, at intervals of a month or more, for the consideration of half a
dozen cases at a time. Under the new system of referring men of military age to
the Labour Enlistment Complaints Committees, the Labour Advisory Boards
would only be likely to deal with elderly men, and it was not worth while to maintain the machinery of argument and emotional appeals for their benefit.
(L.R. 107/55; and Labour Advisory Boards minutes).
  [2] Cf. *Report on Enquiry into Industrial Agreements* (Cd. 6953 of 1913).
  [3] M.W. 72469/4.
  [4] M.W. 164535.

the trade union official to his branch members during the war, and on the Ministry's position with regard to local labour difficulties. Between March and September, 1917, when between 2,000 and 3,000 time-keeping cases per month were under observation by the Department's officers, a total of only 6, 31, and 9 (say five per month) were reported to the trade unions.[1]

Works Committees.—There was probably more prospect of success in the treatment of so purely "domestic" a question as bad time-keeping by works committees, where these were prepared to deal with the subject. The Department, as has been said, took no official action in the delegation of discipline to committees including workmen ; but isolated experiments were reported to it in the later stage of the war.

Thus, in July, 1917, the works committee of a Bilston firm[2] considered grievances raised as to the administration of the time-keeping bonus, and had access to the books to settle them. The Phœnix Dynamo Company had a scheme under which a man could choose whether to be fined by the works time-keeping tribunal or the munitions tribunal.[3] The works committee of a Huddersfield firm[4] administered a bonus, subject to stoppage for bad time-keeping or misconduct. The Sunbeam Motor Car Company, Wolverhampton, had a committee which helped the management in time-keeping, and was credited with a reduction of hours lost by 4,000 a week among 3,000 employees.[5]

A year later an example of co-operation was reported from the shop committee of the Britannia Iron Works, Bedford. "The man's record card is handed to the committee, which decides (very justly, according to the Chief Investigation Officer) whether he is to be reported to the Labour Enlistment Complaints Committee."[6]

The coal miners' pit committees, in 1916, undertook to deal with absenteeism among their fellow-workmen.[7] An interesting example of a similar agreement was made with the sanction of the Department in July, 1917, between the Cleveland blast-furnacemen and coke-oven men and the Cleveland Ironmasters' Association.[8] By this agreement a committee of three workmen, chosen by the trade union (with three representatives of the employers "if desired"), was set up at each works, and was empowered to inquire into any charges of bad time-keeping brought by the management, to give warning and advice to any workman who might appear to need it, and to inflict fines up to 20s., subject to the provision of the Truck Acts. A central committee was set up for the district, with power to inflict fines up to 40s. or to submit cases to the Ministry of Munitions, so long as munition tribunals should exist.

---

[1] I.R. 107/16.   [2] C.E. 3997.
[3] C.E. 768.   [4] C.E. 2753.
[5] M.W. 130574/19.
[6] (Printed) *Weekly Report* No. 153, IX. (3/8/18).
[7] See reports of the conferences of the Miners' Federation of Great Britain in November and December, 1916.
[8] M.W. 130574/19. See also p. 112.

Clearly, cases of bad time-keeping were not among the first which newly established works committees would normally undertake, although the prevention of lost time was included among the possible duties suggested for them by the Ministry of Labour in its *Recommendations on the Functions of Industrial Councils and Works Committees*, issued in January, 1919.

(e) ORGANISATION.

The foregoing methods of dealing with time-keeping were mainly methods of deterrence, whereas good time-keeping under normal circumstances is admittedly largely dependent on good workshop organisation. Attempts to prevent lost time during the war threw light on its connection with three special aspects of management.

Methods of wage payment.—The effect of a time-keeping bonus was often discussed during the war, and employers were specially asked to make notes on its effects in their periodical returns to the Department. The opinions thus received varied greatly. On the whole it appeared to be difficult to make such a bonus large enough to be an effective incentive, except in the case of low-paid workers, such as certain labourers, women on timework, and boys, especially apprentices. Even with these, opinions differed as to the efficacy of such a bonus.

It was suggested early in 1917 that time-keeping conditions might possibly be attached to the newly arranged periodical wage advances in the engineering trades. The Committee on Production (who were familiar in their hearings, especially in those concerning the shipbuilding trades, with charges by employers that their workers lost so much time as to neutralise any claim to wage advances)[1] were, however, against such a proposal when consulted informally thereon.[2]

Apart from this possible course, methods of payment for overtime early came under consideration. An attempt was made in some trades and districts, and was fostered by the Admiralty and the Ministry of Munitions, to keep overtime work as a privilege for good time-keepers, or only to allow the calculation of overtime, with payment

---

[1] Cf. Committee on Production hearings, 12 August, 1916, and 12 January and 27 February, 1917.

[2] The opinion of one of their members on this point sums up one important aspect of the relation of wage payment to time-keeping.

" Any general scheme of the sort would be greatly resented by men generally and by the unions as casting a slur on the whole body for the misdoings of a minority, a large part of whom are slackers past redemption and with whom the unions are willing and anxious to deal by disciplinary means. It also involves highly controversial issues. Prior to the war there was much controversy about a guaranteed week, workmen generally wishing for the regularity which a guaranteed week gives, employers generally leaning to the freedom given to them by the system of payment for hourly or daily work. That system undoubtedly taught men in certain industries to believe that it rested with them to choose whether they should work or not, and the effect of that teaching cannot be undone in a moment. It is very difficult for employers during the war to reverse their attitude and make increases of wages dependent on men surrendering their comparative freedom as to hours of work under penalty of being deprived of the increases in hourly payment to which they consider themselves entitled owing to an increase in the cost of living." (M.W. 151449/8.)

at increased rates, after the normal number of hours' work had been performed.[1] The story of these negotiations belongs, however, to the history of wages.

No generalisations as to the effect of methods of wage payment on time-keeping were possible from the extent to which the Department was able to examine the problem.[2] On the whole, time-keeping tended to be less good among piece-workers than among time-workers, and it was sometimes urged by opponents of the Ministry's efforts to promote the adoption of payment by results, that this would operate against attempts to secure regular attendance at work.

Hours of Work.—The statistics obtained from controlled establishments failed under war conditions to show any general correlation between overtime worked and time lost. It became, however, increasingly clear that the absence, under the "one-break" system, of early work before breakfast led directly to better time-keeping. Thus in November, 1917, the following returns were sent in by controlled firms engaged in general engineering[3]:—

	No. of Firms.	Workpeople.	Avoidable loss per head.	Percentage of employees losing over six hours per week.
One-break system ..	147	47,000	1·1	1·9
Two-break system ..	5,062	150,000	2·2	4·7

Later reports agreed that loss of time was reduced by more than one-half as a result of a later morning start. The movement for a shorter working day with one break, which was growing in the year 1917-18, and which marked a reversion to the pre-war experience of many enlightened firms, was opposed largely because of the dislocation, involved by the change, in established agreements as to standard hours and wages. It was primarily for this reason that the Department was unable, under war conditions, to take the initiative in this movement for the reorganisation of the working day.[4]

Welfare.—Much stress was laid by the Welfare and Health Section on the importance of good working conditions and considerate supervision in securing regular attendance at work, and a model system of recording the time-keeping of individuals was prescribed for national factories and recommended to controlled establishments. The position with regard to time-keeping among women was summed up as follows by the director of the Women's Welfare Section of the Department after an intensive study of a number of cases of alleged bad time-keeping referred in August, 1918, for investigation.[5] (The women as a whole were said to come out well from this inquiry, except in five firms with bad working conditions.)

---

[1] Cf. first Report of Committee on Production, February, 1915; Third Report of Committee on National Expenditure, 1918; M.W. 151449, etc.

[2] Cf. *Final Report of Health of Munition Workers Committee* (Cd. 9065 of 1918), Section 8.

[3] Monthly Reports on Time-keeping.

[4] See p. 132 ff.

[5] L.R. 107/70.

" Prevention is better than cure, and for women moderate hours, no work before breakfast and good supervision by a first-rate welfare supervisor are the conditions which produce good time-keeping."

The experience of munition firms appears to show that this constructive view of the requisites for good time-keeping applies, *mutatis mutandis*, to workers as a whole.[1]

IV. Some Conclusions.

The Departme..t, in order to secure good time-keeping and the maximum output of munitions, utilised in varying degrees the force of public opinion ; deterrence, through the agency of munitions tribunals and the Labour Enlistment Complaints Committees ; and the co-operation of workers through the Labour Advisory Boards, trade unions, and, to some small extent, works committees. With the problems of factory organisation it was not possible to deal constructively during the war, except—and this was important—in so far as welfare conditions were involved. The Department's experience showed (1) that the elimination or reduction of lost time involves scientific study of " optimum " hours of work, of methods of wage payment, of welfare conditions, of the reaction of health on efficiency ; (2) that therewith careful record keeping, especially by the larger firms, is desirable ; (3) and that in so far as unpunctuality is a psychological or moral failing, much could be done by public opinion, *e.g.*, through a works committee, but that there are limits to its efficacy unless some " sanction " is in the background such as penalties inflicted by an industrial court.

The chief investigation officers sometimes expressed to the Department their doubt of the efficacy of this apparently thankless branch of their activities. Towards the end of the war period, however, they reported that definite results were visible. Thus the Chief Investigation Officer at Glasgow, whose time-keeping scheme, though originated

---

[1] An official decoration for good time-keeping was considered.

On 15 March, 1915, Lord Kitchener had made the following statement in the House of Lords : " I feel strongly that the men working long hours in the shops by day and night, week in and week out, are doing their duty for their King and Country in a like manner with those who have joined the army for active service in the field. I am glad to be able to state that His Majesty has approved that where service in this great work has .been thoroughly, loyally and continuously rendered, the award of a medal will be granted on the successful termination of the war."

A small committee, under the chairmanship of Sir George Younger, was appointed by the Minister in November, 1916, to consider the fulfilment of this pledge. Various tests of " thorough, loyal and continuous " service were considered, and the possibility of using time-keeping records for this purpose was specially investigated. But the unsatisfactory character of almost all such records, and the obvious administrative difficulties involved, caused the abandonment of a time-keeping, or indeed, of any statistical test. In January, 1918, the committee reported that no general reward could be recommended, but that the King's pledge would be admirably fulfilled by grants under the Order of the British Empire for specially good munitions service.

Parliamentary Debates (1915). *H. of L.*, XVIII., 724 ; HIST. REC. R. 320 47.

in his office, was substantially the same as that in other areas, gave statistical evidence of improved time-keeping during the summer of 1918, and, reviewing its operation after the Armistice, considered the work to have been really successful. " In so far," he wrote, " as this area is concerned, employers and works managers generally have extended a warm welcome to the time-keeping officers, and have expressed full and frank appreciation of the work done.   In most cases it has been intimated that the system initiated by these officers will be carried on at any rate as regards the recording of habitual offenders, and this is a practical recognition of the value of a system which was at the outset criticised by many firms as an additional burden on an overworked staff.   The discipline was generally accepted by employees without friction.   It is a significant fact that less than 1 per cent. of prosecution cases have been defended by trade union officials."[1]

Deterrence is clearly only one method, and not the most permanent, of preventing loss of time in the working day.   It is on account of its fundamental connection with welfare—*i.e.*, the improvement of factory conditions, and the provision of good environment for the industrial worker, with the co-operation of labour for this end—that an account of the Department's time-keeping policy has a place among these chapters.

---

[1] L.R. 107 and (Printed) *Weekly Report*, Labour Section.

CHAPTER VIII.

A FEW LOCAL EXAMPLES OF WELFARE REGULATION.

The widely varying range of the control of working conditions under the Munitions of War Acts may be illustrated by a few brief records of the material side of welfare provision in particular centres. No attempt has been made to gauge the " human " and personal side emphasised by enthusiasts for the welfare movement.

The system as a whole had naturally most ample scope in the Government establishments and national factories, although there were very complete expositions of a " welfare " policy with regard to labour in a number of controlled firms.

I. Woolwich Arsenal.

In the group of factories comprised in Woolwich Arsenal every difficulty involved in the problem of labour supply and regulation in war time was focussed, on account, first, of the very large scale on which production was carried on, in a necessarily limited area, and, secondly, of the high standard and very varied character of the output.[1]

The following statistics as to the numbers employed and the rapidity of their growth illustrate the first point without further comment :—

Date.	Men.		Women.		Boys.		Total.
1 August, 1914	9,466	..	125	..	1,275	..	10,866
2 January, 1915	19,378	..	194	..	3,059	..	22,631
4 December, 1915	37,749	..	609	..	7,540	..	45,898
13 May, 1916 ..	44,025	..	8,104	..	7,704	..	59,833
30 December,1917	41,000	..	25,700	..	6,000	..	72,700

The second outstanding characteristic caused special difficulties with regard to the maintenance of a supply of skilled workmen, in face of the Department's policy of dilution and the claims of military service, which, from the outbreak of the war to the end of 1917, removed 11,250 men from the Arsenal. The welfare department at Woolwich, was entrusted with the execution of the work connected with the badging and debadging of skilled Arsenal workmen, the enforcement of the Schedule of Protected Occupations and of the Military Service Acts, the employment of war munition volunteers, and the conduct of cases before munitions tribunals.

While questions concerning the supply of labour thus necessarily involved a large amount of administrative work, much detailed care was given to welfare and working conditions in the Arsenal.

---

[1] C.E. 1947/15 ; HIST. REC./H./346/3 (Memorandum on the work of the Woolwich Welfare Department, by Mr. A. H. Self).

Housing.—Before the war, Woolwich, like most industrial centres, had been overcrowded and a building scheme was under consideration. With the importation of 60,000 fresh workers for the Arsenal, the pressure for housing became intense. To meet this, a garden suburb was built at Well Hall, providing accommodation for 1,298 households, and seven estates of five-roomed bungalows were developed, providing at the end of 1918 for 2,654 families, a number later increased. These were managed by the Arsenal welfare supervision department. Residential hostels were erected to accommodate 750 boys, 2,600 women and 2,000 men, four of these being under the direct supervision of the department.

Transit.—The local congestion in transit was one of the most acute causes of fatigue to the Arsenal workers in 1915 and 1916. This was impossible to cure completely, but it was greatly remedied by the provision of better omnibus, tram and railway services, by the establishment of a river ferry controlled by the welfare department, and by a careful arrangement of the shifts of work of the different factories within the Arsenal, in order to distribute the 60,000 to 90,000 passengers as far as possible at intervals in the 24 hours.

Canteens.—These were provided partly by private enterprise, but increasingly by the welfare department. Early in 1918 the canteens supplied through the welfare department were able to serve 80,000 to 90,000 meals daily. Their takings were £1,000 per day, they employed 1,000 workers, and their supply depot issued daily 20 to 25 tons of foodstuffs. The canteens latterly opened by the department were carefully planned on modern lines, and quick efficient service was insisted upon.

Hours of Work.—Examples of the very long hours worked at Woolwich up to the autumn of 1916 have been already quoted.[1] They were caused by the demand for output from the Arsenal workshops, with their special equipment of experienced workmen and machinery, and by the congestion in traffic and housing which made it impossible to substitute three eight-hour for two twelve-hour shifts in the 24 hours. They were, however, the subject of vigorous protests by the Health of Munition Workers Committee and the Hours of Labour Committee in the course of 1916, and from the late autumn the overtime and the weekly number of shifts per worker were shortened, though they remained heavy as compared with those in very many controlled establishments. Sunday work for women was abolished in the course of 1917, and at the end of 1917 the Sunday day shift was cancelled.

Welfare Work for Boys.—A special section of the department dealt with the welfare of the 6,000 to 7,000 boy workers on whom the effects of very long hours, high earnings, and continued repetition work, in the great majority of cases without industrial prospects, bore heavily. Six special welfare supervisors for boys were appointed, and efforts were made both to reduce the number of boys employed on

---

[1] See pp. 88, 101.

unskilled work by the substitution of women, and to diminish the bad effects of long journeys superimposed on the day's work by refusing to engage those boys who lived more than an hour's journey from their work, and by offering some amenities such as a summer camp and evening clubs. Boys, however, under the abnormal conditions under which they were living showed little desire for ordinary clubs. There was heavy " wastage " and frequent changes in the boys employed. Between the outbreak of war and the Armistice, 24,000 boys had.been placed at the Arsenal by the Woolwich Employment Exchange, which in one year imported over 1,100 boys from a hundred distant exchanges.[1]

The Welfare of Women and Girls.—The welfare of women and girl workers was provided for on a very large scale, and, on the whole, under better conditions than the similar work for boys, because women workers and many of the processes on which they were employed were practically new to the Arsenal in 1916 and fresh accommodation obviously had to be provided for them. The following is a general sketch of what was attempted for them (again under very difficult circumstances which rendered the complete attainment of ideals of welfare provision impossible), given by Miss Lilian Barker, who was appointed Lady Superintendent at Woolwich Arsenal in December, 1915.[2]

At the date of Miss Barker's appointment the number of women and girls working at Woolwich Arsenal was about 500. From that time the numbers increased enormously, and when the Armistice was signed, 27,000 women were employed.

One of the most important considerations throughout the work was the selection of the women. Practically every woman was interviewed by the Lady Superintendent personally, and workers were encouraged to come to her or to their welfare supervisor when in difficulties. It was important also that the right woman should be selected for the right work. The medical examination determined whether a woman was fit physically for her work, but it was necessary also to see that a worker for light work, such as fuse making and gauging had deft nimble fingers, that machine workers were not too old, and that the workers for T.N.T. were steady, healthy women. Charge hands and group leaders were mostly women promoted from amongst their fellow workers for their steady and capable work, but for the more responsible posts, such as Principal Overlookers or Assistant Forewomen, it was invariably found advisable to select well educated women, with some experience in organising, who were likely to be popular with the girls and at the same time demand good discipline.

Welfare supervisors were also appointed (at the rate of 1 for every 1,000 women), and their duties were to ascertain that the comforts which had been arranged for the women were utilised. Long fire-proof overalls and caps for the workers in danger buildings, rational clothing (tunic and trousers) for those girls who were working on trucks where skirts were likely to hamper their movements, waterproof garments

---

[1] HIST. REC./R./346/42.   [2] HIST. REC./R./346/33.

for those who were exposed to the weather, were the regulation clothing, which it was part of the supervisor's duty to see was properly worn and regularly changed.

For the general health of the worker it was necessary to ascertain that every factory was properly ventilated, that seats were provided for the girls, that there was a break during the morning when they could get light refreshments (a 10-minutes' break in the five hours' morning spell was introduced after some months' experience of women's employment at the Arsenal), that there were ample canteens where they could get nourishing food at a reasonable cost, and that there was a quiet rest room attached where they could rest after their meals if they so wished. Women working on powders such as T.N.T. were provided with special clothes for canteen wear, so as to preclude any danger of their eating their food in gowns that had become impregnated with powder. Abundant ablution rooms, cloak rooms and shifting rooms were provided, and were daily inspected by the supervisors; bathrooms were also erected where the workers on T.N.T. could bathe, whenever they wished, in the factory time.

To provide recreation for the workers, evening classes were started in conjunction with the London County Council, in subjects such as singing, first aid, home nursing, gymnastics, elocution. Concerts in connection with these classes were held fortnightly at the Woolwich Town Hall, and frequent dances and entertainments were given by the girls. Football, hockey, country rambles, and all sports were organised and largely appreciated by the workers, while evening clubs were opened for those of the workers who did not live too far off to profit by them.

Holidays were arranged for both the workers and their children. This was a great help, as it was often difficult for a mother to arrange to go with her children and leave her work. There was also a small convalescent home, and here girls were sent when they showed signs of fatigue or breakdown. The home was used largely as a preventive, rather than actually as a home for the sick. In the last year of the war, holiday houses were organised, and to each of these a party of girls was taken by the supervisor in charge of the factory from which the girls were drawn.

Homes for the babies of the workers were another necessity, and two crèches, for the children of either married or unmarried workers, were started. These were staffed with qualified nurses, under the supervision of the Advisory Committee on Women's Employment attached to the Employment Exchange, together with a Home for Ailing Babies and an Infant Welfare Centre, inaugurated by the American Red Cross Society.

With the signing of the Armistice, the duties of the welfare department at Woolwich became more arduous. Meetings were held in all the factories, at which the women were asked, if they could live without working, to take their discharge immediately. Also those who had a trade, and could return to it, were advised to do so at once. The vacancies that were occurring for clerks in the Army Pay Corps, and for V.A.D. members, were made known, and every girl was asked to come to the Lady Superintendent for advice if she needed it. Numbers of women and girls were put back to domestic service. Lists of suitable advertisements from all the papers were noted each day, and every woman who wanted work and could not get it for herself, was helped as far as was humanly possible. Widows, particularly the pre-war widows with no pension, were the first consideration, and the majority of these were placed on salvage and sewing work for the Dockyard.

II. " Welfare " in a National Factory.

It is impossible to produce either a composite portrait or a wholly typical sample of the control of working conditions in one of the 200 national factories. The Department had probably most complete scope for an effective welfare policy at the National Projectile Factory at Birtley, and the National Explosives Factory at Gretna, both of which were free from the special difficulties which beset such a policy at Woolwich. The detailed provision made in the one case for a Belgian community of 6,000 established in the bare fields of County Durham, in the other for a factory population of 24,700 and a settlement population of 13,485 planted by the Department in the solitude of the Border country, is described in detail in connection with the history of the Department's housing policy.[1]

The following notes, supplied by a member of the staff, give a bare outline of the formal provisions for welfare—on a less comprehensive scale than was possible at Birtley or Gretna—at the Cardonald National Projectile Factory.[2]

" From June, 1916, to December, 1918, the Welfare Supervisor passed through her hands into the factory 6,121 individual girls, who had been sent for selection from the Govan Labour Exchange. On interviewing a girl her record was written on a card which was placed in an index in the Welfare Office, and this card had the whole subsequent history of the girl's career from start to finish. Usually we had from 2,200 to 2,500 women workers. The following table gives the exact numbers with the length of time they spent in the Factory, and incidentally illustrates the shifting employment among women factory workers :

Number of Women Workers Employed June, 1916, to December, 1918.

Time in Factory.	Left.	Paid off or demobilised on completion of Contract.	Total.	Percentage of Total.
Two years and over ..	99	.. 780	.. 879	.. 13·6
Eighteen months and over	368	.. 331	.. 699	.. 10·8
One year and over ..	492	.. 310	.. 802	.. 12·4
Six months and over ..	652	.. 417	.. 1,069	.. 16·6
Under six months and over two weeks ..	1,297	.. 1,002	.. 2,299	.. 33·6
Two weeks and under ..	325	.. 68	.. 393	.. 6·1
Unknown	313	.. —	.. 313	.. 4·9
	3,546	.. 2,908	.. 6,454	

---

[1] Vol. V, Part V.   [2] Hist. Rec./R./346/26.

" The total number of workers started was 6,454. Of this number 3,546, or 55 per cent., left or were dismissed ; 2,908, or 45 per cent., were dispensed with owing to alterations and restrictions or were demobilised.

" *Hours of Work.*—Our shifts were never reduced from the 11½ hours day and 12½ hours night. For the first two months we worked seven days and seven nights per week. The Saturday half-holiday was conceded in April, 1917, and Sunday work knocked off.

" *Welfare Staff.*—This consisted of : Assistant Welfare Supervisor, Night Superintendent, Linen Room Superintendent, four Nurses, 36 Forewomen, and an Outdoor Welfare Visitor, whose duty was to call upon any workers who were off duty through illness, to enquire into cases of distress, and to collect information regarding lodgings for the benefit of new employees coming from the country.

" *Ambulance Rooms.*—These, one for men and one for women, were also in charge of the Welfare Department and were staffed by four trained nurses, one for each room on each shift. The cases handled included dressings, sometimes exceeding 100 per day. Records of all ambulance cases were made and kept by a specially appointed clerk on a quadruplicate form. One copy was sent to the Works Manager to be used as Certificate for illness or absence, and in order that he might take action in case of accidents to provide against recurrence, and collect evidence in case of an enquiry. Another copy was sent to the Secretary's Department, as notification in view of the case involving compensation. The third copy was sent to the Welfare Supervisor, for enquiry from the Welfare point of view, and to follow up in case of the patient being laid up either at home, in lodgings, or in hospital. The fourth copy on a stiff card remained in the Ambulance Room, as their record, and space was provided on the back for the subsequent history of the case. The Factory Doctor visited the Ambulance Room once a week, when the Welfare Supervisor brought to him for examination girls about whose health and strength there was doubt ; compensation cases and cases of possible malingering were also then dealt with.

" *Cloak Rooms.*—The Girls' Time Offices and entrance doors opened straight into the Cloak Rooms, from which one set of doors led into the Factory and the other into the Canteen. A double row of basins with hot and cold water, clean roller towels at any meal hour and change of shift, and an ample supply of plastic antiseptic soap, were placed down the whole length of the room, and the hat and coat racks were divided by a wooden partition to form separate rooms for each shift ; these were sub-divided into sections, numbered and labelled with the Forewoman's name. There were also regular dressing rooms for those who had to make a complete change, such as crane and transport girls. A forewoman (with a staff of four charge hands and four cleaners) was responsible for order and cleanliness on each shift ;

petty thieving was in this way reduced to about nothing, and the free fight which heralded the change of shift and each meal hour during the first two months ceased to exist.

" *Discipline and Conduct.*—The technical training and the actual production of the girls was in the hands of the various foremen, but all matters of conduct and breaches of discipline were dealt with by the Forewomen, except in the case of serious breaches, which were dealt with by the Supervisor. No worker was dismissed or left the Factory without the knowledge and consent of the Welfare Supervisor, who went into each case individually. Her consent was also necessary for the promotion of an ordinary worker to be charge hand.

· " *Factory Clothing.*—The supplying and cleaning of the different uniforms and overalls worn by the girls was looked after. Each suit or overall was washed at least once a week, and, in some operations where soiling was more frequent, as many as two or three changes per week were supplied. Special garments were also available for particular jobs, such as woollen jerseys and oilskin suits for outdoor occupations, clogs, gloves, etc., and thick corduroy suits for Crane Girls and Transport Workers in winter.

" *The Canteen.*—This did not come under the Welfare Department, except the Girls' Dining Hall, which was also used as a Recreation Room, and which had special Forewoman, Charge Hand and staff of cleaners. It was found advisable to provide within half-an-hour after starting, a cup of cocoa or beef tea at a nominal charge ; also at 4 o'clock on both shifts a cup of tea was provided free to every worker.

" *Fatigue Study.*—As a result of much thought it was decided to select one of the best and most practical forewomen to undertake the duties of studying all of the operations in succession, in order to provide data for the study and elimination of Fatigue. The Armistice was signed before the scheme could be started.

" *Crèche.*—In 1917 it was decided to obtain sanction for the establishment of a crèche, having accommodation for 60 or 70 babies, especially children of soldiers' wives and widows working in the Factory. The idea was enthusiastically taken up by the workers, and within a short time there was raised by voluntary subscription and other means £1,200, or a quarter of the total cost.

" *Extra Official Duties.*—In addition to the foregoing the Welfare Department undertook the dispensation of the money collected from the workers for distress purposes, chiefly through the offices of the Welfare Outdoor Visitor. The Welfare Supervisor was also a member of the Hospital Committee, which was responsible for issuing admission forms to any of the workers requiring hospital or convalescent treatment. The Welfare Supervisor was responsible for convening the Girls' Recreation Committee. This Committee provided a piano, gramaphone and library for the Dining Hall ; they also rented a

V–3   G 2

Recreation Field, which they equipped with garden seats ; they founded three different Girls' Football Teams, and were responsible for organising many Red Cross Entertainments, both in the Canteen and in various Hospitals round about the City. They also defrayed the cost of many picnics for wounded soldiers."

III. Progress in the Smaller Controlled Firms.

In contrast to the large scale examples already quoted, the following accounts by welfare officers of the Department illustrate the limits of practicable improvements in certain small controlled establishments :—

(1) A small firm employing, in June, 1916, 55 women (in addition to men) on springs and axles for Lewis gun carts, etc.

The work was said by the factory inspector to be heavy and very dirty, the women of a " rough Black Country type," working from 6 to 6 and 6 to 1 at about 16s. a week. The factory was old and inconvenient, with no arrangements at all for washing. The management was said to be " not really unsympathetic, but the need to consider welfare conditions for their workers had not struck them." By October, 1916, on the recommendation of the welfare officer, one of the women employees had been made responsible for the discipline of her fellow workers, some washing arrangements had been made and everything was much tidier. A year later (when the numbers had grown to 500 men and boys and 100 women) the welfare officer reported that caps and overalls had been provided for the women workers and there was general improvement. " Although it will always remain a rough place of the usual Black Country type, the arrangements are satisfactory on the whole."[1]

(2) An old established firm of bolt and nut makers, whose head was said to be " ready and anxious to do anything for the welfare of his workers."

Here in June, 1916, there were 300 women employed—" a good type whose fathers and mothers had been in the trade. There were women of 70 years old who came when they left school ; their daughters and relations were also working." Their earnings were said to average 14s. 6d. per week of 54 hours. Discipline was wholly by men. There was no provision for washing except one broken basin, since the girls were said to prefer to use the " suds " from their work. The welfare section recommended the appointment of a woman supervisor, the provision of a mess room and of means of washing. By the date of the Armistice no welfare supervisor had been appointed, but washing arrangements were somewhat improved and a canteen had been built despite real difficulties as to a site.[2]

(3) " A small factory founded in the eighteenth century, with dirty and rather dark shops, next to a refuse heap, two miles from anywhere."

[1] C.E. 1260/15.   [2] C.E. 1227/15.

Saucepans, stewpots, hand grenades, were being made in February, 1916, by 60 women and 300 men. The factory possessed a mess room. The girls made any complaints to the foreman " with the cook as intermediary." The welfare section recommended the appointment of a forewoman to look after the girls, better washing accommodation and a cloak room. By October, 1918, a woman charge hand had been detailed to act as supervisor, the place was a good deal cleaner, and two or three basins had been provided, but no further washing arrangements had been made as the girls were said to prefer to use buckets. The firm stated that it was not doing well financially and could not afford to provide a cloak room.[1]

As has been said, some of the most complete systems of provision for industrial welfare were to be found in certain controlled establishments. In others, especially in the smaller factories, progress had often perforce to be slow, as measured by the rate of acceleration applied to industry during the war.

---

[1] C.E. 1918/15.

CHAPTER IX.

CONCLUSIONS.

I. The Significance of the Munitions Welfare Movement.

(a) WELFARE AND THE DEPARTMENT'S LABOUR POLICY.

The significance of the welfare movement among munition workers cannot be fairly estimated without some reference to its contemporary setting.

The Department's policy with regard to welfare and working conditions was a logical complement to its control of the supply of labour as well as of war material. If the maximum output of munitions was to be obtained, it was clearly essential to have a reliable supply of labour. Hence the different restrictions on labour imposed by the Munitions of War Acts. To a great extent, these restrictions and the welfare measures of the Department were negative and positive aspects of the same policy of securing stability and efficiency of labour in the interests of output ; and their efficacy can be judged best in conjunction. Thus, the much criticised "leaving certificate" rules, under Section 7 of the Munitions of War Act, were issued in order to keep restless workers from moving from factory to factory ; the same end could be, and was in many firms, reached, apart from their standards of wages, by the provision of good conditions and considerate management. Bad time-keeping, as has been pointed out in detail, could be dealt with either by deterrent or constructive treatment; petty disputes and strikes—virtually forbidden under Part I. of the Munitions of War Act, but constantly occurring—could be prevented in many cases by good standards of discipline, and by exercise of the "tact" which employers frequently said was the first requisite of welfare supervision.

It is indeed possible to over-estimate the connection between these two sides of labour regulation. No improvement in working conditions or friendly intervention in individual firms would, of course, prevent strikes on industrial principle, nor would they cure fundamental antagonisms between capital and labour. Thus while much of the industrial unrest among munition workers centred in the Clyde districts, where working and living conditions tended to be bad, it also expressed itself in frequent strikes in the Coventry engineering works and in the new aircraft factories, where special consideration had been given to the workers' comfort. But with full acknowledgment of its limitations in this respect, the welfare movement should be considered as a complement to the so-called "industrial compulsion" of the Munitions of War Act and its first amendment.

(b) Industrial Welfare and other Social Movements.

The period of the war coincided with a marked development of civic consciousness, taking form in multitudinous common activities, prescribed by Government Departments or organised spontaneously, and controlled by " local representative committees " drawn from all classes, including labour. These operated with varying effectiveness to meet many common needs, and supplied a training ground in combined action for social welfare outside the sphere of normal municipal administration. It coincided also with a notable increase of interest in and provision for health, public and individual, and with a marked rise in the standard of living of the working class as a whole, and especially in the position of the " bottom dog "—the unskilled workman—together with that of women and young people as wage earners. The movement for a parallel improvement in working conditions was a natural corollary to these three lines of development. Were the works, it might be asked, in which was passed the greater part of the waking day of the industrial worker to be isolated from the effects of these and similar movements ?

The demand for better working conditions, as distinct in this case from shorter hours, was beginning to become effective among wage earners before the end of the war ; and the movement for " joint control " in industry was preparing to give expression and direction to this through the welfare committees attached to the National Industrial Councils in certain industries and the growing welfare activities of works committees.

(c) Some Current Opinions.

This movement towards industrial welfare was, as has been already indicated, not without criticism.

Apart from conservative opposition in some cases to changes in organisation and from reluctance in other cases, chiefly of bad relationship with their workpeople, to provide anything beyond essentials for their benefit, employers complained of the expense involved. The standard of industrial welfare set by the Department, despite Government allowances towards part of the cost, involved a firm, it was said, in payments of a large amount for wages and salaries for unproductive workers—charwomen, canteen waiters, cloakroom matrons, cooks, charge-hands, nurses, welfare supervisors, doctors. Such provision, in so far as it was primarily for the benefit of women workers, must affect the standard of wages payable to women in industry,[1] while, if it was for the benefit of men and women workers alike, greatly increased efficiency of labour was required in competitive production to compensate for such expenditure. To this objection the Department could reply by quoting the emphatic opinion of a number of successful employers, who asserted from their own experience that " welfare pays," by improved timekeeping, by more efficient labour, by the prevention of disputes in the works, by the checking of labour wastage, and by change of " tone " in the works

---

[1] Cf. L.R. 5581 *passim* for representations on this point by the Employers' Consultative Committee.

which was reflected in output and factory costs. It was, however, a type of criticism that could not be readily and completely disposed of, especially in the smaller firms, where such expenditure inevitably worked out at a comparatively high rate per head of the employees, and in firms where provision for welfare did not produce an immediate increase in efficiency or smooth working.

The attempts of the Department to popularise provision for industrial welfare were to some extent handicapped by the fact that p opaganda for its adoption by employers began almost at the same time as energetic propaganda to induce workmen to accept the dilution of labour. " What are the employers getting at ? " was a question reported in the early stages of the welfare movement by those in touch with the trade union rank and file. Welfare measures were, it was said, an attempt to increase output, desirable indeed during the war, but leading ultimately to employers' profits.[1] This suspicion recurred, as the efforts to persuade the workmen to agree, in fact as we.l as in theory, to the suspension of trade union privileges was followed by growing industrial fatigue, by resentment among certain types of workers over the " debadging " of skilled men, and over the Department's efforts to hold the balance between the interests of the skilled and unskilled workmen (as in the Trade Card negotiations of 1916-17 and the granting of the $12\frac{1}{2}$ per cent. bonus of 1917-18), and at the same time to support the adoption of systems for payment by results in which some workmen feared that their standard rates were to be submerged. In practice, workers were commonly very ready to avail themselves of good accommodation and the help and friendship of supervisors, nurses and doctors ; in theory, distrust of bureaucratic intervention and of capitalist " philanthropy " reappeared at intervals ; while certain types of the workers felt and urged that they were being offered *panem et circenses*—subsidised[2] canteens and recreation grounds —in place of the reconstruction of industry. By the date of the Armistice, workmen as a whole, like those represented by the Woolwich Trades Council,[3] probably fully accepted the welfare movement, whether inaugurated by employers or by a Government Department, in so far as it had actually come their way. A large number, however, claimed to control it ; *i.e.*, to have an effective say in the adjustment of their working conditions, meals, ventilation, starting hours, discipline, as well as of hours and wages.

Outside critics sometimes said that this work of spreading the welfare of munition workers was beyond the sphere of a temporary Department created for the rapid production of war material, and that it should, in fact, if undertaken at all, have been left to the Home Office. This has already been discussed, and it has been represented that a new " extra-legal " standard could best be reached by an employing Department, exercising no compulsory powers, for which public

[1] " The more we produce, the more idlers will have to waste, and the more skilled men we will be able to spare for Churchill to play Napoleon with." (General Secretary's letter. Boilermakers' *Monthly Report*, November, 1919.)

[2] Appendix I.   [3] See p. 49.

opinion was not yet ripe, and unhampered by the disciplinary duties necessarily exercised by the Home Office in the enforcement of the Factory Code.

But apart from this question of relations between Departments, it might be asked whether it was in principle desirable to centre the workers' welfare in either a Government Department or an individual firm. Should the State thus take power to enforce (as in the Munitions of War Amendment Act and the Police, Factories, etc., Act of 1916) not only the necessary minimum required for efficiency of output, but also the amenities of industrial life, such as those offered by canteens ? This, it might be argued, was indeed an advance on the spirit of factory legislation bequeathed by Shaftesbury and his supporters and acquiesced in by employers in the forties of last century.

Further, should such amenities, from whatever source instigated, cluster round any one place of employment ? The firm could thus absorb the seven ages of life of a workman, who might, without exaggeration, attend the factory crèche as a baby, play on its recreation ground as a child, join its works school and scout troop as a boy, belong to its football club and social institute as a youth, bring up his family in one of its cottages, receive medical treatment during illness or accident in later life with financial help from the management or the works sick fund, and end his days as the pensioner of the firm or the works benefit society. One disadvantage in such comprehensive schemes is, as has been suggested by a well-known employer,[1] the temptation to use them as a form of advertisement and thus lose all the advantage aimed at therein as a link between capital and labour and a stimulus to *esprit de corps* in the factory. The theoretical objections to such a connection between the workman and the individual firm have been already discussed ; they appear equally in all criticisms, from the point of view of either capital or labour, of " prosperity-sharing " or profit sharing as between capital and labour. Apart, however, from this problem of industrial relationships there is a further point of principle involved in the question (which was raised in another form, in the trade union world, by the unofficial Shop Steward movement)—should the locality or the works—the tie of neighbourhood or of occupation—be the centre of the workers' interests other than those strictly connected with the earning of wages ? With the shortening of the working day and the growth of leisure for the manual worker, this question became of practical importance. The experience of the Ministry of Munitions did not, however, continue long enough for its solution.

II. Some Effects of Control by the Department.

Leaving these unsettled questions of principle, some results of the Department's policy with regard to welfare and working conditions

---

[1] HIST. REC./R./346/105.

among munition makers may be summarised. These results were often singularly incongruous in appearance, though not in fact, with the ostensible aims for which the Department was created.

(a) RESULTS IN MUNITION WORKS.

1. The welfare policy of the Department ensured a standard of physical comfort for nearly 350,000 workers in national factories and government establishments, much above the minimum required under the Factory and Workshop Acts, and it stimulated a similar provision of canteens, rest-rooms, ambulance rooms and other material comforts, to a greater or less degree, in a large proportion of the other controlled establishments, in which at least 400,000 women munition workers were employed. This increased comfort was extended, though to a considerably less extent, among a million and a quarter men and nearly a quarter of a million boys similarly employed by controlled firms and in national factories.[1]

2. It pushed forward the movement, existing in a very limited number of factories before the war, to focus in some one responsible person, or section of the management, the care of the health and physical needs of a firm's employees. The title of " welfare supervisor," or " welfare department," was an admittedly cumbrous description of the functions of such an officer or group of officers, but was generally adopted at the time as a description of their rapidly extemporised duties. By the date of the Armistice 550 supervisors of women, and 275 boys' supervisors had been appointed from the Department's panel, and it was estimated that there were 1,000 women supervisors of different grades in the munitions works of the country.

3. The Welfare Section stimulated the provision of special training for this new branch of factory administration, so that training for welfare supervision or its equivalent was, even after the special needs of the munition factories ceased, a recognised part of the programme of the social science schools of most universities. The Department was not able definitely to standardise the training or the equipment required for these officials, though careful consideration was given to the subject. Nor did it enforce their appointment, except in most of the national factories and in those in which T.N.T. work was done. But it created and fostered a demand for them, and greatly increased the quantity and quality of the available supply.

4. The Department similarly organised and greatly extended the sphere of the works doctor, through the appointment of such officials to a large proportion of the national factories. These doctors, with the specialists at head-quarters, to a great extent diminished, though they did not prevent, the dangers to workers of handling the poisonous sub-

---

[1] See Vol. VI., Part IV., for detailed statistics.

stances required for the supply of explosives.   Their work, and the studies of physiological effects of fatigue, of good and bad ventilation, and other conditions of employment, made by experts connected with the Department, led to improved conditions for munition workers, but also showed how large a field of industrial hygiene remained to be explored either by official or unofficial agencies.   Efforts to regularise work and improve time-keeping equally showed the need for more detailed future study of the subject, in connection both with the workers' health and with factory organisation.   During the war, however, the Department could claim to have improved time-keeping among munition workers by methods of deterrence exercised by investigation officers and munitions tribunals, and by the more positive action of improved transit and organised welfare.

5. Through this policy of promoting health and comparative comfort in factories the Department entered on the far more difficult problem—difficult, because psychological rather than material—of labour management.   The acceptance of munitions tribunals, established chiefly to enforce a simple standard of workshop discipline, was, to some extent, a recognition, equally by employers and workers, that labour management on the one side and the observance of discipline on the other was, at least in time of war, of national and not merely of local or sectional importance.

6. The establishment of the welfare supervisor in factories, warmly recommended by the Welfare and Health Section of the Department, was also an acknowledgment, new to many firms, that the handling of labour needs special care.   The special training of forewomen and women charge-hands, one of the solutions of administrative difficulties suggested and in a few cases introduced for the small factory or the firm with scattered branches, or equally, the promotion of the welfare supervisor to a definite position on the staff with rank as a manager, was a recognition of the need for some such special allocation of powers and for improvement in the detailed management of labour, so far, at least, as women were concerned.   The welfare supervisor, often an unspecialised social worker thrust into the position to "look after" the women and young people in a factory, tended steadily to obtain definite functions, whether as a nurse or a games mistress on the one side, or an "employment manager" or "apprentice master" on the other.

The scope of welfare supervision was still indeterminate at the date of the Armistice, though there seemed to be, as has been indicated, some tendency to separate the "managerial" from the "social" side—the control of employment from the provision of recreation. But whatever the developments of the supervisor's position (and these must obviously vary with the age and type of workers and the size of factory concerned), its significance remained unchanged, as a recognition of the "human needs of labour" and the need for some substitute for the lost personal touch in the big industry between over-busy representatives of capital and of labour.

Probably it was from this point of view that most welfare supervisors approached their work during the war.

7. The Department was closely concerned with problems of hours of work for munition workers, but its staff, as has been said, approached the administrative problems of regulating hours from wholly different points of view.[1] No ideal arrangement was possible during the war, but, in conjunction with the Home Office, the Department shortened the hours of munition workers after the extreme pressure of 1915 and the first eight months of 1916 was over, and secured the adoption of such shifts and breaks in long spells of work as should secure as much rest as then appeared possible for women and boys and girls. Incidentally, in dealing with the workers' holidays, with the regulation of overtime and with the proposed curtailment of the normal working day towards the end of the war, constant evidence was received both of the vigour of the survival in twentieth century Britain of local industrial usages and also of the dominance of wages questions in current industrial problems.[2]

The Department built, or promoted the building of, 11,738 flats and houses for munition workers. It provided hostels for more than 23,500 workers and secured further accommodation in a large number of other cases, together with lodgings and billets in private houses for munition workers. Two complete colonies at Birtley and Gretna were created by it, and its influence dominated the social life of the working-class population of a number of the smaller towns, such as Carlisle, in and near which munitions were produced.

8. In addition to its comprehensive housing policy, the Department provided directly for canteens and messrooms in the great majority of the 150 national and government factories, while the Central Liquor Control Board approved. on behalf of the Department, the canteens of some 740 controlled establishments and recommended the writing off of their capital cost to the extent of almost £2,000,000. During the last nine months of the war the Department controlled the food supplies of these canteens, which were estimated to be available if required for a million persons daily.

These two sections of the Department's activities are recorded in detail elsewhere,[3] but reference to them is unavoidable in an account of the general policy of industrial welfare of the Ministry of Munitions.

9. In carrying into effect this policy of control in the interests of efficiency, the Department maintained the principle that the State should, to a great extent, finance the emergency cost of such provision—a principle adopted on a very wide scale in the Government's housing policy of 1918-19. The proportion of such expenditure from which the owners of a factory were thus relieved is indicated in detail in Appendix I.

---

[1] See p. 100.   [2] See pp. 120, 131, 132.   [3] Vol. V., Parts IV. and V.

(b) The Progressive Adoption of Welfare Standards.

The above is a short summary of the action taken by the Department to ensure the efficiency of munitions labour in a time of continued stress and to realise in some degree its responsibility as a model employer. The machinery for these ends had, like that of the shell factories, in many cases to be rapidly improvised, and the results of its working cannot be measured accurately, although they undoubtedly diminished the bad effects on the workers of their efforts to " deliver the goods."[1]

The welfare movement stimulated by the Department was not, however, confined to munitions works. The *Factory Inspectors' Annual Report* for 1917-18 bore witness to the permeation of standards of welfare to the non-munition trades, such as

" cotton and woollen and worsted textiles, in laundries, in potteries, in biscuit factories . . where conditions, with honourable individual exceptions, have long been stationary, but here too . . . the new movement has begun to take effect. . . . In these and many other developments moving towards social welfare in non-munition factories in 1917, there is really less sudden a growth than it is apt to be considered. Enlightened workers have been asking for these things, and enlightened manufacturers have been demonstrating for many years that these improving conditions are both rightly demanded and practicable." " Before the war came, the Inspectors knew of a greatly increasing and extending desire on the part of manufacturers to improve the conditions of factory life beyond the statutory minimum, and the Inspectors have steadily worked both to respond to and increase that desire. Now common-sense awakened sees that the pace must be greatly quickened . . . It is not only in controlled and national factories that material advance has been made. The whole spirit of management has quickly changed in many factories and industries where no new welfare order runs, and where State control of profits has not entered."[2]

It is not possible to gauge accurately the extent to which this extension of industrial welfare was directly a reflex action, during the war, of the Department's propaganda, any more than it is possible to say definitely to what extent official control of munition workers' wages assisted in their increase in non-munition trades.[3] In both cases probably the reflex action was considerable. In its control of wages, the outstanding work of the Department was its contribution to the principle of standardisation by its adhesion to the principle of national wage advances under the auspices of the Committee

<hr>

[1] Cf. the medical evidence before the War Cabinet Committee on *Women in Industry*. [Cd. 135 and 167 of 1919].
[2] Cd. 9108 of 1918, pp. 16-17. See also Cd. 340 of 1919 (report for 1918).
[3] See Vol. V., Parts I. and II.

on Production, by its establishment of rates of payment which should be common to the women in all the different munition trades, and by its sanction to the elimination of many of the local differences in wage rates which had outlived the conventions or the economic causes to which they owed their origin. The control of welfare and working conditions introduced even more complex, though perhaps less contentious, problems than those connected with rates of wages and the working day. But here, too, the Department succeeded to a great extent in setting and reaching a standard. It did this, not primarily by compulsion, but by offering examples, advice or information, together with financial concessions. It utilised for this purpose its unparalleled position as an employer and the right of entry into factories exercised by its various officials. Much of its work had necessarily to be temporary, and welfare supervisors looking round in 1919 on deserted workplaces and canteens, might feel that the welfare movement had been as transitory as the workers. It is, however, fair to conjecture that this was not the case. Employers in many districts had seen the success of welfare measures on a large scale. Workers had, despite discomforts of overcrowding and long hours, been employed in a large proportion of the larger factories under good conditions, with consideration as definite as numbers would allow for health and general well-being. The tide that bore back " munition girls " after the Armistice to small workrooms or laundries or other industries, or possibly to domestic service, ensured the permeation of welfare standards to other employments and to more backward places. The effects were similar, though probably less, in the case of men munition makers. The transplanted workman, as he ceased to be required, e.g., for " diluted " labour in the big engineering shops, or for work in one of the aeroplane factories in which welfare conditions were as a whole good (but in which the advent of workmen from some dozen different trades caused almost insoluble difficulties of wages and hours), took back—in some cases at least—a standard of a reasonable degree of civilisation of industry. By July, 1918, 40 per cent. of the men and nearly 28 per cent. of the women engaged in industry were employed on munitions work in its widest sense,[1] and the welfare movement had therefore a wide possible sphere of influence.

This permeation of standards of industrial welfare, like the training in *esprit de corps* and common action obtained, for better or worse, by the workers aggregated in the big munition districts, was clearly one of the indirect social results of the production of war material for the Ministry of Munitions.

III. The Bequest of the Welfare Movement in Munitions Work.

The production of munitions put back the standard of hours of work, of the regulation of wages, of the liberty of labour to those of

---

[1] See Vol. VI., Part IV.

the reigns of George IV., or, in some degree, of Queen Elizabeth.[1] In face of this retrogression, the first Minister of Munitions foretold in February, 1916, the contribution to social progress of the welfare movement lately inaugurated by his Department.

"It is a strange irony, but no small compensation," said Mr. Lloyd George, "that the making of weapons of destruction should afford the occasion to humanise industry. Yet such is the case. Old prejudices have vanished, new ideas are abroad; employers and workers, the public and the State, are all favourable to new methods. This opportunity must not be allowed to slip. It may well be that, when the tumult of war is a distant echo and the making of munitions a nightmare of the past, the effort now being made to soften asperities, to secure the welfare of the workers, and to build a bridge of sympathy and understanding between employer and employed, will have left behind results of permanent and enduring value to the workers, to the nation, and to mankind at large."

If the welfare work of the Ministry of Munitions did not reach this ideal, yet, in addition to the immediate results attained, it left in 1919 a definite bequest to the progress of industry.

(a) A CONTRIBUTION TOWARDS "SCIENTIFIC MANAGEMENT."

It gave, and advertised, a demonstration of the application of scientific methods of labour control, as outlined by the Health of Munition Workers Committee and by other experts. This

---

[1] The Department was more than once reproached for its reversion to "Elizabethan principles" of labour regulation. (Cf. Vol. V., Part II., pages 67 and 116, and *Parliamentary Debates* (1916), *H. of C.*, LXXXV., 1734, etc.) The analogy between some of the provisions of the Munitions of War Act of 1915, and the Statute of Artificers of 1563, is of at least historic interest. Section seven of either Act limited the worker's right to fresh employment without a leaving certificate, and imposed penalties on both workman and employer for contravention of this provision. Equally, the employer's right to dismiss the worker was limited in either Act. The Statute of Artificers gave power to the State, as represented by local J.P.s, to fix wages, in accordance with cost of living and other circumstances, both for men and women, with penalties for employers exceeding these rates. (Cf. Sections 4(2) of the Munitions Act of 1915, and 6 and 7 of the Amending Act of 1916). It anticipated the Hours of Labour Policy of (different) sections of the Ministry of Munitions in fixing hours of work during part of the year at from 5 a.m. to 7 or 8 p.m., which equalled the working day of the engineer who was doing an "extra quarter" as overtime; in securing two hours for meal-times in this period, and even in providing for rest pauses during work, "half-an-hour at the most for the workman's sleape when hee is allowed to sleape, the which is from the mydst of May to the mydst of August." It anticipated the Ordering of Work Regulations for good order and time-keeping under Section 4 (5) of the Munitions of War Act, by its special provision for regular attendance "upon paine to lose and forfayte one peny for every hour's absence, to be deducted out of his wages that shall so offende," with ve y heavy penalties for insubordination during working hours. Even the prohibition of strikes by the Munitions Act was anticipated by the Act of Queen Elizabeth in section 10, which forbade a workman, under punishment of £5 fine and one month's imprisonment, to leave unfinished the building of a church, ship or mill—"work of national importance." The powers taken by the sixteenth century statute to obtain forced labour for employers (sections 3, 5 and 17), were not, however, despite the current catchwords of "industrial compulsion," re-asserted in the Munitions Acts.

application was admittedly very imperfect, but it marked a definite step forward in methods of production in this country, on lines similar to those followed at the same time by some of the "scientific management firms" of the United States, but avoiding the rather grotesque expedients of certain American pioneers.

(b) The Correlation of Agencies.

It began to break down the barrier, both within and without the factory, between industry and what is vaguely called "social" work, *i.e.*, the improvement of conditions of life by official and unofficial action. The war, in part, lifted the veil over factory life and lessened the gap existing between the administration of social and industrial laws. It may fairly be claimed that it is to the advantage of both forms of administration to bridge this gap, and that the welfare movement in munition factories was a step towards this. Thus the welfare supervisor (under whatever title) was able to supply a valuable link between the employees of the large factory and the application of recent social and industrial legislation in connection with Workmen's Compensation, Social Insurance, War Pensions, Trade Boards, etc.— legislation which is apt to prove a burden to the busy employer, and to lose much of its benefit to the employee, without intelligent and comparatively leisured interpretation. Similarly, attention was drawn from the other side to the need of co-operation between the life of the factory and the work, *e.g.*, of the school doctor, the club worker, and the continuation school. The Welfare Section left clear sign-posts to guide advance in this direction.

(c) A Demonstration in State Socialism.

The assumption by the Department of responsibility for the efficiency and the general well-being of munition makers led its officers, as has been said, into a number of apparently incongruous activities. The following is a small selection from the subjects thus considered :—

The provision of a factory herd of cows (for T.N.T. workers) ; the relative merits of cocoa and milk as a beverage for such workers ; the energy value contained in suet puddings ; the cost of hockey sticks and boxing gloves ; the erection of swings ; the purchase of flower seeds ; the establishment of play centres for children ; the choice of models, utilitarian and æsthetic, for factory caps and overalls ; the requirements of a boys' holiday camp ; the pros and cons of "mixed clubs" ; the area of washing trough required per worker ; the merits of different kinds of soap and soap boxes ; the comparative advantages of crèches and of their own older relatives for the care of babies whose mothers were employed in munition factories ; the overcrowding of tramcars and the supply of ferry boats ; the equipment, down to the last saucepan and floor mat, of hostels or of village centres such as Birtley and Gretna ; the degree of fatigue produced by housework or by shell production respectively (as a factor in decision as to the length of the day or night shift) ; the influence of holidays and of works cinemas as stimuli to output.[1]

---

[1] C.E. 1013/13 ; C.E. 1260/15 ; L.R. 1459/2 ; L.R. 8584 ; L.R. 218/45 ; Hist. Rec./R./346 ; C.E. 437 15 ; L.R. 2258, etc.

This medley of subjects may seem a *reductio ad absurdum* of State socialism or of " grandmotherly administration." Individual welfare, however, and the complex influences, material and immaterial, that lead to efficiency are inevitably varied ; questions such as those enumerated were dealt with at headquarters promptly, and with full recognition that they were essentially matters of local concern ; and the two spheres in which the detailed care of the Department was most exercised, at Birtley and Gretna, fully stood the test of demands for output.

IV. Distribution of the Work of the Welfare and Health Section.

The highly varied work of the Department with regard to the welfare and working conditions of munition workers was, after the Armistice, distributed as follows :—

The care of the welfare of factory boys was attached to the Training Department of the Ministry of Labour ; and an active Boys' Welfare Association carried on, unofficially, energetic propaganda for the spread of the movement.

Similarly the promotion of women's industrial welfare was transferred in part to the Training Department of the Ministry of Labour, while the Employment Exchange Department undertook responsibility for the registration of candidates for supervisors' posts. The Home Office also fostered the welfare movement, and issued in 1919 an explanatory pamphlet on the subject.[1] It also resumed, in full, control of hours of labour of protected persons. A strong central Institute of Welfare Workers further supplied an unofficial organisation for standardising welfare work and making it known.

Legislative provision for the extension of the welfare movement was in full operation when the work of the Department ceased. The Home Office continued to issue welfare orders under the Police, Factories, etc., Act of August, 1916. The Trade Boards Act of 1918 (Section 10) authorised Trade Boards to " make representations " to Government Departments with regard to working conditions in their trades, while in the organised industries an increasing number of Joint Industrial Councils were beginning to consider questions of hours, conditions and training. When the work of the Welfare Section finally closed the introduction of legislation for a 48-hour week for all factory workers had been definitely promised.

The diverse activities of the Extra-mural Subsection were absorbed in part by the Ministry of Health (*e.g.*, in connection with the Maternity and Child Welfare Act, 1918) ; in part by the Home Office and Board of Education (in connection with " Juvenile Organisations Committees ") ; in part by local authorities in the administration of the Education Act of 1918, and by many unofficial local organisations providing for the weekly wage-earner's leisure.

---

[1] *Welfare and Welfare Supervision in Factories and Workshops.*

The scientific research which contributed so much to the Department's work, through the Health of Munition Workers Committee and its own experts, was carried on in a different form by the Industrial Fatigue Research Committee, whose monographs on the relation of industrial conditions to output began to appear in 1919. Attention was concentrated on one very practical side-issue, the prevention of industrial accidents, by special enquiries undertaken, in connection with the Workmen's Compensation Act, and by energetic propaganda carried out in individual works by an unofficial body, the " Safety First " organisation, which took form in 1918, on the lines of a similar movement in America.

APPENDICES.

APPENDIX I.

Welfare Finance.

The cost of welfare provision in munitions works was borne to a very considerable extent by the taxpayer, inasmuch as a large proportion of such expenses was deducted from the surplus contributing to the munitions levy or the excess profits tax.

(a) " INTRA-MURAL " WELFARE.

Canteens and messrooms.—In November, 1915, it was agreed by the Department that the cost of the *provision* of canteens and mess-rooms in controlled establishments might, in calculating the profits of such establishments for the purpose of the Munitions Levy, be written off to the extent approved by the Canteens Committee of the Central Control Board (Liquor Traffic). From January, 1917, when the Munitions Levy was abolished, the Commissioners of Inland Revenue applied the same principle to the assessment of Excess Profits. In July, 1918, when the Central Control Board was no longer responsible for munitions canteens, the Commissioners of Inland Revenue stated that it was outside their powers to continue this arrangement, and proposals for direct Government grants towards the further provision of canteens, up to a yearly value of £565,000, were laid before the Treasury and were under consideration when the Armistice terminated the whole scheme of State help for canteens in controlled establishments. In November, 1918, up to 65 per cent. of the cost was virtually being paid from the taxes.

In national factories the Department undertook to provide canteens, and in many cases the cost of the canteen was included in the general cost of the factory as a whole.

Running expenses of canteens in controlled establishments were met from sales or provided by the firm, and might not be included in the factory working expenses, which were exempt from the Munitions Levy or Excess Profits Duty. A prolonged discussion with the Treasury on the question of responsibility for the payment of running expenses in national factory canteens ended in January, 1917, in a compromise. The Ministry undertook to pay (1) capital cost of building, installation, and equipment ; (2) cost of maintaining buildings ; (3) current cost of lighting and heating ; (4) cost of cleaning, if done by the factory staff. The remaining expenses, including salaries, fuel, etc., must be met from, the sales.[1]

It has already been explained that the majority of these canteens did not pay their way, but that those responsible for their establishment

---

[1] HIST. REC./H/346.1/1,2. HIST. REC./R/346/134,135.

represented that on educational grounds such loss might be condoned, and that it was impossible to apply to them the standards of profit and loss applicable to ordinary working-class restaurants.

Shortly after January, 1917, an accounting system was installed in national factories, in consequence of which the percentage of net loss to total takings of 20 to 23 per cent. up to 31 March, 1917, was reduced in the following half-year to 13·78 per cent., and for the half-year to 31 March, 1918, to 6·43 per cent. For the half-year ending 30 September, 1918, in which the accounts of 113 canteens were audited, the net losses submitted to the Treasury were £49,010 15s. while surpluses amounting to £6,865 1s. 2d. were carried forward in the accounts of 30 canteens. For the half-year ending 31 March, 1919, during the very difficult period of canteen trading which followed the Armistice, losses of £67,268 14s. 4d. were shown, while the surpluses carried forward were reduced to £4,526 2s. 10d.

In addition, national factory canteens under the management of caterers or voluntary societies were assisted by the Ministry to the extent of £11,268 in the period from 31 March, 1917, to 31 March, 1919, inclusive.[1]

Canteens under the Inspection Department showed losses to 31 March, 1919, amounting in all to £6,699 15s. 8d., while a surplus was shown in the Inspection Depôt canteen at Park Royal of £2,060 2s. 11d.

Between November, 1915, and November, 1918, 867 schemes of canteen provision in controlled establishments had been approved, and writing off allowances had been recommended to the value of £1,909,135. At the date of the Armistice, 733 privately owned munitions works, with 870,000 employees, had canteens.

On 21 August, 1918, Mr. Kellaway quoted the total number of canteens available for munition workers as 900, providing for a million, and used daily by 500,000, and involving a capital cost " to the Government " of £3,500,000.[2]

Cloakrooms, rest rooms, first aid rooms, etc.—In 1916 it was intimated to firms that the cost of this provision would be allowed to be written down to such an amount as would fairly represent their value to the owner at the end of the period of control.[3] Up to this point their cost might be deducted from excess profits, in whole or in part, if approved by the Welfare Section.

It was agreed in February, 1918, between the Board of Inland Revenue and the Department, that the provision of ambulance rooms, first aid equipment, etc., would in general be allowed as a working expense, but if the cost appeared excessive (*e.g.*, over £500), or if the rooms seemed to have a permanent post-war value, a suitable writing off allowance would be recommended to the Board of Inland Revenue. The provision for welfare accommodation, messrooms, lavatories,

---

[1] HIST. REC./R/346/39. The accounts of the canteens at Woolwich Arsenal, Gretna, Waltham and Enfield are not included.
[2] (Printed) *Weekly Report*, No. 156, IX. (24/8/18).
[3] M.W. 183899. Cf. C.E. 758/15.

cloakrooms, was rather less liberal. Small sums below £100 might be charged as a working expense with the approval of the Welfare Section. Those under £1,500 might be recommended for writing off up to 50 per cent. of their value ; while firms wishing to spend more than £1,500 were referred to their District Surveyor of Taxes.

Non-controlled establishments were directed to apply to the Board of Inland Revenue direct for permission to charge the cost of these buildings as a working expense or to claim a writing off allowance.[1]

In national factories, cloakrooms, messrooms, and first aid rooms were provided and maintained as a factory cost.

Welfare supervisors.—The salaries of welfare supervisors might be written off if they were approved by the Welfare Section, *i.e.*, were appointed from the Department's panel or formally approved after appointment.

Overalls and protective clothing and seats in factories.— Reasonable expenditure, approved by the Department, was held to be a working expense. This usually covered the supply of two caps and overalls per woman employed in any one financial year.

The provision of stools was held to be capital expenditure. No writing off of their cost was allowable except for renewal.[2]

The Department represented to the Treasury, on 5 January, 1917, that the cost to controlled firms of providing welfare accommodation, with the salaries involved, should be treated on the same liberal footing as that of canteens, either by writing off the cost or by direct Treasury grants, on the principle that subventions for such purposes should be made in a manner readily comprehensible by those directly concerned. It was further urged that such grants would meet the case of those firms which had no excess profits. The Treasury, however, on 20 February refused to sanction the principle of direct grants for such ends. In passing the Munitions of War Amendment Act in 1916, " it was clearly the intention of Parliament that the employer should be responsible to the Minister for the conditions of employment in his establishment ; but the proposed practice of making grants from public funds towards the cost of canteens and other amenities would result in the transfer of responsibility from the employer to the Minister."[3]

At the end of 1918 it was calculated that the cost of welfare provision (including salaries, but excluding cost of canteens) worked out at £2 per head as initial cost, £1 per head as yearly cost, in three average firms with about 1,000 workers. The expenditure sanctioned by the Department for such provision in a typical month in the last year of the war amounted to £14,000 among 38 firms.[4]

[1] Hist. Rec./R/346/135.
[2] M.W. 183899.
[3] M.F./Gen./231. M.W. 151437. M.W. 28683/5.
[4] Welfare Officers were informed that recommendations for new buildings or alterations should be based on the " minimum necessary accommodation required of the simplest and most economical kind," both on account of the increasing need for economy in labour and materials and of the opposition to " dilution " raised by unnecessary recommendations. (12/6/17, etc.). Hist. Rec./R/346/120.

(b) EXTRA-MURAL WELFARE.

Expenditure on extra-mural welfare was small by comparison with the cost of intra-mural work, partly because of the obviously lesser need for buildings, land and salaries ; partly because, where such need existed, the Department was commonly asked only to supplement private effort.

Recreation Schemes.—Munitions firms began to develop recreation schemes, with the approval of the Department, toward the end of 1916.   Joint civic recreation schemes developed in 1917.

It was arranged in February, 1918, that when a controlled establishment incurred expenditure on a recreation scheme sanctioned and approved by the Welfare and Health Section, that section should recommend to the Board of Inland Revenue that contributions by the controlled owner be allowed as a working expense up to an amount not exceeding 10s. per head of those benefiting by the scheme.   Such expenditure might not normally be devoted to the purchase of land or construction of buildings.[1]   It was intended to cover initial, not running, expenses.   If such provision appeared to have a substantial post-war value which would remain in the firm's ownership, allowance was made " not by way of treating the expenditure in whole or part as a working expense, but by granting a writing-off allowance, the Welfare and Health Section recommending to the Board of Inland Revenue such allowance as they considered reasonable, having regard to the probable post-war value.   Where a firm disagreed with the writing-off allowance recommended, it was open to the owner to approach the Board of Inland Revenue, when his liability to Excess Profits Duty for the final accounting period was under consideration, and claim under Section 40 (3) of the Finance (No. 2) Act, 1915,[2] a deduction of any amount by which the difference between the cost and post-war value of the asset in question exceeded the writing-off allowance already granted.

The Treasury was " prepared to consider " similar applications for national factories ; and, in fact, allowed the Finance Department, on the recommendation of the Welfare and Health Section, to make a grant up to 2s. 6d. per head of the numbers employed.   This 2s. 6d. grant was the most usual form.   The money so accruing was used both for capital and current expenditure.   In some cases, especially in the smaller establishments, a larger sum was required.   Wherever more than 2s. 6d. was sought, special Treasury sanction had to be obtained.

---

[1] L.R.W. 1108.

[2] " Where it appears to the Commissioners of Inland Revenue, on the application of a taxpayer in any particular case, that any provisions of the Fourth Schedule to this Act should be modified in his case, owing to a change in the constitution of a partnership . . . or to the necessity in connection with the present war of providing plant which will not be wanted for the purposes of the trade or business after the termination of the war, or to any other special circumstances specified in regulations made by the Treasury, those Commissioners shall have power to allow such modifications of any of the provisions of that schedule as they think necessary in order to meet the particular case."

Uncontrolled firms were given the same privileges with regard to claims for recreation expenses, subject to the approval of the Home Office instead of the Ministry of Munitions.

Crèches.—In 1917 the Treasury approved grants of 75 per cent. of the cost of the establishment, extension and equipment of day nurseries for the children of munition workers, and 7d. per head maintenance grant for each 12 hours attendance. The total expenditure was as follows :—

			£	s.	d.
19/3/17 to 31/3/17	..	..	..	1,999	14	3
1/4/17 to 1/4/18	..	..	..	11,210	11	11
1/4/18 to 1/12/18	..	..	..	7,990	0	0
			£21,200	6	2

Forty-one nurseries were assisted. They were inspected by the Board of Education, which audited the accounts for payment of grants.[1]

Hostels.—On 7 July, 1917, the Treasury sanctioned an expenditure of £5,000 on private hostels, " whose existence has been of proved value to munition workers, and may be expected to be of value during the continued activity of the munition works of the district." This sum might be spent on (i) grants towards the capital expenditure incurred in starting or carrying on hostels, and (ii) maintenance grants at the rate of not more than 6d. per head per diem in the case of six clearing hostels.[2] In the case of these last hostels, there were special and obvious difficulties in making them self-supporting.

This grant was renewed in August, 1918, by which time grants had been made to 16 of the hostels inspected by the Welfare Section. The total sum expended up to December, 1918, only reached £4,837 4s. 9d., leaving a surplus of £5,162 15s. 3d. on the Treasury grants.

The grants made consisted mainly in sums of from £100 to £300 to small hostels, provided by semi-" charitable " bodies.

Institutions, etc.—The sum of £470 was spent between 17 August, 1917, and 12 June, 1918, on grants to seven institutions helping munition workers—the Barrow hospital, the Hereford general hospital, the Lancaster district nursing associations, etc. Small sums were also sanctioned and paid to the Travellers' Aid Society (£15) for help to munition girls on journeys in 1917, and in payments on account of a " sickness and emergency fund."[3] Only £186 had been spent on account of this fund by the end of November, 1918, and of this £100 went to the expenses of an emergency hostel for the large number of women and girls, including munition workers, stranded at Holyhead owing to the overcrowding of the cross-channel boats in the summer of 1918.

---

[1] L.R. 2960.   [2] L.R. 2710/2.   [3] L.R. 2710.

These grants were made in small sums by the district welfare officers, *e.g.*, for travelling expenses and in case of sickness, and, except in extreme urgency, " with the approval of headquarters in each case."

The upkeep of works hospitals, but not their provision, except in so far as the cost was increased by war conditions, might be sanctioned as a working expense.[1] Special payments of 3s. and 4s. a day to hospitals, for in-patient treatment to T.N.T. workers, were authorised.[2]

The Maharajah's Fund.—This fund consisted of £6,000, presented by the Maharajah Scindia, on 22 July, 1915, with two additional sums of £50 and £20.   It was given in January, 1916, to the Welfare Section for the benefit of munition workers, and was spent on such matters as pianos and books for hostels, grants for recreation clubs, tools and seeds for munition girls' hostels, swings for munition workers' children, a camp for Woolwich boys, lectures by the Y.M.C.A. National Council, etc.   £4,385 18s. 6d. had been spent at the end of November, 1918.

---

[1] Cf. C.E. 1017/15. (October, 1917.)
[2] C.M. 4/2733 ; L.R. 218/2.

APPENDIX II.

(CHAPTER VI, pp. 107 ff.)

Sunday Labour. Statistics, 1916-17.

(a) EMPLOYMENT ON SUNDAY LABOUR IN CONTROLLED ESTABLISHMENTS ON NON-CONTINUOUS PROCESSES.

	1916			1917				1918			
	Jan.-Feb.	April-May.	Nov.-Dec.	Mar.-April.	Aug.-Sept.	Oct.-Nov.	Nov.-Dec.	Feb.-Mar.	Mar.-April.	April-May.	May-June.
Total number of firms employing Sunday labour on non-continuous processes.	812	593	632	514	333	222	356	450	576	469	419
Total number of employees in firms working on Sunday: Men	—	—	575,205	480,454	285,024	210,518	249,941	284,252	421,418	335,134	274,231
Women	—	—	184,068	147,602	160,134	100,892	120,780	132,342	165,190	148,741	148,713
Average number of employees working per Sunday Men	—	—	106,251	76,782	41,407	38,335	40,293	42,225	69,685	43,440	29,808
Women	—	—	13,828	10,329	7,061	6,999	6,681	4,119	11,673	7,138	6,191
Number of firms working every Sunday.	—	—	455	243	258	175	253	301	295	216	276
Number of firms in which women are employed every Sunday.	—	—	78	16	51	33	54	57	40	25	45

(b) PERCENTAGE ON SUNDAY LABOUR OF TOTAL EMPLOYED IN VARIOUS CLASSES OF ESTABLISHMENTS.*

Males.

	1916.			1917.								
Month	Oct.	Nov.	Dec.	Jan.	Feb.	Mar.	April.	May.	June.	July.	Aug.	Sept.
Week ending	15 Oct.	12 Nov.	17 Dec.	14 Jan.	11 Feb.	18 Mar.	15 Apr.	13 May.	17 Jun.	8 July.	12 Aug.	16 Sept.
Government Establishments:												
Royal Factories	28·0	26·5	23·0	23·0	21·5	15·0	21·0	10·0	10·0	9·5	13·8	10·9
National Projectile Factories	11·0	10·0	28·5	24·5	10·0	10·0	8·5	5·0	6·5	7·0	8·3	8·9
National Shell Factories	9·0	8·5	10·5	5·5	5·5	6·0	5·0	4·5	5·0	4·2	1·6	4·3
National Filling Factories	4·0	5·0	5·0	10·0	11·5	7·5	9·0	6·0	6·0	6·7	2·1	1·7
High Explosives and Propellants	33·0	40·0	29·0	31·0	35·0	33·0	15·5	32·5	29·0	27·6	26·2	21·6
TOTAL, including Miscellaneous	20·5	20·5	24·0	21·5	18·0	15·0	18·0	11·5	11·5	11·2	12·2	10·7
Non-Government Establishments:												
Metal Trades	8·0	7·5	8·0	7·5	8·0	8·5	7·5	·5·5	6·0	5·4	—	6·3
Chemicals and Explosives	19·5	19·0	21·5	21·0	21·0	19·0	18·0	17·5	15·5	15·4	—	15·6
TOTAL, including Rubber, Wood Trades and other Trades	8·5	8·0	9·0	8·5	8·5	8·5	8·0	6·0	6·5	5·8	—	6·7

Females.

Month	Week ending	1916 Oct. 15 Oct.	Nov. 12 Nov.	Dec. 17 Dec.	1917 Jan. 16 Jan.	Feb. 11 Feb.	Mar. 18 Mar.	April. 15 Apr.	May. 13 May.	June. 17 Jun.	July. 8 July.	Aug. 12 Aug.	Sept. 16 Sept.
Government Establishments :													
Royal Factories		7·5	6·5	7·0	9·0	2·5	3·0	3·5	3·5	1·0	2·9	7·7	3·3
National Projectile Factories		8·0	6·0	22·0	16·5	6·0	8·5	6·5	3·5	2·0	2·9	3·3	3·0
National Shell Factories		8·0	11·0	11·0	4·5	5·0	1·5	1·5	1·0	1·0	0·3	0·0	0·3
National Filling Factories		11·5	6·0	1·0	6·0	11·0	4·0	2·0	2·0	1·5	0·2	0·0	0·1
High Explosives and Propellants		37·5	44·5	33·0	30·5	32·5	34·5	33·0	33·0	27·5	28·4	25·2	26·4
TOTAL, including Miscellaneous		11·5	9·5	10·0	10·5	10·0	7·5	6·5	6·0	4·5	4·8	5·0	4·7
Non-Government Establishments :													
Metal Trades		2·5	8·0	2·5	1·5	1·5	2·0	1·5	1·0	1·0	1·1	—	0·9
Chemicals and Explosives		11·5	12·0	13·0	12·5	13·5	8·5	7·0	7·0	6·5	6·0	—	5·9
TOTAL, including Rubber, Wood Trades and other Trades		3·0	3·0	3·5	2·5	2·5	2·0	2·0	1·5	1·5	1·5	…	1·4

* The figures given in the table are obtained by calculating the actual numbers engaged on each Sunday as percentages of the mean of two proximate monthly returns of total numbers employed,

APPENDIX III.
(CHAPTER VI., pp. 115 ff.)
Overtime, 1916-17.

(a) AVERAGE NUMBER OF HOURS' OVERTIME GAINED PER HEAD OF MALES EMPLOYED ON OVERTIME.

Week Ending	1916.				1917.						
	15 Sept.	13 Oct.	17 Nov.	15 Dec.	12 Jan.	16 Feb.	16 Mar.	13 Apr	18 May.	15 Jun.	3 July.
Trade Group :											
Iron and Steel	14·0	12·5	12·5	12·0	12·0	11·0	11·0	10·0	10·5	11·5	11·0
Tinplate	16·0	14·5	13·5	14·0	13·5	12·5	15·5	13·5	13·0	13·5	12·5
Wiredrawing	10·0	9·5	10·0	10·0	10·0	9·5	10·0	9·0	9·5	9·5	10·0
Hardware	8·0	8·0	7·5	8·0	8·0	8·5	9·0	7·5	8·5	8·0	8·0
Engineering	12·0	11·0	11·0	12·0	11·5	11·5	11·0	11·0	11·0	11·0	11·0
Electrical Engineering	13·0	9·5	10·0	10·0	10·0	10·5	10·0	10·0	10·5	10·0	10·0
Shipbuilding	11·5	12·5	12·0	12·5	12·0	13·0	13·0	12·5	13·0	12·0	12·5
Cycle and Motor	10·5	10·5	10·0	10·5	9·0	9·5	9·5	9·0	9·0	9·0	9·0
Railway Carriage and Wagon	7·5	8·5	9·0	9·0	8·0	9·0	9·5	8·5	8·0	8·0	9·5
Carriage, Cart and Wagon	10·5	10·0	10·0	10·0	10·5	10·0	10·0	10·0	8·0	8·0	9·0
Tools, Cutlery, etc.	9·5	11·0	9·5	9·5	9·5	9·5	9·5	9·0	10·0	9·5	9·5
Small Arms	10·5	9·0	10·5	10·5	10·5	10·0	11·5	12·5	8·0	12·5	12·5
Scientific Instruments	10·5	10·5	10·0	10·0	10·5	10·0	10·0	9·5	9·5	9·0	9·0
Jewellery, etc.	9·5	10·0	9·0	10·0	10·0	10·0	13·0	9·0	8·5	10·0	11·0
Other Metals	10·0	9·5	9·5	9·5	10·0	10·5	9·5	9·0	9·5	9·5	9·5
All Metal Trades	12·0	11·0	11·0	11·5	11·0	11·0	11·0	10·5	11·0	11·0	11·0
Chemicals	11·0	11·0	11·5	10·5	11·5	10·0	11·5	11·0	11·5	10·5	11·0
Explosives	13·5	13·5	13·0	14·0	14·5	12·0	13·0	12·5	13·0	12·0	12·0
Rubber	10·5	10·5	10·5	10·5	10·0	9·5	9·5	8·5	9·5	10·5	10·0
Wood Trades	8·5	8·0	8·0	8·0	8·0	8·0	8·5	8·0	7·5	8·0	7·0
All other Trades	10·0	11·0	11·0	11·5	11·5	10·5	10·0	9·5	10·0	9·5	9·5
TOTAL	12·0	11·0	11·0	11·5	11·5	11·0	11·0	10·5	11·0	11·0	11·0

(b) AVERAGE NUMBER OF HOURS' OVERTIME GAINED PER HEAD OF FEMALES EMPLOYED ON OVERTIME.

Week Ending	1916. 15 Sept.	13 Oct.	17 Nov.	15 Dec.	1917. 12 Jan.	16 Feb.	16 Mar.	13 Apr.	18 May.	15 Jun.	13 July.
Iron and Steel	9·5	7·5	8·5	7·5	6·5	7·5	6·0	5·5	5·5	6·5	6·0
Tinplate	—	—	—	—	9·0	11·0	16·0	6·0	0·0	9·0	7·5
Wiredrawing	7·0	6·5	6·5	6·5	6·0	6·0	5·5	6·5	6·5	5·5	5·5
Hardware	9·5	10·0	4·5	5·5	6·0	6·0	5·5	5·5	6·5	5·5	5·5
Engineering	8·5	7·0	8·5	8·0	7·5	8·0	7·5	6·0	7·5	7·5	7·0
Electrical Engineering	7·5	6·5	7·0	6·5	7·0	7·0	7·0	6·0	7·0	7·0	7·0
Shipbuilding	8·5	10·0	6·5	8·0	6·5	6·5	6·5	6·0	5·5	5·5	8·0
Cycle and Motor	9·0	8·5	7·5	9·5	6·5	6·5	6·5	5·5	5·5	5·0	5·5
Railway Carriage and Wagon	5·0	4·5	5·5	6·0	5·0	5·0	6·5	5·0	4·5	5·0	5·5
Carriage, Cart and Wagon	11·0	11·0	10·0	9·5	9·5	10·0	9·0	10·5	13·0	9·5	9·5
Tools, Cutlery, etc.	13·0	6·0	6·5	6·5	6·5	6·5	7·0	6·5	6·5	6·5	6·0
Small Arms	13·0	9·0	7·5	8·0	6·0	5·0	6·5	8·5	6·0	7·5	6·5
Scientific Instruments	7·0	6·5	5·5	6·0	7·0	7·0	6·5	7·5	6·0	6·5	6·0
Jewellery, etc.	7·0	7·0	6·0	7·5	7·5	7·0	7·5	6·5	6·5	6·5	7·0
Other Metals	7·5	6·5	7·0	7·0	7·0	7·5	7·0	4·0	6·5	6·0	6·5
All Metal Trades	8·5	7·5	7·5	7·0	7·0	6·0	7·0	6·0	7·0	7·0	7·5
Chemicals	4·0	6·0	6·0	10·5	11·0	10·0	9·5	8·0	7·5	6·5	8·0
Explosives	8·5	10·0	11·0	6·0	5·5	6·0	6·0	8·0	8·5	6·5	5·0
Rubber	6·5	7·0	8·0	9·0	8·0	7·5	7·5	5·0	5·5	8·0	7·0
Wood Trades	8·0	7·5	7·5	7·5	7·5	7·0	7·5	7·5	7·0	7·5	6·5
All other Trades	8·5	8·5	8·5	7·5	7·5	7·0	6·0	6·0	7·0	6·0	6·5
TOTAL	8·0	7·5	8·0	7·5	7·0	7·5	7·0	6·0	7·0	7·0	7·0

APPENDIX IV.

(Chapter VI., pp. 122 ff.)

The Shift System in Government Establishments.

Percentage of Employees on Various Shift Systems on a Date Approximating to the Middle of each Month.

Males.

Week ending	1916.				1917.							
	15 Sept	13 Oct.	17 Nov.	15 Dec.	12 Jan.	16 Feb.	16 Mar.	13 Apr.	8 May	15 Jun.	13 July.	17 Aug.
Royal Factories :												
One Shift	—	—	—	—	31·5	30·5	33·0	33·0	33·0	34·5	34·0	34·5
Two Shift	64·0	66·5	66·5	65·5	65·0	66·0	66·0	63·5	62·0	61·5	62·0	61·7
Three Shift	3·5	3·5	3·0	3·0	3·5	3·5	3·5	3·5	4·0	4·0	4·0	3·8
Not stated	—	—	—	—	0·0	0·0	0·0	0·0	—	—	—	—
National Projectile Factories :												
One Shift	82·0	77·0	81·0	81·0 (81·5)	20·5	21·0	32·0	36·5	32·0	38·0	37·5	37·8
Two Shift	—	—	—	—	67·0	79·0	68·0	63·5	54·0	59·5	62·5	62·2
Three Shift	0·0	0·0	0·0	0·0 (0·0)*	0·0	0·0	0·0	0·0	0·0	0·0	0·0	0·0
Not stated	—	—	—	—	12·5	0·0	0·0	0·0	14·0	12·5	0·0	—

	C1	C2	C3	C4	C5	C6	C7	C8	C9	C10	C11	C12
National Shell Factories :												
One Shift	—	—	—	—	18·0	16·5	17·0	19·0	17·5	20·5	22·5	23·5
Two Shift	72·0	73·0	71·0	76·0†	75·0	76·5	70·0	71·0	78·5	76·5	68·0	73·5
Three Shift	3·5	2·0	6·0	6·0†	6·5	6·5	12·0	8·0	2·5	1·5	0·5	1·2
Not stated	—	—	—	—	0·5	0·5	1·0	2·0	1·5	1·5	9·0	1·8
National Filling Factories :												
One Shift	15·5	43·5	45·5	46·5	29·5	30·5	29·5	31·0	33·5	49·0	37·5	34·4
Two Shift	—	—	—	(47·0)‡	42·0	54·0	52·5	45·5	47·0	44·5	41·5	52·6
Three Shift	31·5	1·5	1·5	0·5	10·0	10·0	0·5	7·5	3·0	3·0	4·5	2·7
Not stated	—	—	—	(1·5)‡	18·5	5·5	17·5	16·0	16·5	3·5	16·5	10·3
High Explosives and Propellants :												
One Shift	—	—	—	—	38·0	38·5	44·0	38·5	39·0	41·5	45·0	43·5
Two Shift	—	—	13·5	12·0	6·0	9·0	11·0	10·5	10·5	15·0	11·5	10·7
Three Shift	—	—	39·0	36·0	37·5	39·5	36·5	42·0	36·0	38·0	43·5	44·8
Not stated	—	—	—	—	18·5	13·0	8·5	9·0	14·5	5·5	—	1·0
Miscellaneous :												
One Shift	14·5	13·5	100·0	100·0	100·0	87·0	82·5	80·5	76·0	86·0	74·0	75·3
Two Shift	37·5	47·0	0·0	0·0	0·0	13·0	15·0	12·0	6·5	11·5	20·5	23·7
Three Shift	—	—	0·0	0·0	0·0	0·0	2·5	3·0	1·5	2·5	5·5	1·0
Not stated	—	—	0·0	0·0	0·0	0·0	0·0	4·5	16·0	0·0	—	—

V–3

H

APPENDIX IV—continued.

Females.

Week ending	1916				1917							
	15 Sept.	13 Oct.	17 Nov.	15 Dec.	12 Jan.	16 Feb.	16 Mar.	13 Apr.	18 May.	15 Jun.	13 July.	17 Aug.
Royal Factories :												
One Shift	—	—	—	—	10·5	12·0	9·0	7·5	8·0	11·0	11·0	11·5
Two Shift	69·5	76·5	78·0	81·0	83·0	81·0	84·0	85·0	80·5	80·0	81·0	80·6
Three Shift	4·0	5·0	5·5	6·5	6·5	7·0	7·0	7·5	8·0	9·0	8·0	7·9
Not stated	—	—	—	—	0·0	0·0	0·0	0·0	3·5	—	—	—
National Projectile Factories :												
One Shift	—	—	—	40·0 (44·0)*	8·5	8·0	10·5	11·5	12·5	18·0	17·0	18·0
Two Shift	35·5	42·5	43·5	—	35·5	43·0	46·0	47·0	45·0	39·5	41·5	42·8
Three Shift	49·0	47·5	48·0	51·0 (47·5)*	46·5	49·0	43·5	38·0	39·5	42·5	41·5	39·2
Not stated	—	—	—	—	9·5	0·0	0·0	3·5	3·0	0·0	—	—
National Shell Factories :												
One Shift	38·5	36·5	39·5	43·5†	13·0	12·5	12·0	14·0	8·5	9·0	9·5	12·9
Two Shift	48·0	45·5	45·5	43·5†	43·0	49·0	36·0	41·5	47·0	47·5	43·5	46·7
Three Shift	—	—	—	—	43·5	37·5	50·5	44·5	43·0	42·0	37·5	38·5
Not Stated	—	—	—	—	0·5	1·0	1·5	0·0	1·5	1·5	9·5	1·9

National Filling Factories:

	1	2	3	4	5	6	7	8	9	10	11	12
One Shift	—	—	—	—	11·5	10·0	11·5	13·5	15·5	41·5	30·0	20·1
Two Shift	18·5	24·0	26·5	36·5	28·5	35·0	44·0	25·0	35·0	38·5	37·0	50·6
Three Shift	37·5	27·5	26·5	(28·0)‡	27·0	32·0	9·0	25·0	11·5	12·0	12·5	11·3
				3·0								
Not Stated	—	—	—	(25·0)‡	33·0	23·0	35·5	36·5	38·0	8·0	20·5	18·0
				—								

High Explosives and Propellants:

	1	2	3	4	5	6	7	8	9	10	11	12
One Shift	—	—	—	—	18·0	18·0	18·5	15·5	17·5	17·5	17·5	17·5
Two Shift	—	—	0·0	2·0	0·0	1·0	1·0	1·0	0·5	0·5	0·5	0·3
Three Shift	—	—	83·0	80·0	80·5	78·5	79·0	80·5	80·0	81·5	82·0	82·1
Not Stated	—	—	—	—	1·5	2·5	1·5	3·0	2·0	0·5	—	0·1

Miscellaneous:

	1	2	3	4	5	6	7	8	9	10	11	12
One Shift	—	—	100·0	100·0	100·0	87·0	82·5	80·5	76·0	86·0	74·0	81·8
Two Shift	14·5	13·5	0·0	0·0	0·0	13·0	15·0	12·0	6·5	11·5	20·5	13·8
Three Shift	37·5	47·0	0·0	0·0	0·0	0·0	2·5	3·0	1·5	2·5	5·5	4·4
Not Stated	—	—	0·0	0·0	0·0	0·0	0·0	4·5	16·0	0·0	—	—

* Percentages given in brackets include November figures for a National Projectile Factory which failed to make a return for December.

† Percentages do not include figures for Liverpool (3,546), which made a late return.

‡ Percentages given in brackets include November figures for a National Filling Factory which failed to make a return for December.

INDEX.

CONTENTS OF VOLUME V.

NOTE.—The present issue is subject to revision,
and must be regarded as provisional.

HISTORY OF THE MINISTRY OF MUNITIONS.

VOLUME V

WAGES AND WELFARE

PART IV

THE PROVISION OF CANTEENS IN MUNITIONS FACTORIES

1921.

VOLUME V

WAGES AND WELFARE

PART IV

THE PROVISION OF CANTEENS IN MUNITIONS FACTORIES

CONTENTS.

The Provision of Canteens in Munition Factories.

APPENDICES.

(C191—5296) Wt. 3643/AP5036 9/21 250 Harrow.

1

PART IV.

THE PROVISION OF CANTEENS IN MUNITIONS FACTORIES.

I.—The Canteens Committee of the Central Control Board (Liquor Traffic).

When the war broke out the movement towards industrial canteens was making steady progress. In the case of certain trades and processes (*e.g.*, the explosives trades, manufacture of lead and arsenic, and electric accumulators), the provision of rooms for taking meals was compulsory under the Factory Acts and Regulations, but in the years preceding the war there was a growing tendency for employers to provide not only mess-rooms, but also cheap restaurant facilities for their employees. In this, the food industries—the chocolate and biscuit makers—were the pioneers, their example being followed by soap-makers, dyers, tobacco manufacturers, etc.[1] An enquiry made in 23 large factories in June, 1914, showed that the average number dining daily at these factories was 65,495, of whom 27,373 were males and 38,122 females.

This movement was stimulated by the crusade against the excessive drinking alleged to be prevalent among munition workers, inaugurated by Mr. Lloyd George, then Chancellor of the Exchequer, in his speech at Bangor on 1 March, 1915, and resulted in the creation of a new temporary authority known as the Central Control Board (Liquor Traffic).

In lieu of a policy of prohibition, the policy of exceptional control in limited areas was adopted, and the Defence of the Realm (Amendment) (No. 3) Act became law on 19 May, 1915. This Act enabled the Government to set apart for special treatment in the matter of the liquor trade any areas where, on account of munitions manufacture or transport or the training of military or naval forces, the continuance of the peace time facilities for the sale of intoxicants would interfere with the successful prosecution of the war. The administration of the powers of control entrusted to the Central Control Board (Liquor Traffic), which was established as the prescribed Government authority for the purposes of the Act by an Order in Council of 10 June, 1915, does not concern us here, except in so far as it throws light on the movement for the establishment of industrial canteens.

Among the duties imposed by Parliament on the Board was " the positive and constructive task of facilitating and encouraging, and, if necessary, themselves undertaking the supply of food for munition and transport workers, and they immediately appointed a " Canteens Committee."

[1] Reference to the provision of mess rooms in factories and workshops is to be found in the Annual Reports of the Factory Department since 1893. See, for instance, *Factory Inspectors' Annual Report* for 1909 (pp. 42, 54, 81, 106, 127, 133, 134, 144) ; for 1910 (pp. vi., xviii., 38, 71, 73, 96, 115, 119) ; for 1913 (p. 8).

The membership of this committee was as follows :—

Sir George Newman, M.D. (Chairman, also a member of
Central Control Board).

Major the Hon. Waldorf Astor, M.P.

Sir William Lever (resigned July, 1916).

Mr. William Towle.

Mr. Cane (Secretary).

Mr. Higgins (Assistant Secretary).

(a) GENERAL PRINCIPLES.

The considerations which led the Central Control Board to appoint this committee were expressed in the last section of the Board's first report,[1] issued on 12 October, 1915.

> " It has been necessary in this report to enlarge on the restrictive action of the Board, as it is in that direction that their proceedings have so far been before the public. The Board, however, attach very considerable importance to the constructive side of their work, and this side has received their careful consideration. The Board incline to the view that excessive drinking may often be traced to the want of adequate facilities for food, refreshment, and recreation, particularly in conjunction with long hours and overtime. The improvement of public houses and the provision of canteens may therefore do much to render less necessary the imposition of purely restrictive measures. The Board are accordingly encouraging by all the means in their power the efforts which are being made, by public spirited voluntary societies, or by other bodies interested, to improve the conditions by which adequate facilities for food and drink can be secured in munitions and transport areas."

Quite apart, however, from the liquor question with which circumstances had connected it, the need for industrial canteens, or some equivalent, must have arisen in the course of the second year of the war even amongst a nation of teetotalers. Only less completely than the soldiers themselves the munition workers were a mobilised army, suddenly aggregated in vast numbers in unfamiliar localities, whither the claims of national service or the lure of better wages had brought them. Existing local resources were quite unequal to feeding them. Such conditions encouraged drunkenness, and the institution of adequate arrangements for taking meals would remove the cause of the increased drunkenness ; but the problem was essentially a problem of commissariat, not a problem of Temperance.

> " It devolved upon the Board to secure the supply of proper and sufficient nourishment for the worker, in order to maintain his health, to increase his energy and output, and to diminish or prevent fatigue or exhaustion. The circumstances of the moment emphasised the desirability of vigorous action.

---

[1] Cd. 8117.

The enormous and rapid increase in the number of munition workers, their concentration in well defined districts, the local difficulty in obtaining food at reasonable prices, the distance from the factory at which many of them lived, all these were conditions which made more acute and pressing the whole problem of the food supply of the workers . . . . The real requirement is to supply for large numbers of persons at specified times a suitable dietary . . . . at a reasonable cost.

" In endeavouring to meet this requirement, the Board have proceeded on two collateral lines of action :—
   " (a) The increase of facilities for obtaining suitable meals at public houses, and
   " (b) The establishment wherever necessary of industrial canteens inside or within easy access of the works, supplying both substantial meals and light refreshment at reasonable prices."[1]

Eight months before these words were written, Sir George Newman, Chairman of the Canteens Committee, on 10 September, 1915, made his first report [2] to Lord D'Abernon, Chairman of the Central Control Board, summarising the first three months' work of the committee :—

" 1. . . . . The Board have taken the view that in the first place the employer should be called upon to make canteen provision : failing him, some approved voluntary society should be encouraged to undertake the task ; failing both of these, the Board would consider whether it was desirable for the Board itself to undertake the duty.

" 2. In many places, the Board is informed that employers are themselves providing more or less adequate canteen accommodation, but up to the present we have no complete list of these canteens.

" 3. In regard to the very numerous munitions areas where the employer for one reason or another has not hitherto taken action, I have to report that a number of public-spirited voluntary societies have commenced to undertake canteen provision. In order to co-ordinate such work, the Board has appointed an Advisory Committee consisting of the Canteen Committee plus representatives of such approved voluntary societies. The conditions for approving such societies have been carefully considered, and are set out in due form in prescribed regulations. The Advisory Committee has met several times, and we are now in a position to say that there are over 40 canteens in working order, and over 30 in process of establishment, and a still larger number in contemplation.

---

[1] *Second Report of Central Control Board.* May, 1916 (Cd. 8243).
[2] HIST. REC./R/346.1/1.

"4. The Central Control Board have applied to the Treasury for sanction to make grants in aid of capital expenditure for the provision of canteens by non-profit-making voluntary societies approved by the Board, and the Treasury have sanctioned the grant of a quarter of such expenditure.[1] This grant will be made under prescribed regulations which are of a very simple form."

At the conclusion of this report Sir George Newman wrote :—

"It is desirable that the price of food should be sufficiently low to meet all requirements."

These words serve to indicate the general policy of the Board. But in the course of time the interpretation of this policy became a matter of acute controversy. Should the canteens be indirectly subsidised institutions ? Or, should they, on the other hand, be made to pay their way ? Again, if a policy expressed by the latter phrase were adopted, what precise meaning was to be attached to the phrase ? Here was a problem on which the economy of regimental messes threw no light. In the army a soldier's pay is calculated on the assumption that his board is provided. In industry the provision of food in lieu of wages has long been recognised as a practice injurious to the worker as tending to keep down wages. Such methods of wage payment are therefore prohibited by law.[2]

(b) PROVISION OF CAPITAL EXPENDITURE.

From the first it was recognised that the canteens could not bear the cost of the capital expenditure on their building and equipment. As Sir George Newman's letter above quoted shows, much was due in the early stages to private subscriptions through the channel of voluntary societies.[3] Patriotism suggested that here, as in the case of the Red Cross, was an opportunity for those not actively engaged in the war of contributing to the comfort and well being of those who were. The Central Control Board secured Treasury support for the efforts of these societies,[4] and welcomed the aid which they could render. It soon became clear, however, that the expectation of an uninterrupted flow of public subscriptions to the funds of voluntary

---

[1] The proportion of the grant was shortly afterwards raised to a half.

[2] The Truck Act, 1831, Section 23, provides that " no deduction shall be made from the wages of a workman in respect of victuals dressed and prepared under the roof of the employer unless an agreement or contract for such stoppage or deduction shall be made in writing and signed by the artificer."

[3] The following is the list of approved voluntary societies engaged in this work :—The Young Men's Christian Association ; The Munition Makers' Canteen Committee (Lady Lawrence) ; The National Peoples Palaces Association, Ltd. ; The Salvation Army ; The Church of England Temperance Society ; The Church Army ; The Young Men's and Women's Christian Association (Scotland) ; The Young Women's Christian Association (Scotland) ; The Young Women's Christian Association (England) ; The British Women's Temperance Association (Scotland) ; The Glasgow Union of Women Workers ; The Women's Volunteer Reserve ; The Women's Legion (Scottish Branch).

[4] Third Report of the Central Control Board, p. 10. Cd. 8558 of 1917.

societies was not likely to be realised. After the first excitement was over, the public not unnaturally reflected that the provision of canteens was after all a matter for the employers ; nor did it appear reasonable that charitable contributions should be required in connection with the feeding of a class of workers so well paid as those employed on munitions were reputed to be. The value of the later services of these societies it is impossible to over-estimate ; but they ceased, quite properly, to be of a financial character. " The conclusion forced itself upon the Board " says the third report[1] of the Central Control Board, " that the services of the voluntary societies could best be utilised by employing them to manage canteens erected and equipped by employers."

In these circumstances it became clear that the Board must either render further financial assistance to the societies directly, or must devise some means of persuading employers themselves to provide canteens in their works. The latter course seemed preferable on all grounds, but chiefly because it afforded some guarantee for the permanence of the canteen movement and its continuance after the war. The Board, therefore, approached the Minister of Munitions and sought his sanction for an arrangement under which the proprietors of controlled establishments should be allowed to charge the capital cost of providing canteens at their works against the current profits of the establishment for the purpose of Part II of the Munitions of War Act, 1915. The Ministry, having obtained Treasury sanction, gave authority on 19 November, 1915, for the adoption of this proposal,[2] which meant that about 65 per cent. of the capital cost was paid from the taxes. Buildings so financed were to be maintained permanently as canteens, except by consent of the Ministry of Munitions or the Government Department succeeding it.

(c) WITHDRAWAL OF " WRITING-OFF " CONCESSIONS.

These concessions were originally granted by the Minister, when controlled establishments were subject to the Munitions Levy, under the wide discretionary powers given to him by the Munitions of War Act, 1915, in assessing the liability of controlled employers to that duty. The Munitions Levy was abolished on 1 January, 1917, and the collection of Excess Profits Duty from controlled firms devolved upon the Commissioners of Inland Revenue. The discretionary powers of the Commissioners in assessing liability to Excess Profits Duty were limited. They were, however, empowered to allow persons liable to the tax to write down any buildings or plant which they might provide during the lifetime of the duty to their post-war value. In ordinary circumstances, the post-war value could not of course be determined until after the war, but the Commissioners, feeling bound to honour pledges given by the Minister of Munitions with regard to the canteen concession, agreed to regard it as a case of special depreciation, and allowed the Canteens Committee of the Central Control

---
[1] Cd. 8558 of 1917.   [2] M.W. 45309.

Board to assess the post-war value of a canteen at a controlled establishment as soon as it was completed and in operation, and without waiting for the end of the war.

It was naturally assumed that the transfer to the Ministry of Munitions of the responsibility for canteen organisation would not affect the concession, and that the Commissioners of Inland Revenue would as readily accept recommendations from the Ministry of Munitions as from the Central Control Board. It was found, however, that this was not the case. On being approached the Commissioners explained that they had for some time past had misgivings as to the legality of the concession and on 19 June, 1918, they wrote to the Minister stating that the Commissioners

> "feel that they ought to place on record their judgment that in the circumstances now existing the arrangement heretofore existing, can no longer be regarded as conforming with Revenue Law."[1]

The situation thus created was considered by the Munitions Food Advisory Committee,[2] who referred the question to a sub-committee, with Lord D'Abernon as chairman. The sub-committee considered the alternative system of direct grants from Government funds in aid of the provision of canteens, but came to the conclusion that such a proposal would not be favoured by employers. They recommended strongly the maintenance of a system of writing-off against excess profits, and their conclusions were endorsed by the main committee.

A further effort was made to induce the Commissioners of Inland Revenue to abandon their position, but in a letter dated 26 July, 1918, the Commissioners replied finally that they felt bound, in fulfilment of their statutory duty, to terminate the arrangement hitherto in force.

It was agreed that it would be futile to pursue the matter further with the Commissioners, and on 15 August, 1918, Mr. Kellaway decided that the Treasury should be asked to sanction the payment to controlled owners of grants from Government funds not exceeding in amount 65 per cent. of the actual total cost incurred to provide a fully equipped canteen at a controlled establishment. A letter on these lines was addressed to the Treasury on 11 October, 1918.[3] The total annual expenditure from Government funds if the proposal were approved was estimated at £565,500.

The Lords Commissioners of the Treasury did not reply until 15 November, 1918, when, of course, the entire situation had been changed by the signing of the Armistice. In their letter[4] their Lordships directed that "in view of the cessation of hostilities, no further expenditure, whether by way of direct grants from public funds or the promise of writing-off allowances, should be incurred for this purpose."

---

[1] L.R.F. 120/5.
[2] See below p. 18.
[3] L.R.F. 120/5.
[4] 39136/18 (L.R.F. 120/5).

Some discussion followed as to the course to be adopted in regard to schemes approved but not begun before the Armistice was signed, and it was finally decided on 30 April, 1919, that the approval of such schemes must be cancelled and that the undertakings given in respect thereto must be withdrawn.

To all intents and purposes, therefore, the concession as to the writing-off of the cost of canteens at controlled establishments was in operation for three years, from November, 1915, to November, 1918. During that period 867 schemes of canteen provision at controlled establishments were approved and undertakings were given to recommend the writing-off of £1,909,135 in all in respect of these schemes.

II.—The Health of Munition Workers' Committee.

Closely connected with the work of the Canteens Committee of the Central Control Board was the work of another committee of which Sir George Newman was also Chairman, namely the Health of Munition Workers Committee, appointed with the concurrence of the Home Secretary " to consider and advise on questions of industrial fatigue, hours of labour, and other matters affecting the personal health and physical efficiency of workers in munitions factories and workshops."[1]

When beginning their work, the committee no doubt derived a certain amount of guidance from the experience of those few private firms that had already instituted industrial canteens on their own account. These firms were principally in the food industry, but included also makers of soap, paper, tobacco, cloth and tin boxes. Short of the fully equipped canteen, provision of various kinds and degrees for the workers' meals—rooms for taking meals, facilities for warming up food and so on—was in existence in various places.[2] Some canteens included recreation rooms, gymnasia, baths, educational classes, etc., in addition to the dining room.

The Committee's memorandum on *Canteen Construction and Equipment*[3] deals not only with utilitarian aspects, the lay-out, material of floors and walls, ventilation, etc., but also with æsthetic considera-tion. The very sound principle is laid down that the canteen should be internally and externally as unlike a factory as possible. Plans and elevations suitable for canteens of various sizes are provided.

---

[1] Its membership was as follows :—Sir George Newman, M.D. (Chairman : also member of Central Control Board, and Chairman of Canteens Committee) ; Sir Thomas Barlow, Bart., K.C.V.O., F.R.S.; Mr. G. Bellhouse, Factory Department, Home Office ; Prof. A. E. Boycott, M.D., F.R.S.; Mr. J. R. Clynes, M.P.; Mr. E. L. Collis, M.B., Factory Department, Home Office; Dr. W. M. Fletcher, M.D., F.R.S., Secretary of the Medical Research Committee; Mr. Leonard E. Hill, M.B., F.R.S.; Mr. Samuel Osborn, J.P., Sheffield; Miss R. E. Squire, Factory Department, Home Office; Mrs. H. J. Tennant; Mr. E. H. Pelham (Secretary).

[2] Cd. 8133 of 1915.

[3] Cd. 8199 of 1916—This and other memoranda were summarised in a published pamphlet " *Feeding the Munition Worker*."

The possible methods of management fall under three heads :—

(i) Direct management by the employer himself, if possible with the assistance of a committee of the workers. This would in almost every case necessitate the appointment of a manager or a manageress, to work under the employers or the committee's direction.

(ii) Management by a voluntary society, who would, to all intents and purposes, take over the entire management.

(iii) The employment of an outside caterer.

The choice of any one of these methods must be largely a matter of opinion, but it is very desirable that the employer and the workers should together take a personal interest in the working of the canteen, and this is clearly most easily secured by the first method.

On such lines as these the canteen movement grew steadily. The Munitions of War (Amendment) Act, 1916, empowered the Minister to require the establishment of a canteen in any controlled factory as a condition of approval. Similarly the Police, Factories, etc. (Miscellaneous Provisions) Act, 1916, empowered the Home Secretary by special order to require the occupiers of factories and workshops to make arrangements for preparing a supply of meals to their workpeople. As a rule, however, the movement was left to make its way on its own merits.

III.—Financial Control of Canteens in National Factories.

The Central Control Board undertook in January, 1916, the general responsibility for the organisation of canteens in the Royal Arsenals and in the National Shell, Projectile, Filling and Explosives Factories administered by the Ministry of Munitions :—

After preliminary discussion between officers of the two organisations, a letter was despatched from the Ministry on 3 January, 1916,[1] inviting the Board to

" undertake the general responsibility for the organisation of canteens in the Royal Arsenals, the National Shell, Projectile, Filling and Explosives Factories which are being erected by or for the Ministry. In some cases it is understood that satisfactory arrangements have already been made and in such cases no further action will be necessary. In other cases, however, it will doubtless be found that no provision has yet been made or that further provision is required, and in such cases the Minister desires that the Canteens Committee should make themselves responsible for seeing that there are satisfactory arrangements in operation at all the establishments in question. The Ministry will undertake to provide the building, lighting, heating and equipment of the canteens, and the Minister desires that the canteens should be run so as to be

---

[1] M.W. 28683/7.

self-supporting, including the cost of staff. It is not implied that the Canteens Committee should necessarily run the canteens themselves. It will be open to them to entrust the work to the Y.M.C.A. or any other body whom they approve for the purpose, or to leave it to the Board of Management or other local organisation."

The Board's reply was dated 22 January. After intimating willingness to undertake responsibility for the canteens at national factories the letter continues[1] :—

" I am to enquire whether it is the intention of the Minister that the Central Control Board should relieve the Boards of Management or other local organisations of their primary responsibility in the matter of canteen provision. The Board are of opinion that these local authorities will be eager to transfer to other shoulders the burden of organisation and management where such work is not immediately and directly concerned with the production of munitions of war, and for this reason it seems desirable to make it clear (if such is the intention) that while the Central Control Board will exercise general control and supervision over the provision of canteens at national factories, etc., it will be no part of their functions to organise each individual canteen.

" The Minister's desire that the canteens should be self-supporting is one with which the Board are in full sympathy. They think, however, that its attainment is to be regarded rather as an ideal than as a condition, particularly where women are employed."

The necessary instructions to the various departments of the Ministry of Munitions responsible for the control of the factories and to the factory authorities were embodied in a circular issued on 16 February, 1916, which stated that the primary responsibility for the making of adequate and suitable provision and for the proper management of the canteen when established would rest with the responsible authorities at each factory, subject to the general supervision of the Canteens Committee.

It will be seen that the correspondence had not defined with real precision the scope of the functions to be exercised by the Central Control Board or the extent of the Board's responsibilities. At the time it was scarcely practicable to do so. The sentence in the Ministry letter of 3 January :—" In some cases it is understood that satisfactory arrangements have already been made and in such cases no further action will be necessary " almost implies that once a canteen had been organised and launched upon its career it would require no further attention from headquarters. The Central Control Board do not appear quite to have taken this view. They regarded their immediate task as one of organisation : thereafter they conceived that it would be their duty to keep the canteens under such supervision as would be

---

[1] M.W. 28683/7.

supplied by frequent expert inspection. Both the Ministry and the Central Control Board were agreed that a canteen must be regarded as an integral part of the factory to which it was attached, and that management by an organisation independent of and not subject to the control of the factory management could not be satisfactory. The possibility or desirability of creating a central organisation for the management of canteens, which would have installed its own managers and servants and would have made its own arrangements as to the purchase of foodstuffs and as to tariffs, does not appear to have been seriously considered. The establishment of such an organisation would have involved delay : the conduct of their canteens by an external and independent authority would unquestionably have been irksome and objectionable to the factory authorities, more especially where, as at the outset was generally the case, they were men accustomed to conduct their own concerns without interference. The line of least resistance was thus to leave each factory to make its own arrangements, subject to such expert advice as the factory authorities were willing to accept. The method of central management might, in the long run, have proved more efficient if it could have survived the friction and opposition which its establishment would have engendered, but the fact that it was ignored, despite the suggestive analogy of the Navy and Army Canteen Board, appears to indicate that so far as national factories were concerned it was not within the sphere of practical politics.

The first duty of the Board was obviously to take a survey of the position. It was found that in the majority of the larger factories canteens were in course of provision, sometimes on a large and elaborate scale. In the smaller factories, and notably the National Shell Factories, canteens had in many cases been provided or were in course of provision, and in others it was doubtful whether they were required. The canteens were generally managed by the factory authorities themselves through their own paid servants, but in a few cases the management was entrusted to such associations as the Y.M.C.A. or to outside caterers. To meet this last class of cases the Board caused to be prepared by its legal advisers a form of agreement which regulated the relationship between the factory management and the association or caterer by whom the conduct of the canteen was undertaken. This standard form of agreement provided that the caterer or association should meet the cost of food and of the necessary staff, and that the factory authorities should supply the premises and equipment, should light and heat the buildings, should supply fuel for cooking and maintain the canteen and its fixed plant in repair.[1] Arrangements were made for the supply by H.M. Office of Works (Supplies Division) of the necessary furniture, crockery, cutlery and utensils on the requisition of the Board.

In the course of these preliminary visits and in correspondence which followed thereon the Board found reason to believe that many of the canteens which were in operation were being conducted at a loss,

---

[1] L.R. 2799/62.

and that their management would benefit from close supervision. The Board, therefore, took steps to strengthen their inspecting staff with the view that each canteen should be visited at least once a month. At the same time the need for some regular statement of the accounts of the trading in the canteens began to be felt, as obviously criticism of the efficiency of a trading concern can be of little value unless it be guided by adequate information as to the financial position.

The necessity of initiating a suitable system of accounting for canteens was at the same time receiving the attention of the Finance Department of the Ministry, and on 20 April, 1916, a letter was sent to the Board asking them to agree to a form of procedure in connection with current canteen accounts.   Forms to be used in rendering periodical statements of accounts were sent and the Board was asked to arrange that canteen accounts should be kept separate from factory accounts. It was also suggested that the factory auditors should act as auditors of canteen accounts.[1]

IV.—Canteen Deficits : A Controversial Problem.

Unfortunately at this point a serious disagreement on financial policy between the Board and the Ministry began to reveal itself[2]. Primarily the question at issue was the interpretation of an ambiguous. text.   The Ministry's letter of 3 January, 1916 (already quoted) had said, " The Ministry will undertake to provide building, lighting, heating and equipment of canteens, and the Minister desires that the canteens should be run so as to be self-supporting, including the cost of staff."   The Central Control Board took this to mean that the Ministry would provide not only the capital expenditure on lighting, heating and equipment but also the current expenses, and that a " self-supporting " canteen would be one in which the takings covered the cost of food and staff alone.   The Finance Department of the Ministry on the other hand understood that the Ministry was only to provide the capital expenditure on these items, and that current expenses were in all cases to be covered by takings.[3]

But behind this matter of interpretation lay a difference of principle.   The Board had already stated in their answer of 22 January that they regarded canteen solvency (even as interpreted by their own criteria, presumably) " rather as an ideal than a condition."   Their position was that the canteen habit was a valuable one and that an artificially low tariff, employed as a temporary expedient, might act as an advertisement and thus promote an institution of national

[1] C.R. 3235 and 3259.

[2] The Central Control Board is unable to endorse the account of its views and policy given in this and the succeeding section.   An alternative statement, prepared by Mr. P. R. Higgins, Assistant Secretary of the Board, is printed as an Appendix—see Appendix II.

[3] The two views are stated in detail in C.R. 3269 :—
  (i) Finance Department's view—Mr. Duckworth's letter of 28 July, 1916.
  (ii) The Central Control Board's view—Mr. Cane's reply of 8 August, 1916.

benefit. It was also urged that the encouragement of the canteen
habit and the taking of good healthy meals increased output, and that
a financial loss on the canteen account was more than balanced by a
profit on the factory account. In other words, a losing canteen
promoted " output," and output was the prime concern of the Ministry
and of the nation. They cited in support of their policy " the almost
universal practice of the private employers who have established
canteens for their workpeople."

The standpoint of the Finance Department in opposing the policy
of the Board is set out in a minute by Mr. Duckworth, Deputy Director
of Munitions Finance, on 25 October, 1916.

He showed that there was considerable pressure for the lenient
treatment of canteen accounts ; the Chairman of the Canteen Committee, welfare supervisors, the supply departments, and the managers
of national factories all urged generous treatment.

If interest in the immediate output was the ultimate end of the
canteen movement, it would probably pay the Ministry to provide free
meals ; but if it was admitted that output was sufficiently satisfactory,
and that it was desirable to look ahead and consider the benefit that
would accrue from a general adoption of the canteen habit, then the
prices charged in canteens should be so arranged as to meet reasonable
charges for maintenance. The liberality of the Ministry should
be restricted at the point at which it ceased to be an encouragement
and became a discouragement to commercial firms to provide canteens
for their workpeople. It was dangerous to allow canteen meals to
be regarded as a subsidy in lieu of wages.

Another argument was that as additions to wages were specifically
given to meet the extra cost of living, so the prices of food in canteens
ought to have been raised *pari passu* with the cost of the raw material.
Further, taking the long view, as it was probable that the earnings of
working-class families would be lower after the war, while the price of
food stuffs remained high, it was unwise as a matter of policy to inflate
wages still further by the provision of unduly cheap food.

It is unnecessary to follow in detail the controversy that took place
round these points throughout the year 1916. One unfortunate
consequence was that the canteens themselves remained without
authoritative guidance in financial matters and drifted into habits of
reckless and slovenly finance. When canteens were first opened in
national factories the Central Control Board had issued a form of
trading account and balance sheet, but no detailed instructions as to
the keeping of accounts. As a result, when in January, 1917, the audit
of canteen accounts was begun, it was found that accounts were very
irregularly kept, while in many cases the monthly accounts which were
furnished did not disclose the true trading results, owing to the lack of
definite interpretation of the correct allocation of expenditure between
factory and canteen. In June, 1917, the Controller of Factory Audit
and Costs, under whom a section had been set up to supervise canteen

accounts, issued some instructions to factories, and these were followed in November by a " Memorandum on the System of Accounting for Canteens in National Factories." In his report on canteens in national factories up to 31 March, 1918, the Controller of Factory Audit and Costs wrote :—

> " If an efficient system of accounting and consumption records had been introduced at the outset it is probable that much of the losses incurred would have been avoided."

Early in January, 1917, an agreement was reached on a basis of compromise, and an agreed circular was issued to managers of national factories laying down the following allocation of expenses[1] :—

(*a*) The Ministry were to pay :—

    (i) The capital cost of building, installation and equipment.

    (ii) The cost of maintaining the buildings.

    (iii) The current cost of lighting and heating the premises.

    (iv) The cost of cleaning the room at the beginning of the day, if done by the factory staff.

(*b*) The following were to be included in the price of meals :—

    (i) The prime cost of food.

    (ii) The cost of preparation of meals, including the wages of cooks and the fuel for cooking.

    (iii) The cost of service.

    (iv) The maintenance of equipment.

    (v) The cost of internal management (if any) and cleaners other than those referred to above.

It will be seen that the Finance Department had retreated a considerable distance from the position held in the previous July, when they demanded that all current expenses should be paid for by the canteens. None the less they had secured one essential point. Henceforth canteen charges were placed on a business footing. Both parties, Ministry and canteen, had their several liabilities clearly defined : there would be no further danger of the charge of "camouflaged charity."

Some time, however, necessarily elapsed before all canteens could adapt themselves to these strict conditions. It was one thing to institute a paying tariff in a new concern, quite another thing to introduce it into a concern whose customers had become accustomed to a losing tariff. The task was also made more difficult by the steady rise of prices due to the war. At the request of Dr. Addison, then Minister of Munitions, Sir George Newman submitted on 24 January, 1917, a memorandum[2] on the causes of and treatment of deficits. These were many and serious. All but nine of the national factory canteens showed a deficit, and if the cost of fuel were shifted on to the expenses,

---

[1] HIST. REC./R/346.1/7.   [2] M.F./Local/178/8

as had just been agreed, the number of solvent canteens would be reduced from nine to four.   Sir George indicated as causes :—

(i) the desirability of attracting customers whose natural habit was to bring food from home.

(ii) the concentration of canteen business into one or two short periods, the cost of staff, as is usual where a " rush " business is transacted, being consequently heavy.

(iii) the extra cost involved in serving night meals.

(iv) the performance of unremunerative services, such as the warming up of food and the boiling of water.

(v) the difficulty of finding efficient managers.

Sir George inclined to his former view that these causes combined rendered deficits unavoidable save in exceptionally favourable circumstances, and he expressed the hope that " the development of the canteen habit would not be sacrificed to consideration of finance or the dictates of mere economic pedantry."

The Finance Department were however determined to take a less lenient view of deficits.   As Mr. Duckworth wrote in comment on Sir George Newman's memorandum : " The real danger is lest canteens, and with them the canteen habit, may be definitely destroyed by disregard of considerations of finance."[1] It was unfortunately becoming clear that the Finance Department could not look to the Central Control Board for co-operation in this matter along the lines they intended to pursue.   The deficits continued to increase and it became necessary to establish some new piece of machinery within the Ministry to deal with them.

V.—The Canteens Finance Committee (Ministry of Munitions).

On 1 March, Mr. (later Sir John) Mann, who had succeeded Mr. Lever as Assistant Financial Secretary, summoned a conference at which were present—Sir George Newman, and Mr. Agar, one of the Central Control Board's inspectors, Mr. Webster Jenkinson and Mr. Duckworth, representing the Finance Department, and certain representatives of supply departments at whose factories the canteens were established.   This conference arrived at definite conclusions with regard to deficits in the past and future.   A statement was sent to the Treasury setting out the position and asking sanction for the writing off of past deficits : and a special committee, known as the Canteens Finance Committee, was established to advise the Assistant Financial Secretary with regard to the monthly statements of accounts forwarded by every national factory, and to consider and report upon proposals for the financial and economic control of canteens in national factories. The committee contained representatives of the Finance Department,

---

[1] M.F./Local/178/8.

the Inspection Department and the supply departments.   The business of the committee included[1] :—

  (i) The consideration of audit reports on the working of the canteens.

 (ii) The preparation of a statement for submission to the Treasury with respect to any deficits that might be disclosed.

(iii) The recommendation of payments to canteens where, owing to the poisonous nature of the work, the provision of food could be treated as a special medical precaution.

(iv) The consideration of suggestions for the prevention of deficits.

Mr. Mann, Assistant Financial Secretary, was chairman and Mr. Duckworth, secretary, succeeding Mr. Mann as chairman in September, 1917.   The committee began by meeting once a week, and met twenty-four times in all during its year of existence, April, 1917 to April, 1918.[2]

At the conference on 1 March, Sir George Newman consented to join the new committee, but he did so apparently on the understanding that it was to be a sub-committee of the Canteens Committee, of which he was chairman, including representatives of the Ministry departments concerned.   When he found that the Canteens Finance Committee was constituted on an entirely different basis he took no part in its proceedings and subsequently resigned his membership.[3]

Thus the two committees, the committee of the Board and the committee of the Ministry, worked side by side, entirely separately and not without friction, for the year of their joint existence.

The simultaneous existence of these independent committees can hardly be defended on theoretical grounds.   It may well be maintained, however, that the Finance Department took the best course practicable at the moment in creating for the special purpose, on which it found itself in apparently interminable controversy with the Central Control Board, an instrument of its own entirely independent of the Board, while leaving the Board and its committee otherwise free to carry on those parts of their work around which no controversy had arisen.

---

[1] Hist. Rec./R/346.1/5.

[2] There is danger of confusion between two quite distinct "Canteen Committees."

  (i) The Canteens Committee of the Central Control Board (Liquor Traffic), of which Sir George Newman was Chairman. This committee was in practice indistinguishable from the Central Control Board which it represented : the terms "Central Control Board" and "Canteens Committee" became virtually synonymous in Ministry usage and as such have been employed in this account.

 (ii) The Canteens Finance Committee of the Ministry of Munitions, the institution of which has just been described.   This will be referred to throughout by its title, and never as the Canteens Committee, though that description was often in popular use at the time.

[3] Hist. Rec./H/346.1/3, p. 11.

The problem which confronted the Canteens Finance Committee was the problem of the deficits, as its terms of reference indicate. None the less a study of these terms of reference shows that the title of the committee was in a sense a misnomer. Finance is actually inseparable from organisation. It was the fact that the Central Control Board did not bear financial responsibility that made it an unsatisfactory body for purposes of organisation, once the canteen had been launched and started on its way. Conversely, the financial responsibility borne by the Canteens Finance Committee, more particularly its duties in the matter of the treatment and prevention of future deficits, compelled its activities to extend over the whole range of canteen organisation. At the same time it was not an executive body. Executive powers still resided as they always had done with the factory management, which in the case of national factories was the particular supply department of the Ministry concerned. All the supply departments and each new supply department, as it came to be created, placed a representative on the committee. Thus it was essentially a co-ordinating committee, and in addition to its function of financial criticism, formed the most convenient means of approach to canteens in national factories through their responsible departments.[1]

Thus, in consideration of suggestions for the prevention of deficits, the committee was, in the course of 1917, visited by representatives of the Food Controller, in connection with such subjects as the utilisation of waste products. On another occasion the Food Controller sent a representative to place his views before the committee on the subject of economy in consumption, and secured the support of the supply departments to the lines on which he proposed to address, through selected speakers, the workers in national factories.[2] A further and most valuable contribution from the Ministry of Food was the offer, through the Canteens Finance Committee, of the services of skilled cooks to visit national factory canteens where necessary and give cooking demonstrations. This arrangement dates from 11 February, 1918.

But the *raison d'être* of the committee was the deficits. The seriousness of the situation is shown by the accounts of those national factory canteens, 60 in number, that were audited by the Ministry authorities.[3] Of these canteens only two showed a profit when the various expenses were correctly allocated. The remaining 58 showed a total deficit of over £68,000. The committee at once undertook to cope with the situation. The causes of deficit seemed roughly to fall under two heads : bad management, which often took the form of uneconomical buying, and bad tariffs, which made a deficit inevitable with the best management, and were due in many cases not to bad management but to what the committee considered the bad financial principles inculcated by the Central Control Board. The deficits were

---

[1] Hist. Rec./R/346.1/5.
[2] Memorandum by Mr. Duckworth (Hist. Rec./R/346.1/5.)
[3] See Appendix I.

referred to the several supply departments concerned for enquiry and report. In a few cases the supply departments preferred that the enquiry should come from the Canteens Finance Committee direct, but in the main the practice was for the chartered accountant who received the reports to call the secretary of the committee's attention to deficits and their possible causes, and he in turn referred them for report to the various supply departments.

As a first step in the prevention of future deficits the committee passed resolutions at its first sitting on 4 April, 1917.

(a) The factory manager and canteen manager in each national factory should be formally acquainted that monthly deficits would not in future be allowed to pass without serious question by the committee.

(b) The canteen manager, with the concurrence of the factory manager, should be allowed to raise prices whenever, in his opinion, it might be necessary to do so, in order to avoid a deficit. All such rises were to be reported to Sir George Newman.

(c) Steps should be taken to ensure the provision of punctual and accurate monthly statements of account, and the Ministry's auditors instructed to report at once on any points that seemed to require attention.

(d) Every national factory canteen should be instructed to send up a local purchases sheet monthly so that the committee might be in a position to judge whether the purchases were made economically.

These four resolutions mark the turning point in the history of the Ministry canteen management. Decisive action had at last been taken, and not at all too soon. As a result, and after a year's work, the number of solvent canteens for the half year ending 31 March, 1918, was raised to 17 with a profit of over £6,000. The defaulting canteens audited still numbered 74, but their total deficit for the half year was under £36,000, or a little over half the total deficit shown a year earlier. The percentage of total loss less total profit of sales was reduced from 20 per cent. at 31 March, 1917, to 6½ per cent. for the half year ending 31 March, 1918.[1]

These results even so may appear disappointing. Two considerations should, however, be borne in mind. First, it was no part of the policy of the Ministry to make a profit, as such, out of the canteens. The aim was to make both ends meet. From this point of view in several canteens showing a " negligible " loss the committee may be held to have achieved its purpose. Secondly, it must be remembered that the Central Control Board regarded financial loss as a definite item in their policy of popularising canteens at the taxpayer's expense. The committee could at first only mitigate that system : had they attempted to reverse it, traditionally established as it was in the customers' minds, they would probably have forfeited the custom of the canteens and so defeated their own ends. The continuous

---

[1] See also Appendix I.

rise of food prices during their year of administration has to be borne in mind in estimating the achievement of the committee down to April, 1918, when its responsibilities were taken over by the Food Section of the Labour Department.

VI.—The Work of the Food Section, March—November, 1918.

With the opening of the year 1917, the prospects of a food shortage attracted for the first time the serious attention of the public. A Food Controller figured among the new Ministers created by Mr. Lloyd George's Government on its accession to power in December, 1916. Lord Devonport published his scheme of voluntary rationing in February, 1917. April was the month in which the " U boat " successes reached their maximum. The history of the food shortage and the measures by which it was met belongs to the records of the Ministry of Food rather than to the Ministry of Munitions. It will only be necessary here to touch on those aspects of the story which belong to the history of the canteen movement.

On 24 April, 1917, Dr. Addison, then Minister of Munitions, appointed a committee, known as the Munitions (Food) Committee, to enquire into and make recommendations for the adequate feeding of munition workers. The report of the committee,[1] issued on 7 May, reflected the state of mind of the mass of thoughtful people towards the subject at that date. In common with the rest of the country the committee showed a strong hostility to the idea of compulsory rationing by tickets, and a desire to avoid it at all costs. Indeed, the perusal of this report in the light of later events is calculated to create a vivid impression, both of the difficulties that faced the Ministry of Food at its inception, and of the successful manner in which these difficulties were overcome.

In April, 1918, the general system of rationing the whole population was introduced and the establishment of the Food Section in the Labour Department of the Ministry, superseding both the Canteens Committee of the Central Control Board and the Canteens Finance Committee, was practically coincident with this event.[2] The step had already been foreshadowed in a letter from the Minister (Mr. Churchill) to Lord D'Abernon, Chairman of the Central Control Board, on 13 February, 1918. Mr. Churchill wrote :—

> " I am compelled to the conclusion that the present problems in regard to food, differing so materially both in character and extent from those which gave rise to the activities of the Canteens Committee, render it imperative for me immediately to take a much more intimate responsibility for the feeding of the munition workers than I have hitherto taken or needed to take . . . I feel I am bound to set up within the Ministry of Munitions itself a special department dealing with the subject, and I am now making arrangements to that end.

[1] *Report of the Munitions (Food) Committee.* (Copy in HIST. REC./R/346.1/4.)
[2] *Fourth Report of the Central Control Board (Liquor Traffic).* Cd. 9055 of 1918.

It would be of the greatest assistance to me if you could spare as many as possible of your staff who have been concerned with the working of canteens, and I hope that Sir George Newman will continue to help us with his advice."

On 28 March, 1918, a General Memorandum[1] was issued describing the organisation and functions of the Food Section, of which Mr. Martin Hall became Director.   Its functions fell under three heads :—

(i) To inspect canteens at national factories and to advise the factory management on all questions relating to the feeding of munition workers.

(ii) To inspect the canteens at controlled establishments and to advise their proprietors on questions relating to the provision and maintenance of canteens, and to communicate with the Inland Revenue Department on questions of finance affecting the provision of canteens at such establishments.

(iii) To act as the sole means of communication between the Ministry of Munitions and the Ministry of Food on all questions affecting the feeding of munition workers.

Under this wide reference the Food Section was fully occupied in carrying on the work hitherto performed by the two Canteens Committees which it superseded, and in facilitating, with the help of the Ministry of Food, the provision of the food supplies required by munitions canteens.   It also found itself closely preoccupied in the discussions which arose from the withdrawal by the Inland Revenue Department of writing-off privileges referred to above.[2]

VII.—Growth of the Canteen Movement.

The following table[3] illustrates the growth of the canteen movement :—

	September, 1916.		March, 1917.	
	Number of Canteens	Number of employees in establishments concerned	Number of Canteens	Number of employees in establishments concerned
Controlled Establishments	300	490,000	420	600,000
National Factories	135	150,000	150	200,000
Total	435	640,000	570	800,000

According to the records of the Food Section, 733 privately owned munitions works employing 871,046 persons were provided with canteens at the time of the Armistice.

When to canteens in controlled establishments the canteens in national factories are added, the number of canteens amounted to over 900, providing for 1,000,000 workpeople, and involving a capital cost to the Government of £3,500,000.[4]

---

[1] No. 73.   [2] p. 5.

[3] The 60 canteens in dockyards are omitted from the table.

[4] (Printed) Weekly Report, No. 156, IX (24.8.18).

Of course as the canteens increased in number, so did the munition works that required them. In March, 1917, the 600,000 employees in controlled establishments provided with canteens represented 36½ per cent. of the total number of employees in controlled establishments, and the 200,000 employees in national factories provided with canteens represented 83½ per cent. of the total number of employees in national factories. The total amount of the allowances from current profits of controlled establishments which the Board had up to that time (March, 1917) undertaken to recommend for the provision of canteens was £785,000, and the total payments made in subvention of voluntary societies amounted to £12,570. These figures (which refer solely to controlled establishments) work out at a Government expenditure of £1 6s. 8d. per employee. But the accommodation of these canteens did not suffice for the simultaneous feeding of all the employees in the various works, and taking the unit of canteen accommodation, the cost in September, 1916, worked out at £6 11s. per place.

From a pre-war standpoint the growth of the movement had been rapid. The third report of the Central Control Board (April, 1917) concludes :—

> " There can be little doubt that the industrial canteen will become a permanent and essential feature of the modern factory. From the worker's point of view this is a great step in advance. To eat a carefully prepared meal in wholesome and cleanly surroundings is not merely a matter of health and efficiency, but is a direct preventive of alcoholic excess. The absence of civilising influences from factory industry has been its condemnation in the past. The industrial canteen aids in the destruction of this traditional reproach, and the stimulus imparted to the canteen principle during the last two years may be claimed as a substantial contribution to the humanisation of industry."

As regards national factories the canteen equipment was approximately complete, but the bulk of the munition workers were in controlled establishments, and here only two fifths had access to canteens. One reason was that the great majority of controlled establishments were too small to necessitate separate canteen accommodation. Of the 4,000 controlled establishments in September, 1915, more than half had less than 200 employees, and another quarter between 200 and 500.

Even as regards the controlled firms employing over 500 workers, the canteen movement had not reached half of the total number (900) by March, 1917. The reasons for this limitation were summarised, as follows, by Sir George Newman, in September, 1916.

> " The period covered by the activities of the Board in the matter of canteens has been singularly unpropitious to the undertaking by employers of new enterprises not directly connected with the production of munitions. Both labour and

materials of all kinds were scarce and costly, and the delays in obtaining them and in securing the execution of building works have been both harrassing and vexatious. Moreover, many employers of the period under review have been required to take up new processes of manufacture, to adapt their plant or to install new machinery for work novel to them, and in many cases to employ female labour for the first time. They have also been much occupied with the actual work of manufacture under great pressure, and with problems of labour. It is hardly therefore a matter for astonishment that they have not shown eagerness to take advantage of the concession, when to do so could not fail to impose on them a considerable added burden of trouble and labour, and anxiety.

" As regards the attitude of employers in general, it may be said that their objections to the provision of canteens are based as a rule on practical grounds, *e.g.*, that they have not available space, that they are not sure of making excess profits, that there is no demand from the workers, or that the management are already overworked. There is evidence, they say, of considerable scepticism as regards the usefulness or desirability of a canteen in their particular works, and a want of faith in the likelihood of the success of such an enterprise. Nor can it be denied that there is ground for this scepticism. It must not be overlooked that the prevailing habit among the workers has hitherto been to bring their meals with them to the works or to obtain them from or at home. The domestic budget is as a rule based upon this arrangement, and the weekly payments made by the workers to their wives, parents or landladies are supposed as a rule to cover the provision of the mid-day meal. Additional expenditure on meals at a canteen is, therefore, regarded as a dead loss, especially by the older generation of workers. The disturbance of a time-honoured domestic practice, which is involved in the purchase of meals at a canteen, is thus something of a revolutionary idea. The canteen habit can only by degrees gain acceptance among the working classes and the habit of economy which leads many men and women to prefer food brought from home, even if it be less appetising and less nourishing than the food obtainable in a canteen, is not easily to be overcome."

APPENDICES.

APPENDIX I.

(See above p. 16.)

Trading Accounts of Canteens in National Factories.[1]

(a) TRADING RESULTS.

	Total number of Canteens.	Net Profit on Canteens showing Profit. £ s. d.	Number of Canteens showing Profit.	Net Loss on Canteens showing Loss. £ s. d.	Number of Canteens showing Loss.
To 31st March, 1917	60	57 19 11¾	2	68,427 8 3	58
From 1st April, 1917 to 30th Sept., 1917 ..	77	3,365 8 2	4	49,226 9 4	73
From 1st Oct., 1917 to 31st March, 1918 ..	91	6,326 8 5½	17	35,539 7 2	74
From 1st April, 1918 to 30th Sept., 1918 ..	113	3,926 12 1	26	49,303 10 4	87
From 1st Oct., 1918, to 31st March, 1919 ..	120	351 6 3	11	66,633 11 4	109
From beginning to 31st March, 1919	132	14,027 14 11	9[2]	269,130 6 5	123

[1] The canteens at Woolwich, Enfield and Waltham Abbey are not included.
[2] These were :—Litherland Explosives Factory ; Glasgow (Mile End) Projectile Factory ; Horley, Leeds (Oulton), and Neasden Central Stores Depots ; Erith and Watford (No. 2) Trench Warfare Filling Factories ; and King's Lynn Wood Distillation Factory.

(b) Periodical Trading Accounts.

	To 31st Mar., 1917.	1st April, 1917 to 31st Sept., 1917.	1st Oct., 1917 to 31st Mar., 1918.	1st April, 1918 to 30th Sept., 1918.	1st Oct., 1918 to 31st Mar., 1919.	Total.
	£ s. d.	£ s. d.	£ s. d.	£ s. d.	£ s. d.	£ s. d.
Sales—						
Canteen Takings ..	337,996 4 6½	332,620 2 8½	453,786 8 1	528,749 8 9	306,956 8 9	1,960,108 12 10
Sundry Receipts ..	570 9 2	651 0 1	989 8 5	2,481 10 11	2,925 7 7	7,617 16 2
Total Income ..	338,566 13 8½	333,271 2 9½	454,775 16 6	531,230 19 8	309,881 16 4	1,967,726 9 0
Provisions Consumed ..	292,818 6 2	270,223 7 10½	334,141 9 5	379,258 18 1	233,725 3 11	1,510,167 5 5½
Gross Profit	45,177 18 4½	62,396 14 10	119,646 5 10½	150,033 17 8	73,733 12 0	450,988 8 9
Gross Loss	—	—	1 7 2½	543 7 0	502 7 2	1,047 1 4½
Percentage on Sales ..	13·36	18·76	26·37	28·27	23·86	22·95
Expenses—						
Salaries and Wages ..	82,539 3 2½	78,805 16 5½	109,080 6 11	147,597 16 1	102,738 18 7	520,762 1 3
Fuel for Cooking ..	13,740 12 2	12,193 2 7½	15,705 6 9	18,063 18 8	12,537 14 2	72,240 14 4½
Repairs and Maintenance	9,808 12 4½	9,299 1 4	12,109 8 2½	15,995 16 3	14,518 13 1	61,731 11 3
Printing and Stationery	1,508 17 4½	1,758 15 11½	2,572 18 3½	2,696 8 6	1,767 0 11	10,304 1 0½
Carriage, Motors, etc ..	563 13 1	356 13 11	495 7 2½	1,240 19 7	1,472 2 5	4,128 16 2½
Travelling Facilities ..	1,181 10 9	1,070 2 4	1,388 5 7	2,051 0 3	1,013 7 5	6,704 6 4
Overalls	432 15 0	274 7 10	200 5 11½	840 8 5	355 9 1	2,103 6 3½
Discs	—	—	187 15 3	945 2 6	1,478 15 2	2,611 12 11
Interest	1,121 3 10	2,394 6 5½	3,832 16 8	1,102 15 0	2,113 4 3	10,564 6 2½
Rent, Rates, etc.. ..	38 19 5	51 11 8	118 2 4	422 2 8	292 14 0	923 10 1
Cash Deficiencies ..	—	—	60 15 6	22 7 10	98 15 11	181 19 3
Miscellaneous	3,182 8 7½	2,704 17 5	4,095 17 1½	6,370 4 1	4,052 2 6	20,405 9 10
Total	114,117 15 10	108,908 16 1	149,847 5 9	197,348 19 10	142,438 17 6	712,661 15 0½
Total Expenditure..	406,936 2 0	379,132 3 11½	483,988 15 2½	576,607 17 11	376,164 1 5	2,222,829 0 6
Net Profit on Canteens showing Profit	57 19 11½	3,365 8 2	6,326 8 5½	3,926 12 1	351 6 3	14,027 14 11
Net Loss on Canteens showing Loss..	68,427 8 3	49,226 9 4	35,539 7 2	49,303 10 4	66,633 11 4	269,130 6 5
Percentage of Loss, less Profit on Sales..	20·23	13·78	6·43	8·58	21·59	13·01

24

APPENDIX II.

(See above, p. 11.)

Extract from Memorandum on the Supervision of Canteens in National Factories, by Mr. P. R. Higgins, Assistant Secretary to the Central Control Board (Liquor Traffic), September, 1919.

(The substance of what follows here has been incorporated above, pp. 11–14.)

* * * * *

In the course of the discussion on trading accounts it became apparent that a difference of opinion existed between the Liquor Control Board and the Finance Department of the Ministry of Munitions as to the interpretation of that passage in Sir H. Llewelyn Smith's letter of 3 January, 1916, which runs as follows :—

> "The Ministry will undertake to provide the building, lighting, heating and equipment of canteens, and the Minister desires that the canteens should be run so as to be self-supporting, including the cost of staff."

The Finance Department read this passage as meaning that while the Ministry would provide a building fully equipped, all current charges thereafter for food, wages, fuel for lighting and heating and cooking, the maintenance of fixed and portable equipment and cleaning should be borne by the canteen from the trading receipts. The Liquor Control Board held that the meaning was that the canteen should bear the prime cost of food and the wages of the staff employed and nothing else.

The text of the letter is ambiguous and will support either interpretation. Being unable, therefore, to rely upon it both parties appealed to first principles and the criteria suggested by each are quoted below. The view of the Liquor Control Board is outlined in a letter to the Secretary of the Ministry of Munitions, dated 8 August, 1916 :—

> "If it be once admitted that a canteen in an industrial establishment cannot be expected to be a self-supporting institution on a commercial basis like a restaurant established by private enterprise, the decision as to the charges of which it should be relieved must depend upon practical considerations and must be based upon experience which will show how far such canteens can be self-supporting without jeopardising their entire usefulness."[1] . . . .

Both sides were agreed that once the strict commercial principle was abandoned the allocation of current charges as between factory and canteen was arbitrary and each suggested a different canon for determining their incidence. The Liquor Control Board proposed to base the allocation on "practical considerations" of providing meals at prices attractive to the workers : the Finance Department advanced

[1] The view of the Finance Department, as expressed in a memorandum by Mr. G. H. Duckworth, has been quoted in the text. (*see above*, p. 12.)

the view that the closer the approximation to the strict commercial basis the greater would be the willingness of the average employer to establish a canteen at his works. The Liquor Control Board considered that insistence on the strict commercial basis of charges would imperil the immediate usefulness of the canteens, and they were evidently of opinion that the creation of a demand for canteen facilities on the part of the workers was the best means of securing the permanence of the canteen movement. The Finance Department did not think that a development of the canteen habit stimulated by the sale of meals at less than the commercial price could be permanent, as private employers could not afford to maintain canteens on such lines. Both parties agreed that the prime cost of food and the wages of canteen staff must be met from canteen takings, and as these items represent together about 90 per cent. of the current charges in a canteen the field of discussion was narrow. It admitted, however, of controversy and accusations from the one side of "economic pedantry" and from the other of "disregard of considerations of finance" show that the discussion was not always conducted with amenity.

Ultimately, the question was settled by a compromise embodied in a circular issued by the Finance Department on 15 January, 1917, and signed by Mr. (now Sir) John Mann, the Assistant Financial Secretary. By this circular the various charges were apportioned between factory and canteen as follows :—

" (a) The Ministry will pay—

(1) The capital cost of the building, installation and equipment.
(2) The cost of maintaining the buildings.
(3) The current cost of lighting and heating the premises.
(4) The cost of cleaning the room at the beginning of the day, if done by the factory staff.

" (b) The following charges should be included in the price of meals—

(1) The prime cost of the food.
(2) The cost of preparation of meals, including wages of cooks and fuel for cooking.
(3) The cost of service.
(4) The maintenance of equipment.
(5) The cost of internal or domestic management (if any) and cleaners other than those referred to in (a) (4) above."

The circular in question included an important paragraph on the question of deficits on canteen trading.

" 3. *Deficits.*—It is believed that with proper management the apportionment of expenditure indicated above should enable the canteen to be self-supporting and, unless in exceptional circumstances, deficits upon canteen working will not be chargeable against the factory or other Ministry funds.

"4. If deficits are already being incurred on the working of the canteen, or if the margin of profit has been relatively small, the foregoing instructions may necessitate a revision of the tariff. Before that step is taken, however, reference must be made to the Canteen Committee of the Central Control Board (Liquor) Traffic . . . . "

The Liquor Control Board had found in the course of their periodical visits that the majority of the canteens were working at a loss. Trading accounts were returned by 35 canteens for November, 1916, and of these only nine showed a profit on the month's trading. Even in these cases it was doubtful whether a profit would have been realised if the apportionment of charges prescribed in the circular of 15 January, 1917, had been followed.

The obvious suggestion was to raise prices. In the view of the Control Board, however, the causes which gave rise to deficits on trading were too varied and complex to be removed by this simple remedy. For the information of Dr. Addison, who had asked for a statement on the subject, the causes of deficits were summarised in a memorandum presented by Sir George Newman on 24 January, 1917. Briefly, the causes were :—

(i) The danger if prices were too rapidly advanced that the men and women employed, who were not accustomed to spend money on meals away from home, would cease to purchase and would revert to the practice of bringing food to the works ;

(ii) The concentration of canteen business in one or two short periods, the cost of staff as is usual where a " rush " business is transacted being consequently heavy ;

(iii) The necessity of serving meals at such times of the day or night as the hours of working in the factory demanded, although at certain periods profitable working might be out of the question ;

(iv) The performance of unremunerative services, e.g., the warming-up of food or the supply of boiling water. A canteen is not merely a restaurant but is also a place of general resort during meal times, and many who use it make no purchase or only a trifling one ;

(v) The difficulty of attaining efficient management. Canteens in national factories were working-class restaurants on a large scale, and the number of persons qualified to manage them was extremely limited. The ordinary " coffee-shop " caterer, though he could manage a small business efficiently, was not capable of handling the canteen business, the details of which he could not keep in his head. It was necessary, therefore, to train persons, and preferably women of superior social and educational standing, in the business, and this could not be done in a day."

       *   *   *   *

On 1 March, 1917, Mr. Mann, the Assistant Financial Secretary, summoned a conference to discuss the whole question. At this conference there were present Mr. Mann himself, Sir George Newman, representatives of the Finance Department of the Ministry and representatives of certain of the supply departments responsible for the control of the factories at which canteens were established. The whole question of deficits was discussed rather diffusely, and the suggestion was finally made by Mr. Mann that the Canteens Committee should form a sub-committee "including a few people representing various departments in the Ministry directly concerned for the purpose of focussing discussions, tracing details of management and preparing results of the working of canteens in Government factories." Mr. Mann proposed certain individual as suitable members of the committee. Sir George Newman replied that he was in entire agreement and warmly welcomed the suggestion.

A proposal for the creation of a committee was accordingly submitted to the Minister on 8 March, 1917. It was not, however, the proposal agreed to by Sir G. Newman at the meeting on 1 March to set up a sub-committee of the Canteens Committee of the Liquor Control Board with co-opted members from the Ministry. The committee, whose constitution was approved by the Minister, was an entirely distinct one, with representatives from six departments of the Ministry and only one representative from the Canteens Committee. The proposal was approved by Dr. Addison on 12 March, and Mr. Mann agreed on the 15th of that month to take the chair and appointed Mr. G. H. Duckworth, of the Ministry Finance Department, as secretary of the committee.

No specific terms of reference were approved by Dr. Addison, but in the invitations to attend the first meeting it was stated that :—

"The business of the committee will include :

(a) Consideration of the audit reports on the working of the canteens ;

(b) Preparation of a statement for submission to the Treasury with respect to any deficits that may be disclosed ;

(c) The recommendation of payments to canteens where, owing to the poisonous nature of the work, the provision of food can be treated as a special medical precaution ;

(d) The consideration of suggestions for the prevention of deficits."

In welcoming the suggestion to establish a sub-committee, Sir George Newman was probably glad to have an opportunity of bringing the Canteens Committee in its relation to canteens at national factories into closer touch with the supply departments concerned. A committee on the lines originally suggested by Mr. Mann would probably have served a very useful purpose as it would have enabled the Canteens Committee to bring at once to the notice of the representative of the supply department any defects of management revealed by the reports of the committee's inspectors, and reciprocally it would have been practicable for the supply departments to ask for investigation in any case in which they were dissatisfied with the management of a canteen. A great opportunity was thus lost.

It actually happened that two committees existed side by side for almost 12 months (from April, 1917 to March, 1918), each of which was charged with certain responsibilities in relation to canteens at national factories. It was difficult if not impossible to draw any line of demarcation between the functions of the two committees, as each deemed it to be its duty to secure the efficient and economical management of the canteens and friction was unavoidable. The Canteens Committee of the Liquor Control Board pursued its efforts along the lines which had been followed since January, 1916, and undoubtedly succeeded in "keying up" considerably the standard of management. The Canteens Finance Committee for its part pressed for a reduction of the deficits on trading, and thus kept constantly before the supply departments and factory managers their responsibility for the proper conduct of their canteens. Sir George Newman subsequently resigned his membership of the Canteens Finance Committee, whose meetings he had never attended, and thereafter the two committees followed their several ways.

The position was, however, one of unstable equilibrium, and it was inevitable that each party should from time to time endeavour to secure a fresh definition of its powers and responsibilities. The details of the various discussions are of little interest as they affected the actual conduct of the canteens or the mode of their supervision scarcely at all. The Minister in January, 1918, was considering a recommendation from the Assistant Financial Secretary (Sir H Hambling) that the whole question of the proper authority to supervise canteens should be submitted to a Council Committee, when the sudden shortage of meat and the anticipated difficulty of obtaining food supplies of all kinds convinced the Minister that he must assume direct responsibility for the feeding of munition workers. A new section, called the Feeding of Munition Workers Section or, more usually, the Food Section, was accordingly constituted as part of the Labour Regulation Department. This section absorbed the functions both of the Canteens Committee and of the Canteens Finance Committee.

Contents of Volume V.

Note.—The present issue is subject to revision
and must be regarded as provisional.

HISTORY OF THE MINISTRY OF MUNITIONS.

VOLUME V

WAGES AND WELFARE

PART V

PROVISION FOR THE HOUSING OF MUNITION WORKERS

1921

PART V

PROVISION FOR THE HOUSING OF MUNITION WORKERS

u

CONTENTS.

(C197) 5260 Wt.3643/A.P.5036 7/21 250 Harrow

CHAPTER VI.

Special Aspects of the Housing Problem.

CHAPTER VII.

The Elizabethville Colony, Birtley.

CHAPTER VIII.

The Gretna Townships.

APPENDICES.

INDEX.

CHAPTER I.

INTRODUCTORY.

From its foundation the Ministry of Munitions was confronted by an urgent housing problem. Certain centres in which big armament firms had existed or in which, at any rate, there was highly developed engineering industry, were already seriously congested, and the establishment of national factories, very often in these same districts, was further to intensify the problem.

Since the outbreak of war the construction of working-class houses by private enterprise or the activity of local authorities had, owing to the scarcity and high cost of both labour and material, been practically at a standstill. Such areas, too, as the Clyde, the Tyne, Barrow, Sheffield, Birmingham and Coventry had already experienced a pre-war shortage of housing accommodation.[1] Thus in Coventry there had recently been a marked decrease in the number of houses built every year; in 1911, 1912 and 1913 the numbers were respectively 1,211, 894 and 838; in 1914 there was a slight increase to 977, but it was totally inadequate to meet the normal demand of the town apart from the rapidly increasing and abnormal needs of the Coventry Ordnance Works.[2] In Birmingham also the Birmingham Small Arms Company, which in March, 1915, had under discussion a proposed increase of 4,000 rifles a week on their output, entailing an additional staff of 8,000 persons, named the housing difficulty as a serious hindrance to the scheme. They emphasised the already grave lack of accommodation for their ordinary workpeople and considered it would be well to deal with the provision of houses concurrently with the building and equipping of their new factory.[3]

The principal action taken by the Government previous to June, 1915, had been the initiation of a housing scheme for Woolwich Arsenal, where before the close of 1914 the expansion of staff was so enormous and the difficulties of housing so correspondingly great as to render remedial action a necessary war measure. It was accordingly agreed at a conference held in January, 1915, between representatives of the Local Government Board, the Treasury, the War Office and the Office of Works, that the Office of Works should undertake the task. Land was immediately purchased at a cost of £40,381 15s. 3d., and at the time of the Ministry's formation the work of constructing 1,298 houses and flats was well under weigh.[4] In addition the War Office had assisted Vickers with loans towards the provision of houses for munition workers at Erith, Crayford and Barrow.[5]

---

[1] This pre-war shortage, partly caused by uncertainty as to how the Finance Act of 1910 would affect building speculation, was universal; in the South Wales Coalfields there was a deficiency of 40 to 50,000 houses (Commission on Industrial Unrest).

[2] L.R./11636/6.　　　　　[3] 94/R/30.

[4] *Report from Committee of Public Accounts* (1917), Appendix 5.

[5] *Ibid.*, Appendix 12.

The acute shortage of housing accommodation at armament centres had also been dealt with under the Defence of the Realm Act, an amendment, dated 16 March, 1915, making it lawful for the Admiralty or Army Council " to take possession of any unoccupied premises for the purpose of housing workmen employed in the production, storage or transport of war material."

The Ministry was faced with a problem which has here to be considered, and which was at once serious and complicated. Its primary interest in housing was to secure and increase output, the welfare or social side of the question was but the means to an end ; and the permanent interests both of the State which provided the house and of the workman who lived in it were subordinated to the needs of the moment. This attitude coloured the policy of the Ministry during the war. From motives of economy and speed, temporary buildings were preferred to permanent ones, save where the latter would obviously be needed after the war. In addition to the more obvious methods of solving the problem of housing the munition worker, the Ministry also sought a way out of the difficulty by the improved organisation of billeting arrangements and by the development of transport facilities.

The whole situation was changed by the Armistice and the permanent houses have formed a preliminary contribution towards a wide scheme for State provision of housing, and as such their administration assumed a new importance ; while the temporary buildings, although in urgent demand during the months succeeding the Armistice, necessarily proved less satisfactory as a contribution to the housing question.

For the same reason that the problem of housing during the war was regarded essentially as one of output, its solution was not confined to one department, and, in addition to the Housing Section (attached in the first instance to the Parliamentary and General Branch of the Ministry of Munitions, and from August, 1917, to the Labour Regulation Department), the Explosives Department, the Aircraft Department, and the Woolwich authorities all undertook responsibility for housing schemes. It was not until after the Armistice that housing matters could be centralised in a single department, administering the schemes in accordance with a considered policy.[1]

The question of rents again was prejudiced during the war. So long as it was necessary to attract workers to a particular locality and keep them there, it was impossible to enforce the Treasury proviso of an economic rental, which would have been almost invariably higher than the prevailing standard.[2] It was not until after the Armistice that a firm stand in the matter of rents could be taken.

These and other difficulties, of which not the least arose from lack of material and labour,[3] must be taken into account before a true estimate of the Ministry's achievement in providing housing can be obtained.

---

[1] See below, p. 32.   [2] See below, pp. 12–16.   [3] See below, p. 24.

CHAPTER II.

HOUSING ADMINISTRATION.

I. Departmental Organisation.

The admitted importance, and even urgency, of housing schemes for the employees of Government contractors, and particularly of armament firms, made it very desirable that the Treasury should early lay down definite procedure. Accordingly on 15 June, 1915, they addressed a letter to the Ministry on this subject. They defined the policy hitherto adopted in dealing with housing, which was to limit grants of housing loans to schemes for houses urgently needed in areas where war work was being carried out and where the Department concerned was prepared to testify to the need. Every effort had been made to restrict capital expenditure or to reduce it to a minimum. They therefore laid it down as a fixed principle for the Ministry of Munitions that, wherever possible, only temporary accommodation sufficient for the needs of the moment should be provided, and definite proof that this was impossible would be required before schemes for more permanent construction were adopted. Temporary housing could not be assisted out of the Local Loans Fund, but would be a matter of arrangement between the Ministry and its contractors. When, however, it was conclusively shown that permanent accommodation was essential, the Treasury was prepared to ask the Public Works Loan Board to assist either local authorities, societies or individuals. In practice permanent housing was only sanctioned where it was certain that it would be required to meet the needs of the normal population after the war.[1]

The Ministry of Munitions accepted the dictum thus laid down by the Treasury of the paramount importance of providing temporary rather than permanent accommodation, and the policy now initiated was to remain the guiding principle throughout.[2]

It was obviously necessary early to define the future relationship between the Ministry and the Departments concerned with the administration of the Housing of the Working Classes Acts. Much depended on which was likely to be of most use to the Ministry, the Local Government Board or the Office of Works. It was felt that on the whole, though the Office of Works had a larger technical staff of architects

---

[1] Treasury letter, 15 June, 1915 (Copies filed in C.R.V./Gen./360 and L.R./112/140).

[2] L.R.112/140. Some exception was raised to the proposal that permanent houses must represent the permanent needs of the neighbourhood. It was felt that there might be an artificial demand for houses due only to war conditions which it would be impossible to meet by temporary accommodation, even though the post-war need might be doubtful. (Memorandum by Mr. Wolff to Mr. Beveridge, 22 June, 1915.)

more widely distributed throughout the country, the Board had a more intimate knowledge of housing and the statutes which affected it. In the first instance, accordingly, the Ministry applied to the Local Government Board—in whom (under the Housing Act of 1914) was vested authority to deal with the provision of houses for persons employed by Government Departments—as to what help they would give in cases which were referred direct to the Ministry, and, more especially, whether the service of the Board's Inspectors would be available to check contracts and to decide whether temporary rather than permanent accommodation should be provided. A conference was held on 21 July, 1915, with Mr. Dickenson, head of the Housing Department of the Local Government Board, who promised all assistance in his power.

There was, however, the question of overlapping and consequent disagreement with the Office of Works, to whom the Public Works Loan Board, where application was made otherwise than by a local authority, submitted all plans and specifications. It was therefore considered advisable to approach the Public Works Loan Board as to whether in case of provisional housing for munition workers they would accept recommendations from the Ministry based on advice received from the Local Government Board without reference to the Office of Works.[1] As a result of conferences the Public Works Loan Board, while not definitely binding themselves, stated they would be predisposed to accept the Ministry's recommendation. Procedure was also discussed with the Committee on New Issues, who agreed that if the Treasury received a definite statement from the Ministry based on expert advice from the Local Government Board they would recommend the scheme to the Public Works Loan Board.[2]

The Ministry and the Local Government Board in consultation together next arrived at a form of procedure which was followed in cases where permanent accommodation was decided on. In the first place inquiry was made on the spot through the Local Government Board's Inspectors as to the housing situation in the locality concerned. The Board then made a report based on these investigations, stating the amount and nature of temporary or permanent accommodation which should be provided. In the case of permanent housing, where there was a willing local authority that authority would usually be asked to undertake the work, the Public Works Loan Board advancing the money in the ordinary way if desired. Where no arrangement was made with the local authority, either the firm concerned was asked to undertake a housing scheme or the Ministry undertook the work direct through their offices or agents. In either case the Local Government Board lent the assistance of their professional staff of architects and engineers. When the work was carried out by a local authority as agent for the Ministry the Board assisted in the supervision of contracts and inspection of work.[3]

[1] L.R./112/141 ; C.R.V./Gen./361.
[2] C.R.V./Gen./361.
[3] Hist. Rec./H/346.2/1.

It was decided from the first to work as far as possible through the Departments concerned with housing instead of setting up an elaborate new organisation, thus not only effecting a saving in public money but also securing continuity of policy.

Early negotiations had been carried on by the General Secretary, but in October, 1915, when schemes were being actively arranged, it became necessary to establish a special section in the Ministry to deal with matter relating to housing. This section remained under the direct control of the Parliamentary and General Branch until 1917 (under Mr. Lascelles), while the work was actually administered by the Assistant General Secretary (Mr. Vernon). As a result of Mr. Churchill's re-organisation in August, 1917, the housing section was transferred from the Secretariat to the Labour Regulation Department.

On 29 October, 1915, a Director of Housing Construction was appointed to work under the general direction of the Secretary of the Ministry of Munitions.[1] This appointment was intended in the first instance to supply the direct supervision necessary to temporary schemes (with the exception of those undertaken by the Explosives Department). The duties included the preparation of plans for temporary housing and all arrangements relating to tenders and contracts ; the terms of all contracts had to be submitted to the Finance Department for approval. When permanent housing under the supervision of the Local Government Board and temporary schemes were undertaken in the same locality the Local Government Board co-operated with the Director of Housing Construction in such matters as the construction of roads and sewers which affected both undertakings.[2] From 1917 onwards the Director of Housing Construction also controlled any permanent housing scheme which was not undertaken by local authorities.[3] To these duties were added as time went on the examination of bills for repair work, the certification of payments and contracts sent in by local architects and the arrangements for the supply of equipment.[4]

In March, 1916, when the first schemes were approaching completion, a Director of Housing Management was appointed.[5]

As will be seen, other branches of the Ministry, the Inland Transport Department and the Central Billeting Board, working both independently and in co-operation with the Housing Section, shared the task of providing housing accommodation for munition workers.[6]

---

[1] Mr. Henry Holloway, a member of the well-known building firm ,held this appointment until the end of 1916, when he was succeeded by Mr. Robertson, architect to the London County Council.

[2] L.R. 112/138. The temporary scheme at Sheffield was an exception to the general rule, the Sheffield Corporation acting as agents for the Ministry.

[3] L.R. 112/138. Mr. Lloyd George enumerates this as part of the Director's work in his letter of appointment, 29 October, 1915.

[4] L.R. 112/127.   [5] This post was held throughout by Sir Robert Carlyle.

[6] By 1918, the large number of Departments whose sanction or co-operation was required for a housing scheme was a source of considerable delay. In addition to negotiations with the Treasury, the Local Government Board and local authorities generally, a permanent scheme was dealt with at various stages in its career by the Central Billeting Board, the Works Construction Sub-Committee of the War Priorities Committee and the Munitions Works Board. An attempt was made to simplify the procedure in March, 1918. (L.R. 112 51, 58, 77.)

After the Armistice a Controller of Housing (Mr. Duckworth) was appointed, with the Directors of Housing Construction, Housing Management, and Housing Finance reporting to him and their sections brought together under one root.[1]

In the course of 1919 various new duties were added to the work of the department. Thus it took over the control of temporary bungalows at Woolwich from the Chief Superintendent of Ordnance Factories, and of a housing scheme at Queen's Ferry from the Explosives Department.

In October, 1919, the Construction Section was taken over by the Office of Works. The Management and Finance Sections continued some time longer as part of the organisation of the Ministry of Munitions, the official transfer of the Housing Department to the Office of Works bearing date as from 1 July, 1920.

II. The Finance of Housing Schemes.

(a) METHODS OF FINANCING SCHEMES.

It was at first assumed that expenditure on housing would come under Contracts Finance.[2] The increasing importance of the housing question and the magnitude of the sums involved made it imperative, however, that it should have a separate financial existence, and, as a result of late negotiations between the Treasury and the Ministry, housing schemes have appeared separately among the sub-heads under which the Munitions Vote was accounted for. The Treasury also laid down that separate reference was required in respect of all expenditure on housing of munition workers.[3]

The Ministry undertook the control of all expenditure connected with temporary schemes entered upon either by the Housing Section or the Explosives Department. Tenders and contracts were arranged for by a Ministry official and were in all cases submitted to the Finance Department for approval.[4]

---

[1] A Departmental Housing Committee, under the chairmanship of Mr. Duckworth, met weekly from the beginning of 1919 to secure correlation of principle and action on the part of each section. Co-ordination with the Housing Committee of the Local Government Board was insured by the appointment of the Director of Housing Construction as liaison officer with that committee, and with H.M. Office of Works by the appointment of a representative of that Office.

[2] The Treasury letter of 23 June, 1915 (copy in L.R. 112/140), laid down that it was the duty of the contractor to arrange and pay for such accommodation as was necessary (recovering doubtless the net cost in the price of his products), but that, in special cases, financial assistance might have to be given by the Contracts Department to individual contractors. On 2 July, Sir Hubert Llewellyn Smith agreed to discuss the finance of housing with the Treasury on this basis.

[3] Treasury letter of 24 February, 1916 (copy in 15/Munitions/377), and Treasury Minute of 24 January, 1916 (copy in C.R./2979). It was agreed early in 1916 that expenditure on account of temporary quarters for workmen outside Woolwich Arsenal should be taken to the Ministry of Munitions Vote and not to the Ordnance Factory Vote. The expenditure for Housing under the Munitions Vote has been £1,097,018 17s. 3d. in 1915-1916; £2,084,635 9s. 8d. in 1916-1917; £1,163,749 16s. 1d. in 1917-1918, making a total of £4,345,403 13s. (Appropriation Accounts, 1917-1918 p. 4.)

[4] L.R. 112/138.

The different methods employed by the Ministry for subsidising permanent housing schemes fall under the following heads : (*a*) grants to local authorities; (*b*) assistance given to controlled establishments ; (*c*) arrangements for post-war ownership.

Grants to Local Authorities.

On 4 October, 1915, the Ministry forwarded to the Treasury the terms of agreement into which, after consultation with the Local Government Board, they proposed to enter with local authorities undertaking permanent housing schemes. The scheme was to be carried out by the local authority under Part III. of the Housing of the Working Classes Act, 1890, the Public Works Loan Commissioners advancing money in the ordinary way, if so desired. The Ministry was to bear, by way of grants towards the excess cost over pre-war building rates, such proportion, not exceeding 30 per cent., as should be determined by the Local Government Board after negotiation with the local authority. A condition of all grants was that the Government should have the option of tenancy for munition workers during the war.[1]

The Treasury, in reply, was inclined to take exception to any assistance of local authorities from public moneys, and laid down the proviso that the discretion of the Local Government Board should be limited to 15 per cent. of the total in assessing the amount of excess cost to be borne by the Ministry.[2]

Meanwhile, owing to the extreme urgency of the question the Ministry had anticipated Treasury approval and had already entered into arrangements with local authorities from which it was too late to withdraw, committing themselves to 20 per cent. to 25 per cent. of the total cost. The Minister accordingly requested authority covering the arrangement arrived at and asked that the limit for future cases should be raised to 20 per cent. of the total cost. The Treasury gave the covering sanction required on 12 November, but refused to alter their decision to limit excess cost borne by the Ministry to 15 per cent.

As events proved, no further appeal to the Treasury was needed, for the provisional arrangement made proved to include the four schemes which alone were financed in this manner.[3]

---

[1] C.R.V./Gen./361.

[2] Their Lordships pointed out that the local authority had no vested interest in the pre-war price of building, nor was it likely that there would be a rapid fall in building prices after the war, owing to the amount of reconstruction work. Moreover, the workmen for whom the houses were required would be earning high wages and could afford to pay an adequate rent (Treasury letter 14 October, 1915, copy in C.R.V./Gen./361).

[3] L.R. 112/49. The lowest grant made by the Ministry was 13½ per cent. to the Lanarkshire County Council. Coventry Corporation claimed 32 per cent. on pre-war cost or 24 per cent. on present estimated cost, but eventually compromised on 20 per cent. including the cost of roads and sewers. The Ministerial grant to Sheffield was also 20 per cent. over the whole scheme. The highest grant, 25 per cent. on buildings and 10 per cent. on roads and sewers, was to Dudley Corporation, who provided the sites both for permanent and temporary schemes, charging a nominal rent for the latter. Negotiations for similar arrangements at Newcastle and Dartford fell through owing to the local authority's refusal to agree to the terms offered by the Ministry (C.R. 2913 ; L.R. 1153/13 ; L.R. 11636/12).

The Ministry retained a financial interest in the due execution of these schemes; all contracts were made by the local authorities under their supervision and were approved by them before being signed. Once the houses were ready for occupation, Ministerial responsibility ceased.[1]

Assistance given to Controlled Establishments.

Direct grants to local authorities had provided for permanent housing schemes to meet the requirements of a national factory or a works extension paid for by the Ministry. Other financial arrangements were made to meet cases where controlled establishments undertook contracts of the first importance whose fulfilment was not possible without the provision of additional housing. These arrangements included either (i) a loan from the Ministry, (ii) a charge against excess profits, or (iii) a direct grant from the Ministry.

With regard to (i), loans direct by the War Office[2] or Ministry of Munitions were usually made at the current rate of interest, varying between $4\frac{1}{2}$ per cent. in 1915 and $5\frac{1}{2}$ per cent. in 1917. Since 1915 the Ministry advanced money only on evidence of an equivalent value of work done.[3] A period of 20, 30 or 40 years was allowed over which the loan was repayable.[4] The Ministry also allowed that loans should be written down to replacement value, to be decided at some fixed date after the war.

These loans were the subjects of formal agreements between the Ministry and the firms. The agreement concluded with the Austin Motor Company for the loan of £75,000 to provide 251 houses may be quoted as summarising the general policy. The value of the houses was to be determined two years after the war and any depreciation on the original cost was to be written off. The company was to pay $5\frac{1}{2}$ per cent. on the loan during the period preceding valuation. If they elected to pay off the debt during this pre-valuation period the property would be re-conveyed to them at their own expense. After valuation had been made the company was to wipe off the debt in

---

[1] L.R. 112/138.

[2] In 1915 the War Office made a loan of £150,000 to Beardmore to construct workmen's houses at Dalmuir, and £75,000 and £50,000 to Vickers for the same purpose at Barrow and Crayford respectively. (D.F.3/P.A.C./22; Hist. Rec./ R/346.2/6.)

[3] D.F.3/P.A.C./22. The Controller and Auditor General drew attention in 1916 to the fact that two years after the date of the advance to Beardmore only about three-fourths of the loan had been expended and that the contractor had therefore had for a considerable period the use of large sums at a low rate of interest (*Report of Controller and Auditor General*, 1916-1917). It appeared that in this case under Scottish law, which differed fundamentally from English, the payment of the loan had to be made on the execution of the agreement. The latter provided, however, that if the loan were applied to any other purpose than housing, the balance outstanding should then be charged with interest at 5 per cent. instead of $4\frac{1}{2}$ per cent. A settlement was made with the firm on these lines.

[4] The general rule was 40 years; the Aluminium Co., Dolgarrog, had 20 years and Austin's had 30 years.

thirty annual payments, continuing to pay 5½ per cent. interest, or they might, if they wished to, pay it all off at once.[1]

Other firms which received assistance in this manner were the Aluminium Corporation, Dolgarrog, the Aircraft Manufacturing Company, Hendon, the British Cellulose Company at Spondon, Dorman Long and Co., Grahame-White, and Vickers.

The second method of assistance given to controlled establishments was writing off from excess profits. In certain instances private firms, willing to undertake to provide accommodation for their employees, were deterred by the great increase in the cost of building. In the beginning of 1916, to meet such cases, a special arrangement, practically equivalent to a State grant, was initiated in the case of Brotherhood of Peterborough,[2] by which a part of the cost of a permanent housing scheme was allowed to be charged against excess profits. The essential characteristics of this form of grant, which was very generally applied to controlled establishments over the next twelve months, was that it involved no direct outlay by the Ministry ; the excess profits were intercepted on their way to the Treasury and the remainder of the expense was borne by the firm.

The basis of allowance to the firm was the difference between the present and pre-war cost of providing the accommodation. The total amount of excess cost thus arrived at was not written off to the firm, but a certain proportion, varying according to the particular case and decided after investigations by the Ministry. Occasionally, as in the case of Vickers' scheme for 100 houses at Weybridge, the amount of writing-down allowed on the entire cost was to be reviewed at the end of the period of control but was in no case to exceed 50 per cent.[3]

Plans and estimates for schemes financed in this manner were in every case submitted to the Ministry. Certain conditions were also imposed ; it was stipulated that rents were to be approved and that the houses should be reserved for munition workers during the period of control.

In two instances direct grants were made unconditionally to firms. In this way Dorman Long and Co. received 25 per cent. of the total cost of their scheme for 300 houses at Redcar as a grant and the remainder on loan at 1 per cent. above the bank rate. A small scheme for 15 houses undertaken by the Appleby Iron Co., Ltd., at Scunthorpe, also received a grant from the Ministry of 20 per cent. of the expenditure.

Arrangements for Post-war Ownership.

By the end of 1916 the disadvantages of methods hitherto adopted for financing permanent schemes became apparent. Schemes undertaken by local authorities were delayed by the trouble they experienced

---

[1] L.R. 11773/7.

[2] The firm was carrying out a large contract for 6-in. and 8-in. howitzer sights which required the best class of labour (M.W. 50016 ; C.E. 266/23).

[3] C.R.V./Gen./9 ; HIST. REC./R/346. 2/1.

in obtaining labour and the difficulty of fixing the amount of the subsidy. Writing-off from excess profits of private firms was also unsatisfactory : for not only is it a radically unsound principle to intercept revenue before it reaches the Exchequer, but also it is not on general principles desirable that employers (often indeed themselves disinclined to become builders or owners of house property) should be the landlords of their workmen.

The principle of post-war ownership was first adopted in the case of a scheme for 350 houses in Mid-Lanarkshire which it had originally been decided to treat on the basis of a direct grant of a percentage of the cost to the local authority. Prolonged negotiation on these lines carried on from May, 1916, to the close of the year broke down as the local authority demanded a higher percentage (30 to 40 per cent. of the cost) than the Ministry would grant. It was therefore arranged that the work should be carried out in the first instance at the expense of the Ministry, that the firms concerned should make a contribution of £20 per house in return for first claim on the tenancy, and that the local authority should agree to take over the houses three years after the war at their market value as determined by valuation.[1]

The Treasury accepted this principle of post-war ownership,[2] and from 1917 onwards insisted on a definite agreement for the post-war ownership of all permanent houses constructed by the Ministry ; though in the case of Barrow-in-Furness, where the terms offered were rejected by the Corporation, the Ministry, with Treasury consent, remained owners of the property.[3] The Local Government Board were also prepared to agree to the proposed arrangement provided that they themselves were consulted.[4] Certain conditions common to all post-war agreements may be summarised as follows :—

(1) The Ministry was to build so many houses which the local authority or firm, as the case might be, undertook to buy at a fixed date after the war. (2) The price to be paid was to be determined either by mutual agreement, or failing this, by a valuation by an approved neutral valuer. (3) The management of the property might be handed over by the Ministry during the period of the Ministry's ownership on terms to be agreed upon between the two parties.[5]

When a local authority accepted the post-war ownership of a scheme initiated for the benefit of a special firm, the latter was made,

---

[1] Hist. Rec./R/346. 2/1.

[2] L.R. 112/127, 147. The Treasury regarded the proposal as satisfactory only in those cases where the local authority could not be persuaded to build, where controlled establishments would only build on condition that a considerable part of the cost was charged to excess profits, or where the utmost possible use had been made of such expedients as the erection of temporary hutments and the requisition of empty property.

[3] See below, pp. 48–50.

[4] L.R. 112/47. The Local Government Board pointed out, that while continuing to give all assistance in their power, their limited architectural staff would prevent them undertaking the management or supervision of very extensive schemes.

[5] L.R. 112/26.

wherever possible, to contribute. Thus with regard to the Shirehampton scheme, the National Smelting Company agreed to pay 25 per cent. of the difference between the cost of erection and the valuation at which the property was taken over after the war. In this case the agreement for post-war ownership was tripartite, the contracting parties being the Minister, the National Smelting Company and the Corporation of Bristol. The terms gave the company the option of purchase two years after peace ; if they failed to exercise the option, the corporation was to purchase at market value three years after the termination of war.[1]

One great advantage of post-war ownerships was that the Ministry, by becoming directly responsible for construction, was in a position to ensure that it was carried out as rapidly and continuously as possible. The financial merits, as compared with the system of direct grants, were uncertain, and as time went on it became increasingly difficult to make an agreement which was considered speculative and hazardous by the local authorities, naturally unwilling to bind their successors to such terms. At Coventry, at Barrow and at Irlam, indeed, both the local authority and the firm refused to consider post-war ownership, and in this instance the Treasury had to waive the question and to agree to the Ministry holding the property until a suitable purchaser was found.[2]

The economic rent on 70 per cent. of the expenditure insisted on by the Treasury[3] also complicated the question. It involved in all cases an increase over the rents already prevailing in the district and the local authorities feared that, while the higher rents might be obtained during the war period, they would be unobtainable at a later date, and that any valuation on the basis of "market" value would, in fact, be made on the basis of the high rents available, with a consequent loss to the local authority. It was therefore found necessary in some cases to postpone the period of valuation from three years (the ordinary limit set) to seven, by which time wages might be expected to have reached their normal post-war rate.[4] An alternative basis of valuation also appears in the later schemes ; thus both at Lincoln and at Letchworth the agreed basis was "replacement" value after the deduction of a reasonable allowance for depreciation.[5]

The public announcement that some system of State-aided housing would be undertaken after the war added to the difficulties of negotiating post-war ownership ; local authorities and other prospective post-war owners had, and could be given, no general guarantee from the Ministry that the State-aided schemes would not undersell the housing schemes which they were asked to take over.[6]

---

[1] L.R. 112/26.   The option was to enable the company to make over the houses to the Avonmouth Garden Suburb.

[2] L.R. 112/26.   [3] See below, pp. 12–16.   [4] L.R. 14260.

[5] L.R. 112/77 ; L.H. 84.

[6] At Irlam and Glengarnock, however, a promise was made that the rents of Ministry houses should be reduced to the level of those put up by the local authority under the Housing Act, as soon as the latter were ready for occupation.

The lengthy negotiations resulting from these uncertain conditions impeded progress. As permanent schemes were only undertaken where houses would be wanted after the war and advantageous disposal was therefore practically certain, the Ministry decided in April, 1918, to ask the Treasury that arrangements for post-war ownership might be dropped. About this date, however, the Treasury created a precedent by waiving post-war ownership in the case of the Barrow scheme, and, as no other cases were then pending, it was decided that future schemes might be decided on their merits.[1]

(b) The Question of Rent Determination.

The rents of permanent houses under those early schemes where the local authority was subsidised were fixed by the Ministry, the Local Government Board and the local authority in consultation.[2] In Coventry, for example, the rents fixed for the Stoke Heath Estate were 9s. 6d., 10s. 6d. and 11s. 6d. for different types of three bedroomed houses, representing a full economic rent on the outlay.[3] What happened here typifies the difficulties besetting the question of an economic rent. Both the Local Labour Advisory Board and the Coventry Ordnance Works pointed out that these rents were out of proportion to those charged in other parts of the city, which ranged from 4s. 6d. to 7s. 6d. for similar accommodation, and that men would sooner be very uncomfortable than pay them. At the instance of the Ministry the Corporation accordingly in the autumn of 1916 reduced the rent by 6d. on each house. These reduced rents left no balance and the Corporation considered that any further change meant that the houses would become an annual charge upon them. In March, 1917, the tenants formed themselves into a Stoke Heath Tenants Defence Association and threatened a " no rent " strike. They appealed to the Minister to receive a deputation, but as the Minister neither was the owner of the houses nor controlled the rents he did not feel called on to interfere.[4] The Corporation was eventually obliged to readjust the balance sheet and reduce the rents to 7s. 11d., 8s. 11d. and 9s. 11d. respectively, at which sum they subsequently remained.[5]

The policy of post-war ownership, as seen above, introduced a new element of ministerial ownership in later schemes, and the Treasury stipulated that rents should be fixed at a rate which would provide an economic return on at least 70 per cent. of the cost. This percentage appears to have been adopted to some extent by chance, for when rents were fixed for the Farnborough scheme, the rents paid in the district and the cost of the houses were taken into account, and sanction asked for a rent considered fair under the circumstances. The same method was applied to the Mid-Lanarkshire scheme, under which the policy of post-war ownership was first adopted. The rent thus arrived at happened to provide an economic return on 70 per cent. of the cost,

---

[1] L.R. 112/77. The Local Government Board also considered at this date that post-war ownership schemes were wrong in principle. (L.R. 112/58.)

[2] L.R. 11636/70.

[3] L.R. 11636/12 ; Hist. Rec./R/346. 2/23.

[4] L.R. 11535/70.

[5] L.R. 112/118.

and this proportion, which was intended to represent a rough estimate of the probable cost of building immediately after the war, was henceforward required by the Treasury as the basis of assessment.[1]

Both the Treasury and the Ministry favoured an economic rent on 70 per cent., or even a higher proportion of the cost, since the high wages obtained made it possible for tenants to pay, and the establishment of the principle of paying rents on the cost of building would undoubtedly make the position of housing easier after the war.[2] Certain difficulties, however, hampered the carrying out of this policy. The chief lay in the fact that the rents of pre-war houses were everywhere considerably lower than could be charged on the 70 per cent. basis. This difficulty increased as time went on, for while the cost of building doubled during the war, the pre-war rents remained standardised under the Increase of Rent Act and accentuated the grievance of those called upon to pay the higher rents of new houses. Labour organisations, too, though they expressed the view, in principle, that an uneconomic rent was unsound, and a subsidised rent meant a subsidised wage (and this especially where a private firm was concerned), tended to abandon the principle when faced with an immediate demand for higher rents.

It was further found that when a housing scheme was undertaken to attract labour from another district, the object of the scheme was likely to be defeated if too high rents were asked.[3] At Glengarnock, for example, the houses which were intended to attract workmen, already living at low rents and in good employment, occupied an isolated position and were unlikely to let in the open market. Rents based on 70 per cent. of cost would have been considerably higher than those obtaining in the neighbourhood, and on the recommendation of the Scottish Local Government Board certain concessions were asked from the Treasury, who refused to sanction any rent not yielding the stipulated economic return. It was only after considerable negotiation and delay that rents were fixed on this basis.[4]

The most serious opposition to the required economic rent came from Scotland, where an increase was involved of from £6 to £10 on the prevailing rents. The rents of the Mid-Lanark houses sanctioned in January, 1917, led to considerable agitation by Local Trades Councils and Tenants' Defence Associations, combined with threats to strike. The Ministry refused to give way, and after prolonged conferences

---

[1] HIST. REC./R/346.2/23.   The full economic rents for the Farnborough houses would have been 18s. 7d. for a house containing 3 bedrooms, living room, parlour and bathroom, and 13s. 7d. for 3 bedrooms and a living-room. Treasury approval was given to rents of 14s. 6d. and 10s. 6d. respectively. (Printed) *Weekly Report*, No. 113, XVI. (13 October, 1917).

[2] HIST. REC./R/346. 2/23.

[3] At Queen's Ferry, owing to the high cost of construction and to the importance of allocating and retaining labour on dangerous work, it was not considered possible to charge economic rents and the annual loss on the whole scheme was about £1,000 yearly. (95/2/118.)

[4] Report of Housing Section to Mr. Churchill, May, 1918 (L.R./11636/11). Treasury approval was not given until August, 1918. (Printed) *Weekly Report*, No. 153, IX. (3/8/18).

with the local organisations and a concession to the local authority by which post-war ownership by the Ministry was extended from three to seven years, the scale of rents was accepted in May, 1918.[1]

The schemes launched in 1918 showed a growing discrepancy to the prevailing standard of rents, not only of pre-war houses but of houses built during the war, and it seemed probable that serious discontent would be caused by " fixing " such high rents.   At Barrow, economic rents worked out at 15s., 16s., and 17s. per house, while the price of pre-war accommodation ranged from 5s. to 6s. 6d.[2]   At Lincoln the estimated rent on 70 per cent. of expenditure was 20s. 6d., while the prevailing local rent was 6s. 6d. to 8s.[3]   Coventry furnishes perhaps the most striking example, for of the two permanent schemes undertaken in 1917 and 1918 respectively, the rents on a 70 per cent. basis for the former were 9s. 6d. to 10s. 6d., while for the latter, it was stated in October, 1918, they would have to be fixed at 16s. 9d.[4]

Experience showed that this question of an economic rent perpetually threatened labour troubles, and at the instigation of the Labour Department of the Ministry[5] a conference was held with Sir Robert Chalmers on 22 October, 1918.   It was then agreed as a general rule that rents for permanent houses should be fixed to give an economic return on 70 per cent. of the estimated cost of the building and 100 per cent. of the cost of land.   Application was to be made to the Treasury in cases when it was thought undesirable to fix rents on this basis.

There was no change of policy after the Armistice, though the Housing Department recognised that the provision of subsidised houses was likely to open the way to abuses, and that once the period of immediate stress had passed, building ought to be treated as an economic proposition.   A rent representing a return on the entire cost could not, however, be introduced at once, and it was felt that an insurance payment of 30 per cent. on the part of the Ministry was justifiable during the exceptional conditions following the conclusion of the war.   Even on this basis the rents were unacceptably high, and during the 18 months following the Armistice there were many threatenings of rent strikes, while strikes actually took place at Coventry and Woolwich.   The determination of rentals also caused delay in carrying

---

[1] L.R. 6028/12, 112/18; HIST. REC./R/346. 2/23 ; (Printed) *Weekly Report*, No. 140, IX. (4 May, 1918).

[2] L.R. 10/77.   These rents were strongly opposed by the Corporation, whose views were awaited on 22 November, 1918.

[3] HIST. REC./R/346. 2/23.   [4] HIST. REC./R/346. 2/23; L.R. 11636/64.

[5] L.R. 112/142.   The Finance Department regarded the question as one of expediency.   Mr. Duckworth in a Minute to A.F.S., dated 22 August, 1918, pointed out that there was no question of inability to pay on the part of the tenant, whose present earnings and economic rents on even 100 per cent. of the cost of building would probably compare favourably with a similar relation between pre-war earnings and pre-war rents.   The 70 per cent. basis had been fixed as a fair compromise between a full economic rent under war conditions and the economic rent that would be required under normal post-war conditions, and was adopted with the deliberate intention of avoiding fluctuations later and the possible increase of rentals on old tenants at a time when the earnings of the working man would certainly be lower and the cost of living possibly as high.

out agreements for post-war ownership, since local authorities and firms alike were inclined to favour a lower rent in order that the purchase price might be correspondingly decreased.

The Ministry as a rule made no stipulations as to the rents fixed by firms carrying out housing schemes, and in most cases pre-war rents prevailing in the district were charged. A notable exception was the case of the Austin Motor Company, who, anxious to have an economic return on the financial outlay, charged and, after some initial difficulty, obtained 18s. 9d. a week each for 50 brick houses and 14s. for bungalows.[1]

The rents of temporary cottages were fixed originally on expenses entailed in capital cost, depreciation, rates and administrative expenses.[2] The same difficulties as were experienced with regard to the rents of permanent houses applied to the temporary cottages. The earlier assessments—which averaged 7s. 6d. for a three-bedroomed and 6s. for a two-bedroomed cottage[3]—were invariably in excess of the prevailing rates. In addition, the type of one-storeyed cottage was at first disliked. At Dudley, for example, where the rents were exceptionally low, ranging from 5s. to 2s. 6d., rents of 7s. 9d. and 6s. 3d. were asked for the Ministry's temporary cottages. This, combined with the initial unpopularity of the one-storeyed wooden bungalow, resulted in a notable failure to let. In June, 1917, there was a change in the management, and this, together with the reduction of the rents to 6s. and 5s., had such good results that, whereas at that date only 43 per cent. of the cottages were let, by May, 1918, 90 per cent. were reported to be occupied.[4]

As time went on it became increasingly impossible to obtain a rent which provided anything approaching a full economic return on outlay. The rents of semi-permanent cottages, sanctioned for Barrow in October, 1917, were fixed at 9s. 6d. for a bungalow with three bedrooms and 7s. 6d. for one with two bedrooms. The first rent represented an economic return of 52 per cent. on the capital cost and the second of 45 per cent. The Treasury protested against these low rents, but on an assurance from the Ministry that it was impossible to obtain a higher rental for this type of house, they gave their consent to them on 28 March, 1918.[5]

Allied to the question of an economic rent is that of charges made in the Ministry's hostels. The original intention was that charges should cover all expenditure and provide interest on a sinking fund and capital.

---

[1] Although the rents were fixed so high the loss to the firm was ultimately heavy, for the cost of erecting the bungalows (which came from America and had to be pieced together by British workmen) in particular far exceeded the estimate. Some of the conditions of the Corporation of Birmingham's bye-laws also involved very heavy expenses.

[2] A certain number of cottages at Gretna were furnished and, by arrangement with the Treasury, an extra charge representing 17½ per cent. of the cost of the furniture was added to the rent. (HIST. REC./H/1122. 7/19.)

[3] These rents included rates and water but not light.

[4] D.F. 3/P.A.C./22 ; L.R. 11513/3.

[5] L.R. 10726/7.

Prices were fixed in 1916 before experience had been gained as to running hostels and on the assumption that the buildings would be fully occupied for the life assigned to them.   They averaged an inclusive price for the women's hostels of from 13s. to 14s. 6d. a week, though in one case, at Slade's Green, the charges were as low as 11s. 6d.[1]   The usual charge for men's lodging was 6d. a night ;   at the Dudley Hostel board was fixed at 14s. 6d. a week.   The weekly charge in Gretna hostels for board and lodging was 18s. for males and 12s. for females.[2] The charges for clearing hostels averaged about 2s. a day.[3]

Owing to the general increase in prices and the unpopularity of hostels at the outset, these prices did not cover expenses and the charges for hostels opened in 1917 were fixed on a higher scale.   The question of revising the prices already existing was fraught with some difficulty. An economic rental would in most cases have exceeded local charges for lodgings and hostel tenants would have been worse off than the majority of their fellow-workers.   Although, in principle, the trades unions objected to hostel charges being so low that they did not cover expenses,[4] there was considerable opposition to any suggestions of a rise.   However, in July, 1917, the Abbey Wood hostels were raised from 14s. 6d. to 17s. and Slade's Green to 13s. 6d.   An economic charge at this date was estimated to be, for women, 15s. 6d. a head per week in a large hostel and 19s. in a small hostel ;   for men, 17s. in a large hostel and 20s. in a small hostel.[5]

The revision of prices at the Coventry hostels was carried out under specially difficult conditions.   Owing to labour unrest it was not until November, 1917, that it was decided to raise the charges to 15s. a week. Very serious labour trouble was then threatened, resulting in important changes in the administrative staff of the Government colonies, so that it was not actually until February, 1918, that the changes were introduced.

In October, 1918, following on a bonus of 5s. a week awarded to women, it was decided that an inquiry should be made into the charges at women's hostels.   It was found that the general cost of board, apart from lodging, was about 13s. 6d. a week in a normal hostel when reasonably full.   It was therefore decided to raise all hostels to a standard charge of 17s. 6d., the increase to date from 2 November.[6]

---

[1] D.F. 3/P.A.C./22 ; Memorandum on Housing filed in the Housing Section.

[2] Hist. Rec./H/1122. 7/19.

[3] The inclusive charge at Gloucester was 10s. 6d. a week, which was raised to 14s. 6d. in 1917.   (Hist. Rec./R/346/131.)

[4] Hist. Rec./R/346/118 ;   D.F. 3/P.A.C./22.   The Secretary of the Coventry Branch of the National Federation of Women Workers reported that some agitators went so far as to say that a hostel run by a private firm resembled a compound for black labour.

[5] Hist. Rec./R/346/118.   These figures were composed in every case of a maintenance charge (including salaries, rents, rates, etc.) of 5s. per head, the remaining figure covering the cost of catering.

[6] (Printed) *Weekly Report*, No. 163, IX. (12/10/18).   Lodging charges were raised to 4s. a week at the same time.

III. The Management of Housing Schemes.

(a) TYPE OF ACCOMMODATION PROVIDED.

The type of permanent accommodation provided was much the same in all cases, that is to say the ordinary type of working-class dwelling, a two-storey brick cottage containing two or three bedrooms, a kitchen and a living room. A bath was usually provided but not a separate bathroom. In Scotland " flatted " tenement dwellings with somewhat inferior accommodation were often provided.

Temporary housing was supplied either as cottages, colonies or hostels. In two cases—those of the large Explosive Factory at Gretna and the National Projectile Factory at Birtley—the Ministry provided a complete temporary village, each with its own schools, churches, hospital, shops, institutions, etc.[1]

Temporary cottages were generally single-storey buildings, some with five rooms (kitchen, scullery and three bedrooms) and some with four. They were equipped with either gas or coal stoves for cooking and heating and were lighted by gas or electricity, whichever was cheaper. They were constructed of wood while it remained comparatively plentiful and cheap, but after the beginning of 1916 concrete slabs, treated with waterproofing compounds, and timber framing were used to form the walls.[2] The estimated life of the wooden houses was 15 years and of the concrete from 15 to 20 years, but their life could be extended almost indefinitely if properly repaired and maintained. These temporary cottages could be spaced as closely as 25 to an acre. In 1917 a more solid type of semi-permanent cottage, estimated to last 30 to 40 years and consisting either of one-storey bungalows with two bedrooms or two-storey bungalows with three bedrooms, was introduced at Barrow and Scunthorpe.[3]

Colonies or hostels were composed of long one-storeyed hutments divided into single and double cubicles and accommodating about 100 to 130 persons,[4] each block of hutments being provided with lavatories and baths. In addition to the dormitory blocks a colony was provided with an administrative block containing offices and rooms for the Superintendent, and Staff Dispensary and sick room. Recreation rooms and wash-houses, where minor laundry operations could be undertaken, were also provided. All buildings were heated with hot-water pipes and radiators and lighted with electricity or gas. This type of accommodation, which was found to be particularly convenient when a large number of women workers were brought from a distance, necessitated separate buildings for catering purposes with properly equipped kitchens. The Government colony at Holbrook Lane,

---

[1] See below, pp. 58–78.

[2] At the beginning of 1917 the Ministry received stringent instructions from the War Cabinet to practice the utmost economy in the use of timber for constructional purposes and to substitute brick wherever possible. (L.R. 112/47.)

[3] HIST. REC./R/346.2/6 ; L.R. 10726/7.

[4] The Sheffield " Colony " for men accommodated only 30 workers.

Coventry, was of this type ; the dining hall seated as many as 2,800 at one time and the workers could all be served within a quarter of an hour.[1]

With regard to clearing hostels, which were established to serve as clearing houses through which newcomers could be passed on to suitable lodgings, it was found in every case that houses already in existence could be adapted for the purpose.

(b) THE MANAGEMENT OF COTTAGE PROPERTY.

At the beginning of 1916, owing to the approaching completion of the various temporary schemes, it became necessary to draw up a scheme of management, and in March, 1916, a Director of Housing Management was appointed. This part of the work was done with the assistance of Messrs. Barlow and Appleton, whose services were lent to the Ministry by the Bournville Trust. These experts advised as to the proper allowances for cost and management, wear and tear, depreciation, bad debts, empties, etc., and undertook a systematic inspection of the Ministry's temporary property.[2]

The principle was that the direct management of all temporary schemes belonged to the Ministry ; in practice the management was occasionally delegated to some approved person or society. The problem differed according to the nature of the scheme, that is whether cottages or hostels and colonies were concerned. Birtley, which embodied every type and scheme stands apart.[3] The temporary cottage schemes at Coventry, Dudley and Scotswood were placed in charge of officials appointed by and responsible to the Ministry, who collected the rents and saw to the carrying out of repairs. At Sheffield, where the only other scheme of this type was carried out, the Corporation exercised during the war the general supervision of the cottages on behalf of the Ministry.[4]

The Ministry took no active part in the management of the permanent houses built by local authorities or controlled establishments. Those permanent houses, however, which in 1917 and 1918 were erected at the entire cost of the Department were managed by the Housing Section of the Ministry, which had hitherto undertaken the temporary schemes. Occasionally the management of the property was handed over to the post-war owner during the Ministry's ownership ; thus Colville's undertook the factorage of the Glengarnock

---

[1] HIST. REC./R/346. 2/6 ; *Report from the Committee of Public Accounts,* Appendix XII., etc. The other colony in Coventry, Whitmore Park, was at first served by the canteen carried on under the direction of White & Poppé, but this proved unsatisfactory and control was taken by the Ministry.

[2] L.R. 112/31, 34 ; HIST. REC./R/346. 2/3.

[3] An officer of the Ministry was in residence here, but his responsibilities were limited to seeing that the moneys due to the Ministry were properly collected and accounted for and that repairs were duly maintained : the real management rested with the Belgian Government.

[4] HIST. REC./R/346. 2/3, etc. The cottages were part of large schemes including men's hostels and colonies, all of which the Corporation undertook to manage.

houses on a payment from the Ministry of 7s. 6d. per house per annum. In the same way during the war the Shirehampton estate was managed by a committee nominated by the Board of Management of the Avonmouth Garden Suburb subject to certain supervisory powers retained by the Ministry.[1]

(c) THE MANAGEMENT OF HOSTELS.

The maintenance and management, including furnishing and catering, of hostels and colonies for men and women were until November, 1918, carried out by the Housing Section, acting in conjunction with the Welfare Department.

It was the practice for the Ministry to maintain direct control over women's hostels and colonies.[2] In June, 1916, those at Woolwich were undertaken by the Welfare Department of the Chief Superintendent of Ordnance Factories in order to avoid difficulties likely to arise if the management of the hostels was completely separate from the management of the Arsenal.[3] A colony was placed under the management of a Lady Superintendent appointed by the Ministry and assisted by a staff of matrons and maids. A separate matron was appointed for every hostel. The standard ratio of the staff to the number of residents was one matron and three maids to every hundred girls.[4] A permanent staff, however, could not be added to at a moment's notice or dismissed unless there was good reason to suppose that a hostel would remain permanently empty, so that in many cases the staff was high in comparison with the number of residents.[5]

In the case of men's hostels the Ministry might delegate direct control. Thus at Sheffield the management was handed over to the Corporation, who received all rents and payments which were paid in to the credit of the Ministry; all accounts against the estate were certificated by the Town Clerk or City Treasurer and forwarded to the

---

[1] L.R. 10724; L.R. 11747/15. In 1918 Miss Octavia Hill's system of house property management was introduced at Barrow, Dudley, Coventry, Sheffield, and, later, at Shirehampton. The aim was to secure the wise government of the houses by appointing educated women to act as agents to the landlords, and in this way to have full power over the management of the house.

[2] An exception was made in the case of the women's hostels for Messrs. Austin at Birmingham which were to be managed by the company on the following terms: (1) The general scheme of management, including numbers, staff, salaries, charges and appointment of Lady Superintendent, was to be submitted for ministerial approval. (2) The hostel was to be open for the inspection of the Welfare Department. (3) The Ministry reserved the right of taking over direct management if necessary. The hostel at Slade's Green was managed under similar conditions by the Y.W.C.A. (L.R. 15744/3.)

[3] Hist. Rec./H/346. 2/5. An agreement was made that rates of charges should be similar. These hostels were handed over to the Y.W.C.A. to manage.

[4] The inconvenient arrangement (necessary, however, for the maintenance of discipline) of the Colony blocks which in most cases were separated from one another, made it necessary to have a matron in every block to supervise the girls.

[5] D.F. 3/P.A.C./22. At one time it was in the proportion of one to five at Coventry.

Ministry for payment. Here the plan adopted was to farm out the hostels (accommodating 13 or 28 workers) to housekeepers who paid £2 or £4 a week according to the capacity of the hostel and were allowed to charge each workman 3s. 9d. a week for lodgings and make their own terms for catering. In the same way each colony of 30 workers was let to a co-operative society for £15 a month, the same charge being allowed to be made for lodging. These rents assumed that accommodation was fully occupied, and as this, in Sheffield, proved not to be the case, the agreement had to be modified and the rent paid to the Ministry reduced to 2s. 6d. per week per worker in occupation. Later the whole management was transferred to the Housing Department of the Ministry.

At Dudley a general manager to the whole property was appointed by the Ministry, but hostel keepers were appointed under somewhat similar conditions.[1]

Clearing hostels were generally managed by local agents for the Ministry. Thus at Lancaster, where a clearing hostel was established for Vickers' National Projectile Factory, the arrangements were handed over to the Lancaster Advisory Committee on Women's War Employment. The management of the clearing hostel at Gloucester for Quedgley Filling Factory was undertaken by a local committee.[2]

---

[1] L.R. 11513/3. The hostel keepers at Dudley paid £4 per week clear of rates to the manager and undertook to give precedence of tenancy to munition workers, keep the place clean, and provide meals to the workmen who paid 3s. 6d. for lodging, 1s. for the key of their lockers and extra for food.

[2] L.R. 16820 ; Memo. on Housing filed in Housing Section.

CHAPTER III.

HOUSING SCHEMES CARRIED OUT BY THE MINISTRY.

I. The First Housing Programme (1915–16).

A definite housing programme, especially in relation to the new programme of guns and shells, was the first necessity, and on 4 August, 1915, Mr. West's department was asked for estimates. A list of requirements was accordingly drawn up showing the estimated numbers (including the percentage of married men) wanted in connection with (1) the new gun programme, (2) the new ammunition programme, (3) the new gun assembling factories.

This statement formed the basis of further discussion with the Treasury; there were indications—for example, at Sheffield and Newcastle—that local authorities, if assisted, were prepared to undertake permanent schemes, and the Ministry pointed out that, though the temporary scheme was of course cheaper absolutely, a permanent scheme might prove cheaper from the Treasury point of view. The Treasury remained firmly in favour of temporary accommodation and were prepared rather to face a subsistence allowance to married men on the same basis as that granted to munition volunteers. The percentage of married men to be accommodated was likely to be high—varying, according to the estimate, between 50 and 80 per cent.—and the Ministry was extremely opposed to the Treasury suggestion of subsistence allowances, as likely to be successful neither for employers nor employed.[1]

The statement of requirements was next sent to the Local Government Board (both for England and Scotland), whose Local Inspectors were instructed to report fully on the possibilities of accommodation in the various centres.[2]

---

[1] L.R. 112/141 ; C.R.V./Gen./361. Mr. Beveridge minuted on 25 August, "Subsistence allowances are not so attractive a problem that we should desire to extend them ; it is also unsatisfactory to have married men separated for a long time from their families where it can be avoided." Sir Hubert Llewellyn Smith considered the suggestion " preposterous." About the same date the Treasury had suggested to the Army Council this method for relieving the ever-increasing housing difficulties at Woolwich. The Army Council, however, rejected it as not practical and substituted a building scheme for temporary houses, at the same time handing over a number of married quarters in barracks hitherto occupied by unmarried soldiers. (M.W. 3697.)

[2] L.R./112/141 ; M.W. 5593/2.

The following results as to requirements were obtained from the Board's investigations[1] :—

AREA.	Estimated No. of Employees.		Estimated No. to be housed.	No. of permanent tenements provisionally suggested.
	Male.	Female.		
England—				
Birtley ..	4,000	80	3,600	Doubtful.
Coventry ..	1,350	1,000	1,200	600 (doubtful).
Dudley	2,000	2,000	3,600	300
Erith	1,500	1,500	3,000	100
Newcastle ..	1,700	—	1,530	650
Sheffield ..	9,950	50	9,000	800
Scotland—				
Glasgow and District.	4,000	1,500	600	100–150
Total	24,500	6,130	22,530	2,550–2,600

According to these returns, in six out of seven districts in which the provision of further housing accommodation was essential, a certain amount of permanent housing was suggested. In the seventh case, that of Birtley, a National Projectile Factory to be run entirely by Belgian labour was to be established and plans for a temporary village were already being prepared by the Office of Works in consultation with the Belgian managers of the factory.[2]

General Treasury sanction was given to this estimate of requirements on 14 October.[3] With regard to permanent housing their Lordships recognised " as a practical problem it will be necessary in some cases to embark on permanent housing schemes, and the number of permanent tenants contemplated (2,600) does not on present information appear to them excessive or beyond the powers of the Public Works Loan Board to finance in the ensuing year."[4]

---

[1] HIST. REC./H/346. 2/1, Appendix B. The accommodation at Manchester (Armstrong Whitworth), Nottingham (Cammell Laird & Co.), Long Eaton and Liverpool was reported to be sufficient for the demands likely to be made on it ; it was also probable that facilities already existing at Barrow, Lancaster and Houston would prove adequate. About the same date returns as to the additional number of munition workers likely to be employed in districts in which there were no national factories at the moment were compiled by Divisional Officers of Labour Exchanges. According to these returns, of a total of 56,500 (37,000 men and 19,500 women) more or less satisfactory accommodation for 36,000 workers was reported to be available. The most urgent needs from the Ministry point of view were likely to be at Derby (Rolls-Royce and the National Shell Factory), Selly Oak (Austin Motor Company), Gloucester (National Filling Factory), Woolston (J. J. Thorneycroft), Acton (Hayes Filling Factory) and Harlesden (Park Royal Filling Factory) ; less pressing needs were those at Huddersfield, where a National Shell Factory was under consideration, and at Norwich. (L.R. 112/137.)

[2] The Office of Works subsequently withdrew and the work was carried out by the Director of Housing Construction of the Ministry. For a complete account of Birtley see below, Chap. VII.

[3] Treasury approval had to be sought on each scheme separately.

[4] C.R.V./Gen./361 ; L.R. 112/49. For arrangements now made as to grants to local authorities see above, p. 7.

At the date of the Treasury sanction negotiations had already reached an advanced stage with local authorities in all the districts concerned. At Coventry without further delay the Corporation undertook a subsidised scheme for 600 permanent houses, with the stipulation that they should be primarily for the use of the Coventry Ordnance Works.[1]

At Sheffield a permanent scheme had to be abandoned because of failure to reach agreement as to terms. The question was resumed in the beginning of 1916 and arrangements then made by which the Corporation undertook to build 261 permanent houses, aided by a grant, and also to supervise a very large temporary scheme of cottages and hostels initiated by the Ministry.[2]

The Corporation of Newcastle already had a scheme for 688 permanent houses under consideration and the Ministry offered a grant of £45 per house on condition that the houses were ready for occupation by 31 March, 1916. Partly owing to their inability to keep to this time-table and partly to the increase in the cost of labour and materials the Corporation abandoned their plans and the Ministry was obliged to fall back on a scheme of temporary cottages. This change of plan caused considerable delay, and it was not until 25 February, 1916, that Treasury sanction was received for the full number of 600 cottages.[3]

In the Dartford and Erith districts negotiations with the local authorities also failed. Here the Minister freely exercised his statutory power to take possession of unoccupied premises, commandeering schools and other public buildings to such purpose that from 4,000 to 5,000 persons were housed without additional construction. The immediate necessities of Vickers were thus met, while three hostels were planned at Slade's Green to meet the requirements of the Thames Ammunition Company.

The needs of Woolwich Arsenal and of the Explosives Department had not for special reasons appeared in the Ministry's estimate of 4 October.

At Woolwich, as has been mentioned above, a large permanent scheme had already been carried out by the Office of Works, but the continued extension of the Arsenal, where the numbers employed rose from 10,866 in August, 1914, to over 44,000 in October, and where a further increase of 20,000 was expected for factories in course of erection, made it necessary to consider further housing accommodation. Sites were arranged for at Plumstead, Eltham, Greenwich and Abbey Wood and plans drawn up for the provision of 1,500 units of married quarters, 5 hostels for boys, 10 for women and one for men, each to contain 100 workers. Treasury sanction was obtained for this enterprise on 12 December, 1915, at a cost not to exceed £345,000 for the married quarters and £41,275 for the hostels.[4]

---

[1] For Coventry see below, pp. 50–54.   [3] Hist. Rec./R/346. 2/12.

[2] M.W. 50675/16.   [4] M.W. 39697, 39697/3 ; C.R. 2913.

The Explosives Department always carried out their housing schemes independently of other departments of the Ministry. Early in July, 1915, when their new factories—which from their nature were in isolated districts—were still under construction, the question of housing the workers was discussed. A housing branch was then set up to work in co-operation with the Local Government Board, who lent the services of their chief Town Planning Inspector to the Explosives Department.[1] The most important of their schemes was undertaken in 1915 and was for the erection of a complete village at Gretna, comprised partly of temporary and partly of permanent buildings for upwards of 10,000 workers.[2]

No additional houses were provided at Queens Ferry while the explosives factory was merely under construction, although some four to five thousand builders' workmen had to travel daily long distances by train. The number of operatives for the factory was estimated at half this number, but it was essential that certain skilled workers, foremen, etc., should live near at hand in case of emergency. After an unsuccessful attempt to arrange a scheme with the Rural District Council, the department therefore proceeded to erect its own township at Mancot. The original plan, laid down in January, 1916, was for three hostels (two for men and one for women), a hospital, and sixteen cottages for foremen. Considerable additions were made later and the township eventually had a population of 800 persons.[3]

It was not till about the beginning of March that all the principal schemes were established, so that the summer of 1916 found most of them seriously in arrears. There had been a very bad spring, with continuous rain and snow, which had caused a general delay of several weeks. But the main hindrances to progress, which were to become more and more accentuated as time went on, were already active. The chief was the difficulty of obtaining labour. The type of workmen, available as not liable to military service, was necessarily inferior through age, physical defect or inexperience, and it was difficult to get exemption for a better type of man. The great scarcity of plasterers and plasterers' labourers specially held back the work.[4] Shortage of material was not at this stage acute, but haulage was a difficulty, while the railway companies showed increasing inability to accept and forward plant and materials.[5]

The permanent schemes showed the worst delay. According to the stipulated time-table the Coventry houses were to be finished by 26 June ; at that date none were actually ready and the scheme was

---

[1] 74/U/42.

[2] For a complete account of Gretna see below, Chap. VIII.

[3] 95/2/118.

[4] In June, 1916, the Local Government Board reported that 246 houses of the Dudley scheme were in progress and only 254 workmen engaged on them. A complaint here was that the rate of pay was so good that the workmen became dilatory and left work on the slightest pretext. (L.R. 11513/4.)

[5] L.R. 11513/4 ; C.R.V./C/15.

not completed until the middle of October. At Sheffield, where the contract time expired on 31 July, there were, on 12 August, 73 completed, 69 nearing completion, 56 at the roofing stage, 58 begun and 5 not begun. The Dudley permanent houses were not finished until the beginning of 1917.[1]

The temporary housing at Sheffield carried out by the Corporation was five months late. The Woolwich hostels, on the other hand, built under the supervision of the Director of Housing Construction were within a week or two of scheduled time.

The schemes hitherto enumerated had been undertaken for the most part in connection with new factories under construction. Plans had, therefore, to be based upon an estimate of the labour requirements of these factories and the extent to which such requirements could be met by local resources without the importation of fresh labour. Estimates were compiled by the departments concerned but necessarily depended to some extent upon conjecture. To delay action until the need for fresh construction had been demonstrated by experience would have resulted in delaying the operation of the new factories. It was also not possible to determine with certainty the actual output required from a factory and consequently what the labour employed by it would be. Again, hostels were the quickest and cheapest means of meeting the problem when it was most urgent, but it was only by experience that their unpopularity, due to the dislike of the discipline and supervision inherent in hostel life, was discovered.

In the circumstances it was inevitable that some miscalculation should be made in the earliest schemes. The most serious of these was in the case of Sheffield, where a temporary scheme was carried out for 4,627 workers, of whom 937 were to be housed in 473 cottages and 3,690 in hostels and colonies. These numbers were based on the needs of two National Projectile Factories which were to be established in the city, and of the large extensions to many other works engaged on munitions. They were not, indeed, calculated to meet the full estimated requirements, which a letter from Vickers, written in December, 1915, and signed by representatives of Firth, Hadfields, Cammell Laird and John Brown, gave as 8,000 workers to be accommodated by June, 1916. These figures were based on the assumption that the National Projectile Factories in the town would be worked by imported male labour, but, as events turned out, it was found possible to use female labour, a large part of which was available in Sheffield. This did not greatly affect the future of the temporary cottages, which let readily and were furnished and in occupation by the middle of 1916. The effect on the hostel and colony blocks was disastrous : in July, 1916, 117 out of 140 hostels were complete and only five partially occupied while seven out of 28 colonies were complete and occupied. Various expedients were adopted to meet the situation ; the hostels and colonies were thrown open to all munition workers and a number of the hostels were converted into cottages, all of which let rapidly. Thirty-two hostels were later moved to Northwich for the use of the

---

[1] L.R. 112/25 ; L.R. 11513/4.

Explosives Department,[1] and others were taken over by the Admiralty and Vickers. By this means the waste was considerably reduced.[2]

There was miscalculation at Dudley, though here, too, action was only taken after strong representations by local firms. The cottages were at first reserved for munition workers, but as such tenants failed were thrown open to ordinary tenants. The rents were high and the houses themselves, one-storeyed bungalows, were particularly unattractive in appearance. A reduction in rents improved the position considerably but the cottages were never popular.[3]

Later schemes benefited by these experiences ; it was recognised as a mistake to build at once for the full numbers asked for, and wherever hostels were erected they were put up block by block as required.[4]

II. Schemes undertaken in 1916–17.

The first housing programme had been designed to meet the requirements of places wherever national factories or factories constructed at the expense of the Ministry were established. The housing problem was not limited to such places, but was equally acute where firms were carrying out large contracts involving a huge increase in the number of their employees. The principle of a direct government grant to local authorities in such cases was not approved and other arrangements (which have already been discussed)[5] were made when a permanent scheme was decided on. For though, in theory, the Ministry continued to be in favour of temporary rather than of permanent housing schemes, in practice the preferability of the latter had often to be conceded.

Important permanent housing schemes were undertaken as a result of the extension of the steel programme in 1916–17, more particularly for Scottish firms,[6] but 160 cottages were also put in hand for the Partington Steel Company at Irlam, and Dorman Long and Company were assisted in building 342 cottages for their employees.

Again, the development of aircraft work from 1916 onwards led to the importation of labour into certain districts and a consequent

---

[1] The cost of pulling down, removing and re-erecting these hostels was £47,830 and the estimated cost of new huts was £43,200, a difference of £4,630 only. A low estimate of £17,920 was originally made for removal on the understanding that the huts were in sections and could be easily moved, which proved not to be the case. Financial sanction was given to this estimate, but the contract entered into was on a cost plus percentage basis which falsified the estimate to the above extent. The removal of the hostel was justified on two grounds, the saving of time and material, the former of vital importance in connection with the ammonium nitrate programme. (D.F. 3/P.A.C./22.)

[2] D.F. 3/P.A.C./22 ; Memo. on Housing filed in Housing Section.

[3] At Woolwich the calculations had also been in excess, provision being made for 8,326 workers, whereas in April, 1917, only 3,730 were in occupation. *Report from Committee of Public Accounts*, 1915-16, p. 13.

[4] *Report from Committee of Public Accounts*, 1918, p. 117.

[5] See above, p. 6.   [6] See below, pp. 54–57.

demand for housing. At Farnborough, where the Royal Aircraft Factory was established, 250 permanent houses were put up in 1917 at the request of the War Office. These houses were Government property and were put up by the Office of Works. At Hendon, the Grahame-White Company and the Aircraft Manufacturing Company were assisted by the Ministry to undertake schemes for 125 and 250 houses respectively.

The establishment of new spelter works at Avonmouth in 1916–1917 also led to proposals for housing the employees there. The Treasury at first refused to sanction any scheme, but strong pressure was brought to bear on the Ministry both from private quarters and from the Bristol Corporation. Sanction was finally obtained from the Treasury to erect 150 houses, on the Bristol Corporation agreeing to assume post-war ownership and the company concerned, the National Smelting Company, contributing towards the cost of the scheme.[1]

All temporary schemes continued to be carried out at the expense of the Ministry. Among the more important temporary schemes in 1916 and 1917 were those to supply accommodation for workers at National Filling Factories. No provision had been made for these factories in 1915 as the expectation was that they could be run by local female labour without importation from outside. This expectation was in most cases completely falsified and no class of factory has involved such large movement of labour or raised more serious and difficult housing problems.[2] In the spring of 1916 demands for housing began to come in. Large schemes were taken in hand for Coventry. The King's Norton Metal Company asked for immediate accommodation for 800 workers in the Woolwich neighbourhood. Colonies for about 500 workers were immediately put in hand at Abbey Wood and were ready for occupation by July. Further accommodation for 500 women was taken over from the Arsenal authorities at the beginning of 1917. In some cases it was found possible to deal with imported labour without actually constructing new temporary accommodation. In these cases it was often convenient to establish a clearing hostel to which labour could be sent by Employment Exchanges and thus distributed among available lodgings. Clearing hostels were without exception adapted from houses already existing. One was provided by the Ministry at Gloucester as a centre of distribution for the Quedgley Filling Factory ; four, including the Judges Lodgings, were at different times established in Hereford and one in Lancaster.[3]

Contracts arranged with Messrs. Austin of Birmingham at the beginning of 1917 involved the employment of over 3,000 women. The inspection staff was expected to number about 400 and the Ministry erected hostels (Lickey Hostel) for their reception. A second hostel (Longridge) to accommodate 780 was designed for other workers. In

---

[1] Cf. also Barrow, Coventry and the Scottish schemes.

[2] *Report from the Committee of Public Accounts*, 1917, p. 218.

[3] HIST. REC./R/1122. 3/38. At Lancaster on the outbreak of war there were about 500 empty houses and lodgings for 9,000 people. Vickers secured these houses on very advantageous terms and registered the lodgings.

addition Nazareth House, taken over by the firm from a Roman
Catholic community, was adapted for 450 workers, while the firm also
arranged for 50 motor buses, each transporting 29 workers to and from
Birmingham.

Mention must also be made of the accommodation for munition
workers provided since the beginning of the war by an ever-increasing
number of private hostels. These hostels were run by philanthropic
or semi-philanthropic concerns as, for example, the Girls' Friendly
Society, the Young Women's Christian Association, the Young Men's
Christian Association, the Roman Catholic Church, the Church of
England or the Church of Scotland. They were subject to inspection
by the Welfare Department of the Ministry, and often acted in conjunction with Labour Exchanges. The number of private hostels for
munition workers in 1917 was 224 for men, 269 for women, 2 for
boys and 8 clearing hostels.[1]

The Ministry felt that the claims of the private, and especially of the
clearing, hostels for women to support were very strong. Charges had
to be made on a low scale, girls came and went quickly, bad debts were
inevitable. Any charge above 16s. 6d. was impracticable, and with this
sum it was impossible, from 1917 onwards, to cover the costs where less
than 300 were concerned. The smaller types of hostel, taking about
40 tenants, were more popular than the large ones and had a better
influence, besides being in many areas the only ones available. In
June, 1917, Treasury sanction was obtained for the expenditure of
£5,000 on those hostels which had been of proved value to women
munition workers. This sum was applied as grants in relief of capital
expenditure and also as a maintenance rate not exceeding 6d. per day
in the case of the clearing hostels. During the year July, 1917–July,
1918, sixteen hostels, of which five were clearing, were relieved. The
Treasury grant was renewed for 1918–19.[2]

III. The Housing of Munition Workers in 1918.

A noticeable feature in the last year of the war was the general
character of the demand for houses, and more particularly for those of
a permanent nature. Building, as has already been noticed, had been
at a discount for some years previous to the war and this had been

---

[1] M.W.L.R. 2710/2.

[2] M.W.L.R. 2710/2. The largest grant, £1,349 13s. 9d., was made to the
Belmont hostel, Kirkcudbright, run by the Y.W.C.A., for educated women
employed as apprentices at the Galloway Engineering Works. The majority
of private hostels were for munition workers, though other classes of workers
were provided for. In the Nottingham area the women's hostels only included
30·2 per cent. of munition workers while all the men in hostels were on munitions.
At the same date ten out of the eighteen women's hostels in the Bristol area were
for munition workers. In the Leeds area, of 475 women and 4,558 men living in
private hostels, 52 per cent. of the women and 96 per cent. of the men were on
munitions. In the Newcastle district a great number of hotels, public halls
and schools had been adapted by the Admiralty for men on Admiralty work.

followed by more than four years' warfare, during which ordinary building of working-class houses had been at a standstill. The increasing difficulties of labour and material compelled the Ministry to reduce demands to a minimum and to rule out proposals that did not concern munition workers. Wherever possible existing buildings were adapted as hostels,[1] and hostels were built in such a way as to be capable of conversion at any time into blocks of temporary cottages.[2] No new permanent schemes were originated in 1918, though negotiations begun in the preceding year were now, as at Lincoln, Shirehampton and Scunthorpe, carried to a successful conclusion.

Two causes, however, helped to ameliorate the conditions affecting the housing of munition workers by the Ministry in 1918— the reduction of the munitions programme and the effects of the legislative creation of " Special Areas."[3]

One direct result of the reduction in programme was the closing down of the King's Norton Factory, with the result that their hostels were set free for Vickers' employees in the Erith and Crayford districts. For the same cause, plans for a hostel for 500 women belonging to the Coventry Ordnance Works were indefinitely postponed. Side by side with the reduction of munitions was the extension of the shipping programme, and the Ministry arranged with the Admiralty that any accommodation set free by displacement of munitions labour in shipping centres should be placed at their disposal. Otherwise each Department remained responsible for providing for its own workers.[4]

Questions affecting both Admiralty and Ministry were most likely to arise in the Clyde district, where at the beginning of 1918 the Admiralty proposed to introduce about 4,000 men. The conditions here were so notably bad that the reduction of programme did not materially ease the housing position, though plans under consideration for a hostel for 400 women at Cardonald Filling Factory were abandoned in consequence.

Turning to the question of " Special Areas," a new regulation, 2 A (2), of the Defence of the Realm Act had been passed in the autumn of 1917 to protect the munition worker from the growing practice among landlords of selling their houses to new tenants in order that the existing tenant might be evicted. The price paid for the house was put sufficiently high to represent in a capitalised form a higher rent than had hitherto been paid, thus enabling the landlord to evade the Increase of Rent Act under which he could not raise the rents on the

---

[1] The Ministry adapted for this purpose houses at Barrow, Bristol, Hereford, Highgate, Loughborough (3), and Newbury in 1918.

[2] This was done at Coventry, when the women's colony was half empty, 6 hostel blocks being converted into 59 cottages at a cost of £60 per cottage. The Queen's Ferry hostels had been constructed from the first with temporary dormitories and living rooms capable of conversion into semi-detached cottages.

[3] See below, p. 48,

[4] L.R./112/42, 57 ; (Printed) *Weekly Report*, No. 141, IX. (11/5/18).

existing tenant.[1]   Under this regulation, however, the Minister was empowered to declare any area where munition work was being carried on a special area where he considered the ejection of munition workers from their dwelling-houses would impede work.   While the order remained in force, no munition worker in a special area could be ejected from his house so long as he paid his rent and observed the other conditions of tenancy, always excepting that relating to the delivery up of possession.

Barrow and Coventry had been scheduled as special areas at the close of 1917, and on 30 January, 1918, Birmingham, where the eviction of munition workers had caused special hardship and discontent, was added to their number.[2]   Other districts declared special areas under this regulation were Scunthorpe, Birkenhead, Erith, Dartford and Selby.   In April, 1918, the Increase of Rent and Mortgage Interest Amendment Act, by providing that an owner who bought his house after 30 September should not be deemed a landlord for the purpose of the original Act, removed the main cause of complaints and made it unnecessary to schedule further areas.

The Ministry's housing schemes, equally with other enterprises, were closely affected by the progressive rise of prices.   The cost of building labour approximately doubled itself during the war, and added to it was the increased cost of material arising from additional cost of transport, of freightage and of labour in manufacture.   As a general consequence it was found that where any interval elapsed between making an estimate for a scheme and inviting tenders, the latter showed an increase over the estimate which had to be revised.

The increasing uncertainty of conditions made it more and more difficult for the Ministry to place contracts by competitive tender. In 1917, the contractors for the Glengarnock houses had stipulated before signing their contracts that any increase of wages over current wages brought about by an award of the Board of Trade should be borne in the proportions of two-thirds by the Ministry and one-third by the contractors.[3]   In July, 1918, it was reported that contractors themselves could not obtain quotations from merchants and from haulage firms and were in consequence unwilling to give close estimates. In two cases where competitive tenders were invited, most of the contractors protected themselves by provisions and restrictions which

---

[1] L.R.H. 40.   Occasionally the landlord effected a fictitious sale under an arrangement by which the incoming tenant paid down a sum of money for an option to purchase without any real intention of completing the purchase.   The only justification of the landlords was that while tenants were profiting by abnormal conditions and letting lodgings to munition workers, they themselves were prevented from taking any advantage of the enhanced value of their property.

[2] L.R.H. 8599; L.R.H. 40.   During September, 1917, thirty-six cases of ejectment affecting 398 tenants were made.   In October, 1915, the Birmingham landlords were reported as among the worst offenders in raising rents.   (Printed) Weekly Report, No. 13, VII. (23/10/15).

[3] (Printed) Weekly Report, No. 103, XI. (4/8/17).   Any concession on this point had been refused in the Coventry Corporation scheme in 1915.   M.W. 54793/16; L.R. 11636/12.

practically made their tenders not binding, while firm offers tended to be so high as to be prohibitive.[1]

An examination of the comparative cost of housing schemes at different periods is instructive. In the earliest contracts under Ministry schemes, made at the close of 1915 or the beginning of 1916, for permanent brick houses of the three-bedroom type, the cost worked out at £300 to £315 each, including roads and sewers.[2] This represented an increase of 20 per cent. on pre-war prices.[3] In May, 1918, the current price for a similar workman's dwelling was approximately £575, the costs differing slightly according to districts and facilities for getting materials and labour.[4] In 1920 the houses nearing completion at Irlam, Barrow, Coventry and Lincoln were estimated to cost over £1,000.

The cost of the earliest hostels and colonies erected in 1916 was from £30 to £35 per worker, including £5 for furnishing and £5 for land, road, sewers, etc. The smaller hostels, holding about 30 workers, cost £5 more.[5] In August, 1917, the cost of building, exclusive of roads and sewers, was £20 for the larger type and £40 for the smaller type of hostel, to which had to be added a sum varying between £17 10s. and £20 for total furnishing equipment. Prices continued to increase and in May, 1918, the cost of temporary hostels was from £50 to £70 per head.[6]

The cumulative result of the difficulties of labour and building was that schemes were badly behindhand; at the time of the Armistice there were in various stages of progress eight schemes for permanent houses at Barrow, Clydebank, Coventry, Glengarnock, Irlam, Lincoln, Mid-Lanark and Shirehampton, and one scheme for semi-permanent houses at Scunthorpe. The number of permanent houses involved was 1,460, and of semi-permanent 36. The houses under erection at Barrow, Coventry and Irlam were to remain the property

---

[1] (Printed) *Weekly Report*, No. 150, IX. (13/7/18).

[2] C.R. 2913. The cost at Coventry was £312, including £41 for roads and sewers; at Dudley £315, including £33 for roads and sewers, and at Glasgow £300. The cost of the Woolwich permanent scheme was very high owing to urgency of requirements. The scheme included 1,086 cottages and 212 flats and the average costs worked out at approximately £622, including cost of lands, roads, sewers and fences.

[3] This is the basis of the grant to local authorities at this date.

[4] Report of Housing Section to Mr. Churchill, May, 1918. This estimate was for a house containing 10,000 cubic feet, with a 16 foot frontage, 25 ft. depth, two storeys each 8 ft. 6 in. clear, a living room, scullery, bath, lavatory, fuel and food cupboards and three bedrooms.

[5] C.R. 2913. *Report from Committee of Public Accounts*, Appendix XII. The Sheffield hostels were estimated to cost £31, £32, and £33, according to the site.

[6] HIST. REC./R/346/118 ; Report of Housing Section to Mr. Churchill, May, 1918 (L.R./11636/11). No schemes for temporary cottages were undertaken after 1916, when the cost was £140 for the three bedroom type and £120 for the two-bedroom type. The semi-permanent cottage which supplanted them in 1917 and 1918 cost about £445 for the larger and £380 for the smaller type. (C.R. 2913 ; L.R. 10726/7.)

of the Ministry, since ownership agreements had not been arranged ; the remaining schemes were to be handed over either to local authorities or to firms at dates varying from three to seven years after the termination of the war.

As regarded completed schemes, there were at Barrow 202 semi-permanent houses which were ultimately to go to the Corporation but were in the meantime managed by the Ministry ; 250 houses at Coventry, though temporarily managed by Messrs. Siddeley Deasy, were Ministry property, as were 250 houses at Farnborough managed by the Royal Aircraft Factory. In addition to permanent or semi-permanent houses, there were a number of temporary cottages and huts, as well as hostels and colonies.

IV. Housing after the Armistice.

All the uncompleted schemes, with the exception of those at Barrow, Coventry, Irlam and Lincoln, were finished by the spring of 1920. It was early decided that no new constructional work should be undertaken by the Ministry ; but towards the end of 1919 a certain amount of work was undertaken in converting hostels under the control of the Housing Department into houses.

Though constructional work decreased after the Armistice, the Ministry's activities in connection with housing management naturally increased as more houses became ready for occupation. In April, 1919, there were 1,502 houses, in addition to nearly 4,000 bungalows, which were, or would be, managed by staff appointed by the Ministry, while 464 houses at Glengarnock and Coventry were managed by firms under Ministry supervision. The rents collected at this date amounted to about £3,000 a week.

During the 18 months following the Armistice the future administration of the Ministry's housing schemes was constantly under discussion. In the spring of 1919 unsuccessful attempts were made to transfer the responsibility either to the Ministry of Health or to the Office of Works. In August the Cabinet decided that the Office of Works should be responsible for construction, and that management should not be undertaken by the State, but should be transferred to local authorities. By the spring of 1920, however, no schemes had been so transferred, and in April the Disposal Board was instructed to arrange for the sale of all house property belonging to the Ministry. Before these instructions could take full effect it was decided to transfer the Housing Department in its entirety to the Office of Works, such transfer to date from 1 July, 1920.[1]

---

[1] A list of the Housing schemes administered by the Ministry when it handed over to the Office of Works is given in Appendix II.

CHAPTER IV.

BILLETING (1917–1918).

I. The Billeting of Civilians Act.

The use of lodgings as a valuable subsidiary means of housing mobile labour had always been exploited. Early in 1915 the North East Coast Armaments Committee, seconded by the Lord Mayor of Newcastle, had appealed to all lodging-house keepers and to private houses near engineering and shipbuilding yards to take in munition workers, resulting in accommodation for 7,000 men. The Glasgow and West of Scotland Armament Output Committee had made a similar appeal.

The demand for houses and lodgings consequent on the influx of munition workers into certain areas led landlords to take advantage by raising rents. Their action caused much adverse parliamentary debate in the autumn of 1915 and Government was asked to consider the advisability of introducing a bill to establish fair rents and security of tenure as an emergency war measure. Some of the abuses instanced were very flagrant. At Erith, tenants had had their rents raised from 9s. 6d. to 10s. 6d. a week in December, 1914, and from 10s. 6d. to 12s. in September, 1915 ; ejectments were frequently asked for by the landlord but the magistrates and County Court declined to turn out the tenant. In one case where the man could not get an ejectment order he raised rent from 8s. to 12s. so as to force possession. The rents in a block of tenement houses at Glasgow had been raised in August, 1915, £3 19s. 4d. per quarter on a yearly rental of £13 16s. per annum and the tenants only given a few days' notice of the rise. The action of the landlords on the Clydeside was indeed the cause of considerable unrest and nearly 10,000 Glasgow tenants were said to be resisting demands for increased rents.[1] At the same time the rises asked by landlords were nothing when compared with the increases demanded and obtained without difficulty by tenants from their lodgers.

Following on questions raised in the House of Commons the Minister of Munitions initiated inquiries into the raising of rent which had taken place in munitions areas. Reports received from 14 areas, including Birmingham, Liverpool, and Newcastle, did not indicate that, as a whole, the attitude of landlords had been unfair or improper. There were certainly bad instances of rapacity—the landlords of Birmingham were cited as the worst examples—but in several cases

---

[1] *Parliamentary Debates* (1915), *H. of C.*, LXXIV. 1566, 1572, 1284 ; LXXV. 354.

when rents had fallen owing to trade depression before the war, they were now no higher than in previous periods of good trade.[1]   General evidence, however, pointed to the need of reform,[2] and on 23 December, 1915, royal assent was given to the Act known as the Increase of Rent and Mortgage (War Restriction) Act, 1915, which made it impossible during the war (and for six months after) for landlords either to increase the rent of small dwelling-houses or to increase the rate of interest on or call in securities on such houses.[3]   It should be noted, however, that this Act, while it consulted the interest of the tenants as against the landlords, provided no protection for the lodger against the tenant, who at the time of the passing of the Act was already in many instances demanding lodging rates which were more than double those paid for the whole house.

As time went on the capacity of munitions districts for lodging accommodation became to some extent organised.   The various Employment Exchanges and Labour Advisory Committees kept lists of lodgings for imported workpeople, supplemented, where women were concerned, by the Advisory Committee on Women's War Employment.   Mayors of various towns issued appeals to local householders and instituted registers of available lodgings.[4]   In many cases the organisation of lodgings was carried out by the extra-mural welfare officers of the Ministry assisted by paid investigators.[5] Improved transit facilities, whether by rail, omnibus or tram, also made it feasible for workers to lodge some little distance from their work.[6]

Despite these arrangements it became evident by the spring of 1917 that, while available lodgings were by no means exhausted,[7] certain abuses needed reform which could only be carried out effectively by statutory authority.   The abuses were, broadly speaking, the prevalence of overcrowding, together with the unconscionably high lodging rates which were demanded from imported workers.

Contributory reasons impelling the Ministry to take decisive action were the increasing difficulty in getting material and labour, so that any additional proposal for extra building or housing

---

[1] (Printed) *Weekly Report*, No. 13, VII. (23/10/15).

[2] A further advance in rents at Glasgow led to strikes on 17 November, 1915, in protest among the employees of the Coventry Ordnance Works and Messrs. Fairfields.   (Printed) *Weekly Report*, Nos. 17, 18, VIII. (20 and 27/10/15).

[3] Acts of Parliament, 5 & 6 Geo. V. Ch. 97.   The houses so protected were of rentals not exceeding £35 in the London Area, £30 in Scotland, and £26 elsewhere.

[4] Municipal action was taken at Newcastle, Birmingham, Morecambe, Lincoln and Chelmsford.

[5] L.R. 112/15; Hist. Rec./H/346.2 2.   L.R. 1459/11.   *Weekly Report*, 1 January, 1916, 18 March, 1916, 4 November, 1916, 8 January, 1917, to February, 1917. In March, 1917, paid investigators were appointed to work under the Local Advisory Committee at Coventry.   By July, 1917, 950 women had been placed in lodgings—an average of 80 weekly.

[6] See below, Chap. V.

[7] At Lincoln the local house agent estimated that lodgings could be found for 1,500 workers.

construction was scrutinised "with almost microscopic care." The position at the moment, moreover, arising out of the shipping situation, was that the Ministry was working on a great scheme to increase the output of iron ore, which would involve the transference of thousands of workers to districts where housing accommodation was poor.

On 29 March, 1917, the Billeting of Civilians Bill was introduced and read to the House of Commons on behalf of the Ministry of Munitions ; on 23 April the second reading was followed by a long discussion ; on 4 May amendments were discussed in Committee ; on 7 May it was read for the third time and on 24 May received the royal assent.[1] The Bill aroused considerable opposition in its passage through the House, mainly on the score of the compulsion which, it was argued, was implied in its provisions. The title of the Act was perhaps misleading as conveying at first sight the impression that compulsion must necessarily be used, whereas the legislation was on lines entirely different from those laid down by the Army Act for the billeting of soldiers.

The main provisions of the Act may be thus summarised :—

(1) The Board constituted under the Act had power to billet persons engaged on any work of national importance, but the rights of the householder were protected in that billets were allocated in the first instance only to such persons as were willing to provide them. In certain cases total exemption was granted.[2]

(2) Provision was made to secure satisfactory discipline in the case of civilian workers not subjected to military or other control whereby any billeted person guilty of violence, drunkenness or indecency could be removed by the occupier as a trespasser, arrested without a warrant, and be subject before a Court of Summary Jurisdiction to a fine not exceeding £20.

(3) Provision was made for board and attendance, for seeing that the accommodation provided was adequate and rates charged reasonable, both as against householder and lodger.

Other clauses guaranteed the householder against loss by ensuring a week's notice from the worker, by providing payment in case of damage, other than fair wear and tear, and compensation for the introduction of any infectious diseases. Penalties were also prescribed for householders attempting to evade the liabilities of the Act.[3]

---

[1] *Parliamentary Debates* (1917), *H. of C.,* XCII. 2127–2182 ; XCIII. 623, 807, 2579.

[2] These exemptions were (i) where a man was to be billeted, a house containing women only, the house of a man absent on military duty, or the premises of any female religious community ; (ii) where a woman was to be billeted, a house containing men only, or the premises of any male religious community ; (iii) bank premises ; (iv) the accredited residence of any ambassador, minister, consul or agent of any foreign country.

[3] Billeting of Civilians Act, 1917, 7 & 8 Geo. V. Ch. 20.

II. The Constitution and Functions of Local
Billeting Committees.

The Minister of Munitions was entirely responsible for this measure, and its administration was entrusted to a Central Billeting Board set up by the Ministry but including also representatives of the principal Government Departments.[1] The Central Billeting Board was established and held its first meeting on 27 June, 1917. The Act provided that the Board should be assisted by local committees, but as these could not be constituted until it had been proved that they were needed, the preliminary investigation was done through the lodging investigators already employed by the Welfare Department. A report was then drawn up on the results of these investigations and a decision taken as to whether the Act should be applied to the district. If the decision were in the affirmative the Board then set in motion the appointed machinery of a local committee, with executive officers, whose constitution and functions were as follows :—

The statutory requirements were that every local committee should include two representatives of the local authority. Apart from this the constitution remained in the hands of the Central Billeting Board. Experience proved that it was not possible to draw up a model constitution applicable to every area, but certain general rules were observed to make it as representative as possible, the principal employers of the workers concerned and the local Trades and Labour Council being asked to sit on the committee. Where women's labour was specially concerned, any women's organisation, and more particularly the National Federation of Women Workers, were asked to send representatives. When possible the landlady class was also represented.[2] Occasionally the manager of the Employment Exchange or the secretary of the Advisory Committee on Women's War Employment attended the meetings *ex officio*, but as a rule officers of Government Departments were not appointed on a committee which was essentially the guardian of local interests. For this same reason the policy of the Central Billeting Board throughout was to allow as much freedom as possible to a local committee with the minimum amount of control from headquarters. The committees were worked on a voluntary basis, the only expenditure being the amount of wages actually lost by labour representatives in attending meetings.[3]

The main function of a local committee was to fix the rates to be paid for board and lodging, basing them upon the market price prevailing in the district for workers of a class similar to those to be billeted.

[1] The original personnel of the Board was as follows:—Chairman, A. H. Marshall, M.P. ; Ministry of Labour, Mr. H. B. Butler, Miss Durham, Charles Duncan, M.P. ; Admiralty, Mr. A. H. Warne Browne ; War Office, Lieut.-Colonel Butler ; Board of Agriculture, Lord Goschen ; Local Government Board, Mr. A. J. A. Ball ; Scottish Office, Mr. Miller Craig ; National Service Department, Miss Markham ; Ministry of Munitions, Mr. Vernon, Mr. Wolff, Miss Hadow ; Secretary, Mr. R. H. Crooke. Under the provisions of the Act two members at least had to be women. (Hist. Rec./R/346. 2/31 ; L.R. 112/17.)

[2] Hist. Rec./R/346.2/31. 43.   [3] Hist. Rec./R/346. 2/2. L.R. 112/15.

The rates decided upon by a committee were submitted for approval to the Board, who in every case accepted them.

A secondary statutory function was the adjudication on claims incurred through defaulters leaving their billets without notice. The anticipation that this would prove an important part of their work was not fulfilled ; in many districts no claims at all were made and the total number was comparatively insignificant.[1]

The third duty of the local committee was to hear and settle complaints between householders and persons billeted. Contrary again to expectations[2] this side of their work did not in practice amount to much ; complaints were of a trifling nature, and were settled by the executive officer without reference to the committee. In no case was a single prosecution for drunkenness, violent behaviour or other disorderly conduct found to be necessary.

The work of assigning applicants to available billets, though laid down in the Act as a function of a local committee, was in practice carried out by the executive officer or some member of the investigation staff. Under his statutory appointment the executive officer was subordinate to the local committee, but in practice, though working in conjunction with the committee, much of his work was independent and he was directly responsible to the Central Billeting Board.[3] In small districts where local knowledge was an asset, the Central Billeting Board appointed a local man as executive officer, but for larger areas such as Barrow and Coventry, where organising ability was required, an officer was appointed from the Ministry. At Hereford and Lancaster, where the labour was mostly female, women officers were appointed.

Working under the executive officer were paid lodging investigators who were appointed locally, and who were as a rule men and women of a superior working-class type. Investigators of this kind had already been employed by the Welfare Section of the Ministry and were taken over by the Central Billeting Board in any district where it was decided to apply the Billeting of Civilians Act.[4] Their duties were to canvass the district, prepare the lodging register and keep it up to date.

III. The Work of the Central Billeting Board.

The method of action adopted by the Board was to hold a local inquiry, conducted as a rule by the Chairman, accompanied by various members of the Board. A careful survey was made of the situation

---

[1] HIST. REC./H/346. 2/2. The number of claims received were 320, involving payment of £226 14s. 9d., of which £82 5s. 6d. was recovered. In general no claim was entertained in excess of the weekly scale settled by the local committee.

[2] See debates in the House of Commons on the passing of the Act, *passim.* *Parliamentary Debates* (1917), *H. of C.,* XCII. 611, 2127 ; XCIII. 623–701.

[3] L.R. 112/14, 15.

[4] L.R. 112/14. The salary paid to investigators (35s. to 40s. for men and 30s. to 40s. for women) compared very unfavourably with the wages earned in other employment, and it was difficult to secure suitable persons to undertake the work.

in each district, by means of personal interviews with employers, representatives of labour organisations, local authorities and any voluntary body which had been dealing with the lodgings question. A report was then drawn up upon which a decision was taken.

It very soon became apparent that the scope of the Board's work must become wider than was originally contemplated and that the examination of the particular circumstances of each district must be from the point of view of housing or hostel accommodation no less than from billeting. It shortly became, indeed, an established policy with the Ministry of Munitions, when a question of war emergency housing arose, to defer consideration until the Board had visited the district and reported on its needs. A local inquiry in a particular area therefore did not necessarily imply that there was a need for billeting.

On the whole the Board encountered very little local opposition in the course of its investigations. Such as occurred was generally caused by an inherent distrust on the part of the workers of the compulsion which was provided for in the Act, but which in no case was it found necessary to enforce. The Cowes Trades and Labour Council threatened to " down tools " if compulsory billeting was resorted to. The workpeople at Vickers', Barrow, resented the Act as " a hypocritical way out of a legitimate demand for working-class houses," and in the same way the Lincoln Trades and Labour Council resented billeting as likely to result in further congestion of working-class accommodation while delaying a housing scheme which was the real solution.[1] The labour organisations also felt that compulsion would be imposed on artisans while the occupants of better-class houses would be allowed to go free. This question, indeed, presented particular difficulties to the Board, for it was found that the scarcity of domestic service, combined with the food shortage, made it in practice almost impossible to call upon the occupiers of better-class houses, who had not been in the habit of accepting lodgers, to provide accommodation for munition workers.[2]

The investigations of the Board disclosed grave evils, both in the matter of overcrowding and excessive charges.

At Lincoln, which was visited in October, 1917, the population had risen from 52,000 to 58,000 during the war, while the normal increase of houses had entirely ceased. Overcrowding was consequently acute (cases were reported of as many as 19 persons living in houses of five rooms), more particularly in the older part of the city, where the conditions were said to be indescribable and had a disastrous effect upon the social and moral welfare of the people. Skilled workmen coming to the town were unable to obtain houses and frequently had to live in a single room with their wives and children, £3 to £5 being offered for the key of a house. Lodging accommodation was exhausted at the time of the Board's visit and Ruston & Company had been

---

[1] HIST. REC./R/346.2/32, 33.

[2] Both at Cowes and Yeovil substantial assistance was given by the occupiers of large houses. (HIST. REC./H/346. 2/2.)

unable to find lodgings for 20 men, newly-imported, who had to sleep on sacks on the messroom floor.

The conditions disclosed on the Tyneside and in the Clyde district were almost equally gloomy. In the former district, where the problem chiefly concerned men, the lodgings were seriously overcrowded. Conditions were such that the municipal authorities refused even to issue an appeal for lodgings and the Board itself felt there was no case for billeting. In the Clyde district a large proportion of the houses were single apartment tenement houses and it was a common occurrence to find two married families in one apartment and two and sometimes three male lodgers. In Coatbridge there was a single house vacant in the Burgh and premiums of £5 were offered in the local press for a key ; the local authority was quite unable to exercise its Public Health Act to prevent overcrowding as there was literally no other accommodation.[1]

At seaside places, where work of national importance was being carried out, while there was no actual shortage of accommodation, a tendency was shown on the part of the landladies to raise the prices or even to get rid of their munition lodgers during their holiday season.[2]

At Derby an association of landladies, formed by the householders in the immediate vicinity of the Rolls-Royce Works, demanded a minimum of 28s. a week from lodgers, and advertised to this effect in the local papers.[3]

On the other hand, evidence was found of a certain amount of voluntary overcrowding. Applicants for lodgings refused to go very far from their work. At Sheffield, the east end of the town, where the principal works were situated, was far more congested than the west end. The same thing happened at Barrow and Coventry. The dislike, too, which was almost an instinct, of anything approaching an institution often left the hostels and workmen's houses empty while overcrowding the lodging houses in their immediate vicinity.[4]

It emerged very clearly from the various inquiries held by the Central Billeting Board that the problem was becoming more and more directly concerned with housing proper rather than with lodgings. As the war prolonged itself war munition volunteers and other workers who had been transferred to strange districts naturally became anxious to bring their families[5] to the new places of employment and the

---

[1] See also below, Chap. VI.

[2] This happened at Bognor, where 25s. a week was asked during the summer months for a single room which in winter cost 10s. a week.

[3] The War Munitions Volunteers Association immediately inserted another advertisement that they would only pay 24s.

[4] At Port Glasgow, for instance, there was a workman's home with 100 vacant beds in that part of the town where congestion in private lodgings was at its worst.

[5] The Act did not provide for the billeting of the wives and families of workers. Applications were often received by the executive officer for family billets and wherever possible the accommodation was provided though no responsibility was taken (HIST. REC./H/346. 2/2). White & Poppé, interviewed by the Board in October, 1917, said the housing situation in Coventry was desperate for married people : all their temporary married quarters were full up.

demand for lodgings, so acute in 1915 and 1916, to a great extent transformed itself into a demand for houses. Good wages also were an encouragement to congestion in that those who had been in the habit of taking in lodgers allowed themselves the luxury of doing without one. Combined with this was the abnormal cessation of all house building, and consequently in all the big industrial centres—Barrow, the Tyneside, the Clyde district, Coventry—and also in districts such as Lincoln or Northwich, where the congestion was chiefly due to war conditions, the Billeting Board is found stating that housing schemes rather than billeting were the solution of the problem. Where, however, it was considered possible that the application of the Billeting Act might help either to postpone schemes entailing large public expenditure or to tide over the period before their completion, local committees were set up.

In addition to recommendations as to housing, the Board embodied in their reports to Departments recommendations strictly speaking outside the scope of their work, based on the result of their inquiries, relating to such matters as the extension of hostel or canteen accommodation, the provision of special medical attendance in connection with a filling factory, the facilitating of a Corporation scheme for the extension of a tramway or the improvements of train services.[1]

The result of the food shortage in 1917 was to make the landlady less willing than ever to take in lodgers.[2] The introduction of rationing somewhat reversed the position, as experience quickly showed that, under the coupon system, it was easier to cater for a large number.

The services of the Central Billeting Board were exercised on behalf of the Admiralty and the Ministry of Munitions ; by far the greater part of its work was done for the latter Department.[3] At the time of its creation it was thought that it might be called upon to act for the Board of Agriculture for billeting women employed on the land, but this never eventuated. In May, 1918, the Board undertook, if occasion arose, to make inquiries for the Controller of Coal Mines as to billets for men transferred to replace colliers released for military service.

The Board conducted 68 inquiries on behalf of the Departments concerned, resulting in the application of the Act to 29 districts where local committees were accordingly set up.[4]

---

[1] In certain cases the Central Billeting Board itself took direct action with regard to transport ; *e.g.*, at Cowes and Hereford an improved service of trains to and from outlying districts was arranged for by them.

[2] In January, 1918, women were reported to be applying for work at the Elswick Works on the grounds that they were giving up keeping lodgers on account of the high price of food.

[3] Inquiries for the Admiralty were carried out at Bognor, Chepstow, Yeovil, the Tyne District, Southampton, Newport and Cardiff.

[4] These Committees were at Banbury, Barrow-in-Furness, Bognor and Westhampnett, Burntisland, Chelmsford, Coventry, Cowes, Dartford, Derby, Erith, Farnborough, Gainsborough, Halifax, Hereford, Huddersfield, Lancaster, Leatherhead and Epsom, Leominster, Littlehampton, Maidstone, Morecambe, Newport (Isle of Wight), Ross (Herefordshire), Sheffield, Southampton, Troon Ulverston, Weybridge, Yeovil.

CHAPTER V.

THE TRANSPORT OF MUNITION WORKERS.

1. General' Arrangements by the Inland Transport Department.

The provision of suitable facilities for the transport of munition workers played an important part in the ·solution of housing diffi-culties during the war. The causes which gave it prominence—the exhaustion of local labour, the supply of labour to isolated factories, the congestion of population in isolated districts—have already been indicated. Since early in 1916 the work of ameliorating the abnormal transport conditions was .undertaken by à special section of the Inland Transport Department. All types of transport—train, tram, motor-omnibus and boat—came within their purview, and certain general principles of action were established which may be summarised as follows :—

(1) When the Ministry expended capital on structural facilities, the transport company concerned was subsidised on the understanding that they should have option to purchase such structures after the war at a valuation to be agreed upon.

(2) Local highway authorities were only given financial assistance where it was proved that extraordinary munitions traffic was likely to injure public roads beyond the normal capacity of the ratepayers to make good damages.

(3) To avoid waste of labour, material and vehicles, no individual or company was allowed to institute a new omnibus service unless it was certified by the departments con-cerned as necessary either for munition workers or other government war service.

Turning to the different methods of transport, arrangements made with railway companies provided some of the most important facilities, and this despite ever-increasing difficulty arising from deple-tion of railway staff and depreciation of rolling-stock. The methods adopted were various : inducement was offered to the worker living some distance off by the issue of cheap railway tickets to people engaged on munition work[1]; halts were erected at convenient points adjacent to factories where no station existed ; alighting platforms built on sidings connecting works with the main lines ; small stations were extended to cope with increased passenger traffic. Train services were also altered to suit the hours of work at factories, and in some

---

[1] HIST. REC./H/2020/2, pp. 158-163.

cases special services were initiated. During the war, 56 halts and other works in this connection were constructed at an approximate cost of £150,000.

A few examples may be given serving to illustrate the importance of the railway extensions. Thus at Lostock Graham Factory, where local labour was exhausted, negotiations with the railway company resulted in special workmen's trains being run from a large industrial town some 20 miles distant. As the nearest station was two miles from the factory, involving a walk through bad country, an adjacent halt was provided and the distance was also further ‧lessened by arrangements with the Canal Company to provide a footbridge. It is. considered that had these facilities not been provided, adequate labour for this important factory could not have been procured.

At Barnbow National Filling Factory, again, some 6½ miles from Leeds, a halt and special train services were provided for the workers ; here the factory developed so enormously that the halt was twice enlarged, and by the close of the war there were as many as 52 special trains arriving daily and conveying 25,000 workers.

Foleshill Station was also considerably enlarged in order to cope with the numerous trains of munition workers for White & Poppé's factory.[1]

A factory at Salfords engaged in the manufacture of important parts of machine guns was greatly handicapped by being not only a considerable distance from the nearest source of labour, but also 2½ miles from the nearest railway station or other means of transport. A line of railway ran within a few hundred yards of the factory, which was unable to obtain any facilities from the company. Negotiations by the Ministry, however, resulted in the erection of a temporary station and a suitable train service which effectively disposed of the labour difficulty.

Arrangements with the railway also made it possible for 6,500 workmen to be brought from Gloucester, Cheltenham and Stroud to work at the Quedgley Filling Factory ; five trains ran each way by day and two by night, the tickets cost the workers 2s. 2d. each, whatever their place of departure, the additional cost ‧for places beyond Gloucester being charged to the factory.[2]

For the same reasons as applied to the railways, it was difficult for tramway companies generally to maintain and develop adequate services for working people. There were special instances, however, where, by the action of the Ministry, tramway and omnibus services were so improved as to enable workers to lodge some little distance from their work. These improvements were not confined merely to more frequent services. Occasionally, as in the case of the Park Royal and Perivale Filling Factories lying adjacent to each other, a

---

[1] The level crossing at this station led to the factory and was a source not only of danger, but of great inconvenience and delay to workers, who were often held up for long periods. At the request of the Ministry an overhead footbridge was constructed. See also below, p. 52.

[2] HIST. REC./R/1122. 3/43.

loopline was laid down for trams, to prevent delay and disorganisation arising at spots where the workers alighted from and boarded cars.   At Erith the Ministry succeeded, after much difficulty, in inducing two local authorities and a tramway company to make reasonable arrangements for through-running.[1] Motor omnibus services, too, were in several instances extended, or even instituted as was done at Chilworth, whose position was isolated, and whose number of workers did not justify the running of a special train.

II. Facilities provided for Woolwich.

The abnormal increase in labour employed by the Royal Arsenal, Woolwich, necessitated special attention to the question of the transport of munition workers.   The growth of numbers, combined with the introduction of double shifts, already in 1915 taxed the transport arrangements to the utmost.   Towards the end of the year the shifts were revised and several hours of arrival and departure were introduced instead of all workers coming and leaving at the same time. This revision helped to meet immediate necessities, but in the spring of 1916 an urgent demand arose for additional labour at the Arsenal. This labour had to be recruited from new areas, necessitating the strengthening of existing services and the introduction of new ones.

New omnibus services were immediately instituted and, together with those already existing, were strengthened from time to time, so that when the Armistice was signed there were upwards of 300 omnibuses running in the Woolwich area for the conveyance of workers to and from the Arsenal.

The increase of tram services was more difficult to accomplish. There were three lengths of single tramway lines in the centre of the town of Woolwich, which acted as a bottle-neck, and it was evident that further development of the services was impracticable without certain alterations of the track.   After some delay, caused by lengthy negotiations with the Woolwich Borough Council, to whom the tramways belonged, and the London County Council, it was arranged to double the tracks.   The revised tramway service, providing an increase in cars of 15 per cent. between 5 a.m. and 9 a.m. and 27 per cent. between 5 p.m. and 9 p.m., came into operation in July, 1917.

The provision of additional ferry service between the north and south banks of the Thames at Woolwich was an important asset. Not only did it relieve the congestion on tramcars and omnibuses, but it is also estimated to have saved several thousand workers at least forty minutes' journey each way daily.   The question was taken up in August, 1916, and in March, 1917, the service was started between a site on the north bank near Gallions railway station to a point directly opposite within the Arsenal itself.   The operation of this ferry was undertaken by the Arsenal authorities and, apart from its valuable service in maintaining output, brought in a revenue of about £160 a week.

---

[1] Mr. McElroy, General Manager of the Manchester Tramways, carried this through on behalf of the Ministry without remuneration.

CHAPTER VI.

SPECIAL ASPECTS OF THE HOUSING PROBLEM.

During the war circumstances combined to give a special character to the housing question in certain areas. Any history of the Ministry's activities in connection with housing would be incomplete without some detail of the steps taken to face the particular form of the housing problem raised in Barrow, Coventry and the Clyde area.[1]

I. Barrow.[2]

In August, 1914, Barrow-in-Furness was a town containing some 70,000 inhabitants.[3] Its situation, peculiar and isolated, is at the north-west corner of the Lancashire coast. Between it and the Irish Sea on the west is Walney Island, a treeless barrier reef, inhabited only in the centre and connected with the mainland by a bridge. The main industry of the town was already centred round Vickers' works, where for three years previously a steady average of 18,000 workers had been employed. Other large employers of labour were the Barrow Hematite Works and Paper Pulping Works.[4] It is incontest-able that the numbers employed, the wages paid, the house rates paid and the houses built by Vickers were so greatly in excess of similar engagements by other firms or by the Corporation itself as to make the firm, even under peace conditions, a dominant influence in conditions at Barrow.

The residential part of Barrow (exclusive of the houses built by Vickers) is on the mainland, where the ground rises from west to north-east. The houses are, with few exceptions, working-class houses built of red brick, roofed with slates and, except in the main streets, flush with the pavement. The principal streets are broad, well paved and planted with trees, and there is also a public park. Rented houses are the exception in Barrow, for the most part the working-man owns his own house.

---

[1] The history of the unique housing experiments at Gretna and Birtley is related elsewhere. (See below, Chaps. VII and VIII.)

[2] Based on Memorandum by Mr. G. H. Duckworth (copy in HIST. REC./R/346/2); L.R.H. 10/7, 27, 77, 99; 10726/7, 47; 4, 300/44; and Weekly Reports of the Labour Section.

[3] The population on 31 December, 1913, was 68,523 and on 31 December, 1914, 75,368 (HIST. REC./R/346. 2/4).

[4] The latter closed down during the war owing to the scarcity of timber.

The industrial part of the town lies on the west and south-west edge of the mainland. Vickers' works occupy a site at the south-west corner, known locally as Old Barrow. At this point Walney Bridge gives access to the island on which are the two settlements, Vickerstown North and Vickerstown South, built for Vickers' workpeople. On the outbreak of war these townships included 1,000 houses or about one-fourteenth of the whole town of Barrow. Many of these houses had been built and were managed by an estate company established by Vickers. The houses themselves, erected about 1901, are two-storeyed buildings of varying accommodation, with red tiled roofs and rough cast walls. There are small front gardens but none at the back, though neighbouring allotments are available for growing vegetables. The whole district has the appearance of a strictly kept model village.

Like most other towns of any size, there was already on the outbreak of war a shortage of houses at Barrow, estimated at between 1,000 and 2,000. Vickers, anticipating the influx of munition workers, foresaw the demand for fresh house room and took early steps to meet it. Before the close of 1914 they asked for and obtained from the War Office a loan of £75,000 towards the erection of 253 permanent cottages. These were supplemented by 263 houses built by two estate companies, in which Vickers had a financial interest, from funds borrowed from the Barrow Town Council. All these houses were situated in the Vickers townships and were earmarked for Vickers' employees. They were similar in type to those already in existence, with two rooms on the ground floor and three bedrooms, and were completed before the close of 1915. In addition the firm erected a model lodging house for between 300 and 400 men and a hostel, without cubicles, for 104 girls.

The Ministry became directly concerned in housing at Barrow at the beginning of 1916 when accommodation had to be found there for a number of inspectors and examiners on the staff of the Chief Inspector, Woolwich. An arrangement was then made with Vickers by which the firm undertook to build 90 houses, receiving a grant of £97 (to be written down from excess profits) on each house. In return, the houses were to be at the disposal of the Ministry; they were of a slightly better type than others belonging to the company, built in pairs with a garden both at the back and front, with a large kitchen and living room, a scullery and three bedrooms.

The additional 600 houses thus obtained were by the summer of 1916 inadequate to keep pace with the needs of a population which rose from 75,368 at the close of 1914 to 79,206 in 1915 and by the end of 1916 was to attain to 85,179. The extended scheme for dilution, involving the employment of 2,000 women, introduced among Vickers' employees at this date led to a strike, which emphasised so strongly the necessity for providing accommodation for imported labour, more particularly female, that an order temporarily prohibited the importation of more women into Barrow until proper housing could be provided.[1]

---

[1] Hist. Rec./H/1124/1. This order was withdrawn in November, 1916.

It was obvious that temporary hostels furnished the quickest means of housing these women, and the Ministry now took over certain buildings in Barrow and handed them to Vickers to adapt and manage as women's hostels, the Ministry supplying the necessary furniture. In this way three hostels to hold 160 women were completed by December, 1916. These hostels, which barely touched the main problem, were not at first a great success ; the women, who were mostly of a very poor class, disliked their restrictions and preferred to crowd into private lodgings.

In November, 1916, Vickers wrote to the Ministry, " The congestion in housing is now at breaking point," whilst the Barrow Corporation, particularly the labour wing, began an active agitation both in committee and council.[1] Lord Harrowby was asked by the Ministry to investigate conditions at Barrow. His report, dated 23 December, 1916, substantiated this statement as to overcrowding and he recommended that 100 houses and a number of standardised hutments should be built at once, while more buildings should be converted into hostels.[2]

It seemed certain that any further scheme would have to be initiated by the Ministry, for Vickers, who had already spent £623,330 on housing in Barrow, refused to spend further capital on what was probably a war emergency and largely occasioned by the needs of the new howitzer shop, which was Ministry property. They were prepared, however, to assist any scheme by selling a freehold site within a mile of their works at a special price. The Ministry accordingly undertook a scheme for 250 houses which were eventually to be taken over by the Corporation. Treasury consent was obtained, but matters came to a climax in the summer of 1917, before the scheme could be put into operation, and it was merged in a more extensive one undertaken as the result of popular feeling.

In June, 1917, commissioners had been appointed to inquire into the causes of industrial unrest throughout the country. The position in Barrow at this date speaks for itself. The employees of Vickers now numbered some 35,000, nearly double their pre-war strength. Of these 6,596 men and 2,647 women had been imported into Barrow and over 5,000 employees came by train from Ulverston, Dalton, Millom and other small places within a radius of 20 miles.

A report of conditions at Barrow made to the commissioners on their appointment by one conversant with conditions there puts the housing question in the foreground of industrial grievances.

"For the majority of workers here there is no home life. In some instances the wife is engaged on munition work, but in the majority of cases she is occupied with looking after lodgers. . . . The number of beds occupied by night and day on the Box and Cox principle is very high and runs into thousands. The married man returns home to find his wife clearing up for the lodgers and his own meal not ready—in fact, with children,

---

[1] L.R.H. 10/99.   [2] L.R.H. 10/99 ; Hist. Rec./H/1124/1.

lodgers and husband the wife has her hands full—with the result that one or the other is neglected and naturally becomes dissatisfied. Also, I would point out the very inadequate provision for maternity cases. In many homes it is impossible to deal with them, at any rate with decency. Cases have been brought to my notice where nine persons have lived in one room, sixteen in one small house, and a bedroom is occupied by two grown-up sisters and their two brothers 16 and 17 years of age.''

The commissioners took evidence at Barrow on 9 July from representatives both of labour and employers. They were given various instances illustrating the conditions indicated above, but these must be regarded in the light of later events as cases of individual rather than typical hardship.[1] Their mere existence, however, combined with such incontrovertible evidence as was furnished from the official figures for the last six years of the Barrow Borough Treasurer,[2] confirmed the necessity for strong remedial action.

While expressing themselves much impressed by the work done by Vickers, the commissioners stated that there was no evidence before them that either the Government or the municipality had, up to now, taken any practical steps to deal with the problem.[3] They strongly recommended that the War Cabinet should take the matter in hand.

The report of the Industrial Unrest Committee brought conditions at Barrow into prominence. Immediately following on it the Central Billeting Board held a local inquiry on behalf of the Ministry. They met with conflicting testimony both as to overcrowding and the amount of lodging accommodation available, Vickers maintaining (on the strength, it was said, of an out-of-date register) that there was still suitable lodging room for 700 women.[4] Lodgings at any distance from the works were, however, very unpopular. This was partly due to the town tramway service, which was infrequent and bad. Mr. G. H. Duckworth has described the scenes which took place on the tram

---

[1] The Archdeacon of Barrow later stated that, although he was not prepared to say that they might not have occurred, the " horrible examples " mentioned by the Unrest Committee were not within his knowledge and he had not been able to obtain confirmation of them from his clergy. (HIST. REC./R/346. 2/4.)

[2] The figures were as follows :—

	Number of Houses 31 March	Population 31 December	Numbers per House.
1912	12,902	65,257	5.06
1913	13,259	68,523	5.17
1914	13,626	75,368	5.53
1915	13,983	79,206	5.66
1916	14,588	85,179	5.83
1917	14,791	—	—

[3] Evidence taken in one day was necessarily not exhaustive. As indicated above, action had been taken both by the War Office and the Ministry of Munitions in the matter.

[4] Members of the Board who made a personal inspection found serious cases of overcrowding. Families were being housed in railway carriages and caravans, and the share of a bed in a small room was in many cases the best lodging available.

routes at the changings of shifts; men clambered up the outside, standing and sitting everywhere in such a way that the car's back appeared to be broken and the mud guards flapped against the track as the car moved along; it was impossible to collect half the fares or for a tithe of the men and women to get a place.

The Billeting Board considered that the real need was for houses rather than further exploitation of lodgings, but a local committee of the Board was nevertheless set up and local investigators appointed whose work proved of great value.[1]

Meanwhile, the Poor Law Guardians, the Women's Labour League and other public bodies in Barrow were petitioning the Minister, and a question was asked in Parliament as to whether immediate action was being taken in view of the Industrial Unrest Report.[2]   On 2 October the War Cabinet decided that a scheme for 1,000 houses was to be proceeded with.[3]   This decision was announced in the press a few days later, when it was stated that the semi-permanent houses would begin to be ready by Christmas, 1917, and would be finished by March, 1918, when the permanent houses would begin to be available.

In addition, action was taken with regard to the ejectment of munition workers.   The Committee of Industrial Unrest had called attention to the abuse, while admitting that the total of ejectment orders made since 1915 was not large, being in fact 42 out of a total of 88 cases entered.   The Justices at Barrow, however, regarded the matter as one of extreme urgency, considering that unless some drastic step was taken giving them power to refuse ejectment warrants, strikes and rioting were to be anticipated; the Town Council and Trades Council also sent deputations to the Ministry to the same purpose.   Remedy was found in a fresh regulation, 2A (2) of the Defence of the Realm Act, dated 29 September, 1917, which empowered the Minister of Munitions to declare any area where munitions work was being carried on a special area.   Barrow and its neighbourhood was constituted a special area on 1 October, which meant that henceforward no munition workers could be ejected from their dwelling-houses so long as they paid their rent and observed the other conditions of tenancy.

The scheme for 1,000 houses was put in hand immediately.   The climate of Barrow, cold and bleak, was unsuited to temporary buildings, but in order to save time it was decided that half the houses should be one-storeyed concrete buildings with hollow walls, of a semi-permanent character guaranteed to last from 30 to 40 years.   The first instalment of these " semi-permanent " houses was started at once on a site in the Roose Road.   Despite very serious labour scarcity, the first of these houses was finished before the close of 1917 and tenants began to enter in February, 1918.

---

[1] HIST. REC./R/346. 2/32.   A total of 4,611 persons (4,004 men and 607 women) were in this way provided with accommodation.

[2] L.R.H. 10/99 ; *Parliamentary Debates* (1917), *H. of C.*, XCVII. 1594.

[3] This included the scheme for 250 houses already approved by the Treasury, to whom no further application was made.

Difficulties had meanwhile arisen with regard to a site for the permanent houses. Two sites in the neighbourhood of the semi-permanent houses had been chosen by the Ministry and Barrow Town Council respectively. The Town Council site besides being unduly expensive would have involved the destruction of a considerable number of allotments. It was finally decided in March, 1918, that the first batch of 150 houses should be erected on the land common to both suggested sites.

By the spring of 1918, however, the position had considerably altered. Already in November, 1917, doubt had begun to be expressed as to the wisdom or necessity of completing the semi-permanent scheme. A recent bread ticket census had shown that overcrowding was not so serious as at first supposed,[1] while improvements in the train service had opened up the Lake District for residential purposes. The trades unions representatives, moreover, expressed strong objections to houses of the bungalow type and asked for a guarantee of their demolition immediately after the war.[2] Their objections were shared by the Town Council, who in addition probably felt these houses would compete in rents with other houses in Barrow. It is likely, too, that the working men of Barrow, who as a rule owned their own houses, were beginning to realise that a housing scheme on so large a scale might too drastically relieve them of their lodgers.[3]

The Barrow Council was interviewed in January, 1918, and the Ministry decided that on the completion of the 202 houses already in hand the remainder of the scheme should be postponed ; this decision was extended shortly after to the 500 permanent houses, of which 250 only were taken in hand.

The reasons for this decision were (1) that the actual shortage at Barrow had probably been overstated ; (2) the relative need as compared with other districts (e.g., Coventry and Lincoln) ; (3) the difficulties of obtaining constructional labour.

There was no later development of the housing question in Barrow. The deficiency of labour proved a cause of delay, and a scheme suggested in June, 1918, by the Corporation and Vickers for houses on Walney Island (where Vickers offered a free site) was refused by the War Priorities Committee on the ground that labour should be

---

[1] The census showed 4½ persons per house as against 6 persons reported from corporation figures.

[2] The late labour unrest was said to have been much more the unrest of the Union Secretaries than of the men themselves. These Secretaries, who were not themsélves manual workers, found that their members were taking less interest in the Union as their wages increased and their spare time was absorbed in earning " over-time." They saw their chance in the prevalent under-housing for an agitation which might lead to higher wages for the lodgers in which the working-man landlords would also benefit. (HIST. REC./R/346. 2/4.)

[3] In December, 1917, house owners near the new sites sent a formal protest to the Ministry against the erection of Government bungalows as likely to depreciate the value of their property both for letting and selling.

E

concentrated on the scheme already in progress.[1] By September,. 1918, the semi-permanent houses were entirely completed, but progress with the permanent scheme was slow. About 8 per cent. of the work was complete at the time of the Armistice, and by May, 1920, 132 houses out of the total 250 were finished. As already stated, both Messrs. Vickers and the Town Council refused the post-war ownership of these houses, and ownership was therefore vested in the Ministry.

II. Coventry.[2]

During the last 20 to 30 years Coventry has entirely altered in character and has become an important centre of the motor-car and bicycle industries. The character and plan of the ancient city has had its influence on war conditions. Industrial expansion had taken place principally in the north of the city, while the railway station is in the south, a mile from the main square and two miles from some of the most important modern works such as the Coventry Ordnance Works and White & Poppé. The narrow main street, which connects north and south, contracts in the centre of the town so as to be capable of a single tramway line only, and the consequent congestion of traffic has, from the point of view of the housing question alone, been a serious drawback, rendering certain quarters geographically unavailable for lodgings.

The nature of the industries peculiar to Coventry, combined with the existence of an armament firm there, made it certain that there would be a considerable access of munition work to the town. A certain amount of requisite labour could be, and was, supplied locally, but by the close of 1917 it was estimated that something like 12,000 men and 20,000 women had been imported into Coventry.

At Coventry, as at Barrow, the housing problem was not created by the war, although undoubtedly aggravated by it. The provision of dwellings had by no means kept pace with the industrial expansion and the shortage of houses was already in 1914 a grievance of some years' standing.

During 1914 and 1915 building did not remain at a standstill : 1,762 houses, mainly working-class in type, were erected by private enterprise. They were inadequate to keep pace with the influx of workers, and the housing problem at Coventry, which was becoming an increasingly important centre of munitions production, was among the earliest considerations of the new Ministry of Munitions. The first scheme inaugurated was to supply the housing requirements likely to arise from the large extensions to the Coventry Ordnance Works in the autumn of 1915. Under this scheme the Corporation, who

---

[1] The local master builders maintained that they could get necessary labour if they were given the contract and that the company engaged on the scheme could not obtain labour because they were an outside firm.

[2] Based on the Weekly Reports of the Housing Section ; L.R. 11636/6, 12, 70 ; L.R. 112/23, 42, 79 ; L.R. 1459/11 ; C.R.V./Gen./130 ; C.R.V./C/15, 124.

already owned 400 houses, were subsidised to build a further 600 on a site of 50 acres at Stoke Heath, adjacent to the Coventry Ordnance Works, who were to have first option of tenancy for their employees. These houses each contained three bedrooms and were similar in type to those already built by the Corporation. They began to be available for occupation in the summer of 1916, and were completed by the close of the year.

Permanent houses were built in this instance in consequence of the acknowledged shortage of houses in Coventry, but it was evident that the demand could only hope to be met by the rapid erection of temporary buildings, and this more specially in view of the preponderance of female over male workers imported into the town. The type of work undertaken by Coventry firms, notably in connection with fuses, was peculiarly suited to female labour and led to a special development of hostel schemes in this town. Messrs. White & Poppé, in particular, were in 1915 constructing, as agents for the Ministry, a National Filling Factory and Fuse Factory at which they expected to employ 3,500 women and 550 men. Their works were isolated from the town and only a certain number of these workers could count on outside accommodation. A scheme was immediately taken in hand by the Ministry to put up 18 hutments for women, each capable of housing 112 persons, with covered ways and dining-halls in common. At the same time 300 temporary cottages were decided on for the men. Further extensions were undertaken early in 1916, to enable White & Poppé to work both a day and a night shift, which necessitated a con- siderable expansion of the original scheme, and for this firm alone hostels (of which the greater majority were for women) for 5,900 workers and 466 temporary cottages were provided by the Ministry during 1916. In the summer of the same year hostels were begun at Barras Heath to provide for 500 girls imported by the Coventry Ordnance Works for their fuse-filling factory.

The requirements of another firm, the Siddeley Deasy Company, for the housing of whose employees the Ministry felt responsibility, were met by a scheme, initiated early in 1917, for 210 houses, of which a certain number (156) were completed only so far as to serve in the first instance as hostels.

Wherever possible existing buildings were temporarily adapted as dwellings : thus the Holy Trinity Church School had been taken over for the constructional staff engaged on building extensions, while the Coventry Workhouse was rented by the Hotchkiss Company to accom- modate 700 munition workers.[1]

The possibilities of lodging accommodation in Coventry were exploited by the Labour Exchange acting in conjunction with the Women's War Advisory Committee. In March, 1917, paid investi- gators were appointed by the Ministry to work under the committee, with the result that by July, 1917, 950 women had been placed in lodgings.[2] Before this date 100 lodgings for a considerable number

---

[1] L.R. 11636/12.   [2] L.R. 1459/11.

of munition workers employed at Coventry had been requisitioned in the neighbouring towns and villages within a radius of from 10 to 17 miles.[1]

Despite these not inconsiderable arrangements made by the Ministry, which had indeed kept the yearly number of houses built up to about pre-war standard, the housing conditions at Coventry were the subject of growing complaint during 1917. On 26 August, the Minister asked for special investigations to be made, stating that he had heard " from several sources that the conditions under which munition girls are housed at Coventry are a scandal and a disgrace. The grossest forms of overcrowding and profiteering prevail and I am not disposed to remain indifferent to such a situation."[2]

The investigation carried out at the Minister's request, followed up by a visit from the Central Billeting Board on 31 October, showed the existence of much discomfort and overcrowding, rather perhaps than actual lack of accommodation.[3] Lodging conditions in Coventry were specially difficult, for here the natural desire of the munition worker to be within easy distance of his work was frustrated to a great extent by the plan of the town (as mentioned above) and the position of the larger works on its outskirts. The number of convenient lodgings was limited, resulting in congestion and profiteering in the favoured districts. An instance was given where one room was occupied by four girls each of whom paid 6s. a week. In another case a clerk paid 35s. a week for a bed and sitting-room.[4]

Those employees who lived in outlying towns had to walk a considerable distance from the station to their work, which, apart from the general discomfort to the worker, resulted in bad time-keeping. The Coventry Ordnance Works averaged the loss of time for employees coming from Nuneaton at 2·45 hours per girl per week. In this case the girls had to walk a distance of two miles from Foleshill station to the works, and the company had hitherto objected to the use of the Coventry " avoiding line " for their employees as likely to upset their munitions traffic.[5] A very general opinion was expressed at this time that yet more hostels were needed for the imported women, who already numbered 20,000 and who were continuing to pour into the town.[6] It is true that, owing to the non-establishment of a night shift,

---

[1] The Daimler Company had 1,200–1,300 employees coming daily from Nuneaton, Leamington and Warwick; workers also came from Rugby and Atherstone.

[2] L.R. 11636/6. The Office of Works had also called attention to the need or houses at Coventry at this date.

[3] The Central Billeting Board considered that the conditions of overcrowding were not as serious or as numerous as might have been supposed.

[4] HIST. REC./R/366. 2/32. A report, which was not substantiated, was made by Siddeley Deasy that girls of a superior class complained that their beds were let in the daytime to men.

[5] (Printed) Weekly Report, No. 95, XV (9 June, 1917).

[6] In October, 1917, White & Poppé had a weekly order at the Labour Exchange for 100 women, the Coventry Ordnance Works wanted 300 women at once and Daimler 200 at Christmas. (HIST. REC./R/346. 2/32.)

the hostels built for White & Poppé had never been more than half full, but the isolated position of the firm rendered this accommodation practically useless for workers in other factories.

The greatest need of all was for married quarters : there were 2,000 war munition volunteers in the town, of whom about 1,500 were married men who could not bring their families to Coventry (and thus incidentally save the Government allowance) because of the impossibility of getting houses. Married men would not come to Coventry, and since the removal of the leaving certificate restrictions the migration had been serious ; the Coventry Ordnance Works, for instance, had lost 320 men out of a total of 9,946 employed.[1]

These uncomfortable conditions, sufficient in themselves to arouse unrest, were undoubtedly accentuated by the general dreariness of the munition workers' life at Coventry. Thus until July, 1917, the only recreation open to the 8,000 workers at White & Poppé was a picture palace one mile away. At that date a welfare association was formed which organised a horticultural society, a philharmonic society, cricket, tennis, swimming and billiard clubs, and established a cinema theatre. Other firms recognised the need for rational amusement and the autumn of 1917 saw a rapid development of recreation schemes.[2]

The Central Billeting Board advised as a result of their investigations that a housing scheme for 1,500 houses should be begun forthwith, and also that immediate steps should be taken to provide further hostel accommodation for the Coventry Ordnance Works. In view, however, of the fact that some 1,200 houses had already been built in Coventry with Ministry aid it was felt that any allotment on such a scale, even if possible, would be unfair to other congested munition districts, and it was decided to initiate a preliminary scheme for 250 houses.[3] The provision of further hostel accommodation for 500 women, which the Coventry Ordnance Works had been urgently demanding since the beginning of the year, was also decided upon and Treasury sanction obtained in November, 1917. This latter scheme was suspended, however, in May, 1918, in view of changes in the labour position.[4]

A serious grievance had been the eviction of munition workers, and this was now abolished by the constitution of Coventry, Foleshill and Stoke as special areas on 3 December, 1917.[5]

---

[1] Hist. Rec./R/346. 2/32. The case was cited of 35 skilled men brought from Oldham, 33 of whom returned home at once owing to the housing conditions.

[2] (Printed) *Weekly Report*, No. 100, XVI. (14 July/17) ; 112, XVI. ,6 October/ 17) ; 124, X. (5 January/18).

[3] (Printed) *Weekly Report*, No. 123, X. (29/12/17).

[4] Report, May, 1918, to Mr. Churchill (L.R. 11636/11).

[5] See above, p. 29. Thirteen cases of eviction were pending at the time of the Central Billeting Board's visit. One firm (White & Poppé) were said to have been prominent in the matter of evictions : they pointed out that their houses had been erected for their own employees and if evictions were stopped all their Foleshill tenants might leave to go to other firms while retaining their houses.

The application of the Billeting Act to Coventry also served to simplify the lodgings problem. An exhaustive canvass of the town was made under the auspices of the Central Billeting Board, and during 1918 billets were found for 2,534 workers of whom 1,620 were women ; all these billets were offered voluntarily, and no necessity arose to apply to those houses where accommodation to the extent of between 4,000 and 5,000 billets was known to be available, but was not offered.[1]

Of the 250 permanent houses which were decided on as a result of the Central Billeting Board's recommendations, 226 were at Radford Road and 24 at Gorton Road. At the time of the Armistice, about 15 per cent. of the work was completed. All the houses at Gorton Road were finished by 1 April, 1919, but a year later only 104 of those at Radford Road were ready for occupation. These houses, like those at Barrow, were owned by the Ministry.

Coventry housing schemes were brought into prominence in 1919 by the rent strike in the semi-permanent houses at Holbrook Lane, which lasted for several months. By the advice of the Treasury, 30 typical cases were selected for prosecution, and after protracted legal delays the matter came before the High Court in March, 1920, judgment being given for the Ministry.

III.　Scottish Housing Schemes undertaken by the Ministry.[2]

Housing conditions had been for many years so grave a social evil in Scotland that any action taken by the Ministry to relieve congestion in those districts which became munition centres could only touch the fringe of the main problem.[3]　The area principally involved was the Clyde district, including Glasgow and other adjacent towns —where there was a tremendous influx of workers both for the Admiralty and the Ministry—and Mid-Lanarkshire, the centre of a most important munitions district including Messrs. Colville's Steel Works at Motherwell, Beardmore's at Mossend, Stewart & Lloyd's at Coatbridge and Airdrie. Some idea of the housing situation in this area as aggravated by the war may be gained from figures showing the increase in the number of workers employed by various firms between August, 1914, and the close of 1917. Thus at Beardmore's Dalmuir works numbers had risen from 5,874 to 10,885 (men and women inclusive) ; at their Parkhead Works from 8,000 to 27,000 ; Barclay, Curle & Company's numbers had risen from 4,000 to 7,000 ; the Fairfield Shipbuilding Company fluctuated between 7,500 and 13,500 ; Weir & Company's numbers had increased from 2,500 to 5,000, while the establishment of a National Projectile Factory at Babcock & Wilcox had brought an influx of from 7,000 to 8,000 workers. These figures are by no means exhaustive.

---

[1] HIST. REC./H/346.2/2. This number of billets does not include changes of billets.

[2] Based on L.R. 2710/2 ; L.R. 105/2 ; HIST. REC./R/346. 2/32 ; and Weekly Report of the Housing Section.

[3] See Vol. IV., Part II., pp. 43, 44.

A neighbourhood already under-housed was not able to supply the needs of this emergency population, and the want of housing accommodation during the war was undoubtedly a serious cause of unrest as well as a danger to public health. The prevailing type of industrial dwelling was the tenement containing either one apartment or two apartment houses. Two-thirds of the population of Glasgow were stated to live in one-room apartment houses in 1917 ; many of these single rooms were occupied by two families, and cases even occurred where each family took in lodgers, resulting in conditions better imagined than described.

The erection of hostels offered a solution where rapid temporary accommodation was needed. In Scotland hostels were only run as private concerns, conducted generally by such religious and philanthropic bodies as the Young Men's Christian Association, the Young Women's Christian Association, the Roman Catholics, the Girls' Friendly Society, and the Church of Scotland. A small grant was occasionally made in special cases such as the Belmont Hostel, Kirkcudbright, run by the Young Women's Christian Association for educated women, or the hostel for boys at Glasgow.[1] A few firms also received Government assistance to put up hostels for their employees, though not on a very large scale.[2] No hostel scheme, indeed, approaching in magnitude the English schemes was inaugurated ; the largest scheme for women, the group of hostels attached to the Georgetown Filling Factory, offered accommodation for 361, while no hostel for men held over 300.[3] The Benbow Hostel, erected by Beardmore's for their male imported workers, had 386 beds which were generally in use, though the restaurant, where the food was both good and cheap, was not popular, as the men thought it savoured of a model lodging house. This objection to the idea of an institution was common to both men and women, and here, as in England, they would often prefer the discomfort of crowded lodgings to the hostels. During the war accommodation was provided in women's hostels for 916 workers ; in September, 1918, 793 women were in residence, of whom 58·4 per cent. were munition workers. About the same date the number of beds provided for men, excluding Admiralty hostels, was 1,172, and the number occupied was 898.

Besides hostels a certain amount of independent building was accomplished by the firms, although after the beginning of 1917 the difficult conditions of the building trade both as regarded labour and materials made it impossible for firms to initiate schemes themselves. Messrs. Beardmore in particular built, during the war, tenement housing accommodation for 937 workers at Dalmuir and also 60 houses in the English cottage style with good gardens for their aviation workers

---

[1] L.R. 2710/2.

[2] Accommodation was put up by Napier & Miller, Admiralty Contractors, Old Kilpatrick, for 108 persons and by the British Aluminium Co., Kinlochleven, for 150, on assisted terms.

[3] HIST. REC./R/346/40.

at Inchinnan.[1]   The Glasgow Corporation also received a building licence in December, 1917, to erect at their own expense seven blocks of workmen's dwellings in the borough.

Finally, the Ministry itself undertook financial responsibility in connection with five housing schemes, making a total of 1,060 permanent houses representing in every case the immediate needs of the munition workers.   These schemes may be summarised as follows.

(1) In the autumn of 1915 the District Committee of Lanarkshire agreed to build 200 permanent houses at Mossend, with the assistance of a grant from the Ministry of 13·5 per cent. of the total cost.   This arrangement was modified later, the Ministry taking over the houses and defraying the net cost while the local authority agreed to purchase at market value one year after the war.[2]   These houses were primarily intended for the workers at Messrs. Beardmore's National Projectile Factory, and also were open later to workers at the steel works extensions.   The progress of this scheme, which was supervised by the Scottish Local Government Board, was greatly delayed.   Three sites had been chosen, but unfortunately in the spring of 1916, after work was well begun, it was found that in one case the steel works extension had encroached and an alternative site had to be found.   The chief cause of delay, however, the difficulty experienced in obtaining labour and building materials, was so serious that in December, 1917, there still remained 32 houses uncompleted.   In spite of some preliminary dissatisfaction at the rents asked these houses let immediately they were ready.

(2) The largest scheme undertaken by the Ministry was one for 350 houses to supply the needs of three firms, Messrs. Beardmore, Colville and Stewart & Lloyd, all engaged in important extensions in connection with the increased output of steel, and likely to require additional housing by the end of 1916 or the beginning of 1917.   These houses were distributed over three different sites, Mossend, Cambuslang and Carmyle.   The scheme was first propounded in May, 1916, but it did not take definite form till the autumn.   This was partly owing to prolonged discussion with the local authority as to the assistance which should be given by the Ministry, the matter being finally settled on a post-war ownership basis.   The firms agreed to make a contribution per house for the right of tenancy.   The houses consisted of 120 timber-framed houses, 50 one-storey brick, 88 two-storey flats, and 92 two-storey brick houses.   The Scottish Local Government Board was authorised to place contracts in December, 1916, but delays occurred common to all housing schemes, including an acute shortage of timber, and at the Armistice 10 per cent. of the scheme still remained to be completed.   The houses were all ready for occupation by the summer of 1919.

(3) Towards the close of November, 1916 it became evident that the extension to Colville's Steel Works at Glengarnock would also

---

[1] Messrs. Beardmore received a War Office loan of £15,000 for housing purposes in 1915.

[2] (Printed) *Weekly Report*, No. 140, IX. (4 May, 1918).

necessitate additional housing, as the type of workmen expected would not stop unless decent accommodation was available. Accordingly preliminary arrangements as to site, plans and post-war ownership of 250 houses were begun by the Scottish Local Government Board in January, 1917. Negotiations were prolonged, partly because the local authority refused to accept post-war responsibility, which was finally assumed by the firm. Treasury sanction was not received until 7 July, 1917, and contracts for the work signed about two months later. Want of labour and material combined with bad weather unduly delayed this scheme ; 50 per cent. still lacked completion at the time of the Armistice and the scheme was not finished until the beginning of 1920. The factorage of these houses as they became ready for occupation was undertaken by the firm, who received 7s. 6d. for each house per annum from the Ministry, which retained certain supervisory powers.

(4) In 1916-17 the Ministry assented to the firm of John Brown, Clydebank, writing off $12\frac{3}{4}$ per cent. of the cost of a scheme for 160 houses. This firm had always paid great attention to the housing of their workers, and these houses, though built in the prevalent tenement type of one or two rooms and a kitchen, were in a good open situation near the works, well built and arranged.

(5) In March, 1917, the question arose of additional houses required by Messrs. Singer in connection with their Combles Fuse Factory, which would be in working order in three months, with a consequent influx of 3,000 workers. The firm secured a suitable site of eight acres and submitted plans for 100 houses. Negotiations fell through in August owing to the Treasury demand for guarantees, which the firm refused to give, as the houses were required for a government factory from which the firm got no profit.[1] The matter was reopened in January, 1918, and a scheme once more submitted to the Treasury, this time with success. The firm now undertook to secure as far as possible tenants from their own staff prepared to accept forewomen from their workshops as lodgers. The local authority of the Burgh of Clydebank agreed to accept post-war ownership. At the Armistice 25 per cent. only of the scheme was completed, but all the houses were finished by the end of 1919.

---

[1] Reports, of Central Billeting Board, 12 November, 1917 (filed in HIST. REC./R/346. 2/32).

CHAPTER VII.

THE ELIZABETHVILLE COLONY, BIRTLEY.

I. The Foundation of the Colony.

The establishment of the colony of Elizabethville, Birtley, was part of a well-considered plan evolved by the Ministry of Munitions, acting in conjunction with the Belgian authorities, to organise Belgian labour in this country along the most productive and harmonious lines. By the summer of 1915 the use of Belgian labour for munition work had become an established policy. An agency had been specially commissioned, under the auspices of the Board of Trade, to recruit suitable Belgian labour in Belgium and Holland, and assistance in the work of recruiting was given by organised labour in Belgium itself. In this way between December, 1914, and the following March some 6,000 men and 9,500 women and children were brought over to England, in addition to the 100,000 refugees known to have reached England at the former date, and in addition also to considerable numbers recruited by private firms.[1]

The attitude of the British trade unions towards the Belgians was one of " assistance, goodwill and encouragement," but mutual dissatisfaction often arose owing largely to differences of race and language, culminating in a memorandum sent in July, 1915, by the Belgian Minister and Socialist leader, Monsieur Vandervelde, to the Minister of Munitions. In the course of this memorandum Monsieur Vandervelde suggested as a solution of this problem of mutual misunderstanding that Belgian munition workers should be placed as far as possible in separate factories, or at least in separate workrooms, under the direct orders of brigadiers and foremen of their own nationality.

> " Thus established in familiar surroundings," he wrote, " where they are accustomed to work energetically, encouraged moreover by wages much higher than they usually earn, our countrymen would work in conditions both material and moral which would enable them to exert all their capacity and all their good will."[2]

---

[1] HIST. REC./H/327 1. The industrial refugees in the first months of the war were chiefly of the poorest class from Antwerp and part of the province of Liège : the skilled workmen clung to their homes, supported by their savings and by unemployment grants from Belgian Workers' Federations. As these sources of supply became exhausted and the war prolonged itself, the heads of the Unions urged their members as a patriotic duty to go and work in English munition factories. Thus, little by little, the industrial regions of Liège, Antwerp and Charleroi were drained of their best workers.

[2] HIST. REC./H/327/1.

At this moment the question of manning a Ministry factory in process of erection at Birtley was very much to the fore, and the practical outcome of Monsieur Vandervelde's suggestion was the establishment of the Belgian Colony of Elizabethville at Birtley.

The early history of the colony is closely bound up with that of the factory, which must now be briefly traced. As a result of conferences carried on during the summer of 1915, Messrs. Armstrong, Whitworth & Company had agreed to erect and manage on behalf of the Ministry two factories for the manufacture of cartridge cases and of large shell respectively.[1] By the middle of July adjacent sites had been chosen near Birtley railway station, about six miles from the Elswick Works, and preparations were in full swing. It was at a meeting held at Armament Buildings on 31 August that the suggestion that Birtley factory should be worked by Belgians was adopted by the Ministry. Messrs. Armstrong, who had already successfully managed Belgians in one of their Elswick Works by grouping them, agreed to this course. The estimated requirements at this date were about 4,000, and the Ministry, through the War Office, got into touch with three Belgian engineers who undertook to find sufficient labour to staff Birtley. At the same time these Belgians submitted proposals to act as joint general managers of the technical department, responsible to Messrs. Armstrong, Whitworth & Company, who would continue to act as agents of the Ministry. An agreement on these lines was drawn up, but never came into effect, for the Belgian managers proved quite unable to deal with the labour problem and were superseded in January, 1916, after several months of mismanagement. The Belgian Government was now approached as to whether they would be willing to manage the factory, when it was completed, and provide the necessary labour, the British Government finding the working capital and the raw material. The Belgian Government agreed on condition that they should work in direct conjunction with the British Government, without the intervention of Armstrong, Whitworth & Company. It was eventually arranged that the firm should remain in a consultative capacity, and also that the cartridge case factory should be walled off and worked by British labour under the management of Armstrong, Whitworth & Company, while the shell factory was to be managed by the Belgian Government and manned entirely by Belgian labour provided by them. These negotiations were embodied in an agreement between the Belgian Government and the Ministry, dated 11 February, 1916, upon which the future relations of the Belgian colony both in factory and village were based.[2]

II. The Plan and Construction of Elizabethville.

It had been recognised from the first that neither the village of Birtley nor the town of Newcastle could furnish adequate accommodation for the Belgians, and during the lengthy negotiations above

---

[1] HIST. REC./H/1122. 4/3. A scheme for a machine tool factory suggested at the same time fell through.

[2] HIST. REC./H/1122. 4/3 ; HIST. REC./R/337/20.

indicated arrangements for a temporary model village had been proceeding. The Belgian directorate visited Birtley in September, and
proposed that a piece of waste land adjoining the factory should be
acquired and collapsible wooden huts at once erected as the nucleus
of a self-contained village, for the administration of which they would
be responsible. The village was to be built entirely by Belgian labour,
which would afterwards go into the factory. The Ministry accepted
the scheme and the Belgian managers got into touch with the Office
of Works. But here as elsewhere their methods produced little practical
results. Nothing had been done by the end of October, and this reacted
disastrously on the labour question. Building did not begin until
November, by which date recruits for the factory were beginning to
arrive, particularly from France and Holland, and, in many cases,
finding no accommodation available, they refused to fulfil their engagements and sought work elsewhere. Moreover, the idea of utilising
the labour recruited for the factory to build the village proved impracticable as the skilled workmen objected strongly to working outside
their trade. The Office of Works, which had been prepared, acting
in consultation with the Belgian directorate, to carry out the work
of construction themselves, withdrew about this date, and the work
was carried out by contract under the direct supervision of the Ministry.

The main lines of the original scheme for the model village as
prepared by the Office of Works were observed by the Ministry.[1] The
residential parts of the village consisted of married workers' cottages,
and of hutments and hostels for single men.

'The cottages, of which 325 were supplied with three bedrooms and
342 with two bedrooms, were all one-storey buildings. The larger type
were composed either of hollow brick, 2-inch breeze slabs, or wood ;
the smaller of wood, lath and plaster ; the roofing in both cases was
felt. Each cottage had a kitchen living-room, combined in the smaller
house with a scullery. The cottages were generally built in blocks of
six. A small garden in front and a yard at the back completed the plan,
which allowed an area of 500 feet and 490 feet to the two types of
cottages respectively.[2] In addition to these cottages there were
seventeen houses of a superior type, built of brick and cement,
and reminiscent in appearance of a Swiss chalet.

Twenty-two wooden hutments known as " barracks," divided up
into dormitories each taking three men, were provided for single workers.
Twenty-four hostels and six bungalows were also provided for the same
purpose, making accommodation in all for upwards of 1,600 workers.
The earlier of these hutments were built of wood and roofed with
cement, but the greater number were of 3-inch breeze slabs. Three

[1] In the original scheme accommodation was prepared for 6,000 workers,
a number never reached. In consequence the 522 two-bedroomed cottages were
reduced to 342 and hostels designed for 600 women were adapted for men.
(C.R. 2913 ; Hist. Rec./H/327/5.)

[2] Hist. Rec./H/327 5. The size of the living-rooms was in the first case
15 ft. by 10 ft. 6in. and a scullery 8 ft. by 6 ft., in the second 18 ft. by 10 ft. 6 in.
The measurements of bedrooms in the three-bedroomed cottages were 11 ft. 3 in.
by 8 ft. 10 in., 10 ft. by 7 ft. 6 in., 8 ft. by 7 ft. ; of the two-bedroomed cottages,
each 10 ft. 6 in. by 8 ft. 10 in.

large dining-halls, with central cooking arrangements, and constructed to seat some 2,500 men at a time, were also erected.

To this accommodation was added, as the communal life developed, the church of St. Michael, a simple structure of wood, cement and plaster; a school capable of holding 500 children ; a large hospital, with operating theatre and X-ray apparatus; a large covered market and public laundries and baths. A post office, attached to the British postal service but served by Belgian officials, a police station and a prison were also provided.

The village was erected on a slight slope on the left of the main road leading from Birtley to Low Fell. It was fenced round and had one entrance. The general effect of buildings such as have been described, all—with the exception of the bungalows—of one storey and all arranged with geometric precision, was one of monotony. Some relief, however, was afforded by the variety of the carefully tended front gardens. The three main roads, too, were broad and well metalled, with a carefully tended path on either side. The side streets were considerably narrower and at first (partly owing no doubt to the bad weather of 1916) retained a close affinity with the marsh from which they had been reclaimed. What was lacking in variety of scenery was supplied by picturesque nomenclature. We find among street-names *General Leman, Cardinal Mercier, Joffre, Haclen, Yser, Liège, Montenegro, Japan, Portugal*, a *Place George V*, a *Boulevard Queen Mary*, and a *Rue Lord Kitchener*. The name of Elizabethville given to the whole village was of course in honour of the Queen of the Belgians.[1]

The interior of the cottages doubtless showed more individuality than the exterior. In accordance with the agreement with the Belgian Minister, the Ministry had undertaken the furnishing both of cottages and hutments. The kitchens of the former were supplied with dressers and ranges, the bedrooms with hanging or corner cupboards. In addition, an adequate amount of simple furniture with bedding and crockery was supplied to each family. The Belgian housewives, as a class, proved themselves capable and thrifty, and with the simple means at their disposal, combined with the good wages earned by the men, made their homes both attractive and comfortable.[2]

The village was supplied throughout with electric lighting and water obtained from Newcastle. All the common buildings and the hutments were heated, but the heating of the cottages was supplied by the tenants. It had its own system of sewerage.

---

[1] Hist. Rec./R/327 30.

[2] The catalogue of sale of the household furnishings of the township in May, 1919, furnishes an interesting comment on the efficient manner in which the Ministry carried out this side of its bargain. The list includes such items as 2,500 chests of drawers of painted or stained wood, 2,500 toilet tables with mirrors, 1,000 upholstered chairs, 12,000 small chairs, 5,000 beds, 6,000 flock mattresses, 15,000 blankets, numerous bedside mats in attractive colourings, and a quantity of tea and dinner services with blue and gilt borders. The houses of the staff were furnished more ambitiously, as indicated by the enumeration in the catalogue of walnut and oak dining-room suites, white enamel or oak bedroom suites, chairs upholstered in leather, overmantels, etc. (Hist. Rec./R/ 327 11.:

The Ministry charged rent to the Belgians based upon the capital
outlay on the scheme.   In order to obtain a sound assessment they
called in the assistance of Mr. Barlow and Mr. Appleton, the Bournville housing experts, and it was agreed to fix the rents at 10s. per
week for the three-bedroomed cottage and 8s. for the two-roomed
cottages.   The charges in hutments and hostels was 6d. a night
It must be remembered that these rents included lighting, water,
furniture and the use of the village market, hospital and other common
buildings.[1]

III.   The Composition of the Colony.

The method ultimately employed of recruiting labour for Birtley
factory from the Belgian army was to have a marked effect on the
character of the village.   As stated above, the elaborate recruiting
arrangements made by the Belgian managers had broken down hope-
lessly by December, 1915.   An examination into the causes of their
failure was made by Mr. Spicer, appointed by the Ministry at this date
co-ordinating officer to represent them in all matters relating to labour
for the Birtley factory.   In the course of his inquiries it became evident
to him that the only remaining source of available skilled labour of the
type required was the Belgian army.   The Ministry therefore decided
to approach the Belgian authorities, and in the agreement which was
eventually made between the two Governments[2] the Belgians made a
specific promise to withdraw up to 1,000 highly skilled men from the
Belgian army.   In addition they instructed their military authorities
to place all Belgian soldiers recommended for discharge at the disposal of Birtley as they left hospitals in this country.[3]

Arrangements were made by which some 500 unskilled soldiers
were trained in lathe work at a munitions school at Loughborough
before going to Birtley.   The Belgian Government also set up a training
centre at Moisson, in France, where men withdrawn from the army
were tested and where wounded soldiers in France were trained for
work at Birtley.

Instructions were also given to the Belgian Employment Exchange
at Aldwych to put any available Belgian labour in touch with Birtley,
but the skilled men from the Front and the soldiers proposed for
discharge accounted for between 80 and 90 per cent. of the labour
employed at Birtley.

The highest number of workers employed in the factory
ranged between 3,500 to 3,700.   These workers were, with a few exceptions, men : owing to questions of discipline it was decided not to

---

[1] In their estimate the capital cost of the entire scheme, including land,
building, furnishing and general charges, was £272,115.   They reckoned that the
total annual charges, including repayment of interest on capital, repairs, water
rates, lighting, heating and management, would come to £33,987.   The total
rents fixed amounted to an annual income of £40,278, leaving a margin which
put the scheme on a sound financial basis.   (HIST. REC./H/327/5.)

[2] See above, p. 59.   [3] HIST. REC./R/327/20.

employ female labour in the factory.[1] Married men, who were in the minority, were joined by their wives and children and in this way the population of the village attained a total of 6,000.

Belgium has its own religious, political and racial dissensions, but one source of dissension was largely avoided by the fact that of those Belgians who came to Birtley, the Walloons were greatly outnumbered by the Flemings. The Walloons, who came from the most important engineering centres in Belgium, supplied the small percentage of skilled labour required, and the foremen, whose relations with the workers were by no means satisfactory at first, were drawn from their number.

IV. The General Administration.

In 1916, Elizabethville was administered by the Belgian Government on strictly military lines ; the workmen were treated as soldiers first and munition workers second. Under the agreement with the English Government it was arranged that a general manager should be appointed to control the factory and its workers and that a Belgian officer, assisted by a force of gendarmes, should be responsible for order in the village. This " chef du village " possessed the powers given him by Belgian military law in case of military offences, and in addition dealt with refusals to work in the factory, insolence to foremen, etc. Offences by Belgian civilians, who were, as above stated, a small minority, were dealt with by the English police and the ordinary tribunals.

Local government was carried out entirely by the Belgians ; the hospital was in charge of Belgian army doctors and orderlies, aided by Belgian nurses ; the church and cemetery were in charge of Belgian chaplains ; Belgian masters and mistresses were supplied to the school by the Belgian Government ; the post office, though attached to the British postal service, was served by Belgian officials ; the retail stores were financed by the Belgian Government and managed by the Belgians.[2]

A representative of the Ministry was in residence at Birtley from the first to act generally as liaison officer. He took full responsibility for all matters connected with the financial side of the factory, paid all wages, based strictly on local rates, and was responsible for providing raw materials and supplies of all kinds. He had an administrative staff of English clerks, interpreters, inspectors, etc., which already in 1916 numbered 500.

During 1916 there was an ever-increasing discontent among the Belgians against the military administration of the village, culminating in a serious riot in December. Their resentment was aggravated by the fact that many of the disabled soldiers had already been treated as civilians elsewhere, and all knew that English soldiers while working

---

[1] HIST. REC./R/327/29.   In April, 1917, out of a total of 3,708 workers, 36 only were women. (HIST. REC./H/1122. 4/37.)

[2] HIST. REC./R/327/4, 15, 20.

at munitions were not under military law. They also showed special distaste to government by gendarmes, whose tradition and views as to the maintenance of order are different from those of the English police, and who in their own country are accustomed to carry arms. Dissatisfaction centred especially around certain applications of military law, notably those relating to the compulsory wearing of military uniform outside the village and out of working hours, and the prohibition from entering English public-houses in the neighbourhood. Disproportionate punishment for minor offences was also complained of, imprisonment for several days being often inflicted for what we should term "misdemeanours." There is no doubt also that their sense of grievance was aggravated by the discomfort attendant on the first year of village life, and a general lack of opportunity for distraction and amusements.[1]

On the whole it was the infringement of personal liberty which was at the root of the discontent, and this did not affect the factory, where nothing stronger than minor complaints such as occur in all factories, or individual instances of jealousy between Fleming and Walloon, are shown to have existed.

The immediate cause of the riot was the imprisonment of a workman for wearing civilian clothes. On the evening of 21 December some 2,000 workmen assembled outside the Gendarmerie and attacked it with stones and bricks. A gendarme who was hit fired a revolver on the crowd, wounding a boy. The attitude of the rioters became very threatening, they attacked the house of the Chief Officer and, supplying themselves with rags soaked in oil, threatened to burn the colony. It was decided by the representatives of English authority to release the prisoner in order to satisfy the mob, and the rioters were thus persuaded to go quietly home. Meanwhile the Belgian manager of the factory had telegraphed to the Ministry, with the result that the Northern Command was instructed to hold itself in readiness to send soldiers to Birtley. Fortunately, intervention by the British military force, which would have rendered a continuation of the Belgian régime impossible, was avoided.[2]

The immediate result of the riot was the withdrawal of the Belgian gendarmes and the substitution of British police. A new "chef du village" was appointed and in various ways military discipline, while not superseded, was relaxed. The tendency was, as time went on, for the British representative to take over more and more administration.

A further consequence, which reacted favourably on the life of the village and considerably strengthened the position of the British authorities, was the establishment of the Birtley munitions tribunal. It was a real grievance that under the arbitrary military rule the Belgians had no court of appeal, and the Ministry felt that some judicial and impartial body was needed to investigate grievances and to deal with breaches of discipline. After considerable negotiations carried on throughout 1917, the Belgian Government finally agreed that a tribunal should be set up under the Munitions of War Act, 1915 to 1917, on

---

[1] See below, p. 65.   [2] Hist. Rec./R/327/10, 15.

precisely the same footing as other munitions tribunals throughout the country. This tribunal, which included three assessors from the staff and twenty-four assessors, both ·Fleming and Walloon, representing different grades and different shops, was also authorised by the Ministry to act as a Court of Conciliation. It held ten sittings up to October, 1918, ninety-four cases were dealt with and fines amounting to £140 were imposed.[1]

V. The Communal Life (1916–1918).

As has already been indicated, Elizabethville was, during the first year of its existence, hampered by various drawbacks. The first Belgians arrived at Birtley in October and November, 1915, to find no houses provided, and numbers were reduced to sleeping on straw in a shed. A disused cinema was hastily fitted up for temporary lodgings and the construction of the village, particularly the hutments, was accelerated. In the spring of 1916 Belgians began to pour in, to find that accommodation for them was by no means ready. The weather added to the general discomfort, the rain was incessant ; there were no roads, no pathways ; pedestrians floundered up to the knees in mud ; a persistent moisture pervaded everything.

By June, 1916, there were approximately 1,000 Belgians, living chiefly in hutments. Life in the village at this time was monotonous. The only place to sit in the evening was the dining-hall ; there was nowhere to write letters, no games or facilities for amusement. Working hours were over by 6.30 and there was no Sunday work, so that long hours of idleness lay heavy on their hands. The men earned good wages and the possession of means for procuring amusement aggravated the enforced dullness of their lives. The language difficulty would have prevented them mixing freely with the English population even had not the military régime placed impediments in the way, in particular the prohibition to enter licensed houses in the district. The neighbourhood, too, was inclined to adopt an attitude, traditionally British, of criticism towards the alien, while the fact that many of the Belgians were obviously of military age was at first misconstrued.

It is little wonder that the general discontent found expression in the riot of December, 1916, though at that date many of the factors which were to make for later harmony were already at work, houses were beginning to be habitable, arrangements were being made to open some licensed cafés, and men were beginning to settle down with their wives and families. The commissariat of the village was also organised in 1916 on semi-co-operative lines ; the wholesale purchase of all food was undertaken by an administrative body known as the Service Économique, financed by the Belgian Government. A central covered market was erected and here all provisions could be bought retail by the villagers. When towards the close of 1917 the food shortage became serious, a Food Control Committee was set up and followed

---

[1] Hist. Rec./H/327/2.   In accordance with the Munitions of War Acts these fines were paid to the Ministry of Munitions and by them to the Treasury.

as closely as possible the English scheme, and all rationed food was obtained through the Service Économique. Shortage of food occurred here as elsewhere early in 1918, but owing to the clear-cut position of the colony and to the excellent work being done at the factory, the Belgians obtained from first to last a generous share of everything.[1]

Commodities other than food were sold by individuals and the village had its street of flourishing shops, which included tailors, boot-makers, drapers and barbers.

Among the most characteristic features of life at Elizabethville were the communal meals, provided primarily for those dwelling in barracks and hostels, but also shared by a large number of other inhabitants. The food was excellent and the charges low.[2] There were at first two large dining-halls grouped round a central kitchen. A third, the Cheval Blanc, was opened about October, 1917, and repro-duced as far as possible the features of a Belgian café-restaurant ; it seated from 600 to 700 workers ; a band played every evening ; and it was licensed for the sale of beer but not of spirits. Under the same roof was the Birtley Recreation Hall.

By degrees the public services became organised. An early com-plaint as to lack of medical treatment was remedied by the erection of a hospital for 100 beds, fitted with X-rays and other modern appliances. A dispensary attached to the factory was also opened in 1916. The general health of the colony throughout was good, the death-rate averaging about 8·54 per thousand. At first funerals took place at Chester le Street, but towards the close of 1916 a field near the village was set apart as a cemetery for the colony.

The schools were originally built to hold 600 children but had later to be enlarged. The girls and infants were taught by Belgian refugee nuns and the boys by army schoolmasters or disabled soldiers who had formerly been schoolmasters. The children were all taught English in addition to French and Flemish.

The Belgian is essentially a creator of " Societies," and, though they were not officially encouraged, many sprang into existence at Elizabethville between 1916 and 1918. These societies were very diverse in character, and all, whether industrial, philanthropic or purely for amusement, had in common a development of the social side by means of concerts, dramatic performances or fêtes, generally organised for the benefit of some war charity. This applies even to the important branch of the Federation of Belgian Metal Workers, which was established in Elizabethville in 1916 and numbered upwards of 3,000 members.

---

[1] Hist. Rec./H/327/4 and 6.   The Belgian's weekly income at this time averaged £5 10s., and compared very favourably with that of miners in the district who were working on short time. At the beginning of the food shortage the colony stores found considerable difficulty in getting supplies, and the industrious Belgian, basket on arm, was soon found ranging the country-side in quest of provisions, a proceeding naturally regarded with jealousy by the miners.

[2] Hist. Rec./H/327/5. The charges were 4d. for a breakfast of coffee with milk and sugar, bread and butter, 10d. for a dinner of soup, meat, potatoes, cabbage and a slice of bread, and 5d. for a supper of soup, potatoes, bread and cheese.

The Vlaamsch Verbond, the Cercle Wallon, and Les Amis de Luxembourg were social clubs. The artistic side was represented by a band, supplied with instruments by the Belgian Government at the close of 1916. This band organised Saturday evening concerts at Birtley Hall and on several occasions gave performances outside the village. An orchestra formed about the same time took part in the concerts organised at frequent intervals for charity. Dramatic societies—the Comoedia, le Cercle Drolatique, l'Union Artistique—flourished. The Union Sportive provided its members with boxing, fencing, and gymnastics, and there were also swimming clubs, football clubs and a very popular troop of Boy Scouts.[1]

To sum up, during the last two years of its existence Elizabethville was sufficiently provided with the amenities of life, the men were well paid, their physical wants were adequately supplied and everything possible had been done to relieve the monotony of exile.

VI. Demobilisation.

The convention of 11 February, 1916, had provided that as soon as possible after the cessation of hostilities, the Belgian workers at Birtley National Projectile Factory, together with their families, should be sent back to Belgium at the expense of the English Government. Methods of repatriation were under consideration of the Committee on Demobilisation and Reconstruction in the summer of 1918, but it was agreed that details must depend upon the prevailing conditions in Belgium at the close of the war.[2]

Immediately after the signing of the Armistice arrangements were started for repatriation. The more outstanding difficulties may be briefly enumerated. A port of embarkation had to be fixed, ships obtained, a service of special trains authorised, the requirements of alien authorities had to be ascertained and met, household inventories had to be checked in the village, transport of luggage—including special licenses for such articles as church furniture and motor-cars—arranged for, and suitable rations provided owing to the precarious conditions prevailing in Belgium.

In spite of what seemed almost insuperable difficulties, the first party, numbering about 1,425, started on 7 December from Hull, and by 20 January, 1919, the village was deserted save for the administrative staffs and a few stragglers detained on medical grounds. With the departure on 5 February of the Belgian administrative staff, this exotic colony, which for nearly three years had flourished in spite of the somewhat bleak and uncongenial conditions prevailing in the North of England, was finally dispersed.[3] Birtley National Projectile Factory was sold towards the end of 1919 to Messrs. Sir William Angus Sanderson, who also rented a portion of the village to house their workpeople. Four hundred houses were transferred to the Ministry of Labour in connection with their industrial training schemes, while the hospital with its equipment was taken over by the Ministry of Pensions.

---

[1] Hist. Rec./R/327/30.   [3] Hist. Rec./R/327/3.
[2] Hist. Rec./R/327/4 and 5.

CHAPTER VIII.

THE GRETNA TOWNSHIPS.[1]

I. Introductory.

In June, 1915, it was decided to erect at Gretna a large cordite factory likely to employ between 10,000 and 15,000 workers. The introduction of such numbers into a rural area, whose population hitherto had amounted to some hundreds only, was bound to raise the question of housing in an acute form. The railway companies were immediately asked to report on the housing in the neighbourhood within a 25 mile radius. Meanwhile the Explosives Department consulted the Local Government Board, whose chief town-planning expert, Mr. Raymond Unwin, in July took in hand the preparation of a scheme, for temporary huts in the first instance, but later extended to include permanent houses, shops, cinemas and other buildings forming the equipment of a modern town.[2]

The adequacy of the neighbouring towns and hamlets to supply sufficient accommodation was immediately tested. With the cutting of the first sod on the site in August, 1915, thousands of navvies and other labourers invaded the district to make roads and railways, construct drains, lay cables for light and power, erect workshops, hutments, messrooms and streets. In October, 1915, there were 5,000 constructional workers on the site, at the beginning of 1916 there were between 8,000 and 9,000, and it was not until late in 1917 that the work of construction was completed.

Indeed, the main housing concern at Gretna up to the middle of 1916 was the accommodation of these workers. Investigation proved that the limit of accommodation within a radius of between three and twenty-five miles of the site was about 4,500 persons. Temporary expedients, not always ideal in character but calculated to obtain the maximum of accommodation in the minimum of time, were employed to provide further housing. Old farm buildings, warehouses, and a distillery were converted into temporary dormitories and kitchens, and a number of wooden hutments erected. Towards the close of 1915 temporary buildings of the new town began to be available, but as they were not required for operatives a certain number of bungalows and hostels were taken over between December, 1915, and June, 1916, and used for construction workers.

---

[1] Except where otherwise stated this account has been compiled from matter filed in Hist. Rec./H/1122. 7/19.

[2] 74/U/42: unregistered papers of Sir H. Llewellyn Smith and Major Corbett.

Operations began at the factory at the latter date and from thenceforward there was a steady flow of workers into Gretna. Operation and construction proceeded side by side for some time,[1] but there was an appreciably growing diminution in the number of construction workers. In many cases, resident construction workers were transferred to the factory as operatives, and were not disturbed in their tenancy, and by August, 1917, the townships, by this time in good working order, were in the full possession of the staff and operatives of the factory.

II. The Plan and Construction of the Townships.

Careful computation, which took into due account the accommodation available in surrounding towns and villages, had shown that, when the work of the factory was in full swing, housing must be provided for about 13,500 persons, of whom 7,500 would be single persons while the remainder would be married employees of the factory and their families. The fact that so large a number of the workers were either unmarried or at any rate living away from home had an important bearing upon the character and class of accommodation, the hostel type predominating.

The first buildings put up in 1916 were looked on as temporary and were built of timber, which then offered the most speedy and economical means of construction. They consisted of four-roomed cottages for married men, bungalows accommodating 9 workers and a housekeeper, and hostels each accommodating from 70 to 100 single workers. As the work proceeded the erection of temporary quarters gave way, owing to the scarcity of timber, to permanent brick buildings. Hostels built at this late date held anything from 100 to 150 workers and were in reality blocks of cottage shells with the internal fittings and partitions left out, and capable of conversion into workmen's dwellings. The brick cottages varied between the " parlour " type with living-room and three bedrooms, and the " living-room " type with three bedrooms. In addition a few houses of a more imposing character were erected for the senior staff.

The wooden buildings were all one-storey, with a resulting effect of monotony. The permanent cottages and hostels had a ground floor and upper storey. The designs differed considerably, while arrangements in pairs or small groups and the alternation of brick and rough cast served to secure some variety. Each house had a garden divided from its neighbours by hedges of privet, thorn, beech or mirabel plums ; their cultivation was left to the taste of the individual tenant, which was stimulated by the institution of a Horticultural Association in the autumn of 1917.

The total number of dwellings erected was 670 timber huts,[2] 54 timber hostels, 310 brick or stone houses and 134 brick hostels,

---

[1] The maximum number of 24,000 workers was attained in January, 1917.

[2] Of these 139 were of the bungalow type, affording double the accommodation of the other cottages and in some cases were run by married workers as small boarding houses.

representing accommodation for 13,485 persons. The dwellings were mainly concentrated in two townships, Gretna and Eastriggs, corresponding to the grouping of the factory's work under two roofs. At Gartleburn, a settlement of temporary wooden huts and hostels was constructed for the factory police and for chemists and workers in the cordite and magazine areas. A few houses were scattered at other points. The following table shows the disposition of the buildings :—

Locality.	Wooden.		Brick or Stone.	
	Cottages.	Hostels.	Houses.	Hostels.
Gretna Township ..	427	47	127	12
Eastriggs	165	16	160	17
Gartleburn ..	32	5	1	—
Other points ..	46	3	22	1

Gretna, the principal township, with an area of 431 acres, was situated in the central part of the factory area on land sloping immediately south to the old village of Gretna Green. The lay-out was divided into two, the older quarter where the temporary wooden houses and hostels were grouped and the newer quarter where the permanent houses and public buildings were established. Three main thoroughfares and numerous subsidiary roads were constructed to link up the township in addition to the existing main road from Carlisle to Dumfries which traversed the site. The Central Avenue running from north to south was the main thoroughfare, and here were to be found the dozen or so buildings, with shops on the street level and flats on the upper floor, which constituted the shopping centre of the township. Here also were the Post Office, the Border Hall, the cinema and other of the principal public buildings. In the south-west the township compound included the stores, the steam laundry, the central kitchens and the bakery which served both Gretna and Eastriggs. The works hospital, beautifully situated on rising ground, stood on the main Dumfries road.

Eastriggs township, with an area of 173 acres, lay at the western extremity of the factory area, and was chiefly inhabited by those workers engaged on the Dornock section. It occupied the site of an old farm, and a fine avenue of old trees formerly leading from the public road to the farm was preserved to form the main thoroughfare. On the east of this thoroughfare were the temporary wooden buildings, and on the west the permanent brick houses. The shops and public buildings were arranged around an open space in a new road leading directly to the factory.

Electric light was laid on in all the houses and public buildings and was used for lighting the streets. It was supplied from the power house at a sub-station in each township.

At both Gretna and Eastriggs the Ministry undertook the provision of permanent churches. These buildings were all interesting and added character to the townships. At Gretna there was a Scottish Episcopal church built on Gothic lines, a Presbyterian church in the Italian style with rough cast walls and red tiled roof, and a Roman Catholic church in the Italian Renaissance style. At Eastriggs the

Scottish Episcopal church was of local red sandstone roofed with north country green slates, and the Roman Catholic church was Italian Renaissance.

Recreation grounds, laid out for football, hockey and cricket, were immediately adjacent to the townships.

Surplus land in each township was cultivated with oats, potatoes, garden produce and hay or grazings. Operations began on 73 acres in the autumn of 1916 and eventually included 2,025 acres. In the season of 1917-18, the food catering department received an average weekly supply of 12 tons of potatoes, 810 cabbages, 7 dozen cauliflowers and periodic supplies of onions, beets, carrots, etc., while surplus supplies were sent as far afield as Glasgow.

The sewerage system installed in such a scattered area was necessarily one consisting of many independent units. The water carriage system was in operation throughout, and the sewerage of both Gretna and Eastriggs was discharged into the tidal waters of the Solway. The system of house drainage in the townships, by which two or more houses shared a common drain and disconnecting trap, has since been adopted by the Local Government Board for the new housing schemes being prepared throughout the country.

III. Organisation and Administration.

(a) GENERAL.

The general administration of the townships was vested in a town manager who controlled—more or less directly—the various services which Gretna, as a highly organised community, was to establish in process of time. An important part of his work was concerned with housing ; the allocation of houses to tenants, the collection of rents (reduced, however, to a very simple basis by a mandate signed by the tenant on entry into possession allowing the rents to be deducted from his salary), the maintenance of repairs and the upkeep of equipment[1] were all directly administered by him.

There were other administrative problems which must be regarded as incidental to the peculiar conditions under which the community sprang into existence and to its isolated position, notably that of the food supply. The town administration had to consider the needs not only of the 25,000 factory workers, who required mid-shift meals, and of the 7,000 residents in huts and hostels for whom they were responsible, but they had also to ensure that an adequate food supply should be available for the ordinary residents. This was secured by the institution of a catering department and a systematized centralisation of stores. Private traders were given facilities for setting up business

---

[1] The hostels and bungalows were furnished by the Ministry according to a carefully prepared schedule, standardized for each class of building. Provision had also to be made of simple furniture for a considerable number of the huts and houses as many of the married operatives and staff came from a distant part of the country. An increased rent was charged in the latter case.

in the town,[1] but in order to prevent a monopoly among them with a consequent exploitation of the consumer, the catering department opened a shop for meat and groceries, and by charging a certain percentage over cost to some extent fixed retail prices in the neighbourhood.

Certain essential supplies, however, remained so uncertain that special steps had to be taken. A large steam bakery was equipped to ensure an adequate supply of bread. A steam laundry, equipped with the most up-to-date plant, was opened in May, 1916, to deal with the enormous quantities of bedding and domestic washing in connection with the hostels, and also with articles of factory clothing such as overalls, dungarees, caps, etc. Three wash-houses were also constructed at points convenient to the groups of hostels where the girls were able to wash, dry and iron their clothes at a nominal charge of 2d. with soap and soda provided.[2]

The organisation of strong measures in case of fire at Gretna, where the handling of inflammable and explosive process materials in the factory area, together with the large number of wooden houses and hutments in the townships, made the fire risks very heavy, was a primary necessity.[3] A professional Fire Brigade was accordingly instituted under the supervision of a Fire Master who reported weekly to the town manager, and three fire stations were set up at Gretna, Blackbank and Eastriggs. As a preventive measure during the air raids a factory volunteer brigade was formed and on occasion rendered valuable service in the extinction of fire. Between 1916 and 1918 the Fire Brigade was called in for 207 actual fires of which ten were of a serious character.

The site of the factory was both in Cumberland and Dumfriesshire, and was in the first instance policed by both counties. When the factory started working, Gretna was formed into a special police area.[4]

(b) PUBLIC SERVICES.

The responsibility for public services (which in the ordinary course of events would have been undertaken by the central or local authority concerned) was to a great extent assumed by the Ministry, more particularly where the maintenance of public health and provision of educational facilities were concerned.

---

[1] More particularly an arrangement was entered into with the Scottish Wholesale Co-operative Society to open branch Stores in each of the townships in 1915. They sold goods at moderate prices sufficient to meet all expenses and leave a fair balance, which, after deducting a charge equivalent to 5 per cent. on the capital expenditure involved, was handed over to the Ministry as rent for the premises occupied. This arrangement lasted till April, 1917, when the Society took over the business on the usual co-operative basis.

[2] The wash-houses, which were a great success among the operatives, were reserved on certain days for the use of private householders, who did not avail themselves of the opportunity to any great extent, preferring to use the washing facilities with which every house was provided.

[3] Within the factory fences strong preventive measures against fire were also organised.

[4] HIST. REC./R/1122. 7/24.

The need of special medical arrangements became apparent while the factory was under construction, and in December, 1915, the Ministry arranged with the National Health Insurance Commission to be responsible for medical attendance required both by workers in the factory and by residents in the factory area.[1] The services of local doctors were secured, surgeries for first aid were established in the area, and arrangements made for infirmary treatment at Carlisle and Dumfries on terms similar to those charged for military patients.

These arrangements with the Commissioners, intended primarily for construction workers, continued, with certain modifications, after " construction " had merged into " operation." With the growth of the community it was found necessary to provide a special medical staff subject to and directly controlled by the Ministry. Gretna was served by one male and two female Medical Officers, Eastriggs by one male and one female, while in August, 1917, an administrative Medical Officer was appointed for the whole district. It was also found necessary to provide hospital accommodation on the spot, and in 1915 a works hospital, which with later extensions accommodated 84 patients, was erected.

The major infectious diseases were dealt with in the usual way by the local authorities, but the Ministry provided and equipped two wards in the Annan Infectious Diseases Hospital and also contributed a moiety of the construction cost and maintenance of a small infectious hospital opened at Longtown in October, 1917, and managed by the Rural District Council. Minor infectious diseases were treated in a temporary Isolation Hospital, replaced in May, 1918, by 05 West Hospital. In October, 1916, the attention of the Ministry was called to the ill-health of a large proportion of the workers caused by bad teeth, and as a result a dental surgery was built and equipped at the Department's expense which dealt with upwards of 1,300 patients.

The sanitary services, on which the general health of the community so greatly depended, were, by arrangement with the Dumfries County Council and the Longtown Rural District Council, undertaken by the Ministry. A staff of sanitary inspectors dealt with all matters relating to sanitary defects and other nuisances and overcrowding ; they took action in cases of infectious disease and maintained an inspection of food supplies.[2] They were assisted in their work by a very

---

[1] The Insurance Commissioners agreed to repay on a cash value basis in respect of insured workers.

[2] The extermination of rats was a matter of serious consideration. Mr. Duckworth, who visited the site in January, 1916, had foretold this nuisance, and had then recommended the appointment of a professional rat-catcher. (Hist. Rec./R/1122. 7/6.) Events justified his forecast : glycerine and other stores disappeared, potato dumps were riddled with holes, drawings in offices were destroyed ; it was estimated, indeed, that each rat caused a loss of one farthing per day by the destruction of food and material. Such damages, combined with the danger from the spread of diseases, led to the appointment of professional rat-catchers in January, 1918. The number of rats destroyed in one way and another was 12,646.

efficient system of scavenging, carried out in the townships under the direction of the town manager and in the factory areas by the factory managers.

As a result of these precautions, the health record of Gretna was, on the whole, satisfactory. The number of deaths was 145, of whom 30 were females. The 1917 epidemics of measles and German measles visited the townships, but not so severely as the influenza epidemics in the following year. The epidemic of June, 1918, attacked about 1,400 persons, but was much lighter in character than the second outbreak of October, when 35 deaths occurred and the schools had to be temporarily closed.

As stated above, the Ministry undertook the provision of educational facilities. Those already existing had been barely sufficient for the needs of the scattered rural district ; schools at Gretna and Dornock together could only take 130 pupils,[1] whereas it was considered that two schools each providing for 500 scholars would be necessary to meet the full requirements of the new community. The Ministry decided to erect these schools and, in order to maintain control over them, to administer them as voluntary grant-earning schools. Duplicate schools, planned on modern and well-considered lines, thoroughly well-lighted and ventilated and with bright, spacious and airy classrooms well supplied with all necessary teaching apparatus, were accordingly erected at Gretna and Eastriggs. The schools were controlled and administered by a local committee under the presidency of the town manager, and were inspected by the Scottish Education Committee. The maximum yearly attendance at Gretna was 396 and at Eastriggs 272, but the construction of both schools was undertaken in portions as the need for accommodation grew, and at the time of the Armistice neither building had been completed.

In conclusion, mention must be made of the means adopted to meet the abnormal increase in postal business, the existing rural sub-office at Gretna Green being of course entirely inadequate. Post offices were established at Gretna and at Eastriggs ; a branch office was opened at Gartleburn and pillar boxes were plentifully distributed over the site. Other offices in the neighbourhood helped to relieve the situation ; thus at Annan an adjoining building had to be borrowed for post office business on the factory pay-nights. Some idea of the vast amount of business transacted is gathered from the fact that during 1917 over two million letters were posted and about the same number delivered.

(c) Social and Recreation Schemes.

The organisation of a social and recreation department as carried out at Gretna was the result of abnormal circumstances and has no parallel elsewhere. In the early days of the factory, it was found that there was an increasing tendency for workers to remain at Gretna for

---

[1] The Scottish side of the Border only was concerned ; on the English side a small school of the Cumberland Education Committee at Blackbank had to be closed as coming within the factory area.

comparatively short periods. A special investigation was held, resulting in the conclusion that the leakage of labour was almost entirely due to the absence of any regular means of recreation for either men or women in their leisure hours. With the object of keeping workers within the factory area and away from undesirable temptations elsewhere, railway services to neighbouring towns had been purposely restricted ; for instance, there were no late evening trains between Gretna and Carlisle except on Saturday, when the latest train left Carlisle at 9.30 p.m. In order to ameliorate these conditions, the Ministry proceeded without delay to erect various places of entertainment and to establish a central and authoritative body known as " The Social and Athletic Association," to which certain clubs and societies were affiliated.

The Treasury, in giving approval to this Association, laid down the broad principle that every effort should be made to render it self-supporting, but at the same time guaranteed indemnification to the extent of £3,000 against a possible loss on the working of the scheme. All social policy was to be determined by the superintendent of the factory, but the general control of the Association was vested in a standing Recreation Committee, composed of the leading officials in the factory and townships.

It was at Gretna, which had developed more quickly than Eastriggs, that a concentrated effort was first made to cater for the amusements of the new community. The pioneer effort of the Ministry was the erection of the Border Hall, with its spacious stage, fine dancing floor, extensive electrical plant and seating accommodation for 1,100 persons. It was erected, equipped and opened in little more than six weeks, to be in time for the first Christmas festivities of 1916. It was, however, determined from the outset that the accommodation provided at Gretna should be duplicated as far as practicable at Eastriggs and this was eventually accomplished. Thus each township became possessed of an institute, a cinema, a spacious hall for meetings, concerts and dances, a Mission hall, smaller buildings for general purposes, and a recreation ground with pitches for cricket, football, hockey and other games. Tennis courts and bowling greens were also provided.

The various clubs and societies which affiliated themselves to the Association were so numerous that it is impossible to do more than enumerate the principal ones. Chief among them was the Choral and Co-operative Society, the majority of whose members consisted, it is true, of members of the staff, but which contributed largely to the general amusement both by the production of such popular pieces as " H.M.S. Pinafore," " The Gondoliers," and " Paul Jones " (each staged for an entire week) and by sacred concerts on Sundays. They were seconded in their work by an Orchestral Society and an excellent Factory Band. Dramatic, horticultural, scientific, temperance, literary and debating societies were all well supported.

The favourite amusement, especially among the girls, was undoubtedly dancing, and every society and club at one time and another organised dances of its own. For reasons of policy the Recreation

Committee encouraged this form of amusement by instituting weekly "Free Dances" and "Popular Shilling Dances" both at Gretna and Eastriggs.

On the athletic side, football constituted the principal attraction during the winter, and at one time sufficient football clubs were in active operation to provide separate Leagues for the two townships. There were also hockey clubs, for both men and girls, and bowling clubs. During the summer the tennis courts were in great demand, and inter-club matches between Gretna and Eastriggs were arranged. Cricket clubs existed but, as was to be expected in Scotland, the game was not very extensively played.

The social history of Gretna would be incomplete without some account of the action taken to control the liquor traffic. During the early constructional period of the factory, when thousands of navvies and other labourers invaded the district, there was an abnormal increase in drunkenness. In August, 1915, the Ministry exercised their rights under the Defence of the Realm Act and took over the public-houses adjacent to the factory. The Central Control Board assumed control in November, and at the beginning of 1916 decided to adopt the principle of State purchase, and before March, 1916, most of the public-houses had been acquired. The sale of spirits was continued in certain cases. Thirteen canteens, licensed for the sale of beer but not of spirits, were subsequently opened under the auspices of the Board. An experiment, tried in co-operation with the Recreation Committee, of using them as recreation rooms when not open for the sale of beer was abused and had to be abandoned.

In conclusion, the Social and Athletic Association carried out the Treasury exhortation to be self-supporting. Its income was obtained in the first instance from annual club subscriptions varying between one guinea for the bowling club and one shilling for societies such as the literary and debating. These were by no means sufficient to cover expenses and the surplus income was obtained from the cinemas. In spite of the fact that the Association paid a yearly rental of £780 to the Ministry for the buildings, the profit from cinema performances were so large that, instead of making any demand on the Treasury guarantee, the Association voluntarily relieved the Ministry of many expenses for which it became responsible under the Recreation Scheme.

IV. Arrangements for Women Workers.

The problem of female labour at Gretna was unique. There was no possibility of drawing the full number of women required from the locality and between 5,000 and 6,000 had to be brought from all parts of the country. The Ministry recognised that the responsibility of their care was incurred, not only during factory hours but in their home lives as well. Early in 1916 they appointed a Lady Welfare Superintendent with a welfare staff, consisting of factory and hostel supervisors, clerical assistants and matrons, numbering, as the factory developed, upwards of 200 persons.

Arrangements for women at Gretna were grouped naturally under three heads—the engagement of labour, the supervision of the worker in the factory, and the supervision of conditions in the hostel. In the first instance the Employment Exchanges were authorised to secure the workers, but their arrival, often at the rate of some 200 persons a day, was arranged for by the Welfare Superintendent, trains were met, travellers were given free meals, medical inspection and enrolment in the factory were arranged for, and finally the worker was personally installed in the hostel to which she had been assigned.

Factory supervision of 11,000 women was complicated by the scattered nature of the factory and the prevalence of the three-shift system. It was carried out by the chief assistant to the Welfare Superintendent with a staff of shift supervisors and matrons of compounds. Welfare work in the factory was most successful. An excellent understanding existed between the girls and those in charge of them. Shift dances, shift concerts and plays, and even shift football matches were arranged by committees composed of staff and operatives, and this co-operation of the girls themselves produced particularly happy results.

The control of women's housing, which included 70 large hostels and 40 to 50 smaller bungalows, was, however, the most important side of welfare work.[1] The women were recruited from many employments; domestic servants, factory hands, laundry workers, shop assistants, farm hands, dressmakers, school teachers and clerks found themselves working side by side. It was essential at the outset to create a homelike atmosphere, which had yet to be combined with strict discipline. With this aim in view, hostel rules were made as simple and as few as possible, matrons and housekeepers were very carefully chosen, and the Lady Welfare Superintendent and her assistants kept in constant touch with every hostel.

Each hostel took the morning, afternoon or evening shifts in rotation, so that all girls housed in any one building were working on the same shift, with a consequent economy of labour and increase of general comfort. The meals were arranged in accordance with the shift; for the afternoon and evening shifts certain meals being provided at the factory. Board and lodging charges, fixed at 12s. in 1916, but rising gradually to 17s. 6d. as wages were augmented to meet the rise in prices, were deducted from the wages of each girl housed in Ministry quarters. Detailed arrangements as to absence, sickness, leave, discharge, etc., were necessary when the girls' pay was so intricately bound up with their presence in or absence from the hostel. But this was only the framework of welfare. The real hostel life, the only one apparent to the girls, was that of a happy, comfortable home; good and plentiful food; clean, comfortable beds in prettily decorated cubicles; large fires in bright, gay mess and recreation rooms, combined with the kindly, sympathetic interest of the matron in charge. Abundant

---

[1] The Lady Welfare Superintendent also controlled welfare work in the Carlisle area, which included oversight not only of two large hostels holding 750 girls, but also a good deal of visiting of the Gretna girls in Carlisle lodgings.

sources of interest and enjoyment were provided for the leisure hours. In addition to the social amusements organised for and indulged in by the community at large, there were hostel picnics on the shores of the Solway in summer, classes in needlework, dressmaking, millinery, first aid, singing, gymnastics and country dancing, cookery, laundry and basket making.

Hostel parties, got up by the matron assisted by a committee of the girls, were very popular at holiday times ; men friends were invited and the programme generally consisted of a short concert followed by a dance. Sales of work were occasionally arranged for war charities. The Girl Guide movement was also introduced into Gretna, with an appreciable effect on discipline both in factory and townships. The Lady Welfare Superintendent acted as Division Commissioner and many of the staff were company officers.

The girls were encouraged to co-operate in the arrangements made for their comfort ; every hostel or bungalow had its spokeswomen, elected by their fellows, who as occasion required met and conferred with the Lady Superintendent.

In short, all care and consideration was lavished on the women workers, whose welfare was considered by the Ministry as second only to the production of cordite.

APPENDIX I.

(CHAPTER III.)

Housing Schemes undertaken for Munition Workers, 1915–1918.

(a) TEMPORARY COTTAGES AND HOSTELS ERECTED BY THE MINISTRY.

Place.	Capacity of Scheme.	Date of under- taking.	Firm or Factory concerned.
Birmingham, Lickey	Hostels for 450 workers	1917	Austin's.
Birmingham, Long-ridge.	Hostels for 780 workers	1917	Austin's.
Birtley	895 Cottages	1915	Belgian N.P.F.
	46 Hostels for 3,000 workers.		
Coventry	466 Cottages	1916	White and Poppé, N.F.F.
Coventry, Holbrook Lane.	32 Hostels for 3,000 workers.	1916	White and Poppé, N.F.F.
Coventry, Whitmore Park.	31 Hostels for 2,900 workers.	1916	White and Poppé, N.F.F.
Coventry, Barras Heath.	5 Hostels for 5,000 workers.	1916	Coventry Ordnance Works.
Dudley	345 Cottages	1916	Harper, Son and Bean, N.P.F.
	10 Hostels for 270 workers	1916	Harper, Son and Bean, N.P.F.
Erith, Slade's Green	3 Hostels for 140 workers	1915	The Thames Am-munition Works.
,, ,, ,,	1 Hostel for 400 workers	1918	Vickers.
Hereford	1 Hostel for 250 workers	1918	N.F.F.
King's Norton, Abbey Wood.	5 Hostels for 450 workers	1916	N.F.F.
King's Norton, Edgwood.	5 Hostels for 500 workers	1917	N.F.F.
Scotswood ..	411 Cottages	1916	Armstrong Whit-worth.
Sheffield	708 Cottages	1916	Firths, Hadfields.
	168 Hostels and Colonies for 2,061 workers.		
Woolwich ..	1,500 Married Quarters ..	1915	The Arsenal.
	16 Hostels for 1,600 workers.	1915	The Arsenal.

(b) PERMANENT HOUSES.

Place.	Number of Houses.	Date of undertaking.	Type of Agreement.	Firm or Factory concerned.
Avonmouth..	150	1917	Post-war Ownership	Spelter Works.
Barrow	253	1914–15	War Office Loan ..	Vickers.
,, ..	90	1916	Writing off from Excess Profits.	Vickers.
,, ..	500	} 1917	Post-war Agreement	General.
,, ..	202 semi-permanent			
Birmingham	251	1916	Ministry Loan ..	Austin's.
Coventry ..	600	1915	Grant to Local Authority.	Coventry Ordnance Works.
,, ..	210	1916	Post-war Agreement	Siddeley Deasy.
,, ..	250	1918	Ministry responsible	General.
Crayford ..	100	1915	War Office Loan ..	Vickers.
Dolgarrog ..	50	1917	Ministry Loan ..	The Aluminium Corporation.
Dudley ..	300	1915	Grant to Local Authority.	Harper, Son and Bean, N.P.F.
Erith ..	400	1915	War Office Loan ..	Vickers.
Farnborough	250	1917	War Office Property.	R.A.F.
Guildford ..	28	1914–15	Writing off from Excess Profits.	Dennis Bros.
Hendon ..	250	1917	Ministry Loan ..	Aircraft Mfg. Co.
,, ..	225	1917	Ministry Loan ..	Grahame-White Co.
Irlam ..	160	1917	Post-war Agreement	Partington Steel Co.
Lincoln ..	200	1917	Post-war Agreement	General.
Oldbury ..	70	1916–17	Writing off from Excess Profits.	Accles and Pollock.
Peterborough	48	1916	Writing off from Excess Profits.	Brotherhood.
Redcar ..	300	1917	Ministry Loan and Grant.	Dorman, Long.
Scunthorpe ..	36 semi-permanent.	1918	Post-war Agreement	John Brown & Co.
,, ..	15	1918	Ministry Grant ..	Appleby Iron Co.
Sheffield ..	261	1915	Grant to Local Authority.	Firths N.P.F.
Spondon ..	158	1918	Ministry Loan ..	British Cellulose Co.
Stocksbridge	319	1916–17	Writing off from Excess Profits.	Samuel Fox.
Weybridge ..	100	1916	Writing off from Excess Profits.	Vickers.
Woolwich ..	1,086 houses. 212 flats	1915	Royal Arsenal responsible.	Royal Arsenal.
Scotland :				
Clydebank ..	160	1916	Writing off from Excess Profits.	John Brown & Co.
,, ..	100	1918	Post-war Agreement	Singer's.
Dalmuir ..	530	1915	War Office Loan ...	Beardmore.
Glengarnock	250	1916	Post-war Agreement	Colville's.

(b) PERMANENT HOUSES—*contd.*

Place.	Number of Houses.	Date of under-taking.	Type of Agreement.	Firm or Factory concerned.
Scotland— contd.				
Gretna ..	941 cottages, 97 convertible hostels.	1915	Ministry responsible	Explosives Department.
Mid-Lanark	200	1915	Grant to Local Authority.	Beardmore.
,,	350	1917	Post-war Agreement	Colville, Beardmore, Stewart & Lloyd.
Port Glasgow	400	1917	Writing off from Excess Profits.	Russell & Co.
Queens Ferry	191 6 convertible hostels.	1915–16	Ministry responsible	Explosives Department.

(c) HOUSES ADAPTED FOR HOSTELS, PARTLY OR WHOLLY FINANCED BY THE MINISTRY.

Place.	Capacity.	Date of under-taking.	Firm or Factory concerned, etc.
Barrow	38	1918	Various Firms.
Birmingham	50	1917	For Roman Catholic girls.
Bristol	42	1918	Training Section.
Coventry (Foleshill Workhouse).	50	1917	Clearing Hostel.
Enfield	—	1917	Royal Small Arms Factory.
Farnborough.. ..	123 (3 hostels).	1916	R.A.F.
Gloucester	38	1916	Clearing Hostel.
Hayes	40	1917–18	Clearing Hostel, N.F.F.
Hereford	408 (7 hostels).	1917–18	Clearing Hostel and N.F.F.
Highgate	50	1918	Training Section.
Lancaster	50	1916	Clearing Hostel.
Loughborough ..	93 (3 hostels).	1918	Training Section.
Moss End	70	1916	N.P.F.
Newbury	86	1918	Inspection Bond.
Perivale (Workhouse)	—	1917	N.F.F.

V-5

APPENDIX II.

(CHAPTER III.)

Housing Schemes administered by the Ministry on 1 July, 1920.

(a) HOUSES AND BUNGALOWS.

i. Complete (Permanent Schemes) :—

Mid Lanark	250 houses	Shirehampton	..	..	150 houses	
Moss End ..	200 ,,	Coventry (Gordon Road)		24	,,	
Clydebank	100 ,,	Coventry (London Road)		214	,	
Glengarnock	250 ,,	Queen's Ferry	..	..	900	,,

ii. Complete (Temporary and Semi-permanent Schemes) :—

Sheffield ..	710 houses	Scotswood	..	..	410 houses	
Dudley ..	333 ,,					
Barrow-in-Furness.	202 ,,	Woolwich ..	..	..	2,654	,,
Coventry (Holbrook Lane).	465 ,,	Woolwich (Archery Rd.)[1]		41	.,	
		Birtles	..	..	900	,,

iii. Incomplete (Permanent Schemes) :—

	Sanctioned.	*Complete.*
Coventry (Radford Road)	226	104
Barrow	250	154
Lincoln (Wragby Road)	200	43
Irlam	160	12

iv. Schemes belonging to the Ministry, but not administered by the Housing Department.

Gretna
{ 601 wooden huts
55 wooden hostels
325 brick or stone houses
30 brick hostels[2] }

Langwith 41 houses
Pembrey 17 existing houses taken over from Messrs. Nobels

(b) HOSTELS.

Edgwood (Men's Hostels), Eltham (Women's Hostels) and Sheffield.[3]

---

[1] Converted Hostels.

[2] Capable of conversion into cottages.

[3] These were the only hostels occupied by tenants. There were also a large number of untenanted hostel buildings in various stages of disposal.

APPENDIX III.

(CHAPTER VI.)

Woolwich Housing Schemes.[1]

The housing problem in Woolwich and its immediate neighbourhood early assumed importance, owing to the influx of thousands of workers at the Royal Arsenal. On the outbreak of war, the numbers employed totalled 10,866 ; they had more than doubled themselves by January, 1915, while in May, 1917, they had reached 74,467. This rapid growth sufficiently indicates the urgency of the housing question, which was further complicated later by the introduction into the neighbourhood of many thousands of fresh workers for the Abbey Wood National Filling Factory and for the Thames Ammunition Company, the King's Norton Metal Co., and other firms.

The steps taken by the Government to meet the housing difficulty included the erection of both permanent and temporary accommodation. The former method was adopted by the War Office, from whom the Ministry took over a large scheme for permanent houses begun early in 1915. The Ministry of Munitions, mindful of the serious depression at Woolwich and Erith after the South African War which led to working-class houses remaining vacant, concentrated on the provision of temporary accommodation. Attempts were also made to improve existing transit facilities so as to import workers from a distance, and extensions were made both to omnibus and train services, while a new ferry greatly facilitated the employment of workers from the North of the Thames.[2]

(a) PERMANENT HOUSING SCHEME.

On 8 January, 1915, the Local Government Board, the Treasury, the War Office and the Office of Works, acting in conference, decided to embark on a building scheme for permanent houses at Woolwich. It was agreed that the work should be undertaken by the Office of Works, and the Department immediately proceeded to acquire the necessary land on the Well Hall Estate, near Woolwich. At the outset it was intended to erect 1,000 houses, but later, in order to cheapen the scheme, a certain number of flats were substituted, bringing the total number of dwellings to 1,298. The Local Government Board laid down that the scheme should be on the best town-planning lines, and twelve houses to the acre was adopted as a standard. The houses

---

[1] Bas d on M.W.39697, 39697/2, 3, 5 ; L.R.H/8/9, 10, 115 ; O.F./Buildings/23 ; Eastern/2/1605 ; M.F./Gen./1490 ; HIST. REC./R./346.2/1, 5, 11, 24 ; HIST. REC./ H/346/3 ; Report of Committee of Enquiry into Royal Ordnance Factories and of Minutes of Engineering Sub-Committee (HIST. REC./R/1122. 11/19) ; Minutes and Reports of Departmental Housing Committee, Jan., 1919–July, 1920 ; *Report from Committee of Public Accounts* (1917), Appendices 5, 12 ; (Printed) *Weekly Reports* No. 79, XII (10.2.17) ; No. 82, XII (3.3.17) ; No. 95, XI (9.6.17).

[2] See above, p. 43, for some account of transport facilities.

differed as to the amount of accommodation : 116 of the first-class
contained three bedrooms, a bathroom, living room, parlour, extra
room on the ground floor and a scullery; 357 of the second-class had the
same accommodation with the exception of the ground floor room,
while 613 third-class houses had three bedrooms, a living room and
scullery. The flats, of which there were 212, had each two bedrooms,
a living room and scullery. The weekly rents, which were fixed on
the recommendation of the valuer to the London County Council,
were 14s. 6d. to 16s. 6d., 12s. to 14s., 10s. to 11s. 6d. for the three
different classes of houses. The rent of the flats was from 7s. to 7s. 6d.
a week.

The governing consideration in the erection of these dwellings
was urgency. Work was actually begun on 1 February, 1915; by
September, 1915, about 1,000 were finished (of which the greater number
were occupied), and the beginning of December saw the completion
of the scheme. The maximum of speed was not attained without
correspondingly heavy expenditure, and the total estimated net cost
of the scheme was approximately £808,000, which worked out at the
high average cost of £622 per house or flat, including land, roads,
sewers and fences.

An arrangement was made with the Housing Department of the
London County Council and was in operation during 1917, by which
they managed the estate on the lines followed on their own estates in
return for a remuneration of 4½ per cent. on the gross rentals.

(b) TEMPORARY SCHEMES.

At the same time as the Well Hall Garden Suburb was started
the Government took steps to ensure the rapid erection of 3 temporary
hostels for boys and 50 huts, to serve as married quarters, at Plumstead.
The extension to the Arsenal shops in the summer of 1915 and the
proposed introduction of a large number of women workers compelled
the new Ministry almost immediately to face the necessity of providing
additional housing accommodation. In the first instance efforts were
made fully to exploit local resources. Enquiry made as to the accommodation available in the district under the control of the naval or
military authorities resulted in 70 married quarters being taken over
from the garrison. A site on which roads and sewers were already
constructed was obtained by the War Office from the London County
Council, who had abandoned a building scheme there on the outbreak
of war. On this site the Ministry proposed to erect 350 temporary
huts, but investigation showed the site to be low-lying and broken
by holes and ditches, which made any layout without previous filling
a matter of difficulty, and eventually only 125 huts were erected.
Married quarters were also erected on the Corbett Estate, Eltham,
and in October, 1915, Treasury sanction was sought for a further 1,500
huts and for several hostels. In December, expenditure up to £345,000
for huts and £41,275 for hostels was sanctioned, which provided for 1,500
huts at a cost of £230 each, 5 boys' hostels, 10 hostels for women,
each accommodating 100 workers, and an experimental hostel for men.

It was anticipated that the factories in course of construction and nearing completion at Woolwich at this date would employ an additional 20,000 workers. It was impossible for many of these to live at a distance as existing transit facilities were already wholly inadequate in spite of attempts to improve them, and in March, 1916, it was reported that the housing situation at Woolwich was "almost hopeless." Scores of men imported through various agencies threw up their work after a week or two because they could find no accommodation, while two months later, when attempts were made to shorten the hours of Arsenal workers, it was found impossible to introduce the three-shift system among women as suggested by the Hours of Labour Committee, since lack of housing space prevented the importation of sufficient women.

During the summer of 1916 building operations were hurried on, and the situation improved. By the end of the year, under the temporary schemes begun by the War Office and those instituted by the Ministry, there were already erected or in course of construction (a) seven estates of about 2,700 temporary bungalows at Woolwich, Greenwich and Eltham ; (b) hostels, opened by the War Office, to accommodate 300 boys, and others being constructed by the Ministry for 500 boys, 1,000 women and 100 men. Later extensions were made to these, and other hostels were opened for men, so that by 1917, when the Arsenal employed 74,467 workers (including 25,000 women), between 3,000 and 4,000 men, women and boys were provided for in this way.

Bungalows were also put up on the Well Hall Estate, on the Churchfield Estate, a site at Plumstead owned by Queen's College, Oxford, on the London County Council site at Greenwich, on the Corbett and Bostall estates at Eltham and Abbey Wood, and at East Wickham, Lodge Lane and Shepherd's Farm, all of these sites being either loaned to the Ministry or acquired under the Defence of the Realm Act.

In addition to these plans for the benefit of Arsenal workers, the Ministry had in 1915 initiated hostels at Slades Green for 140 operatives at the Thames Ammunition Works, and later at Edgwood for 500 from the Abbey Wood National Filling Factory, while 5 girls' hostels, originally constructed for Arsenal workers, were taken over in 1917 for the use of girls at the National Filling Factory. The King's Norton Metal Company and Messrs. Vickers also organised hostels in the district in connection with their works.

Practically all the huts at Woolwich consisted of five rooms : living room, scullery and three bedrooms, and in some cases there was a bathroom. The question of rents formed the subject of prolonged negotiations between the Treasury and the Chief Superintendent of Ordnance Factories early in 1915, before the plans passed under the Ministry's control. Three different bases were proposed : (a) the rents of house with similar accommodation in the locality, (b) a fair return on capital outlay, and (c) the maximum readily obtainable. The Chief Superintendent urged the last as the only practicable course, since the aim in building had been to induce men to come into the

district in order to work at the Arsenal, and these would be unwilling
to pay more than 5s. or 6s. per week. The actual cost of each hut
worked out at the unusually high figure of £325 owing to the abnormal
conditions and rapidity of construction. Thus calculating on a 20
years' life at 4 per cent., the rentals should be 19s., while the economic
return on 70 per cent. only of the outlay, as required by the Treasury,
would make the figure 15s. In May, 1915, the Treasury fixed the rents
at 9s. 6d. and 10s. per week, which, during the year 1917–18, brought
in a return of 2½ per cent. on the capital outlay. By August, 1918, all
the huts available were occupied at these rates.

Some of the hostels were placed under the direct control of the
Arsenal Welfare Supervision Department, as this facilitated smooth
working as regards the allocation of separate wings to the different
shifts to ensure quiet for sleep and similar details. Others were leased
either to local committees or to organisations such as the Y.M.C.A.,
but with a special agreement to ensure their use as hostels for Arsenal
workers. For example, in the case of the boys' hostels the lessee
undertook to use the building as a hostel for Arsenal boys only, to
be responsible for the physical and disciplinary control of the boys
and to provide for medical treatment when required. The Chief Superintendent of Ordnance Factories supplied equipment and paid rates
and taxes, and the lessee paid a rent of 1s. per week for every person in
the building. The total charge to the boys was not to exceed 12s.
per week, but, subject to these conditions, the lessee made all arrangements for management and service at the hostels. The hostel charges
made to women for rent were from 1s. 3d. to 1s. 9d. per week, according
to the class of accommodation provided, while men were charged 1s. 6d.
per week.[1] The houses and bungalow huts were far more satisfactory
than hostels from the economic standpoint and gave rise to little anxiety
until the post-war period.

The huts were not so rapidly occupied as the permanent houses
during 1916–17, and bad " slumps " in letting were experienced after
the August air raid in 1916, and the bad weather late in the year.
The reports on the bungalows showing the number occupied each week
indicate a tendency throughout the whole period from 1916–18 for the
numbers to rise in summer and decrease in winter, when the huts were
inevitably somewhat damp and cold. In some cases the unavoidable
minimum of discomfort was augmented by lack of permanent ventilation
or by inferior timber. The worst estate for letting in 1916 was the
Corbett Estate, the whole of which was low-lying and nearly twenty
minutes' walk from trams and shops. The municipal services, policing,
scavenging, fire protection, etc., for all the estates were undertaken
by the Woolwich Borough Council, and the huts were accordingly
subject to rates. The roads were usually in a very bad state as they
were only constructed for temporary use and were much cut up by army
lorries taking short cuts.

The success of the hostels varied very considerably, some proving
extremely popular while others were never used to their full capacity.

---

[1] These charges were considerably less than those ordinarily prevailing in
hostels, see above, p. 16..

The most successful year of their administration was from March, 1917, to March, 1918, when the largest numbers were housed, and at the end of 1917 the position was considered satisfactory as few difficulties arose in management and rents were rarely in arrears. The fact that it was impossible to keep the hostels full, however, caused them to be run at a considerable total loss. Thus the St. George's hostel for boys, which showed a profit up to March, 1918, showed a deficit in the following nine months owing to the Arsenal policy of replacing boys with women and girls, while by February, 1919, two hostels run by the Y.M.C.A. had losses of £4,066, and two others directly controlled by the Arsenal lost £6,282 and £9,817 respectively. These last two hostels with one or two others were still open in the spring of 1919 when they were being run at a loss which reached some £302 per week on the men's and £218 on the women's, while roughly a third only of the women and a half of the men were employed at the Arsenal. By June the staff which administered the hostels had been transferred to the Ministry of Labour ; one hostel was closed and it was arranged that the Chief Superintendent of Ordnance Factories should retain the others only so long as they were required by the Arsenal.

(c) THE POST-ARMISTICE POSITION.

The cessation of hostilities made little difference to the demand for huts, which remained full throughout 1919, but after the Armistice the better type of tenants tended to move away as they found work elsewhere, leaving a very rough element in possession. Owing to complaints of cold and damp an abatement of 2s. 6d. a week as coal allowance was allowed for the first three months of 1919. In spite of this concession, in February, 1919, a rent strike occurred which threatened to be serious. An organisation known as the Government Hutments Protection League was formed to conduct a campaign against the administration of the estates, and in the first week of March the number of those refusing rent was 414 against 1,049 who paid. Misstatements were made in the press and rioting and demonstrations occurred, chiefly with a view to terrorising the rent-paying householders, who formed the majority, into joining the strike. In most cases refusals to pay were due to pressure from strike-leaders, as in the case of the troubled housewife who dared not pay " because the League of Nations told her not to," while sometimes actual fear of ill-treatment by the more lawless section prevented compliance. A statement from one of the non-strikers showed that the leaders were chiefly non-Arsenal men or unemployed ; they demanded a 5s. reduction in rent, but there appeared to be no real ground for this step, as a long waiting list of applicants for vacant huts were prepared to pay the current rates. At the end of March the temporary reduction of 2s. 6d. was made permanent and the strike collapsed.

In 1919–20 the management passed from the Chief Superintendent direct to the Ministry, but the system was not satisfactory. Some of the estates were taken over by the London County Council, and efforts were made to relinquish state-ownership of the remainder.

INDEX.

Printed by H.M. STATIONERY OFFICE PRESS, Harrow.

CONTENTS OF VOLUME V.

NOTE.—The present issue is subject to revision,
and must be regarded as provisional.